NEW WORLDS, NEW WORDS

EXPLORING PATHWAYS FOR WRITING ABOUT AND IN ELECTRONIC ENVIRONMENTS

RESEARCH AND TEACHING IN RHETORIC AND COMPOSITION
Michael M. Williamson and David L. Jolliffe, series editors

New Worlds, New Words: Exploring Pathways for Writing About
and In Electronic Environments
John F. Barber and Dene Grigar (eds.)

forthcoming

The Rhetoric and Ideology of Genre: Strategies for Stability and Change
Richard M. Coe, Lorelei Lingard, and Tatiana Teslenko (eds.)

Marbles, Cotton Balls, and Quantum Wells:
Style as Invention in the Pursuit of Knowledge
Heather Graves

Listening to Learn: Basic Writers and Basic Writing in the
Contemporary Academy
Susanmarie Harrington and Linda Ader-Kassner

Multiple Literacies for the 21st Century
Brian Huot, Beth Stroble, and Charles Bazerman (eds.)

Identities Across Text
George H. Jensen

Against the Grain: Essays in Honor of Maxine Hairston
Michael Keene, Mary Trachel, and Ralph Voss (eds.)

Unexpected Voices
John Rouse and Ed Katz

Directed Self-Placement: Principles and Practices
Dan Royer and Roger Gilles (eds.)

Principles and Practices: New Discourses for Advanced Writers
Margaret M. Strain and James M. Boehnlein (eds.)

NEW WORLDS, NEW WORDS

EXPLORING PATHWAYS FOR WRITING ABOUT AND IN ELECTRONIC ENVIRONMENTS

edited by

John F. Barber
Dene Grigar
Texas Woman's University

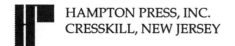
HAMPTON PRESS, INC.
CRESSKILL, NEW JERSEY

Library of Congress Cataloging-in-Publication Data

New worlds, new words : exploring pathways for writing about and in electronic environments / edited by John F. Barber, Dene Grigar
     p. cm. -- (Research and teaching in rhetoric and composition)
    Includes bibliographical references and indexes.
    ISBN 1-57273-333-0 -- ISBN 1-57273-334-9
    1. English language--Rhetoric--Study and teaching--Data processing. 2. Research-Methodology--Study and teaching--Data processing. 3. English language--Rhetoric--computer assisted instruction. 4. Academic writing--Study and teaching--Data processing. 5. Research--Methodology--Computer assisted instruction. 6. Academic writing--Computer assisted instruction. 7. Authorship--Data processing. I. Barber, John F. II. Grigar, Dene. III. Series

PE1404.N49 2001
808'.042'0285--dc21   00-054218

cover design by Dene Grigar

Hampton Press, Inc.
23 Broadway
Cresskill, NJ 07626

We shall not cease from exploration
And the end of all our exploring
Will be to arrive where we started
And know the place for the first time.
—T.S. Eliot

We dedicate this book to each other, and to our friends-colleagues who have all been a part of this journey and "exploration."

John F. Barber and Dene Grigar

CONTENTS

BY WAY OF PROLOGUE:

A DISPATCH CONCERNING SUSPENSE, SIGNS, AND SHAPES

Hugh Burns

New Worlds, New Words: Exploring Pathways for Writing About and in Electronic Environments is a collection of essays—or dispatches—about the suspense of language, the signs of technology, and the shapes of literacy at the edge of the new millennium. These dispatches establish a fresh common ground for writing about and in electronic environments. All of these dispatchers have visions dancing in their heads about teaching with technology. The new work in this collection concerns how these imaginative techno-rhetoricians explore, describe, demonstrate, and understand the evolving forms of digital discourse. As the editors who stimulated these dispatches, John Barber and Dene Grigar challenged each contributor to write of what will have come to pass.

This wonderful assignment sounds straightforward enough, except for one uncertainty: the future. The certainty, however, for all of these scholars is that language, technology, and literacy will interact to sculpt tomorrow's times. But what remains uncertain and suspenseful is *just how* language, technology, and literacy will interact to sculpt tomorrow's electronic spaces.

This much about these collected dispatches is true: The future imagined herein promises more suspense, many signs, and many shapes.

SUSPENSE

By way of prologue, read these dispatches and suspend disbelief. Suspend your traditional assumptions about what an intellectual text is and what it may become. Realize that tomorrow will be the best of quantum times and the worst of quantum times. As net-dwelling writers and teachers, we will be suspended and connected in golden ways, as Czeslaw Milosz in "Tidings"[1] reminded us.

> . . . we lived in a golden fleece,
> In a rainbow net, in a cloud cocoon
> Suspended from the branch of a galactic tree.

Be forewarned. The new kinds of text demonstrated in this collection are coming in the next millennium. The new *ethos* described here will spring from activity, the community activity of private conversations. The new *pathos* examined here will incorporate the sound and fury of public chat and idle talk. The new *logos* illustrated here will derive facts and artifacts from writers talking in virtual places. Again, be forewarned. Although these classical rhetorical duties are not exactly the intellectual, persuasive acts we have come to expect as academics, a new dynamic of *ethos*, *pathos*, and *logos* will exist and will be studied. In studying these words and worlds, there will be wondrous mystery—and hope. For in the future writing will happen naturally in electronic environments. And thinking as well.

If writing methods become increasingly more digital, then research methodologies will necessarily and naturally change. Like an archeologist's suspense, techno-rhetoricians will dig in digital sites. Cynthia Haynes and Jan Rune Holmevik define our new research work as "hacking into time" and consciously see writers resisting the traditional ways of organizing and controlling the flow of information. When they suggest that writers will publish themselves as message and messenger, they are right. Look for the signs of a new rhetorical suspense in that old canon of invention, arrangement, style, memory, and delivery.

SIGNS

By way of prologue, be assured humans beings will be humans communicating through digital learning environments. People will be connected through electronic networks, and they will seek to be more connected with each other. Be mindful of the signs, and there will be many. Milosz, in "Tidings," reminded us again.

> And our net was woven from the stuff of signs,
> Hieroglyphs for the eye and ear, amorous rings.

As to these signs or hieroglyphs for using collaborative and cooperative technologies for writing specifically, *New Worlds, New Words* offers a commentary on a variety of topics pertaining to wired life. These dispatches suggest many of the contributions a collaborative writing environment such as MOO can provide. For example, as amorous rings perhaps, MOOs are a delight to ponder. Yet in terms of sociology and education, MOO-space and MOO-activity will remain difficult to assess in terms of learning to write and teaching to learn. Dene Grigar reports of the interesting tensions between what MOO texts seem to be—oral discourses—and what they really are—written texts. Will assessment need to be so difficult in the future? The answer is no, but be forewarned: Text was, is, and still will be *techne*. Many students are finding these virtual writing journeys "awesome." Will yours?

Another sign is that these dispatches lay a groundwork for what will be considered *writing for publication* in the late great age of print. Today, as these scholars publish in the traditional form, some here demonstrate new forms and new possibilities. They can play. They can be serious. They can critique inside and out. Victor Vitanza reminds the audiences in cyberspace and just out there that "no matter how silly, the writing is serious." The contributors describe and imitate a writer's life in the virtual world as it will have become, avoiding the pretense of a writer's life as it should be. In the verisimilitude of an imagined online reality, these dispatches contain many more signs as to what writing will be and could become.

These dispatchers are deeply concerned with technology. They see how their credibility as teachers is linked to future technology. In matters of teaching writing in collaborative electronic spaces, credible outcomes will ultimately be more important than manufacturing a cyber-charisma. Tomorrow's writers learning to write in the online school zone will be measured by their collaborative performances as writer *and* reader. Teachers of writing will also profess to believe certain truths and practice them as professors as well. Every teacher of writing will have become a student of technology as well as a writer engaged in teaching in virtual dimensions—synchronously and asynchronously. Teachers will come to know enough technology to translate rhetorical principles into pedagogical practice. Big signs will be posted. *Writers at Work. Readers Crossing.* These dispatches, if properly understood, do not allow writing teachers to linger in the land of the theoretical.

These dispatches, therefore, foreshadow many new shapes for literacy practices.

SHAPE

By way of prologue, remember that many of the several revolutionary agendas in imagining new worlds and new words have to do with knowing better how literacy shall sculpt our times and spaces. Milosz concluded his "Tidings":

> A sound reverberated inward, sculpturing our time,
> The flicker, flutter, twitter of our language. . . .

Like language, the flicker, flutter, twitter of technology will also reveal and conceal literacy.

The explosion of information will continue to increase rapidly. As the digital world is never static, the technological skills for learning digital literacy will lag behind the bleeding edge developments. A new set of dynamic literacies will be shaped by practice, if not by design and if not just in time. Such electronic environments allow every writer who wishes to be published to publish—whether an audience wishes to read it or not, whether or not the message is worth publishing. The contradictions of learning, teaching, writing, and reading remain and are exposed when the newest technologies shape writing and literacy differently. There is no doubt that such new paradigms mean new navigational tools for literacy immersion. The theater of all of this, as John Barber suggests, contains the rise and fall of dramatic action. Interconnected players starring on many virtual stages will produce, direct, write, and perform the new world's literacy scripts.

Although there is no guarantee that teaching language skillfully online will produce a skillful writer and thinker, these dispatches suggest that we had better be as realistic as we are creative.

- We will need to understand the integration of verbal and nonverbal literacies in electronic environments. Myka Vielstimming's dispatch directs attention to the visual and verbal tension among the new words and new worlds. Jeff Galin and Joan Latchaw predict how abnormal discourse may just become the norm, just as integrating implies a new inner shape.
- We will need to publish more of our students' work, so Nick Carbone defines the shape and the invigoration of

academic publishing as we move writers "from print to pixel."

- We will wonder what we should improve. Dickie Selfe foreshadows how working professionals and writers at work may create a dynamic of blame, thanks to the "speed up" of new words and more words. Michael Day suggests how we will distill quality from quantity to shape these new world research design possibilities.
- We will be asked to prepare writers for the *real world*. Judith Kirkpatrick imagines the shape of a pedagogy for rediscovering method in an age dedicated to serving up "information age skills."
- We will learn to trust in the coherence of hypertext and the fluidity of language. Mick Doherty's dispatch, as well as his with Sandye Thompson, comments on how the commentary mode is already outside the linear norms.

These energetic demonstrations of scholarship, as well as the others, certainly shout for the learners, teachers, writers, and readers among us to start our literacy engines.

Before reading these dispatches, therefore, I prescribe a modest self-examination about your commitment to the shape of literacy today and tomorrow.

- Have you the energy and the motivation for integrating new digital tools for composing?
- Have you come to understand a better way to write and to teach writing when using electronic environments?
- Will your current literacy tools meet your future instructional goals and professional expectations?
- What strategies are you developing to integrate new forms of writing in your curriculum?

These are some of the questions you should ask yourself as you read and study *New Worlds, New Words*. You will soon have more. Indeed, in these narratives and expositions, you will find more links between teaching acts and learning consequences. These dispatchers have left something for you to do. You must write dispatches of your own. The confluence of technology and thought is bringing a renaissance in knowledge-making. You are there. Study these dispatches from this band of sages and scribes with an eager expectation of what writing will have become in the first, great age of digitext.

May their new words help sculpt your new worlds. We invite your dispatch.

May our students write well and prosper.

NOTES

1. This and following quotes from Milosz, C. (1978). Tidings. In *Bells in Winter* (C. Milosc & L. Vallee, trans.). New York: The Ecco Press.

introduction

OR PHILOSOPHIZING ABOUT THE ART AND TECHNE OF WRITING IN THIS BOOK[1]

Dene Grigar and John F. Barber

1.   Δεινιὸν γάρ που, ὦ φαῖδρε, τοῦτ᾽ ἔχει γραφή, καὶ ὡς ἀληθῶς ὅμοιον ζωγραφία. καὶ γὰρ τὰ ἐκείνης ἔκγονα ἔστηκε μὲν ὡς ζῶντα, ἐὰν δ᾽ ἀνέρῃ τι, σεμνῶς πάνυ σιγᾷ. ταὐτόν δὲ καὶ οἱ λόγοι· δόξιας μὲν ἂν ὡς τι φρονοῦντας αὐτοὺς λέγειν, ἐὰν δέ τι ἔρῃ τῶν λεγομένων βουλόμενος μαθεῖν, ἕν τι σημαίνει μόνον ταὐτὸν ἀεί. ὅταν δὲ ἅπαξ γραφῇ, κυλινδεῖται μὲν πανταχοῦ πᾶς λόγος ὁμοίος παρὰ τοῖς ἐπαΐουσιν, ὡς δ᾽αὕτως παρ᾽ οἷς οὐδὲν προσηήει, καὶ οὐκ ἐπίσταται λέγειν οἷς δεῖ γε καὶ μή πλημμελούμενος δὲ καὶ οὐκ ἐν δίκῃ λοιδορηθεὶς τοῦ πατρὸς ἀεὶ δεῖται βοηθοῦ· αὐτὸς γὰρ οὔτ᾽ ἀμύνασθαι οὔτε βοηθῆσαι δυνατὸς αὑτῷ.[2]

2. In comparing writing to the art of painting—that is, written rhetoric to visual rhetoric—it seems to us, these words of Plato, presumably of Socrates, present a false notion of writing, a notion that has been with us for thousands of years. It is this: The written word appears static, like images in a painting, and in its static form it relays the same idea over and over again. Additionally, it is silent, and because it cannot speak up for itself, the written word is always in danger of being

sullied—misread—by those who feign knowledge of its meaning. Thus, like art, writing falls into the realm of the material world of shadows, mirror images, and objects, that place where ignorance prevails. This is what Plato says in the *Phaedrus*. What Plato wrote about writing.

3. Plato innovated as he conserved, for he was, to be honest, a man of his time. Only a few hundred of years before Plato was born, writing reemerged in Greece, after having been lost during a long, dark age. Some believe that the desire to preserve Homer's texts was the reason for writing's re-development. But certainly, Athens in the time of Plato was in transition, strenuously holding on to the oral ideal even as oral discourse was committed to writing. For Socrates, Plato, and others, orality upheld order of the past and promoted reason. It was tradition, φυσις (>Physis). Writing—the upstart, νομος (>Nomos)—Plato said, fostered misunderstanding, mistranslation. But that he wrote down Socrates' dialogues, his seemingly oral discursive genre, opens up the possibility that Plato saw advantages to writing even as he railed against it. Perhaps he grudgingly understood that any word expressed is as corruptible as the idea behind it or the person who interprets it. Orality is as permanent as the wind that carries it; writing, as the reed-paper that it is marked on.

4. But this possible understanding about the evolving *and* eternal nature of writing is not among those openly expressed. Instead, Plato declares that writing is static, that the written word says the same thing over and over again (μόνον ταὐτὸν ἀεί). But worse than static, writing is dumb and requires human intervention in order to make sense. Writing, manifesting itself simply as marks on a roll of papyrus, does not make knowledge itself, nor can it express its meaning like a wise philosopher can express meaning. Extended logically, this argument suggests that if words are dumb, then they are also ignorant, since knowledge for Plato is expressed in oral discourse, in communication with others, in the dialectic. Knowledge conveyed in writing, then, is false, as untrue as a shadow masquerading as the thing that casts it, as misleading as firelight is when compared to the sun's light. The other—the words spoken by a philosopher—are the epitome of truth, transcendence, the ideal. At the very worst, written words are manifestations of irrationality, emotion run amok. More than 2,000 years later, Sven Bikerts in *The Gutenberg Elegies* echoed Plato's lament against the written word—that is, the word written *digitally*—as if Birkerts' words, like Plato's, have somehow escaped Stanley Aronowitz's notion of the ineluctable intertwining of writing and technology. The master's biases live on in light of our progress.

5. We, the progeny of Western thought, do refer to writing as technology—an innovation of humankind, proof of the preeminence of the human spirit, a mark of progress from primitive preliterate sensibility. Τεχνή (> Techne). A craft, a skill, a cleverness of the hands directed by the mind. Man-made invention dependent on intelligence, talent, manual labor: Like the cultivation of grain, the irrigation of desert lands, the weaving of flax, the production of pottery, the manipulation of the computer keyboard to locate data within the computer's memory banks or outside of them on the internet. Technology, electronic or otherwise. Manifestations of rationality. Rationality as a model for order.

6. Because technology requires rational thought, Plato saw it as something more akin to science than to art, for art was divinely inspired and not produced from any real knowledge or any particular skill.[3] Plato's artist, the poet, the purveyor of stories, was merely a conduit through which the gods spoke, and art merely "a stream of emotion which flows from poet to actor, and from actor to audience."[4] By attacking the poet, Plato also sets a trap for artists of all types, even artists of written discourse and their art, writing of all types. It is all madness, falling under the jurisdiction of the Muses. Manifestations of irrationality. Irrationality as a model for chaos.

7. Plato suggests that our notion of writing and technology is flawed. Writing is not techne, is not technology, does not represent any real progress for humankind because its corruptible nature precludes it from being considered part of the realm of the intelligences, of science. Writing and technology are not the same. They sit in opposition of one another.

8. Yet, Plato is, at best, ambivalent about the underlying nature of writing. Even before the period of transition in which he wrote, not spoke, the *The Phaedrus*, in Book VII of *The Republic* he lays out the path for the intellectual journey from the cave of ignorance to the sunlight of enlightenment, the place of the ideal forms—the good, the beautiful and the true. Change was upon him even then, for as we see in that work, one of the important qualities of the ideal forms is changelessness, their static nature. And stasis here is good. Writing's statis, represented by those never-changing marks on a page that Plato earlier lambastes, can also be viewed as examples of the eternal quality of the ideal forms. It too can be viewed as good.

9. And it was. The Romans picked on this idea implicit in Plato's work. They knew better than to take Plato at his word, not to read

between the lines, not to see the complexity of his thinking, his struggles to make sense of the meaning of writing. Their saying, *Verba volant, scripta manent*, literally means "spoken words fly away, written words remain." Evidence of the ascendancy of the written over the spoken word. Not that long after Plato.

10. Stasis may not have been the only reason for writing's eventual dominance over orality. Perhaps our preference for writing lay in the desire to get the facts straight, to remember what was true about a thing—for truth, Αλεθη(> Alethe), literally means "not forgetting." Truth, then, implies remembering what one sees, what one hears, what one knows. In an oral culture, the ability to know truth requires a good memory. The invocation of the Muse at the beginning of an epic attests to the nervousness even poets, known for their prodigious memories, must have felt when attempting to recall thousands of lines of verse before an audience. The truth, indeed, can be painful.

11. The rise of the importance of writing during Plato's time, evident in Plato's own work, implies that a need for long-term preservation of facts might have arisen. Or perhaps data had become too complex to remember without making note of it somewhere for later contemplation. Or perhaps both. But somebody (or somebodys) needed to safeguard the important artifacts of culture—the plays, the epics, laws, legal documents, the names of the dead—so that none of it would be forgotten, lost. Even in *The Phaedrus*, Plato wrote, not spoke, his tirades against writing, as if we could not see the contradiction in this undertaking. And so an idea committed to writing aids in the process of not forgetting, appears as solid as truth, and pursuing truth lies at the core of any intellectual investigation. Art or techne, the main point is seeking truth, so it seems to us.

12. But in the Humanities, art always takes precedence over craft, for art carries with it the cachet of creativity, of beauty. Apollo. Delian reason. The light of the sun. Technology, on the other hand, means motors and machines and chips and sprockets, the stuff of sweat and tedious laboring. Cogs in the wheel, the antithesis of heroic endeavors. Hephaistos, the Roman Vulcan. The dark underworld of ignorance. The lame smithy god, cuckolded by Beauty, Apollo's sexy stepsister.

13. The philosophical concepts of writing and technology, therefore, create tension for those of us in the Humanities who compose writing with computers, who live some of our lives in computers'

virtual spaces. For if writing is art and manipulating a computer is techne, how, then, do we reconcile the two enterprises, and what happens when they are, indeed, conjoined in the act of writing online, where text can be scanned, stretched, shrunk, synthesized, shaped, shaded, structured, secluded, seduced? Could Aphrodite have found Hephaistos attractive if she really tried?

14. These questions lie at the heart of the anti-technology rhetoric in regard to using computers to write, teach, and conduct research. The art of writing may, as Plato suggested, get sullied by its contact with those who think they know what writing is saying, particularly those people who are writing it with computers. Or perhaps computer technology may take the art out of writing and relegate it to formulae taught by some software system. Or worse, computer technology, perhaps, may reveal that writing is craft, that it is inextricably linked to process and hard work and is not the stuff of wild poets in turrets inspired by Muses. A blow to the pre-industrialized romantic vision of writing, of the writer, of a time untouched by the words post and modern. Of dichtomized form —> Classical, concerned with underlying form, controlling hierarchies / Romantic, concerned with appearance and the freedom from constraints.5 But it seems to us the notion of form is transformed by process, and process, informed by form. Thus, we see the discussion about writing with computers not as an "either/or," but as a "both/and." Translated generally as "on the one hand, *and* on the other"—the Greekμενδε(>Men de) in the truest sense. Both process and form, both art *and* techne. Extending binaries, distending opposition.

15. Already there are those who have philosophized, theorized, pontificated that using computers and computer technology will fundamentally change how we will write ourselves and the larger surrounding world (our culture) into existence, how we will perceive our culture, how we will interact with one another, how we will rethink our notion that writing is essentially a solitary, heroic endeavor expressed linearly and portrayed as marks graphically reproduced on paper—that using computers and computer technology will take us to the idea that writing is a socially constructive activity produced in concert with multiple voices, multiple persons, will take us back to Plato, with this twist: that writing will yield a *multimodal product* that is more of an ongoing, ever evolving process of change and reinterpretation. With our notion of the μενδε, we will rethink the idea that evolution and change are bad. We will rethink the idea that change and statis cannot, like art and techne, coexist. Not an either/or, but

possibly a "both/and." A re-classical, post-postmodern take on very ancient philosophical point.

16. Such sweeping and prophetic thoughts and claims about the impact of computer technology on the intimate connection between communication, language, and words to create new forms of culture, *new worlds* if you will, have been explored during the past decade. Jay David Bolter, for one, proposes that "electronic writing threatens to redefine historiography in a way that reveals what [Susan] Sontag has called the impossibility or irrelevance of producing a continuous, systematic argument. The same redefinition applies to all academic disciplines in which scholarship is now understood as the producing of systematic argument for publication."[6] Indeed, much of the research literature on hypertext and other current forms of electronic writing suggests that these new communication media will potentially deconstruct the sense of stability surrounding the notions of author, reader, and writing that have long accompanied linear text. Perhaps we will come to see that change and eternalness are both potential in any static condition—that any word expressed is as corruptible as the idea behind it or the person who interprets it. Orality is as permanent as the wind that carries it; writing, as the reed-paper that it is marked on; the *digitalized* word, as eternal as the disk it is saved on, the hard drive that holds its data, the website that archives it, the MOO-space that it appears in, the links taking us to it in a hypertext, the copy paper it is printed on, the wind that carries it spoken.

17. Stability of meaning, then, may no longer be a foregone conclusion in the new worlds of technologically created and defined electronic spaces. Individuals are already staking claim to portions of this evolving cyberspace and fashioning new senses of identity and interaction with others there, already exploring new inner and outer worlds, crossing borders into unexplored territory, moving from one set of values to another. The result: Sometimes anxiety, many times ambivalence, most often discomfort with what Elizabeth Klem and Charles Moran call "an amphibious stage, operating as we do partly in print, partly on-screen."[7] *Ambiscriptuality* we call this overlap of technologies during this transitional age, and this overlap confuses us and causes us tension. Just like it did Plato and Socrates.

18. But this ambiscriptual stage is also one that promises interesting developments and evolution toward more useful or adaptable forms. The dispatches of those exploring writing in electronic environments are useful to those who wish to follow or simply observe, who wish to know what will have become once we make the transition.

19. These dispatches lie at the heart of this book, *New Worlds, New Words: Exploring Pathways for Writing About and in Electronic Environments*, at the heart of our search to know what the future of writing will have become with the union of writing and computer technology. Our theme pursued and pushed by the researchers, theorists, teachers, and students who contribute to this book is that computer-networked technology not only creates (and will have created) new electronic environments (new worlds) but also promotes (and will have promoted) new forms or writer-reader interaction (new words). New Wor(l)ds. These explorers cannot always frame their dispatches, their reports, in familiar words, language, or images we understand. They may, instead, use metaphors, paradoxes, contradictions, collages, fragments, and abstractions that attempt to convey new and different meanings in new and different ways, or to explain the new in terms of the old. Form-givers of new cybernetic design textualities that inform present and future developments. Like Plato's cave of ignorance in *The Republic*. Like Plato's ζωγραφια his paintings, in *The Phaedrus*. Like Klem and Moran's amphibian.

20. "The computer is the ink pen of the future."[8] With this statement, voiced by one of our students, we posit that the technologies of computer networks are, indeed, as Joan Tornow said, "changing the ways people work, play, and learn. They are changing the ways people write and—because our symbol systems are tools of thought—they are changing the ways people think. New conventions are evolving and blurring the past distinctions between writing and talking. The 'talk' that occurs on networks is written talk, a relatively new mode of language with its own peculiar qualities. This new form of language even has a new name—electronic text or e-text. E-text is changing the patterns of when we talk to others—and how we talk. New social webs connect people and institutions in new ways, and information that was formerly sequestered or confined to a select few is now accessible to a larger number of people"[9] searching for knowledge, through both art *and* science, an alchemical union of base elements, mind and digitally archived knowledge. The written and the verbal, electronic and print, *electroverbal* communication and *ambiscriptual* writing in and about electronic spaces.

21. Thus, new worlds requires *new words*. Where language and writing have always been symbols to portray and preserve our thinking, a way of creating reality, the writers-artists in this volume are exploring new language by using words in electroverbal, ambiscriptual ways and treating the electronic spaces where they work as part of the process of

expression rather than as neutral backgrounds. As a result, their new language, their new ways of writing, overcome silence by abandoning language assimilated from the art of language as it has been traditionally practiced. They are also artifacts of what will have been in the future. Incunabular placeholders for what will follow.[10]

22. An understanding of how such technology can (or will) change the forms and functions of writing, has, however, been slow in coming, perhaps due to the rapidity with which technology morphs into new iterations, each filled with new and interesting implications. With the increasing utilization of the World Wide Web, electronic journals, asynchronous and synchronous communications, and hypertextual forms of writing, new electronic environments (new worlds) are emerging and being used as spaces for exploring new ways and new forms of writing (new words) that have the power to change our notions of culture. New worlds, new words, new wor(l)ds.

23. The contributors to this book are conducting and writing about academic research in ways and forms that speak to and test the publication and communication opportunities these electronic technology spaces promote. Similarly, when asked to produce writing publishable in both electronic and print-based formats, they are seeking new avenues for creating work that addresses both environments effectively. Examples of their efforts to make sense of these new spaces abound in this book.

24. Driven as we are by the desire to re-vision, expand, unify— in effect, driven as we are by the notion of the μεν δε —we divide our book into three sections. First, we offer examples of experimental writing showing what writing may become in the future under the influence of computers and electronic environments: Re-vision. In this section we find Victor Vitanza musing about what writing will have become as we "colonize" electronic spaces, Dene Grigar playfully philosophizing about the meaning of reality in virtual spaces, Kathleen Yancey and Michael Spooner uniting rhetoric and the poetic in a hybrid from of textuality, John Barber ruminating on the protean characteristics of emergent forms of immersive narrative promulgated by electronic environments, and Mick Doherty naming, creating, "kludging" the ethos of electronic spaces. Second, we provide theoretical work discussing important issues relating to writing in electronic spaces: Expansion. In this section we find Cynthia Haynes and Jan Rune Holmevik talking about the way publication changes when we move from asynchronous to synchronous spaces, Nick Carbone exploring the

mythos of cyberspace, Michael Day proposing new approaches to research in an electronic age, Jeff Galin and Joan Latchaw offering a new paradigm for scholarship and publishing, Dickie Selfe demonstrating what writing looks like when technology is common in our lives, and Judi Kirkpatrick demonstrating what writing looks like when technology is common in our classrooms. Then, we marry the two concepts of re-vision and expansion in a third section: a series of MOO sessions and subsequent email, hosted and edited by Mick Doherty and Sandye Thompson, in which the authors discuss the theme of the book and the various ideas they address in their dispatches: Unification. And so, practice and theory. Form *and* process. Techne *and* art. Not one *or* the other. Not one *over* the other.

25. In creating this text, we hope to provide a benchmark for the complex and ever changing relations between computer technology, literacy, and culturally situated cognition. All of the contributors to this book are actively engaged in learning and teaching writing in various electronic spaces. All are committed to observing how these environments change writing, writing's forms, writing's functions, even writers themselves. We are interested in the changes writing, filtered through the context of electronic spaces, can bring and will have brought as a way of creating and interacting with a larger surrounding cultural reality. Indeed, we are all interested in taking the initiative to encourage these changes and create new perspectives through which to view the results.

26. We are author-explorers either individually or collaboratively investigating new worlds of writing and finding, or inventing, new words with which to discuss what we are learning and thinking about what writing will have become as it situates itself between oral, print, and electronic cultures in these electronic online computer-facilitated environments. As the trails we pioneer fast become routes traveled by other scholars, researchers, and practitioners in the field, it is time to investigate the new worlds we are discovering and the new words (or new ways of using old words) we are using to describe and position our notions of writing as an embodied practice within new electronic environments that promotes challenging implications for not only the way we communicate, but also why. But because these new contexts are so fundamentally different in concept and because the familiar terms, vocabularies, and images in which they might be framed seem not to suffice, we, like artists, are forced to create and, like scientists, are forced to experiment with new ways of writing about and in these electronic spaces. We are comfortable in the marriage of art and

techne. In the chemistry of their attraction. Aphrodite, over time, in accord with Hephaistos. The future of this harmony is now.

27. Finally, we admit at the outset that our prognostications about new worlds, new words, like some of Plato's views on writing, may well be wrong. But in venturing thoughts, ideas, and scenarios about what will have become of the modalities and issues of writing about and in electronic spaces, we hope to stimulate further discussion regarding the exploration of these environments.

NOTES

1. Based loosely on the style of Ludwig Wittenstein's *Philosophical Investigations*.
2. Plato, *Phaedrus*, 275d-e. Translator, Dene Grigar:
   "A dangerous quality this writing has, Phaedrus—and very much like painting it is. For the images we see in paintings stand like living beings; but, if one questions them, they retain a solemn silence."
   "It is also the same for writing. You may think that it could speak with intelligence, but if someone wishing to actually learn something were to question it about the things it says, then all that person would learn is that it says the same things over and over."
   "And a word once written is tossed about in the dirt alike by those who understand and those who do not—it doesn't know who to speak to. And, indeed, when words are abused or treated unjustly, they always need to fall back on the father for help, for writing does not have the power to defend itself."
3. *Ion*, 533d.
4. Ibid.
5. Robert Pirsig, *Zen and the Art of Motorcycle Maintenance: An Inquiry into Values*, 66.
6. Jay David Bolter, *Writing Space*, 117.
7. Elizabeth Klem and Charles Moran, "Computers and Instructional Strategies in the Teaching of Writing," 132.
8. Michael Watts, a student in John's Technical Writing course, made this astute observation about technology.
9. Joan Tornow, *Link Age*, 1.
10. Janet Murray, *Hamlet on the Holodeck*, 67.

WORKS CITED

Aronowitz, S. (1992). Looking out: The impact of computers on the lives of professionals. In M. Tuman (Ed.), *Literacy online: The promise [and peril] of reading and writing with computers* (pp. 119-137). Pittsburgh, PA: University of Pittsburgh Press.

Birkerts, S. (1994). *The Gutenberg elegies: The fate of reading in an electronic age.* New York: Ballantine.

Bolter, J. D. (1991). *Writing space: The computer, hypertext, and the history of writing.* Chapel Hill: University of North Carolina Press.

Klem, E., & Moran, C. (1991). Computers and instructional strategies in the teaching of writing. In G. Hawisher & C. Selfe (Eds.), *Evolving perspectives on computers and composition studies: Questions for the 1990s* (pp. 132-149). Urbana, IL: National Council of Teachers of English.

Murray, J. (1996). *Hamlet on the holodeck: The future of narrative in cyberspace.* New York: The Free Press.

Pirsig, R. (1976). *Zen and the art of motorcycle maintenance: An inquiry into values.* Toronto: Bantam Books.

Plato. (1963). *The Republic* (F. MacDonald Cornfield, trans.). New York: Oxford University Press.

Plato. (1990). *The Phaedrus* (H. N. Fowler, trans.). London: Harvard University Press.

Plato. (n. d.). The Ion. *"Ion" and Four Other Dialogues of Plato* (pp. 1-16) (P. B. Shelley, trans.). London: J.M. Dent and Sons, Ltd.

Tornow, J. (1997). *Link age: Composing in the online classroom.* Logan: Utah State University Press.

Wittenstein, L. (1968). *Philosophical investigations* (G. E. M. Anscombe, trans.). NewYork: MacMillan Publishing.

CHAPTERS FROM NEW WORLDS:

WRITING IN AND ABOUT ELECTRONIC SPACES

Re-Vision. Form and Process. Experimental writing showing what writing may become in the future under the influence of computers and electronic environments. Dene Grigar playfully philosophizes about the meaning of reality in virtual spaces, Victor Vitanza muses about what writing will have become as we "colonize" electronic spaces, Mick Doherty names, creates, "kludges" the ethos of electronic spaces, Myka Vielstimmig (a compositive author created through and by the collaborative writing of Kathleen Yancey and Michael Spooner) unites rhetoric and the poetic in a hybrid form of textuality, and John Barber ruminates on the protean characteristics of emergent forms of immersive narrative promulgated by electronic environments. These explorers cannot always frame their dispatches, their chapters, in familiar words, language, or images. They may, instead, use metaphors, paradoxes, contradictions, collages, fragments, and abstractions that attempt to convey new and different meanings in new and different ways, or to explain the new in terms of the old. Form-givers of new cybernetic design textualities that inform present and future developments. Like Plato's cave of ignorance in *The Republic*. Like Plato's *zvgrafia*, his paintings, in *The Phaedrus*. Like Klem and Moran's amphibian.

chapter 1.1

A DIALOG ON THE REALITY OF WRITING IN VIRTUAL ENVIRONMENTS

Dene Grigar

AcadeMOO   December 31, 2000   10:34 am

You enter a dark cave. A *fire* burns brightly at few feet ahead of you, illuminating the space just enough so that you can see a low wall ahead. You hear noise coming from behind the wall—it sounds like someone tapping on computer keys. You walk around the wall and see a woman sitting at a *desk* facing the back of the cave. Books and papers are piled up on one half of the desk; a computer takes up the space of the other half. The computer casts *shadows* on the cave walls, and its screen glows in the darkness.

You see fire, a desk, and shadows.
You see Dene sitting at her desk. Warnock, Grube, Turkle, Rushkoff, Whitehead, Guthrie, VV, Mick, and Langham are seated in chairs and talking quietly among themselves.

Dene turns and waves you toward her.

Dene says, "Welcome."

Dene says, "Let me introduce you to this dispatch."
Dene holds up a big sign:

'A Dialog on the Reality of Writing in Virtual Environments'

Dene says, "I hope you don't mind that I record our meeting. We may find this log useful later when working on revisions."

>>A red light on the Recorder flashes to indicate that it has been turned on and is now recording everything that is being said in The Cave.<<

Dene holds up a big sign:

The goal of this dialog is to raise questions concerning the notion of *reality* and its relation to virtual environments, such as the ones we call MOOs and the web, and to the writing we undertake in these spaces.

Dene says, "Before we start, we would like to talk about the way we have decided to present our work. . ."
Dene says, "As you may have noticed, we are writing this dispatch as a MOOlog, the style of discourse found in virtual spaces called MOOs. . ."
Dene says, "Let me explain. . ."

Dene motions to the dark, cavernous space around you.

Dene says, "This space you have just entered is 'The Cave,' a room we have created in the AcadeMOO, a MOO designed for this project. . ."
Dene says, "You probably already know that 'MOO' stands for MUD Object-Oriented and a 'MUD' is a Multi-User Dungeon—or Dimension or Domain. . ."
Dene says, "You may also recognize from the 'dungeon' in the acronym that MUDs originated from the Dungeons and Dragons role-playing game—in the late 1970s MUDs were developed so that participants could play the game by computer. . ."

VV waves at Dene.

Dene says, "Victor, did you want to add anything? I guess I should probably tell you that VV is Victor Vitanza, a well-known theorist of virtual spaces."

VV leaves his chair and joins you by Dene's desk.
VV thumbs to page 405 of _CyberReader_.
VV says, "A MOO 'is a text-based, virtual site where people can communicate by typing to each other in real time or can build virtual objects and share them with others. . . . A MOO is a MUD that is object-oriented. Still more technical. . ."

VV winks.

VV says, "A MOO . . . is a programming language within a MUD that enables its participants to create and manipulate their own virtual objects—say, a room with objects (furnishings).'"[1]

Dene admits that she forgot to mention the idea of manipulating objects. Gregarious leaves its chair and joins you by Dene's desk.

Dene says, "Yes, this concept is important to understand because when we say we can manipulate objects, we are talking about objects written into existence as text, as well as actions relating to those objects that take place as textual activities. . ."

Gregarious says, "Excuse me, Dene . . ."
Gregarious says, "Now that MOOs have been integrated into the web, graphical representations and video stream are available in these spaces, right?"

Dene nods at Gregarious.

Dene says, "Yes, but essentially the programming underlying the creation of the space and objects within that space is textual. And to be honest, may MOOs and other forms of synchronous chat spaces are still textual in nature, their action unfolding textually upon the screen . . ."
Dene says, "It is this textuality that make synchronous environments viable for exploration as writing spaces, as we are trying to show here today."

Gregarious agrees with Dene's assertion.
Dene turns back to you.

Dene says, "Let me explain what I mean about action unfolding in text. Remember that fire you saw as you walked through The Cave . . ."
Dene says, "We have programmed AcadeMOO so that you can type the words, 'Look Fire," and you can actually see a graphical representation of a fire on your screen. It is an object I borrowed from LinguaMOO. . ."
Dene says, "Watch. . .

Look fire.

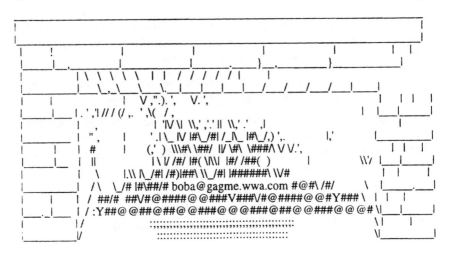

You see a cozy hearth with wood stacked near by . . .
Why not 'light fire'?

Dene says, "If you type 'light fire,' as the note suggests, the program would take you through a series of actions, all text-based, that give the impression that you are indeed lighting a fire, seeing it burn, and hearing it crackle. . ."

Dene says, "MOOs, then, are a form of virtual reality that simulates a real location where people gather and talk . . . "

Dene says, "Even when a graphical interface is present, as in MOOs using enCORE and Pueblo, and we can program a color photograph of a fireplace into the MOO, the MOO environment depends heavily on textual descriptions and representation of the burning of the fire that takes place when we 'light fire.'"

Gregarious thinks it is cold enough in here to build a fire.

Dene says, "So, a MOO's success at recreating reality depends heavily upon the ability of the writer/programmer/creator of that space to produce credible and well-composed text.

VV nods.

VV says, "Michael Heim talks about 'seven divergent concepts currently guiding virtual reality. . .'"[2]

VV flips to page 21 of _CyberReader_."
VV says, "'Simulation,' 'interaction,' 'artificiality,' 'immersion,' 'telepresence,' 'full-body immersion,' and 'networked communications.'"[3]

Dene says, "Well, MOOs certainly exemplify networked communications. We can speak to someone online by typing words on the computer keyboard of computer while others located thousands of miles away can read what we say almost instantaneously on their computer screens and respond as quickly as they can type. As soon as they respond to us, we see an example of interaction, too."

VV nods.

Dene says, "And I guess to a certain extent it represents simulation through its textual and graphical recreation of reality. And that it is 'geared, paved, and wired' reflects its artificiality."[4]

VV says, "And there is a sense of immersion when we inhabit these spaces and take these virtual personae."

Dene says, "Yes, Sherry Turkle tells us that 'when we step through the screen into virtual communities, we reconstruct our identities on the other side of the looking glass.'"[5]

Turkle pricks up her ears when she hears her name mentioned.
Turkle leaves her chair and joins you by Dene's desk.

Turkle says, "Yes, 'we are learning to see ourselves as plugged-in technobodies. . .and we are redescribing our politics and economic life in a language that is resonant with a particular form of machine intelligence."[6]

Dene says, "This brings up a distinction we ought to address because it may illuminate us further on notions of reality. . ."

Gregarious likes Dene's use of 'illuminate' here.
Dene blushes.

Dene says, "That is, the distinction between artificial intelligence and artificial life. Is Helmreich here yet?"

Helmreich leaves his chair and joins you by Dene's desk.
Helmreich waves at everybody.

Dene says, "Helmreich, would you explain briefly the difference between AI and AL?"

Helmreich says, "Artificial Life is a field larely dedicated to the computer simulation—and, some would ambitiously add, synthesis in real and virtual space—of biological systems. . ."
Helmreich says, "Whereas Artificial Intelligence attempt[s] to model the mind, Artifical Life workers hope to simulate the life processes that support the development and evolution of such things as minds."

Gregarious says, "So, it seems, Professor Turkle, that you see virtual spaces as apart from or outside of the self and as places we can connect to and extend ourselves from. . ."

Gregarious says, "But can these spaces be environments that can stimulate artificial life rather than simply simulate real life practices and experiences? And if so, how does that affect our notion of reality and writing within this reality?"

Turkle ponders this point.

Helmreich says, "Excuse me, I think I may be able to help here with 'Artificial Life science Christopher Langton's declaration that life 'is a property of the *organization* of matter, rather than a property of matter itself.' Some have found this claim so compelling that they maintain that alternative forms of life can exist in computers, and they hope the creation of such life-forms can expand biology's purview to include not just *life-as-we-know-it* but also *life-as-it-could-be*—life as it might exist in other materials or elsewhere in the universe.'"7

Gregarious says, "You offer a cogent explanation, I think, in your book _Silicon Second Nature_ about how AL scientists arrived at a view of computers as sources of potential life. Let me see if I can recount it here."

Gregarious clears its throat.
Dene hushes everyone in the room.

Gregarious says, "Computers were first seen as tools we use for computation, evolving next to a 'medium' of expression of mathematical phenomena.' When the universe could be expressed mathematically through computation of data, then scientists could argue the reverse: that computers could be defined as universes or worlds. Once that leap was made, then it didn't take much to connect computers to nature."8

Dene says, "And when computers are linked to nature, then we see a redefinition of physis and nomis, and everything associated with them!"

Gregarious says, "Yes, if ideas about nature (or natural law) change, then notions about what is enduring and conventional and ultimately *right* changes with it. . ."
Gregarious says, "It is difficult for a society when this happens."

Dene says, "Yes, a paradigm shift, to borrow from Thomas Kuhn.

Helmreich nods at Gregarious.
Gregarious bows to Dene.
Dene claps for Gregarious.

Dene says, "So, I guess the question is, what does this mean for notions of reality? . . ."

Dene moves closer to you.

Dene says, "Before we answer this, we should mention very quickly something about MOO discourse, the style of writing we are communicating with.

Dene says, "You may find this style of discourse at first very disconcerting and, perhaps, even inappropriate for academic contexts. . .[9] Dene says, "And to be honest, the informal tone and playful nature of MOO discourse does seem to run counter to the serious business of academic writing. . ."[10]

Dene says, "With so many voices talking and ideas being presented in what seems to be a disjointed, chaotic way, sometimes discussion goes many different directions, and it is hard to reel it back in to the original thread of conversation. . ."
Dene says, "But if you look back at the logs of such a discussion, you will see that much does get done—it is just done differently."
Dene says, "And the more you write in these environments, the less *different* it becomes."

Gregarious says, "I don't mean to interrupt such an eloquent speech, Dene. . ."
Gregarious says, "But you seem to indicate that there are several different types of MOO discourse occurring here: the descriptions and narratives required to create the ambience of the space *and* the conversations, what is called the MOOlog—or in this case the 'dialog'— taking place among the people talking and writing online."

Dene nods at Gregarious.
Dene says, "Yes, MOO discourse, whatever the 'type,' is writing, may seem strange at first to us and unfit for the categories we have constructed for classifying legitimate forms of writing. . ."
Dene says, "But once the novel was new and its form had to be identified, analysed, categorized and eventually accepted. . ."

Gregarious says, "Yes, 'new,'. . . hence the name 'novel:)."
Dene laughs.

Dene says, "But you know, the growing interest in distance learning and the realization that MOOs help to foster intellectual and emotional connections among students and teachers in online and traditional classroom contexts. . ."
Dene says, "Has made teachers and administrators consider MOOs as environments that enhance learning and promote research. . ."

Dene says, "Not to mention, see them as a viable way to reach large online audiences. . ."
Dene says, "Scholars working in these spaces take MOO discourse very seriously. . ."

John teleports in.
You are blanketed in stardust as John lands next to you.

Dene says, "Despite the light-hearted emoting that takes place."

Dene laughs and shakes silver glitter out of her hair.

Dene says, "You know John Barber, the co-editor of this book, right?"

John waves to you.
John joins you at Dene's desk.
Dene smiles at John.

Dene says, "Okay, where were we? Oh, right. For computer mediated communication to be effective, instructional strategies that may seem to a non-user as informal, untraditional/unconventional, or perhaps even silly, are necessary for effective communication in this particular environment. . ."
Dene says, "We hope you'll reserve judgment about the way we are writing this dispatch and dispense with any preconceived notions of what constitutes appropriate scholarly writing until you have completed reading our work. . ."
Dene says, "Now, back to reality. . . I mean, notions of reality."

Dene laughs,
John leans against the desk next to Gregarious.

John whispers [to Dene and you], "Hi, I see you started on time. I'll catch up in a minute. I got caught in some bad traffic driving back from Denton."
John turns to the computer screen and scrolls through the text.

Plato teleports in.
Glaucon teleports in.
Phaedrus teleports in.
You are blanketed in stardust as Plato lands next to you.
You are blanketed in stardust as Glaucon lands next to you.
You are blanketed in stardust as Phaedrus lands next to you.
Plato joins you at Dene's desk.
Glaucon joins you at Dene's desk.
Phaedrus joins you at Dene's desk.

John says, "Did you mention that it is precisely this informality that makes working in a MOO comfortable for students and colleagues."

Dene says, "Yes, I think I did just before you arrived. See, right there. . ."

Dene points to the screen.

Dene says, "But I should probably reiterate that because the AcadeMOO can be programmed so that my friends and I can drink coffee, sit on a couch, watch a video—movements represented on the screen textually and objects, graphically—as we have already said, the MOO environment simulates a *real* space and our actions, *real* interaction."

Plato shutters when he hears the word 'real.'
John smiles at Plato, Glaucon, and Phaedrus.
Dene waves at everyone.

John says, "Real, yes. . . . Yes, Plato. William Gibson defines cyberspace—that is, the space MOOs reside in—as 'consensual hallucination,' so if we all agree that what is happening here is real, then for all practical purposes, it is."[11]

Dene nods at John.

Dene says, "'The electronic frontier',[12] where we live our virtual lives in our virtual offices with our virtual friends. Seems real to me. But I consent to hallucinate with you all. What happens when someone doesn't consent? Is it less than real *just* for the dissenter? How about for the rest of us who continue to consent? Does this become a case of the Emperor's clothes?"

Plato wonders whom this Gibson fellow is.

John says, "William Gibson, one of the preminent cyberpunk authors.

VV says, "I would like to expand upon this topic about MOOs and virtual reality by bringing in Plato's own views of reality. . ."
VV says, "In this way we can get at the heart of traditional notions of reality, notions we have inherited from Plato and others that may be in need of redefinition or, at the very least, reexamination.

Dene nods at VV.
VV turns to Plato.
Plato moves closer to VV.

VV says, "'Before we can understand these, we must grasp the ancient distinction made by Plato among the concepts of 'ideal,' 'actual,' and 'sham' (virtual). . ."
VV says, "Briefly put, Plato assumes a realm of ideal forms for all things. His example of Book 10 of the _Republic_ is a bed: there is 'bedness' (as an abstraction, an ideal, the 'really real') before there can be an actual bed made by a carpenter. . ."

VV says, "An actual bed, therefore, is once removed from an ideal bed. For Plato, a painting of a bed is twice removed and hence it is a sham bed, a simulated bed, a virtual bed—and of no value except to confuse matters. . ."
VV says, "Consequently, Plato would allow the carpenter into his utopia, but not the painter."[13]

Dene says, "So, you are saying that Plato would not place much value on the actions and communications that take place here in AcadeMOO because the environment itself a 'sham,' is unreal, 'twice removed' from the ideal?."

VV nods at Dene.

Dene says, "So Plato then exemplifies that person who would not 'consent' to 'hallucinate' with us?"

John says, "No, not really, he doesn't deny multiple realities, just hierarchizes them. According to Victor, it seems that Plato would view this space as an example of sham reality, a reality which does exist but is of little real value. We should ask him directly."

John turns to Plato.
Dene taps her toes on the cave floor.

Dene says, "John, perhaps this is the world view at work when people say that writing undertaken with computer technology or in electronic spaces is less valuable than writing undertaken in print formats—or more importantly, face to face communication. . ."
Dene says, "This view is interesting because we know Plato believed that techne was 'the science of life . . . a special kind of wisdom,' to quote G. M. A. Grube. . ."[14]
Dene says, "As John and I talked about in the introduction to the book, Plato seems to distinguish between the process behind and the artifact of techne. He likes what we have to do physically with the *tools* of techne, but he certainly doesn't like the *byproducts* we end up with.

John says, "Yes, even today, 2,500 years later, this philosophy is at work. A case in point: Americans love owning and driving their own cars but hate the artifact of millions of people zooming down the freeways at the same time."

John remembers the parking lot he sat in for an hour on Interstate 635 this morning.
VV knows firsthand what John is talking about since he lives near I30.

Plato says, "Dene, I mean Glaucon, '[t]he art of representation . . . is a long way from reality,' don't you agree? Try as you may to mimic nature, but truly a MOO is a mere reflection of the truth, an image of what really *is*.

Glaucon says, "'No Doubt,'15 Socrates . . . I mean, Plato."

Plato eyes Glaucon coldly.
Glaucon blushes at his mistake.

Dene says, "Glaucon's *slip,* it seems, provides us with a perfect lead in to an explanation about Plato's dialogues, since Victor has already alluded to them when he mentioned the _Republic_."

Glaucon wonders if Dene knows what she is getting into having a conversation with Plato about his work.
John thinks Glaucon doesn't know Dene very well.

Dene says, "As you know, Plato is known for his dialogues—works intended for the people of Athens and based on the teachings of his former teacher Socrates. It is believed that Plato wrote Socrates's ideas down faithfully in the early dialogues but moved toward an application of Socratic thought in the later works . . . "
Dene says, "It is difficult to determine if Socrates truly existed, or if Plato adopted Socrates' dialogues as a conceit for his dialogues . . ."

Gregarious says, "I don't mean to interrupt, but I just want to point out that while some may scoff at the conceit of using MOO discourse for constructing a scholarly argument—as you are doing here—they should also question the possible conceit underlying Plato's dialogues—works taken quite seriously among scholars."

Dene says, "Precisely!"

Plato frowns at Dene and wonders why the people sitting around the cave, particularly Dene and Gregarious, aren't shackled.
Glaucon muffles his laughter.
Phaedrus turns his head and laughs softly.

Dene says, "Let me continue . . ."
Dene says, "Because Plato is credited with writing the dialogues, he is generally referred to as the author, though Socrates and others are the speakers . . ."
Dene says, "Plato himself never appears as a speaker in the works, but his name is mentioned in the _Apology_ as one of Socrates's faithful followers present at the trial . . ."16
Dene says, "So, Socrates *may* have spoken the dialogues, and Plato *may* have been the one to write them down. Because Plato is supposedly faithful to his Socrates's teachings, the ideas expressed in his dialogues are often identified with him, too. Hence, Glaucon's

momentary confusion:) . . ."

Dene says, "In essence, Socrates wasn't *real*ly present to deliver the words found in the text but is *virtually* present."

John says, "Do we then refer to Plato's dialogues as sham writing?"

Dene taps her toes on the cave floor and smiles at Plato.
Gregarious speculates that Socrates—whether real or not—becomes Plato's written personae, that Plato *is* Socrates in the dialogues, just as some of us take on other names, genders, personalities in electronic spaces.
Plato thinks Gregarious, like Dene, should spend less time online and more time training in classical thought.

John says, "Plato, I need for you to clarify something for me. You say that if something is not *real*ly, real in the sense that Socrates defines it, it has no *intrinsic value* to society, to the universe?"

Plato nods at John.

John says, "So no matter what knowledge gets made here in this MOO today, or for that matter, no matter what we learn from the books we read, those spaces and that activity are not of value to us?"

Plato nods again.

John says, "Then how do we learn?"

Dene jumps in.

Dene speaks up, "Perhaps Professor Grube would like to join us. His book, _Plato's Thought_ has helped make sense of Plato and his writings for well over six decades now."

Grube leaves his chair and joins you by Dene's desk.
Grube bows politely to everyone stationed around Dene's desk.
Plato thinks the professor's book is brilliant.
Grube bows to Plato and turns toward Dene.

Grube says, "Actually, Dene, we should talk about reality in terms of Plato's notion of the Forms. Let me see if I can shed some light on this topic. I'll . . .how do you say this?. . . *paste in*? what I wrote about this in my book, since you did, indeed, mention my tome."

Plato moves closer to the computer screen.
You squint at the light of the screen.

- - - - - - - - - - - - - - - - - -Grube pastes - - - - - - - - - - - - - - - - - -

'The theory of 'ideas' is the belief in eternal, unchanging, universal absolutes, independent of the world of phenomena; in, for example, absolute beauty, absolute justice, absolute goodness, from which whatever we call beautiful, just or good derives any reality it may have.'[17]

'The theory [presented in the _Phaedo_] is approached from the epistemological side: there exists certain things which we know and which we do not apprehend by means of the bodily senses, and these are the true.'[18]

'On the one hand is the Ideal, 'that which is divine, deathless, intelligible, of one kind, indissoluble, always in the same way identical with itself'; and opposed to this is the phenomenal world 'human, mortal, varied in kind, unintelligible, soluble, never in any way identified with itself.'[19]

'[F]irst, . . . realities such as the good, the equal, the beautiful & c., . . . are absolutely true but cannot be perceived by the bodily sense. They can only be grasped by a process of reasoning akin to the mathematical, by the mind freed as far as possible from the errors of sense. In the second place that there are the realities which the mind saw before birth, as described in the _Meno_, and that we remember them because we are reminded of them by the objects of sense. . . . In the third place these Ideas are unique, stable and eternal, and the contrast is clearly drawn between them and the world of sense. . . . Lastly, these eternal Ideas alone can lead us to a satisfactory theory of causation: no account of a particular thing is possible when it is considered in isolation, it must be brought into a class, the common characteristics it shares with other members of that class must first be understood; and these common qualities, considered abstractly, are the Ideas.'[20]

- - - - - - - - - - - - - - - - Grube stops pasting - - - - - - - - - - - - - - - - -

Gregarious believes that the key here for a contemporary reinterpretation of notions of reality lies in the word 'mathematical.'"
Helmreich nods at Gregarious.

Dene says, "Yes, Gregarious. Hold that thought a minute longer while I clarify what Professor Grube has said."

Dene turns to Grube.

Dene says, "So, let me see if I understand what you are saying . . ."
Dene says, "Plato believes there is a *false* reality we experience through 'the bodily sense,'—material objects revealed through the senses––and a *real* reality we perceive through some sort of intellectual process relating to mathematics—ideas that do not have material form?"

VV retires to the back of The Cave.
Turkle joins VV.

John says, "Does the Ideal Form of cyberspace correspond to the matrix Gibson talks about in _Neuromancer_? If so, it is attainable by only those technosavvy enough—or to put it your way—possessing the ability to reason it intellectually enough to know how to 'jack in' to it."[21]

Dene says, "Hmm. I have to think about that. I thought quickly about the Straylight,[22] which seems to be the antithesis of Plato's sunlight. The false light. Certainly Case is the man who eventually escapes his fetters:) Oh, but think about it—Molly corresponds to Boethius's and Dante's lady who leads the hero through the intellectual / spiritual maze of the cave toward enlightenment, or in this case, a combination of virtual and physical freedom!"

John grabs _Neuromancer_ from Dene's desk.
John clears his throat.

John says, "'The Villa Straylight knows no sky, recorded or otherwise . . . . At the Villa's silicon core is a small room, the only rectilinear chamber in the complex.'[23] Seems cave-like to me."

Plato shakes his head at Dene and John.
Plato turns to Glaucon.

Plato says, "'As for the man who believes in beautiful things, but does not believe in beauty itself nor is able to follow if one lead him to the understanding of it—do you think his life is real or a dream? Consider: is not to dream just this, whether a man be asleep or awake, to mistake the image for the reality?'"[24]

Glaucon says, "Assuredly."

Dene says, "Wait a minute . . ."
Dene says, "Are you insinuating that there is an Ideal notion of a MOO, which constitutes reality. The actual hardware and software going into producing the image of the MOO we are currently experiencing here in the AcadeMOO is second removed from reality . . ."
Dene says, "And the graphical representation on this computer screen is third removed from reality? . . ."
Dene says, "And for this MOO to be good, beautiful, and true it must reside in the Ideal, which resides apart from our senses and our perceptions?"

Glaucon nods at you.
Plato elbows Glaucon and gives him a sharp look.

Plato whispers [to you], "I wish Glaucon wouldn't encourage her—I know where she is going with this."

Dene says, "So the printed representation of the conversation we are having here—what we call the MOOlog—by your definition, would also be considered bad, ugly, and false . . ."

Dene says, "But if you define the Ideal Forms, as Grube suggests, as 'eternal' and 'unchanging' and value them for these qualities . . ."

Dene says, "How is a print form of a MOOlog any less eternal, any less unchanging than the Ideal MOO? What makes it less valuable? I mean, it endures far longer as written discourse than it would as oral discourse—and you certainly seem to value that. . ."

Dene says, "Although it makes sense that you would classify and organize reality to make sense of it—just like Heim does with virtual reality in his work—but how can you hierarchize it like you do? . . ."

Dene says, "Especially when the qualities you identify in your definition of the Ideal Forms are the exact same qualities that define written texts . . ."

Dene says, "This is the same trouble I have with your notion of writing—you seem to say one thing and then do another. It seems like you changed your mind in midstream, or were ambivalent, at best, about writing."

Grube clears his throat, signaling he wishes to interrupt you.

Grube says, "'[I]t has sometimes been supposed that Plato abandoned, or at least fundamentally altered, his belief in the existence of Ideas' but 'there is no evidence to indicate any such change."[25]

Dene says, "Yes, but believing that Plato didn't change his ideas means that even the oral dialogues that Socrates engaged in and the written dialogues Plato produced documenting Socrates's conversation are inferior to the Ideal notion of Socratic reasoning. Can we truly hierarchize Socrates's teachings simply due to the *form* or shall I say, medium, we find it in? . . ."

Dene says, "It would be wonderful if we could meet Socrates face to face, assuming he *is* real . . ."

Plato frowns at Dene.

Dene says, "And have the opportunity to talk to him, but should we devalue his words—his written words—, those found in your dialogue just because they may have been preserved in writing? . . . Aren't the ideas he espouses eternal no matter how they come to us? . . ."

Dene says, "Do we value his words reproduced digitally even less? Are his dialogues located on the Perseus CD or on some site the World Wide Web even less valuable than the print versions?"

John says, "Birkerts would certainly think so."
Dene smiles at John.

Dene says, "Are the ideas generated in this space any less valuable than if we spoke them orally or if they did indeed exist *out there* somewhere in that big sunlit Ideal MOOspace in the sky?"

Plato frowns.

Dene says, "If the Greek definition of *truth* is derived from the idea of *not forgetting*—that is, 'alethe' . . ."
Dene says, "Then, it stands to reason that the preservation of the words, in any format, espousing that truth becomes the topmost goal of knowledge making . . ."
Dene says, "Gertrude Stein herself alludes to this when she says 'the only thing that is different from one time to another is what is seen and what is seen depends upon how everybody is doing everything.'"[26]
Dene says, "And the way in which our epistemology evolves is inextricably linked to the technology available at the time? . . ."
Dene says, "Not only does the medium transmit knowledge (making knowledge dependent upon the medium for its transmission)—we make, but it shapes its message as well. That idea forms the basis of this book, you know. Other people, McLuhan, Berger have argued this—so we are not alone out here."

Gregarious says, "Dene, explain who Berger is for our friend:)"

Dene says, "John Berger, _Ways of Seeing_. Wonderful book. Read it in grad school."
Dene says, "He says that 'every image embodies a way of seeing . . . . The compositional unity of a painting contributes fundamentally to the power of its image.' And he does question the notion of 'value' in our understanding of a work or idea . . ."[27]

Gregarious nods.

Dene says, "From what he suggests, knowledge we make may be valuable no matter what form, no matter what medium it is ultimately expressed in . . ."

Gregarious says, "Good point, Dene. Can we really dismiss the knowledge made in a platonic dialogue even if the conversation between Socrates and Glaucon never really took place? Does that render what Socrates / Plato say less important?

Dene says, "And if there is evidence of knowledge-making archived in a MOOlog, or a website, an email message—is this any less valuable? And even if evidence is not archived, wouldn't the fact we could all

recall the experience mean that it happened, that it was real, that
something may have been gained in the experiencing? . . ."

Dene gets excited when she remembers that the Greek word for cunning
wisdom is from the same root as gain and profit.
Dene jumps up and down.

Gregarious says, "Ah, you are thinking of kerd—for 'kerdea' and
'kerdion'."
Dene grins at Gregarious.

John is reminded of his original comment about Gibson's 'consensual
hallucination.'"

Dene says [to Plato], "You may argue for the concept of *MOOness* of a
MOO, but can you really say a MOO's MOOness exists apart from the
MOO itself? Isn't that problem Aristotle tried to reconcile in his
rethinking of the Ideal Forms? That the sum of a thing's parts are not
less than its whole?."

John is getting confused with all this mooing.
Dene laughs.

Grube clears his throat, signaling he wishes to interrupt you.
Grube says, "'[T]o look upon the ideas as concepts in any shape or form
is a mistake, for a concept cannot by definition exist until the mind has
conceived it, and this Plato quite deliberately refused to admit of his
Ideas . . ."
Grube says, "They are rather the objective reality to which the concept
corresponds, and they exist whether we know them or not.'"[28]

Dene says, "So Plato thinks we don't need MOOs to express MOOness?"
But the useful*ness* of a MOO does insinuate it is *useful*, and usefulness
is key to harmony, another very important concept for you, Plato."

Guthrie leaves his chair and joins you by Dene's desk.

Guthrie says, "W. K. C. Guthrie."

Guthrie smiles politely at you.

Guthrie says, "Think of it this way: 'objects of knowledge, the things
which could be defined, did exist, but were not to be identified with
anything in the perceptible world. Their existence was in an ideal world
outside space and time. These are the famous Platonic Ideas . . . and
which meant form or pattern. In one way then the English word 'idea' is
about unsuitable a rendering as could be found, for to us it suggests
what has no existence outside our own minds, whereas to Plato the
'ideai' alone had full, complete, and independent existence.'"[29]

Dene says, "So, Plato's Forms, what we think of as his Ideal, is the medium by which truth is articulated?"

Gregarious says, "The form *and* the substance of the true . . . and the good and the beautiful, as well."

Dene says, "Then John was right earlier to speculate that the internet may possibly exemplify an Ideal Form since it is an object of knowledge, a thing that can be defined, does exist, but not to be identified with anything in the perceptible world. Indeed it exists outside of time and space, and has full complete and independent existence. And it is a medium. It can be the substance and the form of knowledge."

John scratches his head trying to remember when he said that.

Gregarious says, "Yes, but the problem with that idea is that we can perceive the internet, so it is second removed and, thus, sham reality."

Plato ponders this point for a moment.

Dene says, "Let's take a break from this thread so that we can show this slide we meant to show earlier.

Dene shows "From Dialogues to MOOlogs " Slide #1

* *

We have called this dispatch a 'dialog' because dia-log" refers both to the platonic style of discourse, the *dia*lectic, that we borrow for our work and to the MOO*log* genre common to this electronic environment. It also emulates the kind of discourse that takes place in real-time in a MOO among its denizens and the supposedly real-life conversations that took place between Socrates and various people.

* *

Plato frowns at Dene again when he hears the word 'supposedly.'
Glaucon tiptoes out.

Dene says, "Actually others might call this a 'polylogue,' a term seems to carry both the sense of connectiveness *and* disconnectiveness. . ."[30]
Dene says, "And we are not denying that this phenomenon is not at work here, that this conversation is utopian in some way."

John wonders if Dene plans to edit the MOOlog for publication since there are so many misspelled words and emoting taking place that may be distracting for the reader.

Dene says, "John, normally we wouldn't if the MOOlog was intended for an audience acquainted with the protocols of MOOing. But since we are trying to write for a larger audience, we probably will. I hope doing this won't be offensive to anyone."

John says, "It will sure make it easier to read. It is probably a good idea to clean up the log a bit without losing its original flavor."

Dene nods at John.

Dene says, "But getting back—what interests *us* most about the structure of platonic dialogues, and why we have borrowed the 'dia' in lieu of the 'poly,' is that dialogue is quickly recognizable as a word implying a certain amount of orality inherent in the text—a quality often ascribed, though some people believe erroneously, to electronic writing as well."

Plato turns to Phaedrus.
Phaedrus is sorry to see Glaucon go.

Plato says, "Writing . . . has this strange quality, and is very like painting; for the creatures of painting stand like living beings, but if one asks them a question, they preserve a solemn silence. And so it is with written words.'"

Phaedrus sighs.

Phaedrus says, "'Very true.'"[31]

Dene says, "Okay, this is exactly what I am talking about, Plato . . ."
Dene says, "That you can vilify writing in the _Phaedrus_ on the one hand, and then produce it on the other suggests, perhaps, ambivalence toward a specific quality of writing rather than an outright rejection of it, don't you think? . . ."
Dene says, "Professor Grube here believes that you discussed the Ideal Forms less in your later works *not* because you abandoned them but because you had no longer assumed the notion of the Ideal Form was a claim in need of evincing . . ."
Dene says, "But couldn't we also see your silence as ambivalence? I don't know. But you contradict yourself in many places that just doesn't make any sense."

Grube says, "'Plato's mind was synthetic rather than analytic. He never treats subjects separately. That is why commentators find it impossible to explain his ethics for example without at the same time explaining the rest of his philosophy.'"[32]

Dene says, "Personally I have always felt there are multiple Platos—in other words, like many of us his ideas and views change with time and experience. One Monolithic Plato does not exist, but the Plato of the _Timeaus_, the Plato of the _Symposium_, etc . . ."

Dene says, "And the Plato of the _Phaedrus_ demonstrates the tension between orality and writing in a way that many of us today feel tension between print and electronic discourse."

Mick leaves his chair and joins you by Dene's desk.
Dene wants to remind everyone that Mick is also a contributor to this book:)."

Mick says, "'In all fairness, Plato was not truly criticizing the tool that is writing; he was speculating about, and criticizing the realm he believed the interiorization of that tool would force people to live within.'"[33]

Plato nods at Mick.
Warnock leaves her chair and joins you by Dene's desk.
You think the desk area is getting crowded.

Warnock says, "Remember, 'philosophy is not in the business of providing solutions to problems.' Rather, it 'rais[es] questions about things which might seem to have been settled, or, more often, might never seemed to be questionable at all.'"[34]

Dene says, "So Plato was not necessarily telling us the answer to the question—What is reality—but merely speculating about the nature of it because people may have become complacent in what it *was* and *meant*?"

John says, "Like Cindy Selfe arguing we must 'pay attention to' technology when it becomes transparent in our society—at the point in time when it is fast becoming transparent in our society."[35]

Dene nods.

Mick says, "Or Michael Joyce reminding us that 'technology aspires toward transparency."[36]

Gregarious says, "Plato may have been responding to the growing transparency of writing—when writing as a technology was replacing orality and was inserting itself into a different, perhaps *higher* reality?
Dene says, "It was at that point that it needed to be questioned and thought more carefully about!"

John thinks about that idea for a minute.

Dene says, "But the problem is that so much of what Plato—and Aristotle—have said developed into dogma for us, thousands of years of dogmatic thinking about reality, beauty, women's place in society. It just seems to have been taken *beyond* speculation, or what we call description, and into prescription . . ."

Dene says, "You may wonder why Plato's philosophy has any connection to writing for electronic spaces like MOOs and the World Wide Web since it predates the computers by thousands of years . . ."
Dene speaks up, "Let's see if A. N. Whitehead and Guthrie have anything to say about this topic. Gentlemen, your thoughts?"

Whitehead stops and looks up at you when he hears his name.
Whitehead leaves his chair and joins you by Dene's desk.

Dene says, "Will you say something to our guest about Plato's influence?"

Whitehead says, "We were just discussing this."

Whitehead eyes Guthrie, daring him to interrupt.

Whitehead says, "Well, 'the safest general characterization of the European philosophical tradition is that it consists of a series of footnotes to Plato."

Grube smiles at Whitehead.
Warnock refuses to take sides in this issue.
Whitehead folds his arms and stares at Guthrie.

Guthrie says, "Yes, but as I was saying to you earlier, Plato's philosophy doesn't hold up well in contemporary society—'Aristotle suffers less than Plato if treated on the principles of the Outlines of Knowledge so much in favour to-day'."[37]

Whitehead shakes his head.
Whitehead leaves The Cave in a burst of light.
Dene says, "BRB."

Plato wonders what brb means.

John whispers [to Plato and you], "Means, *Be Right Back*."

Guthrie leaves The Cave in a burst of light.
Dene returns with some notecards.
Dene clears her voice and smiles at everyone assembled around her desk.

Dene says, "Let me explain briefly how Plato has come to influence our culture even today."

- - - - - -- - - - - - - - - - Dene pastes - - - - - - - - - - - - - - -

Let me just say that we are not claiming that our culture follows the thinking of Plato (and Aristotle) because we have made some conscious effort to do so. Rather, their worldviews have left an indelible mark on Western civilization through practical means. For example, any student of the middle ages can tell us that Plato's concepts, particularly those relating to reality found in the _Timeaus_, shaped Augustine's thinking almost 800 years after Plato's death (Knowles 35). Considered by many to be one of the most influential thinkers of his time, Augustine was instrumental in laying the groundwork for early Christian thought in the 4th century A.D. In turn, these ideas were inscribed upon medieval society by the Church, whom Augustine and others after him helped to shape.

Even when Plato's (and Aristotle's) writings were lost after the fall of the Roman Empire and subsequent invasions of Europe by various Germanic peoples, we knew of their teachings from texts that had trickled into the West from the Middle East and Moorish Spain during and after the Crusades. Thomas Aquinas, the father of scholasticism and intellectual thought during the 13th century, is credited for re-introducing Aristotelian thought to Western culture after he had studied Latin translations of Arabic copies and commentaries of the philosopher's work (Grant 52).

Later Cosimo de Medici was instrumental in the dissemination of Plato's texts in the 15th century (Yates 13), an event instrumental in ushering in the Italian Renaissance. In the 17th and 18th centuries science united platonic philosophy with Christianity further and, in doing so, brought Plato to us in the philosophic vision of the orderly, controlled, and "providentially guided" universe during the Age of Reason (Jacob 242). Romantic poets of the late 18th and early 19th centuries fell under the influence of hermeticism, a strange mixture of mysticism, magic and philosophy (Tuveson 152-169) derived loosely from platonic doctrine, and by doing so retranslated Plato for another generation of thinkers (_Hermetica_ 2). In the late 19th and early 20th centuries Aristotle's approach to knowledge-making—what we call empiricism—influenced Modernist thinkers and artists, from William James to Gertrude Stein.

Thus, Plato's—and Aristotle's—ideas have been carried through the ages because thinkers before us found what these two philosophers think significant in some way, and due to this, platonic and aristotelian views on science, the arts, gender differences, politics and philosophy have lived on, in some iteration, to contemporary times.

- - - - - - - - - - - - - - - Dene stops pasting - - - - - - - - - - - - -

Mick says, "'I'd like you to go back to my comment about Plato's reasons for speaking against writing."
Mick says, "His speculating about 'interiorization of the tool'—that is, working in a solitary fashion rather than reaching out to others in a community to make knowledge together in conversation?"

Gregarious sees a connection between Plato's notion of community and this conversation taking place right here in this MOO.

Dene says, "But what is more interesting, perhaps, is the tension we sense between what Plato's texts propose to be, real oral discourse—what he refers to as *Logos*—and what they really are, written texts, which Plato condescendingly calls *logoi,* words that can be subverted by the uninterested or ignorant."

Mick nods at Dene.

Dene says, "Once again it goes back to Plato's anxiety about the *product* of writing—the archivable text of his dialogue that could be subverted without the assistance of the philosopher to explain it."

Gregarious says, "And he does demonstrate a nervousness about this process, too—that the process of working alone will undermine society."

John says, "So both bothered him."

Dene says, "Actually it is change that bothers him. He likes the notion of the eternal because it is where truth can reside. You know, when something is remembered over a long course of time, we tend to think of it as physis, as natural . . ."

Dene says, "Change destroys truth by corrupting its foundations. . ."

Dene says, "I think about that wonderful example Jay David Bolter uses in _Writing Space_, when he is demonstrating the notion of change inherent in the tools we use to think with. I think the excerpt comes from _The Hunchback of Notre Dame_."

John says, "'This will destroy that!' is what I think he wrote."[38]

Plato likes being referred to in the third person when he is standing in the room.

Dene says, "Yes, the idea that, just as the 'printed book' will destroy the foundations of medieval life—the Catholic Church—so will the computer destroy the foundations of contemporary life . . ."

Dene says, "We need to expand our definition of technology to include more than computers . . ."

Dene says, "Avital Ronell, for example, blames the technology of the telephone in her book, _The Telephone Book_ for creating a schizophrenia in our culture."

John says, "I can't remember where I read it but someone argued very convincingly once that the automobile destroyed American society."

Dene says, "Maybe we can see technologies as causing loss *and* gain."

John says, "Do we have a monolithic symbol for our culture—a symbol that represents an institution so powerful that it controls our very lives and the way we think, or is our society so decentered that there is not one thing that will destroy us if it fell?"

Dene says, "Television? It's not a symbol of an institution, but it exerts powerful control over us. But can we further break down our media-driven society with computers than we already have with the introduction of the TV?"

Gregarious locates a copy of _The Medium is the Message_ from the pile of books on Dene's desk.

Gregarious says, "Listen to this quote by McLuhan and Fiore: 'Until writing was invented, man lived in acoustic space: boundless, directionless, horizonless, in the dark of the mind, in the world of emotion, by primordial intuition, by terror. Speech is a social chart of this bog'."[39]

John thinks McLuhan overstates the case a bit too much.
Dene agrees.

Dene says, "I wonder if it only looks like a 'bog' to us? Maybe people living in an oral culture have a different notion of intellectual space than we have today—that the *limits* of their landscape implied by McLuhan can be seen differently? Maybe we can no longer understand this structure since we have been influenced so greatly by writing."

John looks for Dene's copy of Ong's _Literacy and Orality_.

Dene says, "It's not here. I lent it to a student. But I do have a copy of Rosalind Thomas's _Literacy and Orality in Ancient Greece_."

Dene clears her voice.

Dene says, "She says, "Orality is often idealized, invested with the romantic and nostalgic ideas connected with folklore, folk culture, and folk tradition, or the 'noble savage'. . . . In other words [orality] become[s] more than merely descriptive . . . and start to imply a whole mentality or world view which is partly born of a reaction to the modern world."[40]

Gregarious says, "In other words, she doesn't agree with McLuhan."

Dene says, "Actually she says she favors scholars who study 'detailed, culturally specific studies of the manifestations of literacy, in a given society, often eschewing entirely any of the wider claims made for the effects of literacy,' it says here on page 15."[41]

Dene puts the book down.

Plato turns to Phaedrus.

Plato says, "'The man who thinks that in the written word there is necessarily much that is playful, and that no written discourse, whether in metre or in prose, deserves to be treated very seriously . . . that man, Phaedrus, is likely to be such as you and I might pray that we ourselves may become.'"[42]

Dene says, "We are glad you brought up this idea that writing should not be taken seriously, Plato."

Dene turns to you and continues to speak.

Dene says, "As we said previously, similar criticism has been leveled at electronic discourse. Michael Heim, for example, condemns electronic media for its potential to manipulate and disenfranchise the masses."[43]

Dene picks up a pile of books from her desk and holds them out for you to see.

Dene says, "Here are some others: Barbara Garson's _The Electronic Sweatshop: How Computers are Transforming the Office of the Future into the Factory of the Past_, James Brook and Iain Boal's Resisting the Virtual Life: The Culture and Politics of Information_, the Critical Art Ensemble's _The Electronic Disturbance_."

Dene speaks up, "However, there are those, like Langham here, who disagree with Heim and point to MOOs as spaces in the public sphere that are not silent, not a place of 'primordial fear', and will perhaps *re*connect the individual to the community . . ."

Langham leaves his chair and joins you by Dene's desk.
Langham nods and smiles.

Dene says, "In fact McLuhan and Fiore tell us that 'print technology created the public.[44] Electric technology created the mass.'" A belief in complete opposition to Plato's notion of 'interiorization of that tool' Mick brought up earlier."

Dene picks up a copy of _The Virtual Community_ from the pile of books on her desk.

Dene says, "And of course Howard Rheingold talks about the virtual community, or 'social aggregations that emerge from the Net when enough people carry on those public discussions long enough, with sufficient human feeling, to form webs of personal relationship in cyberspace. . .'"[45]

Dene says, "So, Plato, even if you are somehow right to lambaste writing, can you honestly rail against electronic communication?"

Dene laughs at the thought of Birkerts reading this last statement.[46]
Mick wonders who will elegize electronic writing in some future period.

Dene says, "Actually John does this in his dispatch, "Following in the Footsteps."

John shrugs his shoulders and smiles at Dene.
Dene turns to Plato.

Dene says, "But you certainly should see that this electronic discourse does offer opportunities for public discourse, on a grand scale, perhaps much in the same way as oral discourse did for your culture."

Gregarious likes Dene's idea that technology brings about a situation where there is a loss and a gain.

Langham says, "Excuse me, but what I said was that . . ."
Langham says, "'It is possible that MOO is the forerunner of technology that will provide the sort of structured environment needed for the 'common place' of civilized society. If so, we have the median between the oral and the literate extremes.'[47]

Dene nods at Langham.

Dene says, "I didn't mean that electronic discourse *was* oral discourse . . ."
Dene says, "Only that there may be some commonalty."

Dene shows Metaphors for Electronic Forms Slide #2

* *

What Don Langham calls 'the median' between orality and writing, Mick Doherty refers to as 'a new hybrid form.'[48] Elizabeth Klem and Charles Moran think of it as "amphibious."[49] And Janet Murray calls it "incunabular."[50] Certainly we can describe Plato's dialogues as a kind of hybrid that of the oral tradition and the *newer* technology of writing. In fact, Jay David Bolter suggests that very idea in _Writing Space_.[51] He says Plato's dialogues bridge orality with written discourse. John and I describe this transition period as 'ambiscriptual' in our Introduction to this book.

* *

Dene wonders what Plato thinks about this idea.
Plato ponders this point for a moment.

Dene says, "Indeed scholars have long argued that the qualities associated with electronic writing—dynamism, flexibility, and immediacy—makes this kind of writing more akin to orality than to handwritten texts or print."[52]

Dene smiles at Langham.

Dene says, "So, other people have made this connection . . ."
Dene says, "John, will you read the part that is underlined on pages 58 and 59 in Bolter's book since you are still holding it?"

John flips through the pages.

John says, "'The contrast between oral and written texts is important for an understanding of electronic writing, because in some ways the new medium more closely resembles oral discourse than it does conventional printing or handwriting . . . . Electronic text is, like an oral text, dynamic. . . . However, there remains a great difference between oral poetry and the silence of electronic writing.'"[53]

John closes the book and sets it back down on Dene's desk.
Dene types in the URL to Langham's website on her computer.
Dene taps her foot while she waits for the website to load.

Langham says, "Some people see electronic writing as 'Western culture's salvation from print,' while others call it 'electronic skywriting—the fourth cognitive revolution.'"[54]

Dene says, "Bruce Mazlish's book, called _The Fourth Discontinuity: The Co-Evolution of Humans and Machines_, takes it a step further. It is not simply a matter of a cognitive revolution but the realization that there may be taking place a cognitive evolution shared between humans and machines . . ."
Dene says, "George Dyson does a good job fleshing out the evolutionary history and possibilities of machines in his book, _Darwin Among the Machines_ . . ."
Dene says, "And then there is that whole Artificial Life concept sketched out in Helmreich's book we mentioned earlier."

Mick knows a lot of people in academe who would be extremely uncomfortable with those ideas.

Langham says, "'In this revolution, writing will allow us to communicate with speeds approaching that of speech, which is much closer to the speed of thought than other communication media.'"[55]

VV leaves his chair and joins you at Dene's desk.

Dene says, "Which I believe you are suggesting will have a positive effect on society, judging by your use of the phrase 'salvation from print.'"
Dene says, "But this lag time you suggest occurs in even without print texts . . ."

Dene says, "Gertrude Stein was very interested in the speed of cognition . . ."

Dene says, "In _Tender Buttons_, specifically, she explores the notion of the 'linguistic moment,'[56] that moment after we come in contact with an object but before we form its name in our mind. The moment before language is made. The brain's lag time . . ."

Dene says, "And the opening line in Berger's book he says 'seeing comes before words. The child looks and recognizes before it can speak.'"[57]

John laughs at the idea of the brain lagging.

VV says, "Think of it as 'net congestion.'"
Dene grins.

Dene says, "I wonder if there is some connection between the notion of the brain lagging and our ability to discern the Ideal Forms—that maybe if the brain had no lag time, we could comprehend the abstractions, 'the objective reality', far better than we do—assuming the Forms exist."

Gregarious says, "Yes, ironically, while the brain helps us make knowledge it also obfuscates it as well."

John says, "Even those who reject platonism would have to agree that there is a brain bias toward certain kinds of data or information that could possibly lead to new knowledge."

Dene says, "Like knowing that the data in front of you points to a heliocentric universe but the religious views you hold in your mental databanks cannot allow for that knowledge to become truth?."

Plato smiles when he thinks of the pre-Socratics.

Dene says, "So Langham, faster is better? Or rather the immediacy present in speech makes speech preferable to print? Is what we are doing here in this MOO, giving a sense of immediacy that we couldn't achieve in a regular print text? What about MOOlogs? Is the sense of immediacy lost when we download the conversation and print it out? Or is immediacy inherent in the style found in the written material?."

John says, "Literary writers have long been aware that writing in the first person and in the present tense brings the reader more inside the story."

Dene says, "Yes, but in fiction you have the choice to write in three different persons. Here in the MOO we write . . . well, what is this?"

Gregarious think MOOlogs read like a play script, like drama.

Plato thinks it is not like any drama he has ever experienced.

Dene laughs at Plato.

Dene says, "This may be one time you may be agreeing with Aristotle on a topic, Plato. You are right—we don't provide a tragic hero, unless you count our guest here as having to endure great misery in having to undergo such nonsense as this dialog and his one major flaw is that he is overly-polite and will not leave his torment:)."

Dene winks at you.

Grube leaves The Cave in a burst of light.

Warnock leaves The Cave in a burst of light.

Gregarious says, "MOO discourse is highly sophistic writing, based loosely on the 'platonic dialogue,' as you suggested earlier. And so it will either be enjoyed for its playfulness and irreverence or vilified for it."

Dene says, "Yes ...
Dene says, "But getting back to Plato's criticism of writing ... "
Dene says, "I think you, Plato, were arguing, instead, against the silence of writing, rather than the speed of it. And silence suggests ignorance. And ignorance is antithetical to wisdom."

Plato says, "Yes, Written words—'you might think they spoke as if they had intelligence, but if you question them, wishing to know about their sayings, they always say only one and the same thing.'"[58]

Dene says, "Okay, but you wrote this statement, not spoke it orally to an audience—like Socrates probably spoke it—so very possibly your dialogues represent a hybrid form of writing that combined orality with written discourse."

Plato knows where Dene is taking this argument, and he doesn't like it.

Dene says, "Like your dialogues, electronic writing may also be a hybrid form of literacy—one that is part oral, part writing, and also part print, if we consider that we publish texts online in a style that emulates print formats ... "
Dene says, "What we will finally classify it as, I do not know. But exploring it with a traditional ancient literary style that may itself represent a hybrid form, may help us better understand the nature of writing in electronic spaces—and the technologies that produce it ... "

Gregarious says, "And the biases toward it."
John nods.

Dene says, "In fact, there are scholars, like you, Langham, who have argued that electronic writing will indeed spur interest in classical forms of writing ... "
Dene says, "Bolter long made the connection between classical studies and computer technology ... "[59]
Dene says, "And I guess this dispatch may demonstrate that both of you are right."

Dene smiles at Langham.

Dene says, "And, of course, as someone who conceived of writing a MOOlog to talk about Plato's philosophy—before ever reading your essay *or* Mick's discussion about this topic . . ."
Dene says, "I would have to agree that it is quite easy to make the leap from the platonic notion of the dialogue to the textual iteration of a MOOlog . . . "

Dene admits she sees Greek influence everywhere she looks.

Dene says, "But even if you are unfamiliar with ancient genres, you can certainly understand how electronic forms of writing allow for experimentation in styles and subject matter. . . ."
Dene says, "Perhaps because electronic writing represents a space where the constraints normally placed upon formal scholarly writing have not yet been put into place . . ."
Dene says, "And there is that notion that writing in virtual spaces is not *real* writing—it is playing at writing, and because it is playing, we can be *playful*."

Dene thinks about the wonderful presentation she heard at Computers and Writing 1999 Conference by Albert Rouzie about play theory.[60]
Mick retires to the back of The Cave.
Langham tiptoes out.
VV retires to the back of The Cave.
Phaedrus moves away from Dene's desk into the shadows of The Cave in search of Glaucon.

Dene says, "We never explained the background of The AcadeMOO . . ."
Dene says, "It is based on the name of Plato's famous school in ancient Athens, called not surprisingly, The Academy . . ."

Dene smiles when she thinks about Athens.

Dene says, "We should also tell you about Plato . . ."
Dene says, "About 3 weeks ago around 3 o'clock in the morning I was working here in The Cave, my office in the AcadeMOO, trying to create the graphical representation of the fire that you see burning behind you—when someone teleported in calling himself 'Plato . . .'"
Dene says, "Since I had not yet told anyone that I was creating a MOO, I was surprised when he first appeared. But what was even more strange was that this 'Plato' began commenting upon particular philosophical points that I have long been interested in and then applying them to various aspects of technology . . ."
Dene says, "We talked for hours about the representation of reality, stasis and dynamism, knowledge and artificial intelligence, and

improving or destroying our way of life with computers . . ."
Dene says, "He told me that he had been navigating the World Wide Web that evening and somehow he had found his way into my MOO. Although it was obvious he was new to using the internet, he was quick to hit upon the key issues many of us working with electronic technology frequently discuss . . ."

Plato wonders why Dene is so surprised by this.

Dene says, "The sun had come up before I realized that I had not gone to bed and that it was time to leave for work. I had not even had the presence of mind to record our dialogue. But our conversation stayed in my mind for days and days . . ."
Dene says, "He had promised to return at the end of that week to continue our discussion about philosophy and electronic technology, and he requested that I ask some of my colleagues and friends also knowledgeable about these subjects to join us . . ."
Dene says, "Before he left, he insisted that he was, indeed, 'The Plato' I had read and studied in school—and certainly his knowledge of Plato's philosophy was astonishing . . ."
Dene says, "So, we have all been meeting in here for a series of conversations on various philosophical ideas Plato expounded about in his works and their relation to electronic writing and electronic spaces, conversations we have been recording for posterity. . ."
Dene says, "The dispatch reflects one such "dialog" . . ."
Dene says, "We are compelled to share what we have learned with you, and we hope you find what these women and men say about the philosophy and technology as fascinating and illuminating as we do."

John still refuses to believe this virtual Plato is real.
Plato wonders why John is so quick to disbelieve what he cannot see and possibly can never know.
Dene laughs when she hears this.

Dene says, "The personae we take in a MOO represents the person whom we think we are. It is as real as we are."
Dene speaks up, "Maybe Professor Turkle would like to talk about the notion of the reality behind personae for a moment, since she is the far-most authority on the subject."

Turkle leaves her chair and joins you by Dene's desk.

Turkle says, "'MOOs blur the boundaries between self and game, self and role, self and simulation . . . . [P]eople don't just become whom they play, they play who they are or who they want to be or who they don't want to be. Players can use their MUD personae to refine their sense of who they are.'"[61]

John locates a copy of _High Wired_ from Dene's desk.

John says, "Let me read from this book for a moment."

John flips through the pages.

John says, "This is from one of players you cite: 'You can be whoever you want to be. You can completely redefine yourself if you want. You can be the opposite sex. You can be more talkative. You can be less talkative. Whatever. You can just be whoever you want, really whoever you have the capacity to be'."[62]

Turkle smiles at John.

Turkle says, "Yes, 'virtuality is powerful, transitional, and put to the service of [the] embodied real.'"[63]
Turkle says, "I need to go, but I do want to say one more thing . . ."
Turkle says, "'I have often referred to computers as evocative objects for our time, objects that cause us to reflect upon ourselves . . . . MOOs are revealed as evocative objects for thinking about society, education, creativity, reality, and, perhaps most fundamentally, for thinking about the self.'"[64]

Turkle smiles at everyone and waves.
Turkle leaves the Cave in a burst of light.
Dene rubs her eyes and laughs.

Dene says, "The idea that Plato had placed himself into Socrates's trial depicted in the _Apology_ is so similar to the way we place ourselves into MOOspace in these conversations. There is a virtuality involved in Plato's dialogues that is also present here in our dialog."

John says, "Do you think that someone 2,500 years from now will wonder about the realness of our MOOlogs, in whatever form they survive? Will MOOing together in The Cave seem like a conceit to make a point or will it occur to them that it may be real? Will it matter?"

Dene says, "That's a question I often ask: Does the reality of a thing *really* matter if it results in truth and knowledge? To me the question is not *if* Socrates is real and his trial really took place, but that from *that* potential our civilization learned important lessons about integrity, strength, wisdom, etc . . . "
Dene says, "Perhaps some of the notions we demonstrate here will make an impression on someone. Like the idea that we are collaborating to make knowledge . . ."
Dene says, "Even if you don't believe this dialog is really taking place and it is just me writing this dispatch for John's and my book, you cannot deny that I have conferred with others through their ideas in

their books and electronic spaces and that I am not alone in this process. By incorporating these folks's works as I do, I am collaborating with countless other people to make this knowledge in this dialog . . ."

Dene smiles.

Dene says, "Which is why rather than using first person pronouns 'my' or 'I,' denoting personal ownership of a text as we normally may do when talking about a work that we write, you find 'we' and 'us' here . . ."

Dene says, "'We' talk about the ideas expressed in this MOOlog as concepts articulated by all present here . . ."

Dene says, "And I see myself as a facilitator or the synthesizer of the knowledge-making."

Dene says, "There are some other strategies we are using here you may also have noticed."

Dene says, "We have been "chunking text." By limiting discussion to about three to four lines per entry, we can follow the thread of conversation more easily . . ."

Dene says, "Oh yes, you probably noticed the ellipsis each of my entries . . ."

Dene says, "This means that the speaker has not completed her or his thought and requires you to wait before you respond to the comments written . . ."

Dene says, "Oh yes, the reason you can't hear everyone talking and whispering here in The Cave is because in order to be heard by everyone online, each speaker would have to *join us at Dene's desk.* This command allows folks to be heard by those standing in the same area . . ."

Dene says, "We can essentially tune out all these other conversations that way. It is less disruptive to the main threads of conversation . . ."

Dene says, "We can 'speak up' and everyone can hear us, but if we simply 'say' then only those around the desk can hear . . ."

Dene smiles.

Dene says, "Now, we are going to paste in something we have created that explains the connection between the *ancient* philosophy of Plato and *electronic technology*."

You feel a breeze of cold air as Dene whisks off into the darkness of the Cave.

Dene returns with her disk.

- - - - - - - - - - - - - - - - - - Dene pastes - - - - - - - - - - - - - - - - - - -

At first glance, ancient philosophy and electronic technology do not seem at all compatible because Plato's philosophy—and Aristotle's for that matter—predate the computer by around 2,400 years. In fact, most scholars have turned to modern philosophers, like Heidegger or Hegel,[65] or contemporary thinkers, like Derrida or Foucault,[66] to underpin their views of technology. A more careful study of the subject, however, would reveal that much of the thought and perceptions we hold dear and the way we interact with various elements in our culture have been shaped by ideas and world views that have existed long before us—and a whole lot of these thoughts and perceptions came to us by way of Plato, or maybe more precisely, Socrates, who is the speaker in Plato's dialogues.

For example, the hypertextual environment underlying the World Wide Web did not just automatically pop up out of nowhere one day (ex nihilo), but was born over a course of time and engendered by many. Those of us who have studied hypertext theory well know that hypertext has its roots in everything from Vannevar Bush's Memex, to oral discourse, literary writings, and medieval codices (Bolter 21-25). But we should not forget that Plato and Aristotle both shaped the way we categorize and hierarchize information—an important issue when we consider that without the notion of structure, storing and retrieving data from hypertextual environments would be impossible.

The journey from the 100-ton Rockefeller Differential Analyzer developed for winning World War II by MIT's Center of Analysis (Owens 3) to the small boxes filled with silicon and wires that sit on our desks is not a long one, at least as far as technological revolutions go—a mere 50 years (Barber, "Seven Ages of Computer Connectivity"). What's even more amazing is that in less than one decade, our world, once seemingly so broad and expansive, has been transformed into a global village (McLuhan and Fiore, 63), and we, into virtual globetrotters.

Think about it: At any given time of the day any one of us with access to a networked computer and an email account can transport himself or herself anywhere in the world and communicate with anyone else with access to these things. We can navigate the World Wide Web, locate the website of a foreign country, and virtually visit that country, moving from museum to historical site with ease. We can meet with friends online in real-time in MOOs and carry on a conversation as if we are all in the same room together, going so far as even drinking a virtual cup of coffee and lighting a virtual fire in a graphical representation of a fireplace.

It is an awesome journey we take each time we log on, one that takes us to spaces that a decade ago we never knew existed: Web sites, online databases, MOOs, listservs, usergroups, chat rooms, electronic libraries. Even without access to a networked computer or knowledge of these electronic spaces, technology pervades our very existence. We can't open a newspaper without seeing ads for computers, Internet providers, software. We can't watch a commercial on television without a URL address printed on screen promising to provide more information about the product advertised.

In short, computer technology is so ubiquitous now that some of the services it provides are completely transparent and growing more so daily. We don't even think about the computer under the hood of our cars controlling the car's temperature, the mainframe carrying the data about our bank deposit to another branch, or the communications network connecting the air traffic controller to the pilot flying above. But they are all functioning, quietly and relatively efficiently. And as Cindy Selfe warns us, when technology becomes transparent, then we must "pay attention to" it or else it can become dangerous.

There is little doubt that technology is transforming our lives in ways we never thought possible. Besides its capability to connect us to large amounts of information or to one another across vast distances, the computer is also forcing us to think about old issues from a new perspective—from rape (can it really be rape if it's "virtual?") to questions about intellectual property (who owns the rights to documents printed on the web?).

However, climbing at lightening speed as we have been doing toward this precipice we call the Information Age, we have little understanding about what it means to be here or what we ought to be doing with all this information as we move forward in our journey up the rough ascent.

One way to get a handle on the meaning behind these changes caused by technology is through philosophy. Philosophy literally means "love of wisdom." It is the "pursuit of knowledge and the endeavor to live the good life." The knowledge referred to here includes "both knowledge of the world around us (knowledge of what is) and knowledge of the good life (knowledge of what *ought* to be)" (Sprague and Taylor 1).

- - - - - - - - - - - - - - - - - - -Dene stops pasting -

Grube teleports in.
You are blanketed in stardust as Grube lands next to you.

Dene says, "Remember what Mary Warnock said earlier: 'philosophy is not in the business of providing solutions to problems.' Rather, it 'rais[es] questions about things which might seem to have been settled, or, more often, might never seemed to be questionable at all.'"[67]

John nods in agreement.

Dene says, "So, you see, philosophy is an investigation in which we journey on a quest for knowledge—knowledge that sometimes, on the surface, may not seem like something necessary to pursue but, upon closer inspection, *is* . . ."

Dene says, "All of us in this room, The Cave, are not trying to provide you with the right answers *but* instead are trying to ask the right questions relating to various aspects of electronic writing. Reality. Value. Being and Becoming. Harmony . . ."

Dene says, "Journeys, by definition, do not have to be physical—they can be intellectual too."

Dene smiles at the thought of Boethius's _The Consolation of Philosophy_.

John says, "But the beauty of the MOO environment is that it does allow us to "move" physically through the space."

Plato shakes his head when he hears the word 'move'.

Dene notices that Plato is interested in the idea of movement.

Dene says, "Okay, the moving around may be virtual, but there is a realness about this activity of moving—when we type our movements onto the keyboard, we *are* essentially moving data around on a server, which in turn moves us onscreen . . ."

Dene says, "We do experience 'agency, ' as Janet Murray suggests, in our 'immersion' into these environments, so much so that we are in essence able to experience some sort of 'transformation' when we have completed our experience'[68] . . ."

Dene says, "By agency we mean 'the satisfying power to take meaningful action and see the results of our decisions and choices.'"[69]

John says, "Yes. Murray defines immersion as 'is the sensation of being surrounded by a completely other reality. . .'"[70]

John says, "While transformation implies mutability, the ability to enact change."[71]

Dene says, "Which implies movement."

Dene taps her toes on the floor of The Cave.

Plato says, "'The philosopher . . . who holds these things in honour (i.e. mind, intelligence, & c.) cannot possibly accept from those who assert the existence either of one or of many Ideas the theory that the whole of reality stands still . . .'"

Plato says, "'Nor must he listen at all to those who say that reality is ever in every kind of motion, but, like children in their wishes, he must insist on having it both ways; what is immovable is also in motion, the whole and the real are both.'"[72]

Dene says, "Oh, so you are agreeing with us:)?."

Grube says, "Let me translate . . ."

Grube bows politely.

Grube says, "'[T]o be known is a form of activity . . . and the Ideas are at least capable of being known: they are in some manner subjected to an activity and are thus acted upon . . .'"

Grube says, "'And we cannot surely believe that this intelligible world . . . is entirely devoid of activity, life, soul, wisdom, and intellect. Of that which is completely unmoved and inactive . . . there cannot be knowledge.'"[73]

Dene says, "So movement—intellectual or physical or both—is required in order *to know* . . ."

Dene says, "Hence the importance of *the journey theme* in philosophy and literature . . ."

Dene says, " And the quality to evolve, to become, the potential to be other than what we are at a particular point of time."

Dene ponders this point for a moment.
Plato smiles at Dene.

Dene says, "But, Plato, would you view moving around in a MOO as 'sham' movement, like moving around in a dream, even though we are making knowledge here? . . ."

Dene says, "Is there a difference between moving from ignorance to wisdom here in The Cave in our MOO and moving from ignorance to wisdom in the cave in your 'Allegory?' Surely you told that story to move your audience toward enlightenment, although they themselves did not physically move in inch."

Grube says, "The answer lies in _The Sophist_."

Plato says, "Let me quote: 'By heaven, shall we believe that there is no movement, life, soul or knowledge in what supremely is, that it neither loves nor knows, but stands motionless, in proud sanctity, without life or movement?.'"[74]

Grube says, "Yes, '[T]he knowing mind . . . is a principle of active movement and causation.'"[75]

Dene says, "Then evolution is the normal state? . . ."

Dene says, "And the answer is NO—there is no difference between the types of movements! The key seems to be the state of mind, the movement toward knowledge. It doesn't matter where we do it, just *that* we do it . . ."

Dene says, "That is why Boethius was able to journey to knowledge while in his prison cell and Dante journeyed in the afterlife—and, of course, Odysseus around the Mediterranean Sea—and each gained knowledge!"

Gregarious nods.

Dene says, "Okay, but movement—journeys—suggest changing reality, and changing reality is generally connected to the way we view *being and becoming*, which goes right back to the principles underlying the material world where you say we reside and the world of intelligence's where you say the Ideal Forms exist . . ."
Dene says, "In order to find knowledge, we must change reality—the ability to get ourselves from Point A to Point B intellectually, representing movement from one state (ignorance) to another (knowledge) . . ."
Dene says, "Movement implies the state of *becoming*. If we already know, then we are. We don't need to become anything anymore. But if we want to know, then we have to become. But aren't we *being* while we are *becoming*? Doesn't one imply the other?."

John locates a copy of 'Natural and Artificial Intelligence' from the pile of books on Dene's desk.
John flips to page 565.

John says, "Robert Sokolowski says that 'artificial writing promises to do more than writing can do, but it has a foothold in writing: it puts into motion the thinking that is embodied in writing. Our philosophical challenge is to clarify what sort of motion thinking is.'"[76]

Dene likes thinking of writing as motion.

Dene whispers [to John and you], "I love that article. I still find things in it that helps to sort out so much for me."
Dene says, "Of course, the real question is, Do we ever get to the point where we know all and so do not have to move or to become anymore?"

Plato nods at Dene.

Grube says, "Yes, 'Plato insisted upon the possibility of knowledge and upon the existence of absolute values.'"[77]

Dene says, "As we said earlier, actuality and potentiality are both present in written texts, but they are not as readily apparent as they are in hypertextual writing . . ."
Dene says, "That's the beauty of webbed environments—and of MOOs too, since they represent written and electronic spaces . . ."
Dene says, "Maybe the best way to think about it is *that we make meaning while we mean*."

Dene holds up a big sign:

> What are the connections between humans and computers, that is between real life and artificial life?

Dene says, "Maybe the answer to this question lies in Helmreich's text. He has been idling for quite some time now—I think he may have walked away from his computer . . ."
Dene opens _Silicon Second Nature_.

Dene says, "Helmreich provides the 'infomatic view of organisms: "After a while the analogy between the self-replicating programs and living organism becomes so perfect that it becomes perverse to call it merely an analogy. It becomes simpler just to redefine the word organism to apply to both chemical and software creatures . . .'"
Dene says, "'This identification of organisms with programs does not merely indicate a commitment to form over matter, it plays on the popular and scientific conceit that organisms are ultimately nothing other than the unfolding of a genetic plan and that genes equal information structures anagolous to computer programs.'"[78]

Dene says, "The way we answer this question will certainly go far to explain our fear and loathing, so to speak, about computers and other forms of technology."

John locates two books from the pile on Dene's desk.

John says, "The humans in Adolph Huxley's _Brave New World_ are so dehumanized that they do not appear really 'brave' in their world—and the 'savage' who does acts heroically is treated poorly for it."

Dene smiles.
John sets the copy of _Brave New World_ down on her desk.

John says, "And the androids in Philip Dick's _Do Androids Dream of Electric Sheep?_ are so human that they know they do not really dream. . ."
John says, "Which, in Dick's book, is a quality that separates humans from machines.[79]

John sets the copy of _Do Androids Dream_ down on Dene's desk.

Dene says, "John, do you see the copy of McLuhan's book we were using earlier? Will you read the lines underlined on page 53?."

John opens the book begins to read.

John says, "'The instantaneous world of electric informational media involves all of us, all at once. No detachment or frame is possible.'"[80]

John sets _The Medium is the Message_ down on Dene's desk.

Dene claps for John.

Dene says, "Thanks, John. . ."
Dene says, "If we cannot 'detach' ourselves or escape the 'global village,' if our society is becoming truly technocentric in regards to electronic technology, electronic writing, then perhaps the question we all need to ask is . . ."

Dene holds us a big sign.

```
┌─────────────────────────────────────────────────────────────────┐
│                                                                   │
│          What is the best way to live in this environment?        │
│                                                                   │
└─────────────────────────────────────────────────────────────────┘
```

Dene says, "McLuhan and Fiore tell us back in 1967 that 'the medium, or process, of our time—electric technology—is reshaping and restructuring patterns of social interdependence and every aspect of our personal life'. . ."
Dene says, "They tell us that 'it is forcing us to reconsider and reevaluate practically every thought, every action, and every institution formerly taken for granted. Everything is changing—you, your family, your neighborhood, your education, your job, your government, your relation to 'others.' And they're changing dramatically."[81]
Dene says, "So how do we view these changes, this relationship with technology? . . ."
Dene says, "With fear? Anxiety? Anger? With conflict? . . ."
Dene says, "As we suggested earlier, Plato in the _Phaedrus_ lashed out against his own technological shift and at the same time used it to write his diatribe."

John locates a copy of _The Pill Versus the Springhill Mining Disaster_ from the pile of books on Dene's desk.

John says, "Poet Richard Brautigan, however, suggests something else . . ."
John says, "His poem, 'All Watched Over by Machines of Loving Grace' presents a utopian vision of technology and our relationship with it."

Plato has already addressed the notion of utopia in the _Republic_.

Dene says, "But I wonder if you received negative comments about your idealism and over-optimism like Brautigan received from his?"
Dene says, "Or perhaps as *we* may from this MOOlog—although what some people may interpret as idealism and over-optimism we see as an open-minded approach toward a very early iteration of computer technology."

Dene shrugs her shoulders.

Dene says, "Maybe rather than disregard Brautigan's work for its seemingly uncritical approach to technology, we can, instead, see it as an attempt to offer another perspective, one in which we can find harmony with an element in our lives that some of us may find disruptive and regard dubiously at best."

Grube clears his throat, signaling he wishes to interrupt you.

Grube says, "Plato tells us that 'harmony is the essence of goodness and usefulness.'"[82]

Dene says, 'Yes, but isn't it interesting that it is precisely the Greeks who gave us the notion of agon???? As in contest, struggle, test??? The route to heroism was paved in *agon*ies, which runs counter to the notion of harmony!"

Dene shakes her head.

Dene says, "Let's ask John to read Brautigan's poem for us, since he was a friend of Brautigan's *and* is the author of the annotated bibliography of his works.

John opens the book to page 1 and begins to read.

John says, "'I like to think (and / the sooner the better!) / of a cybernetic meadow
where mammals and computers / live together in mutually / programming harmony / like pure water / touching clear sky' . . ."

John smiles.

John says, "Yes, I knew Brautigan when we were both living in Montana. Montana has about the clearest, biggest sky I have ever seen. It is easy to see why his utopian vision would include a clear Montana-like sky, since he loved it out there . . ."

John says, "'I like to think / (right now, please!) / of a cybernetic forest / filled with pines and electronics / where deer stroll peacefully / past computers / as if they were flowers/ with spinning blossoms.'"
John says, 'I like to think / (it has to be!) / of a cybernetic ecology / where we are free of our labors / and joined back to nature, / returned to our mammal / brothers and sisters,
and all watched over / by machines of loving grace.'"

John smiles and gives the book back to Dene.

Dene smiles at John's excellent reading.
Grube claps for John.

John says, "'It has to be!' There is a sense of urgency here . . . "

Dene says, "Maybe he knew something about the tension between humans and machines that we don't yet know."

John says, "I guess his main point is, 'Why live in conflict with something so integral to our lives? Wouldn't it be best to find some way to harmonize with computer technology?—I think he is saying here."

Dene says, "Or make it harmonize with us."

Dene wonders if the movement toward GUI interfaces may be part of this notion of harmonizing the machine.

Dene says, "It is interesting that Brautigan talks about computers as far back as 1968."

John smiles.

John says, "Remember, Douglas Rushkoff talks about the connection between virtual reality, psychedelic drugs, and technology in his article, 'Seeing is Beholding,' in Victor's book . . ."

Dene speaks up, "Rushkoff is here in The Cave with us. . ."
Dene speaks up, "Rushkoff, do you want to tell us a bit about the possible connection between cyberia and the psychedelics of the 60s counterculture?."

Rushkoff joins you by Dene's desk.

Rushkoff says, 'Psychedelics use among cyberians has developed directly out of the drug culture of the 1960's. The first tripsters—the people associated with Leary on the East Coast and Ken Kesey on the West Coast—came to startling moral and philosophical conclusions that reshaped our culture.'"[83]

You think about the raves in more recent times, especially in the cyberpunk novels of Pat Cadigan.

Rushkoff says, "From the principle of morphogenesis, cyberians infer that psychedelic substances have the ability to reshape the experience of reality and thus—if observer and observed are one—the reality itself.'"[84]

Dene says, "So, let me see if I understand what you are saying . . ."
Dene says, "Someone undergoing a psychedelic experience could see a vision like Brautigan writes about—where machines look like flowers and handle mundane tasks for us—and, based upon the notion of morphogenesis, that vision could become reality?"

Rushkoff says, "Yes. 'Cyberians infer that psychedelic substances have the ability to reshape the experience of reality and thus—if the observer and observed are one—the reality itself. It is hardly disputable that, even in a tangible cultural sense, the introduction of the psychedelics into our society in the 1960s altered the sensibilities of users and nonusers alike.'"[85]

Dene says, "So we can make our own reality just by attaining the proper frame of mind? . . ."
Dene says, "Hmmm. This idea fits nicely into Plato's notion of reality . . ."

Dene thinks about this for a minute.

Dene says, "The concept of morphogenesis interests me—I teach mythology, you know, and my students and I spent some time recently studying creation myths . . ."
Dene says, "Morphogenesis in direct opposition of the Logos Doctrine. You know, the creation style found in _Genesis_ and creation stories from other cultures."

Dene waves her arms around.

Dene says, "God said let there be light . . . and there was light. Truly 'ex nihilo'. Creating something out of nothingness. Which reminds me of the way Plato describes creation in the _Timeaus_."

Grube says, "Yes and no. In the _Timeaus_ Plato tells us that '[T]he world is a living being endowed with soul and mind . . . and this soul is spread throughout the universe. It is prior to body, since without it the world cannot live, though this priority is logical only and there never was a time when the world was not; soul once more is the beginning, origin or first principle . . . of life.'"[86]

Plato nods at Grube.

Gregarious says, "Yes, but don't forget that Helmreich reports that many male researchers do indeed feel embued with a sense of the creative force when they program their microworlds."[87]

Dene says, "So reality made from our own minds is not real, but the reality created by the 'world' 'soul' is. Are you suggesting that the Ideal Forms come from this first principle? "

Plato says, "Yes, 'Of divine things he himself is the maker, mortal things he orders his own offspring to bring about. They received from him the immortal first principle of soul and next in imitation of him fashioned around it a mortal body as a carriage for it and within this they built another part of the soul, which holds strange and compelling attributes within itself: first pleasure that greatest bait of evil, then pain escape from good, then rashness and fear, witless councillors, anger that is hard to pacify, hope that is easily misled. These they mix with unreasoning perception and desire that will grasp at everything. Thus of necessity they put together humankind.'"[88]

Dene says, "So, Plato, in your view anything created by humans is automatically flawed and cannot ever match the Ideal . . ."

Plato nods.
John thinks this idea explains human's fear of AI and cloning.

Dene whispers [to John and you], "And the anti-android sentiment expressed by the characters in _Do Androids_."

Dene says, "And the nature of humankind is one of 'rashness', 'fear' and misperception? . . . "
Dene says, "So if we naturally misperceive—because that is our nature—then, how can we know there truly exists the Ideal Forms? Couldn't that too be a misperception? How do you know you haven't erred, Plato, in your philosophizing?"

Gregarious says, "I think the argument boils down to 'patterns,' as Helmreich suggests . . ."

Dene says, "Yes, Helmreich tells us that quantum mechanics holds that 'the only thing that truly exists in the universe is pattern; the substance that supports these patterns is, in some fundamental sense, inessential (in a familiar example, our bodies' molecules, etc., are being replaced constantly. So that we are not so much our matter as the pattern of our matter) . . ."
Dene says, "'This idea that universes are just patterns allows people to claim that 'universes' can be transported from one kind of computer hardware to another; universes are, as the computer science jargon goes, 'portable'.'"[89]

Plato frowns.

Gregarious says, "He says that 'things can be alive or on fire *with respect to* computer worlds.'"

Dene says, "Yes, one researcher told him, 'Life can only be defined with respect to a particular physics. A computer virus is almost as alive as a real virus . . . but only within the physics of the computer memory.'"

John says, "So patterns develop into a truth which goes on to define substance and underlies the form in which substance is articulated in?"

Grube ponders this point carefully.

Gregarious says, "Yes, and to the laws of physics governing the state they appear in, it seems."

Dene sighs.

Dene says, "Plato was right within the mathematical framework he had inherited at his time, but when we expand into current notions of mathematics, his ideas become hopelessly antiquated."

Dene looks at Plato sadly.
Gregarious puts its hand on Dene's shoulder.
Plato knits his brow and hugs Dene.
Plato moves away from Dene's desk into the shadows.

Dene says, "It will be hard for us to let go of these ideas that Plato gave us, but I know we have to in order to make sense of the world we are currently living in . . ."
Dene says, "I had long wondered what we could possibly replace Plato's philosophy with. I guess the answer lies in the theories and ideas generating out of quantum mechanics, artificial life movement, and the work taking place in artificial intelligence . . ."

John nods.
Dene sighs.

Dene says, "Change is frightening for us. But Plato is right in suggesting that our natural reaction to anything new is fear, in which case it makes sense that we would at first reject and rail against computer technology before looking for ways to harmonize with it—as Brautigan hopes for . . . "
Dene says, "It just seems that in a world becoming more and more dependent upon computers and machines, we must understand what being *technocentric* really entails for us . . ."
Dene says, "Thinking about the various views and philosophies that underpin our views and beliefs about technology may help us to achieve some understanding about our connection with technology. It may make our relationship to it less frightening. . . "
Dene says, "Plato's stance on the nature of reality clues us in to some of the underlying reasons we are, indeed, in conflict with machines."

John says, "We raised more questions than we answered."

Dene says, "Yes, but I guess I am wondering why all 'traditional' academic writing has to follow the traditional layout of 'argumentation'? Why can't there be a new style that allows for less emphasis on persuasion and more on group exploration? And if it can, then isn't MOO discourse a perfect environment for this kind of writing?"

John says, "But then you deviate from Plato, because isn't the purpose of his dialogues to persuade the others to see his point of view?"

Dene says, "But Plato is wrong about reality—couldn't he be wrong about our purpose of communicating?"

Dene draws a deep breath.
John turns on the CD player.

You hear music echoing through The Cave. It is Van Morrison's haunting voice. He is singing a song that sounds familiar, but you cannot remember its name. You begin to hum softly to the music. 'Oh, Oh Socrates and Plato they / praised it to the skies / Anyone who's ever loved / everyone whose ever tried. . ."[90]

Dene smiles.

John says, "We need to stop. I am getting tired."
Dene says, "Yes, good idea . . ."
Dene says, "I need to think about what just happened here. . ."
Dene says, "It is painful for me to let go of Plato—and Aristotle—for that matter, they have been a part of my work for so long:(."

John puts his arm around Dene.
John Barber takes a seat on Dene's desk.
Dene holds up a big sign:

The following works were cited or referred to throughout this dispatch.

Barber, John F. "Seven Ages of Computer Connectivity." __Kairos : A Journal for Teachers of Writing in Webbed Environments_. 2.1 Spring 1997. http://english.ttu.edu/kairos/2.1/features/Barber/Ages_information.html.

Berger, John. _Ways of Seeing_. British Broadcasting Corp. and Penguin Books, 1972.

Bikerts, Sven. _The Gutenberg Elegies_. NY: Fawcett Columbine, 1994.

Bolter, Jay David. "The Computer, Hypertext, and Classical Studies." _The American Journal of Philology_ 112 (1991): 541-545.

---. _Writing Space: The Computer, Hypertext, and the History of Writing_. Hillsdale, NJ: Lawrence Erlbaum Associates, Publishers, 1991.

Brautigan, Richard. _The Pill Versus the Springhill Mining Disaster_. New York: A Delta Book, 1968. 1.

Brook, James and Iain Boal. _Resisting the Virtual Life: The Culture and Politics of Information_. San Francisco: City Lights, 1995.

Critical Art Ensemble. _The Electronic Disturbance._ Brooklyn, NY: Autonomedia, 1994.

Dick, Philip. _Do Androids Dream of Electric Sheep?_ . New York: Ballantine Books, 1968.

Doherty, Mick. "MOO a Tool, MOO as Realm: A Response to Don Langham." _Computer-Mediated Communication Magazine_ 1:7 (November 1994). http://sunsite.unc.edu/cmc/mag/1994/nov/moo.html.

Dubnick, Randa. _The Structure of Obscurity: Gertrude Stein, Language, and Cubism_. Chicago: University of Illinois Press, 1984.

Dyson, George. _Darwin Among the Machines: The Evolution of Global Intelligence_. Reading, MA: Helix Books, 1997.

Garson, Barbara. _The Electronic Sweatshop: How Computers Are Transforming the Office of the Future into the Factory of the Past_. New York: Penguin Books, 1988.

Gibson, William. _Neuromancer._ London: Grafton, 1986. 67.

Grant, Edward. "Science and Theology in the Middle Ages." _God and Nature: Historical Essays on the Encounter between Christianity and Science_. Ed. David C. Lindberg and Ronald L. Numbers. Berkeley: University of California Press, 1986. 49-75.

Grigar, Dene. "Defensio Tabularum: A Defense of Archiving Writing Created for Webbed Environments." _Kairos : A Journal for Teachers of Writing in Webbed Environments_. Spring 1997. http://english.ttu.edu/kairos/2.1/.

Grigar, Dene and John Barber. "Defending Your Life in MOOspace: A Report from the Electronic Edge." _High Wired: On the Design, Use, and Theory of Educational MOOs._ Ed. Cynthia Haynes and Jan Rune Holmevik. Ann Arbor: University of Michigan Press, 1998. 192-231.

Grube, G. M. A. 1935. _Plato's Thought_. Indianapolis: Hackett Publishing Company, Inc., 1980.

Guthrie, W. K. C. _The Greek Philosophers: From Thales to Aristotle_. New York: Harper Torchbooks, 1975.

Heim, Michael. "The Essence of VR." _CyberReader_. Ed. Victor Vitanza. Boston: Allyn and Bacon, 1999. 20-35.

---. "The Technological Crisis of Rhetoric." _Philosophy and Rhetoric_ 21 (1) : 48-59.

Helmreich, Stefan. _Silicon Second Nature: Culturing Artificial Life in a Digital World_. Berkeley: University of California Press, 1998.

Hermetica. Ed. and Trans. Walter Scott. Boston: Shambala, 1993.

Jacob, Margaret C. "Christianity and the Newtonian Worldview." _God and Nature: Historical Essays on the Encounter Between Christianity and Science_. Ed. David C. Lindberg and Ronald L. Numbers. Berkeley: University of California Press, 1986. 238-255.

Joyce, Michael. _Of Two Minds: Hypertext Pedagogy and Poetics_. Ann Arbor: University of Michigan Press, 1995.

Knowledge and Value. Ed. Elmer Sprague and Paul W. Taylor. New York: Harcourt Brace and World, Inc., 1959.

Klem E., & Moran, C. "Computers and Instructional Strategies in the Teaching of Writing." _Evolving Perspectives on Computers and Composition Studies. Urbana: National Council of Teachers of English, 1991. 132-149.

Knowles, David. _The Evolution of Medieval Thought_. New York: Vintage Books, 1962.

Kuhn, Thomas. 1962. _The Structure of Scientific Revolution, Second Edition, Enlarged__. Chicago: University of Chicago Press, 1970.

Landow, George. _Hypertext: The Convergence of Contemporary Critical Theory and Technology_. Baltimore: Johns Hopkins University Press, 1992.

Langham, Don. "The Common Space MOO: Orality and Literacy in Virtual Reality." _Computer-Mediated Communication Magazine_1:3 (July 1994). http://sunsite.unc.edu/cmc/mag/1994/jul/moo.html.

"Lexicon of Virtual Culture." http://www.seas.upenn.edu/~mengwong/cyber/cvvc1.html#1.4.

Mazlish, Bruce. _The Fourth Discontinuity: The Co-Evolution of Human and Machines. New Haven: Yale University Press, 1993.

McLuhan, Marshall and Quentin Fiore. 1967. _The Medium is the Message_. New York: Touchstone, 1989.

Morrison, Van. "I Forgot That Love Existed." _Poetic Champions Compose_. Produced by Van Morrison. Caledonia Productions, Ltd.

Murray, Janet. _Hamlet on the Holodeck: The Future of Narrative in Cyberspace_. New York: The Free Press, 1997.

Owens, Larry. "Vannevar Bush and the Differential Analyzer: The Text and Context of an Early Computer." _From Memex to Hypertext: Vannevar Bush and the Mind's Machine_. Ed. James M. Nyce and Paul Kahn. Boston: Academic Press, 1991. 3-38.

Plato. _The Apology_. Trans. Harold North Fowler. Cambridge: Harvard University Press, 1990. 68-145.

---. _Ion._ _The "Ion" and Four Other Dialogues of Plato._ Trans. Percy Bysshe Shelley. London: J.M. Dent
and Sons, Ltd., n.d. 1-16.

---. _Meno_. Cambridge: Harvard University Press, 1990.

---. _Phaedrus_. Trans. Harold North Fowler. Cambridge: Harvard University Press, 1990. 412-579.

---. _Phaedo_. Trans. Harold North Fowler. Cambridge: Harvard University Press, 1990. 201-403.

---. _The Republic of Plato_. Trans. and Intro. Francis MacDonald Cornford. New York: Oxford University Press, 1963.

---. _The Republic_. Trans. Paul Shorey. Cambridge: Harvard University Press, 1990.

---. _The Sophist_. Cambridge: Harvard University Press, 1990.

---. _Timeaus_. London: Penguin Books, 1977. 29-126.

Rheingold, Howard. _The Virtual Community: Homesteading on the Electronic Frontier_. Reading, MA: Addison-Wesley Publishing Company, 1993.

Ronell, Avital. _The Telephone Book: Technology, Schizophrenia, and Electric Speech_. Lincoln: University of Nebraska Press, 1989.

Rouzie, Albert. Applying Play Theory to the Emergent Traditions of the CMC Composition Course. Computers and Writing Conference 1999 Rapid City, SD. 28 May 1999.

Rushkoff, Douglas. "Seeing is Beholding." _CyberReader_. Ed. Victor Vitanza. Boston: Allyn and Bacon, 1996. 31-42.

Selfe, Cynthia L. "Technology and Literacy: A Story about the Perils of Not Paying Attention." _College Composition and Communication_ 50 (1999) : 411-436.

Sokolowski, Robert. "Natural and Artificial Intelligence." _The Informed Reader: Contemporary Issues in the Disciplines_. Ed. Charles Bazerman. Boston: Houghton Mifflin Co., 1989. 562-573.

Sprague, Elmer and Paul W. Taylor. _Knowledge and Value_. NY: Harcourt, Brace, and World Inc., 1959. 1.

Stein, Gertrude. 1926. "Composition as Explanation." _The Selected Writings of Gertrude Stein_. New York: Random House, 1990.

---. 1914. _Tender Buttons_. _The Selected Writings of Gertrude Stein_. New York: Random House, 1990.

Thomas, Rosalind. _Literacy and Orality in Ancient Greece_. Cambridge: Cambridge University Press, 1992.

Turkle, Sherry. "Foreword." _High Wired: On the Design, Use, and Theory of Educational MOOs._ Ed. Cynthia Haynes and Jan Rune Holmevik. Ann Arbor: University of Michigan Press, 1998, ix-xix.

---. _Life on the Screen: Identity in the Age of the Internet_. New York: Simon & Schuster, 1995.

Tuveson, Ernest Lee. _The Avatars of the Thrice Great Hermes: An Approach to Romanticism_. Lewisburg: Bucknell Press, 1982.

Vitanza, Victor. 1996. _CyberReader_. Boston: Allyn and Bacon, 1999.

Warnock, Mary. _The Uses of Philosophy_. Oxford: Blackwell, 1992.

Yates, Frances A. _Giordano Bruno and the Hermetic Tradition_. Chicago: The University of Chicago Press, 1964.

John yawns.
Dene laughs.
Dene holds up a big sign:

Next, you see the works from which each character in this MOOlog
quoted and the page number on which you can find his or her passage
in case you would like to revisit that passage. Those works that do not
list page numbers are generally web sites. Their URL addresses are
listed in the bibliography at the end of this dialog. At times we
mentioned the title of a work that addresses a particular topic. There are
no page numbers for these works.

1. Victor Vitanza, _CyberReader_, 405.
2. Michael Heim, "The Essence of VR," 21.
3. Heim, "The Essence of VR," 21-25.
4. Heim, "The Essence of VR," 22.
5. Sherry Turkle, _Life on the Screen_, 177.
6. Turkle, 177.
7. Stephan Helmreich, _Silicon Second Nature: Culturing Artificial Life in a Digital World_, 8.
8. Helmreich, 76-81.
9. Marshall McLuhan and Quentin Fiore, _The Medium is the Massage_, 8-9. They speak of the "Age of Anxiety," the "innumerable confusions and a profound feeling of despair [that] invariable emerge in periods of great technological and cultural transitions."
10. Dene Grigar and John Barber, "Defending Your Life, or a Report from the Electronic Edge," _High Wired_, 218-222.
11. William Gibson, _Neuromancer_, 67.
12. "The Lexicon of Virtual Culture," http://www.seas.upenn.edu/~mengwong/cyber/cvvc1.html#1.4.
13. Vitanza, 2.
14. G. M. A. Grube, _Plato's Thought_, 222.
15. Plato, _The Republic X_, 598b.
16. Plato, _The Apology_, 34a.
17. Grube, 1.
18. Grube, 16.
19. Grube 18.
20. Grube, 20.
21. Gibson, 37.
22. Plato, _The Republic_, 514a-518b.
23. Gibson, 173.
24. Plato, _The Republic_, 476c. We preferred the translation of this passage found in Grube's book over Paul Shorey's rendering of it (we have been using throughout the dispatch).

25. Grube, 36.
26. Gertrude Stein, "Composition as Explanation," 513.
27. John Berger, _Ways of Seeing_, 7-21.
28. Grube, 49.
29. W. K. C. Guthrie, _The Greek Philosophers: From Thales to Aristotle_, 88-89.
30. Michael Joyce, _Of Two Minds_, 65.
31. Plato, _The Phaedrus_, 275D-276B.
32. Grube, viii.
33. Mick Doherty, "MOO as Tool, MOO as Realm: A Response to Don Langham."
34. Mary Warnock, _The Uses of Philosophy_, 4.
35. Cindy Selfe, "Technology and Literacy: A Story about the Perils of Not Paying Attention," 411-436.
36. Joyce, 65.
37. Guthrie, 122.
38. Jay David Bolter, _Writing Space: The Computer, Hypertext, and the History of Writing_, 1.
39. McLuhan and Fiore, 48.
40. Rosalind Thomas, _Literacy and Orality in Ancient Greece_, 7.
41. Thomas, 15.
42. Plato, _The Phaedrus_, 278a-b.
43. Michael Heim. "The Technological Crisis of Rhetoric, Philosophy and Rhetoric."
44. McLuhan and Fiore, 68.
45. Howard Rheingold, _The Virtual Community_, 5.
46. Sven Bikerts, _The Gutenberg Elegies_.
47. Langham.
48. Doherty.
49. Elizabeth Klem and Charles Moran, "Computers and Instructional Strategies in the Teaching of Writing," 132-149.
50. Janet Murray, _Hamlet on the Holodeck: The Future of Narrative in Cyberspace_, 28.
51. Bolter, _Writing Space_, 111.
52. George Landow, _Hypertext_, 52, 59, 73.
53. Bolter, _Writing Space_, 58-9.
54. Langham.
55. Langham.
56. Randa Dubnick, _The Structure of Obscurity: Gertrude Stein, Language, and Cubism_, 31.
57. Berger, 7.
58. Plato. _The Phaedrus_, 275d-e.

59. Jay David Bolter, "The Computer, Hypertext, and Classical Studies," 541-545.
60. Albert Rouzie, "Applying Play Theory to the Emergent Traditions of the CMC Composition Course."
61. Sherry Turkle, "Foreword," _High Wired: On the Design, Use, and Theory of Educational MOOs_, xi.
62. Turkle, "Forward," xii.
63. Turkle, "Forward," xvi.
64. Turkle, "Forward," xvii.
65. Avital Ronell, _The Telephone Book: Technology, Schizophrenia, and Electronic Speech_.
66. Landow, _Hypertext_; Jeff Galin and Joan Latchaw, "Heterotopic Spaces Online: A New Paradigm for Academic Scholarship and Publication," _New Worlds, New Words_.
67. Warnock, 4.
68. Murray, 154-182.
69. Murray, 126.
70. Murray, 98.
71. Murray, 154.
72. Plato, _The Sophist_, 249c.
73. Grube, 40.
74. Plato, _The Sophist_, 248a-249d.
75. Grube 296.
76. Robert Sokolowski, "Human and Artificial Intelligence," 565.
77. Grube, 3.
78. Helmreich, 123.
79. Philip Dick, _Do Androids Dream of Electric Sheep?_.
80. McLuhan and Fiore, 53.
81. McLuhan and Fiore, 8.
82. Grube, 50.
83. Douglas Rushkoff, "Seeing is Beholding," 39.
84. Rushkoff, 39-40.
85. Rushkoff, 39-40.
86. Grube, 142.
87. Helmreich, 69-84.
88. Plato, _Republic_, 69c.
89. Helmreich, 76.
90. Van Morrison, "I Forgot That Love Existed."

John says, "Time to go."

John waves to everyone.
John heads out the mouth of The Cave and toward the Agora.
Dene smiles and waves goodbye to John.

Dene says, "Thank you for your presence here in this MOO session."
Dene says, "Don't leave yet. Follow John, Victor, Mick, and me to the Agora where we will continue to explore the way in which writing will change in electronic environments."
Dene says, "To do this, type @join Dene."

>>A red light on the Recorder flashes to indicate that it has been turned off. <<

chapter 1.2

IN BE-TWEEN: OR, WRITING ON THE MIDWAY*

Victor Vitanza

I do not portray being; I portray passing.
   —An early Sophist

The world as we see it is passing.
   —Paul of Tarsus

I saw the best minds of my generation destroyed by their REALITY, consuming rationalizations, dragging themselves as if at the dawn of the Enlightenment, through the dark, ever darker, streets protesting for more reality and justice to be realized with an angry fix, angel-headed cultural critics burning for the ancient ideal—really real—connections to the starry dynamo in the machinery of light.

   Hi, I am Victor; I'm a Sophist! I am a Postmodern Sophist. In my case—in our case here this day—such a Sophist is a rhetor (i.e., a speaker) who would w/rite *as if* talking about cyberspace and virtual space and their attendant notions of time. We Sophists have been talking about things Virtual since the fifth century BC. There is nothing new for

---

*Dedication: For Philippe Petit, who walked across a cable between the towers of the World Trade Center, New York, August 8, 1974.

us in that topic. We are virtualists. Virtue for us is virtuosity. And not the ideal, or really real. And yet, although we have spoken of all this, there is something new in time and space. There's, for the lack of a better way of characterizing it all, *a third passing*.

Let's abruptly shift perspectives: We rhetors talk about three different speech acts, or occasions, and genres for speaking. These three genres are ancient, going back as far as human beings can count. And even before human beings took up with counting. These speech acts are deliberative discourse (future), judiciary-forensic discourse (past), and epideictic discourse (present).

Deliberative discourse is concerned with the determining and setting of policy for What we are to do; it is concerned with the future. It is supposed to be practiced by our legislators in real buildings.

Judiciary discourse is concerned about What was done; this speech act attempts to determine the nature of events in the past. It is supposed to be practiced by the judiciary branch and the law courts.

And epideictic, is concerned with—it's hard to say—but there is some consensus that it is concerned with the present, and yet, a sort of eternal present. It is concerned with praise and blame. It is a ceremonial discourse, often practiced during the occasion of a funeral. It is practiced during a *passing*.

I veer away from thinking of this speech act as eternal present, or as merely praise or blame, to thinking of it as a combination of the other two speech acts and specifically in terms of the grammatical tense of the *future perfect*, or *future anterior*, or better put: the *What will have passed*. It is easy to mix together these three speech acts, for they constantly overlap. So, yes, I will mix 'em up, and for a special purpose. And are we not here for a special purpose? Let us lift our heads!

Let me boot up again, and admit more boldly that I am talking about the Dead. I never knew so many could die and so swiftly. So hotly in such a cool medium. I was born into World War II. Born In-Between. I saw the films, the newsreels, the movies, the television series (*Victory at Sea, World at War*), all educational, yet epideictic, films. I never knew so many could be undone. Born In-Between, I live on the Midway. Where the Freak House and the Fun House are to be found. Born through and of Gargamelle's left ear, I live on the Midway.

I know, I understand, but please, Dear Reader, bear with me a little while longer. This talk in writing about death and myself is not merely self-indulgence. This will all have been tied together. Eventually. Inextricably intertwined, Virtually. Perhaps Accidently. Intertwined with what always remains, what will have been said. And *what* remains—always remains—*is* the dead, and what they said and did and what we take them for having said and done. Whether they lived 2,500 years ago or lived with us intimately until 12 noon yesterday. And most importantly, how they themselves and then others represent them as having been.

Our *techne*, in great part, determine our representations of the dead and of ourselves thinking about them. Nietzsche, in a later preface to *Philosophy in the Tragic Age of the Greeks*, spoke of knowing (remembering) "the image of a [person]" by way of anecdotes (p. 25). He wrote three anecdotes each about Anaximander, Parmenides, Heraclitus, and others. (These are the so-called pre-platonics or older sophists who speculated over the nature of passing. And whether there is something or nothing!) Nietzsche's book, his representations of particular pre-platonics, his book of the dead, yet alive, is still of great importance to us today. It is a book about *techne*. When I *re*read Nietzsche's *Philosophy in the Tragic Age of the Greeks* for this chapter, I kept seeing the title as *Communication in the Virtual Age of the Postmoderns*. Or as *"Writing" in the Virtual Age of the Postmoderns*. When I reread Nietzsche's early book, I keep seeing what wants to be said, and how it is to be said at this time and in this place.

Nietzsche, that is, "posthumous man," and his lineage readily make available and strongly suggest to me that in thinking and writing about cyberspace and the future of print culture and especially the In Be -Tween that *I employ*

- the *techne* of literacy (i.e., suggests writing as a means for my thinking, and not electronic media); moreover, this lineage of the dead, yet alive, guides me to select
- literary orality as the means of delivering—in this writing—my embodied thoughts to you; and finally, it suggests
- the genre of the anecdote as my way of knowing. And of the fragment, mixed with the aphorism.

I am well aware that this is a mixed bag, a confusion of approaches. Both contradictory and perverse. I find it beneficial for the time passing, however, to think across contrary coordinates of orality, literacy, and what Greg Ulmer called "electracy" or "chorography" (pp. 48-49).

I am going to speak about the future—that is, future perfect—of Print Culture. At the end of the mechanical age. But I would examine *print culture* in and as passing; and I examine it as how others praise or lament their loss of others or things or—prior to their own personal death—themselves. In that culture. *Writing*—the *techne* of print culture, or of loss, death, and so on—is *passing*, and therein and thereby is the

writer passing, the past passing, and the topic of late print culture—
"death," modernism itself—passing. Obviously, people will continue to
dis/engage in orality and literacy, but these cultures, as dominant
cultures, are passing. And all things associated with them. Yes, I am
talking about not only our death as beings constructed in print culture,
but also even the death of "death," or at least death as we literates have
come to know and experience its passing in the late age of print culture.

What I want to know, however, is not just the image of *a* literate
person passing, but the *image of cyberspace* that others are so excitedly
hysterically reacting to (i.e., needing to find ways of putting a stop to) or
that others are so unthinkingly flowing with (wanting to accept,
embrace, dwell within). My topic is the *book of the dead* in cyberspace and
what it will have made of us and what it will have become. The *book of
the dead*, as I call on it here, is not just a metaphor for cyberspace; it is in
some strange way the very material conditions of cyberspace and
cybertime. More simply put, my topic is cyberwriting in new times and
new spaces. And as Paul Virilio would have it, in third intervals
("Third", p. 6). My topic is of our having been and having passed over
into *something else*. And of what we will be able variously and virtually
to pass for in this something else.

There are so many Humanists who react negatively to any talk
of cyberspace. In that light or darkness, and toward the end of my
discussion, I examine some issues that Mark Slouka deals with in his
War of the Worlds: Cyberspace and the High-Tech Assault on Reality. He is
much disturbed by the death of reality and the death of time and the
overwhelming pull of cyberspace. Yes, the question, the frightening
question is, "Where are we going?" when we have no sense of where or
place in cyberspace! And without coordinates, how are we to engage in
critique? Slouka, however, has yet to admit, like so many of us, that he
himself is a dead man writing! We are all dead men and women,
flatliners, dead Humanists writing and perhaps as strolling through a
bad B-movie, which might get dis/entitled "the night of the writing
dead"!

After Slouka, I briefly retrace some issues raised by Baudrillard
(1994). And then, I touch on Virilio's notion of a third writing, a new
passing, what he calls a "third interval," which is determined by speed,
but a speed determined *not* by Local time as determined by Greenwich
time, or a speed not determined by our triangulation vis-à-vis two
coordinates (cities) and the pole. But determined by a time beyond, yet
not transcendental. By a time of passing. Virilio wrote: "When you come
back to Paris from Los Angeles or New York at certain times of the year,
you can see, through the window, passing over the pole, the setting sun
and the rising sun. You have dawn and dusk in a single window. These

stereoscopic images show quiet well the beyond of the geographical city and the advent of human concentration in travel time. The city of the beyond is the City of Dead Time" (*Pure War*, p. 6). So what I am suggesting is that we are leaving the *city of time*, and "lighting out" for the *cyberterritory of dead time*, the territory of What Will Have Been. This is not to suggest that the Future is Perfect. I am not a e/utopian! It is to say that the future is the past and is passing. To be a revolutionary today, contrary to what Marx (1978) said, all that is necessary to change the world is to change time. When time is changed, space will follow. And writing space, as Jay Bolter argued, will also follow. My sense is that what is happening is not revolutionary, but devolutionary and evolutionary. However, do not at all think that I am talking about history as progress. I am talking, instead, about history itself as passing.

Link: My wife and I have a 5-year-old son, Roman, who at least a dozen times a day comes running . . . flying . . . very intensely . . . like Kramer[1] . . . into a room that we are in, yelling at the top of his lungs: "To Infinnnnnnityyyyy and BeeeeeYoooooooond." *Toy Story!*, of course, is the name of the film. However, it might as well be entitled, à la Baudrillard, *Revenge of the Toys III*.

Link: Everyday, every minute, every second, as William Mitchell in the *City of Bits* suggests, atoms (flesh) are being turned into bits. We are leaving, as Bruce Sterling would say, Meatspace. We are becoming glass! in Cyberspace. We are becoming crystal. Silicon. Covering and highlighting a new time. While Mitchell is optimistic (pp. 167-73), I am not, although I would not say that I am pessimistic, just at times nostalgic and at other times in a statelessness of anticipation of getting to the other side, and yet, I would stay In Be-Tween. I am joyfully pessimistic. And without needing revenge or having it wrecked on me.

Link: "To Infinnnnnnityyyyy and BeeeeeYoooooooond."

Let's speed up. And move toward Intensities. And thereby and there-ever-after, return to drifting, like data trash, in cyberspace. Drifting in the mediascape.

In dis/order to get to drifting, let's turn now to *a new preface* and the *three anecdotes*. What serve as my *next* preface to the anecdotes is

- Sven Birkerts' chapter "Into the Electronic Millennium" (which is an anecdote in itself) from his *Gutenberg Elegies;* then I turn to
- William Gibson's "Agrippa: The Book of the Dead"; and then to
- Bruce Sterling's "Dead Media Manifesto"; and finally, I turn to
- Uncle Tim Leary's fairly recent passing.

1. Birkerts' "Into the Electronic Millennium": Birkerts' chapter opens with a wonderful account of himself and a colleague's buying out a professor's collection of books. Birkerts writes: "As we boxed up the books, we chatted. My partner asked the man if he was moving. 'No,' he said, 'but I am getting out.' We both looked up. 'Out of the teaching business, I mean. Out of books'" (p. 117). From the lower part of the house, the man beckons Birkerts and his colleague to accompany him to the basement. Once down in the very foundations of his house, in the cold expanse of the bottom of his house, the man shows them a computer and says: "I'm changing my life. . . . This is definitely where it's all going to happen." He continues: "The whole profession represents a lot of pain to me. . . . I don't want to see any of these books again" (p. 118).

Commenting on this turn of mind, Birkerts tells us: "Our professor was by no means an isolated case. Over a period of two years we met with several others like him. New men and new women who had glimpsed the future and had decided to get out while the getting was good. . . . It was as if heading to the future also required the destruction of tokens from the past. A change was upon us—nothing could be clearer." After writing of other changes, for example, from orality to literacy, Birkerts tells us of how the electronic media have dug deep and invisibly into the bowels of our world, "creating sluices and circulating through them." The media have created "the interdependent *totality* that has arisen from the conjoining of parts—the disk drives hooked to modems, transmissions linked to technologies of reception, recording, duplication, and storage. Numbers and codes and frequencies. Buttons and signals. And this is no longer 'the future' . . . it is now." Birkerts asks: "Do I exaggerate?" (pp. 118-119).

While one intellectual sells his books and lights out for the territory of pixels and another writes a book and laments the passing of books, yet others (a writer, an artist, and a publisher) develop an electronic book that can be read only once. I am referring to . . .

2. William Gibson's "Agrippa: The Book of the Dead": Gibson (the author of *Neuromancer*) developed, along with the artist Dennis Ashbaugh and the publisher Kevin Begos, Jr., *Agrippa: The Book of the Dead*. Simply put, the text of the so-called book is on a floppy disk (which can be read on an IBM or Apple computer). When the disk is inserted into a disk drive, the words of the story are programmed to scroll automatically up the screen and then to be consumed by a virus. There is no way to save or print out the text. It's a hyperbolic self-consuming artifact. Part of the irony—not only about books and their passing—is that *Agrippa* is a collector's item. To appreciate the various levels of this irony, you have to know something about what comes with the disk.

This disk—given with the deluxe edition, which cost $2,000—is artfully placed within, as Gerald Jonas (1993) describes it,

a 16-by-21 1/2-inch metal mesh case sheathed in Kevlar, the polymer that bulletproof vests are made of. Sheltered inside the case is a book of 93 rag-paper pages bound in singed and stained linen that appear to have survived a fire. The last 60 pages have been fused together to form a block; cut into the block is a four-inch square that holds a computer disk; encrypted on this disk is the text [of the story]. . . . The text of . . . Gibson's story [however] appears nowhere in the book itself. Thirty-two pages contain long sequences of the letters G, A, T, C. This is another kind of code; the letters represent the four building blocks of the DNA double-helix molecule, and the sequences were excerpted from real human genetic material. Seven pages of the book are devoted to copperplate etchings . . . by Ashbaugh [the artist]. These [are] "gene scans" or "DNA footprints." Six of the etchings have been overprinted with early 20th-century advertisements for gadgets like telephones and cameras; a special ink was used so that these reproductions literally wipe off the page at the slightest touch. (pp. 12-13)

The centermentalist idea here is *a book disappears*. This is not about a professor selling his books; it is about a writer sky-writing, that is, writing the *disappearance*. "Writing" that doubly disseminates and dissipates. It is about remembering is forgetting. It is about a collector obtaining at great expense a book that . . . in simulation has withstood time, but is in reality disappearing once again into, as Baudrillard would say, its own pure simulacrum.

If we were to pay the $2,000 to read the text, we would find that it begins with an account of opening a family photo album (manufactured by C. A. Agrippa). The story tells of particular photos and of Gibson, who as a boy opens a desk drawer and finds his father's pistol. Gibson accidentally discharges it twice. Peter Schwenger sees these two discharges alluding to the two explosions in Japan. You see, Gibson's father worked on the Manhattan Project. Gibson, the younger, grows up to write post-post-nuclear fiction, cyber-punk SF. You see, Gibson's father died when his son was 6 years old.

Schwenger has an interesting point, given him by Begos (the publisher): "The singed, disastrous look of the black box's contents takes on a new significance. This 'relic from the future,' as Begos has called it, replicates a typical pattern of nuclear-war fiction. Relic of a past event which *is yet* to take place in the future, the nuclear narrative is transmitted backward to us in the present, which is that future's past" (p. 67).

Wanting to collect the dead, but this time dead media, another cyber-punk writer and friend of Gibson's,

3. Bruce Sterling, writes in his "Dead Media Manifesto":

my good friend Richard Kadrey . . . and myself, . . . recently came to a
joint understanding that what we'd really like to see is an entirely new
kind of book on media. A *media book of the dead,* . . . a book about media
that have died on the barbed wire of technological advance, media that
didn't make it, martyred media, dead media. THE HANDBOOK OF
DEAD MEDIA. A naturalist's field guide for the communications
paleontologist. (*Boing-Boing,* online)

Here, Sterling goes with traditional cause-effect thinking, namely, Let us
learn from the mistakes of the past.

In August 15, 1997, Sterling welcomed his first post from what
he called "Dead Media Necronauts." It is with this post from Dan Rabin
that the list of lost media items begins to be catalogued. Here are a few:

- Prehistoric etched-bone mnemonic devices and lunar
  calendars.
- Preliterate clay tokens of Fertile Crescent area.
- Drumming, shouting, whistling, and alpenhorn networks.
- Pigeon post (e.g., Mameluke Empire, in the 1250s, and
  Reuter's pigeon stock-price network 1849).
- Persian, Mongol, Roman, and Chinese imperial horse
  posts.
- The heliograph (USA 1861).
- Optical telegraphy: French (Claude Chappe 1792), British,
  Swedish, and American optical telegraphy systems.
- Extinct mail and postal systems: Thurn and Taxis (1550
  AD), Renaissance Italian banking networks, early
  espionage networks.
- Nadar's Paris Commune balloon mail. Rocket mail (1992).
- Smoke signals (still in use by Vatican).
- Chinese kite messages, 1232 AD.

Etc. . . . The list, of course, goes on and on.[2]

But lest we forget, not only books are passing, but also people—
our gurus—are passing. Recently, . . .

4. Tim Leary died. 1920-1996: May he rest in pieces. While Leary
was dying, all that was necessary for updates on his progress toward the
great unknown was for us to steer our way to his web page, which gave
us in great detail the kinds and amounts of drugs (prescribed and
otherwise) that he had ingested, inhaled, and injected each remaining
day. It was a hoot, and yet it was something else. Remember: Leary said

that the PC is the LSD of the 1990s. If you have not already, you might visit his Web site. Just turn on, tune in, and boot up. So as to get in touch.

The magazine *Vanity Fair* interviewed Uncle Timothy a few days before he died: They asked, "How would you like to die?" He answered, "I plan to De-Animate—i.e., to snuff my body. Me and my friends are planning the happiest, joyable, organically sensitive Dying Celebrations in human history. . . . Every stage in the process is being filmed and some of it will be broadcast on the World Wide Web. I hope that millions of people will be on-line during the last stages of my celebratory good-bye party." . . . He was asked, "If you could *choose* what to come back as, what would it be?" He answered, "Me, as a hip 21st-century media wizard" (p. 186).

While others are attempting to save the books and save the media, Uncle Timothy was concerned with his brain. So he had plans to have it severed at the very moment of his death so that it might be cyrogenically preserved. According to public records, he remained in one piece. Long live Uncle Timothy.

Link: In Cyber/Space, the ashes of Tim Leary and Gene Roddenberry circle the whirl, threatening to return to us as falling data trash. Soon, very soon, at some pointless in the next millennium, Uncle Timothy will return to bury us. Dig it? The dead-cum-virtual will return to bury us. And to bring us back during the night of the living dead! All this will pass as the boundaries and walls collapse. Everywhere.

Enough of this apparent silliness! Let's get serious, Victor!

I must admit of course that the particular style of writing that I am dis-engaging in, right before you, Dear Reader (Mon Amour), is not new. It's perhaps best labeled as *Modernist Nostalgia*. It is a kind of writing that, no matter how silly it is, is serious; and no matter how serious it is, is silly. It is a kind of writing that ends up parodying or becoming a pastiche of itself. Take, for example, Gibson's *Agrippa*, which has been already parodied. You can find the parody on the WWW. Take, Sterling, who refers to his dead media project as a "modest proposal" (his words)! How am I to take his project seriously? And yet, being a Modernist, I must. And take Leary, who never took his life seriously, although many of us did. And now his death!?

There is definitely a confusion here; things don't *link* as they used to. We have negatively deconstructed binaries; now binaries begin to deconstruct themselves and us along with them. And yet they always have. Call it the revenge of the *Logos*. Or the Revenge of the Object, as Baudrillard would have it. The future is deconstructing us. And perhaps always has. Mark Slouka wants to reestablish the binaries, real and not real, fact and fiction, truth and falsity. In his introduction, "The Road to Unreality," he said: "My gripe, I should point out, is not so much with the technologies themselves as with the general lack of concern over the consequences that many new applications may come to have. I'm a humanist, not a Luddite" (p. 9). In chapter 1, "Reality is Death," Slouka inevitably wrote: "In this New Age, there weren't any facts, just ideologies of the moment; at any given time, the ideologue with the most power and influence got to determine the truth du jour. History, in short—even an event as immutable as the Holocaust—became just a collection of fictions (subjective, indeterminate), a text as susceptible to deconstruction as any poem" (p. 34). I sympathize. As I would, if I were attending a funeral. And we are, indeed, attending a passing. Ours!

If we can only get out of this modernist period! The genre of Modernism (nostalgia) has a great pull on us. I think of Freud's essay entitled "Mourning and Melancholia." Mourning becomes Electra. Does Mourning become electricity? How about electracy? The late age of print culture still has us by the Oedipal eyes. Will we ever get to the virtual writing promised land? Promised space? Will we ever be able to hack our way into the brainstem? My answer is that we already have. Always already have. *At least incipiently have.* We are out and yet within. The future is the past. Even Lyotard talks about Postmodernism as the Future-Perfect, the What will have been. And yet, Arthur Kroker tells us, our post-modernist socius is rapidly becoming "post-modem . . . post-crash society, where everything always speeds up to a standstill." As I say, we are In Be-Tween.

If, when I write of time and cybertime, you, Dear Reader, hear echoes of T. S. Eliot's *The Four Quartets*, don't. There is no central rose garden anymore, where time past and time future meet in time-present. If, when I speak of this style of writing that I am dis-engaging by, you hear echoes of Eliot's *Wasteland*, don't. There is no Sibyl of Cumae in a cage announcing that she wants to die. She is already dead, as we Humanists are dead. There is no culture now fragmented and to be saved or reclaimed, even if for only cynical ends. There is only—Arthur Kroker and Michael Weinstein tell us—Data Trash. After the explosion, there is but data trash. The Electronic-Information Bomb, as Einstein foretold us, has exploded all around us.

But the big difference today is that *differences* we have deconstructed and that have deconstructed themselves are exploding, yet imploding, at an incredible speed: now is then, here is there, the medium is the message, remembering is forgetting, inside is outside, the future is the past, the real (whether ideal or actual) is now virtual, the rational is irrational, the dead bury the living, and so on. Binaries that have been switched from privileged to supplementary positions, and back again, repeatedly, erotically, have exploded, and yet are now collapsing. Gender and Sex, that is, the differences between Male and Female, being switched, and then reswitched, in a whip-lashing vertigo of gender confusions, have exploded as male, female, hermaphrodite, merm, ferm, and so on. Once the conditions for thinking changed, the possibilities for, yes, scientists who are known as geneticists *changed*. At Brown University, Anne Fausto-Sterling (a geneticist) is still discovering new DNA configurations that have her counting beyond five sexes to innumerable sexes.

Yes, the boundaries, the walls, held upright, the borders, clearly defined are coming down, are becoming fluid. In *The War of Desire and Technology at the Close of the Mechanical Age*, Sandy Stone begins pinpointing, also by way of anecdotes, the loss of what communication theorist such as Katherine Hayles have called *homeostasis* (the ability of an organism to maintain itself in a steady-state, an equilibrium). Stone studied with Donna Haraway, the author of "A Manifesto for Cyborgs." Like Sherry Turkle in *Life on the Screen*, Stone is interested in the reinvention of the self into selves by way of technology. But Stone is interested in so much more: un/namely, in her words, she has "fallen in love with the body as prosthesis" (pp. 1-32). If you do not know, I will tell you that Stone is a transsexual and a performance artist and director of the Media Lab at UT-Austin. Stone is dying and re-living proof of someone-cum-many who has moved from *homeostasis* to *autopoiesis* (i.e., self-organization of the body, reflexivity) to possibly an incipient third statelessness that Katherine Hayles would call *virtuality* (in which emergence, or evolution, becomes unpredictable; in which human becomes post-human). Stone, however, is not as given to becoming unpredictable as someone like Orlan, the French performance artist.

What's really (!) causing all this collapsing of binaries, dualities? There is no cause, yet there is an epiphenomenal cause. It is simply *techne*, which is thought of today as *technology*. Again it is human being's venturing from the canny physical and mental world of *homeostasis* to uncanny worlds of statelessness or *virtuality*. And we are not limiting ourselves to our bodies or our natural languages, for we are affirmatively deconstructing the very symbolic system of binary logic/code itself, which is, yes, about to collapse: O/1, off/on, -/+ are being replaced by what is called a boundary or border logic (Meredith and William Bricken) with *one*, perhaps better called a *third*, "operator" known as a "Mark." This border logic, called an irrational logic, has no linear connections; there is, for example, no such thing as cause-effect or metonymy, just as theorist refuse to think of cause and effect in *autopoiesis* or *virtuality*. There are connections, but appositional. The tyranny of the condition of the binary has passed over into—yes, what Plato feared—a third mis/categorization. Sham or simulation. Virtuality. Therefore, can you not connect as you so desire?

- Link: The other day, a graduate student to whom I was speaking momentarily and in a disparingly way about virtual realities and the hyperreal, interrupted me and said: "You know, there is *something downright un-American* about your thoughts." And then he walked over to his desk, picked up Arthur Kroker's book *Spasm* and read: "Virtual America is the USA as an empire of technology, where the will to technique has been so deeply interiorized as the *essence of American being* that technology is no longer an object which we can hold *outside* ourselves, but has become the *dominant sign of American identity.* Or, as Nietzsche said: 'Let the dead bury the living'" (pp. 170-171). And then, the graduate student, whose dissertation I am directing, walked off to meet with his first-year students in the computer-writing lab.

- Link: When I started writing, so many years ago, I was given a pencil and a Big Chief Tablet. When I was in the fifth grade, I was given a fountain pen and better quality paper. (It was a rite of passage for me and others to be given the opportunity to write with permanent black ink!) When I was in high school, I was given the opportunity to learn to type. Although I wrote my assignments with pencil or ink, I was expected to type them before handing them in. When I was 19, I bought my first typewriter because, as I told everyone, I wanted to be a writer. I would compose on my typewriter some, while still writing on paper and then typing it. I would—like many of you—literally cut and paste or tape. When I was 41, I bought my first Apple PC. My life changed again. I brought this computer into my apartment and let it sit there for 3 days. Finally, I took a paper that I was writing on my typewriter and typed it onto a disk. I practiced virtually cutting and pasting. Overnight there was this change: I became an obsessive reviser. *But you know, Dear Reader:* I have undergraduate students in my class who have never used paper and pencil to write, have never used a typewriter at all, who laugh and point when they see one, who have only used a computer to write. It gets even *better*—which is a word that no longer applies—

when I think of a whole new crew of graduate students and especially very new assistant professors in my field who are not talking about Departments of English, or Departments of Rhetoric or Writing or Composition. They are *not* talking about breaking away from English and starting Divisions or Departments of Rhetoric and Composition. They are talking about Departments of Electricity. Do I exaggerate?

• Link: The central most important event in my life has been the assassination of John F. Kennedy. I have seen his head explode in the Zapruder film countless times. Now that present-day technology has refined the film, I have seen near countless times JFK's head re-explode in more vivid color, making it all still *more real than real*. While Gibson's discourse plays one time and is consumed, eaten up by a virus, Zapruder's film plays without end, in a strange loop, and has become the central meme (or mental virus) of my time and space.

• Link: Today, I find Ollie Stone's versions of the JFK assassination more real than, of course, the Warren Commission Report and all the individual accounts, pro or con, about the various assassination conspiracies.

• Link: I have to agree with Baudrillard that the Gulf War never really happened. When a foreign correspondent who was captured by the Iraqis was released at the end of the so-called war, he asked, "How did the war go?" His colleagues in Great Britain were amazed because he who posed the question actually had been *in* the war. However, he counter-responded by saying, "Yes, but I did not see the war *on* TV." Nor, as far as that goes, did anyone else. We saw video war games and selected doctored footage and very little of it. This claim that the war never happened is truly ridiculous and immoral, but it makes insidious and invidious sense. We have moved from hot wars to cold wars now to cool wars. Do people die in cool wars? You bet they do. What has changed, however, is the representation of death. War is simulated, while death is real but more real than real, more horrible than horrible. War and death have become hyperreal. Joining the terms *death-by-friendly-fire*, we now have terms like a *cool-kill*. A *video-kill*.

Let me greatly temper what I have said by also telling you that I was invited to study simulated plane and tank warfare at a number of different levels at Fort Hood, Texas, where I saw pilots get out of apache flight simulators so shaken by their virtual deaths that I felt like a character in Ballard's novel *Crash*, in which death becomes so simulated and repeatedly and repeatedly simulated that is becomes more real than death itself. Simulated death more real than death! Obscene, is it not? First there is reality, then fiction, then the hyper-real. Yes, I have seen ashen pilots get out of Apache flight simulators so shaken by their virtual deaths that they moved like dead men flying. And so the dead bury the living! Do you yet dig it?!

- Link: Yes, I started with a Big Chief Tablet. (As a kid, I always looked at the big chief on the cover and wondered what the connection or link was supposed to be between the native-American tribal chief and my learning to write!) Now I am moving toward writing in Virilio's Third Interval. Everytime I write, I feel the irrepressible pull toward the third interval, and begin to understand that every time I wrote in the tablet I was contributing to the death of the chief's oral culture, by reinscribing print culture.

Now I hesitate to speak of writing in cyberspace and for many reasons, one being that Jay Bolter in his book, *Writing Space*, has best described the new medium and what the conditions for possibilities of "writing" in this space might be and become. As writing *explodes!* At best, I would only suggest how Virilio's notion of time and space *as* third interval *implodes* what we might still call "writing." *Implodes it as telepresence.* Or *transpresence*, contributing to the death of print culture.

For Virilio, there is a fourth temporal condition. If we traditionally have thought of *past* and *future* with the *present* (so-called real time in the middle), Virilio talks of an imminent fourth temporal condition replacing the present tense that he calls telepresence, which not only kills this middle tense, but also the past and the future by collapsing them into the future anterior or telepresence. Into a new epideictic discourse that would reinvent a virtual Athens. In this statusless telepresence there is the potential for absolute speed (the speed of light), which Virilio also calls the third interval. Hence, telepresence and absolute speed are both the third interval. Think of it as travel time becoming immediate time. Think of it paradoxically as travelling (telepresence) while staying at home. Think of it as, yes, also collapsing the two distances of where you are and where you want to travel, becoming one and the same. I know that when I am on the Web clicking, linking, from one site to another, I sense intermittently this collapsing of time and space. I can jump from Tokyo to New York to Sidney to Palermo to elsewhere and elsewhere, while the sun perpetually rises and sets but simultaneously. Yea, the sun simultaneously sets and rises over the cyber-empire. The new world order's newest imperialism.

And how does this simultaneity effect this thing we call "writing"? Let's think for a few sentences about what happens at a MOO. If you do not know what a MOO is, then, let me briefly explain that it is a virtual site, usually located in a server (data bank), where once you are admitted, you can type in simple commands on your monitor that allow you and others to communicate by typing to each other. A MOO is somewhat similar to a chat room, but is by far very different and more subtle in its effects on the typer. When I sign on at a MOO, say, as Big Chief Tablet (my occasional avatar), when I am at a MOO and there are, say, 20 MOO-people writing and communicating, I sense intermittently myself as a writer, or "myself-writing," disappearing, as words cascade down all around my words, in the middle of my typed words and all around and in the "middle interval" of them, cascading all over me, and I lose a sense—again, intermittently—of *who I am writing* in that *third interval*. (Writing in *MOO-space* is not at all like writing in *word processing-program space*, especially if you do not use a client. Not like writing in striated space, but smooth space.) All 20 of us evidently are logging in or travelling from different geographical sites into the same server and we are writing on the same electric big chiefless tablet, and the words, the various drafts, the various "ones"-of-us seem somewhere, but where? together, and not separate. In time or space. (Virilio would say in telepresence.) I in a "real-time-becoming" now have a sense of what a post-structuralist or postmodernist "writer-writing" can be. I have a sense of writing-the-accident. A sense that there is no writer, but especially no reader. Riding and writing the accident. I feel like a character in Ballard's novel *Crash* smashing into and yet caressing others' words. Dying in that writing space, but living on in some other way. I feel that the words bouncing off each other in this smooth MOO space are all surface, without any depth whatsoever, and yet not at all superficial. I feel that no depth psychology or no hermeneutics of suspicion would work here. Things just collapse. The negative denegates itself. And there is only the non-positive affirmative. And smooth surface. Subject and object disappear. Writing un/just appears in a postsymbolic smooth tablet.

Is this kind of writing dangerous? Ethically and politically dangerous? Yes. No. Yo and Nes! It depends on your interests. And yet, realize that the conditions for this "depends-on-your-interests" are disappearing. When writing in electronic environments—and most acutely in MOO-space—*we are writing our disappearance.* We are dead avatars undergoing metamorphosis into something else.

Yes, when in that writing space, I have felt like a character in *Agrippa: The Book of the Dead.* Disappearing yet remembered in some virtual ways, as I have, from time to time, dis/engaged in remembering my grandfather. Will Roman, my son, remember me in this way as he scans across whatever technology will have become?

- Link: In late August 1997, I completed and submitted a manuscript of a textbook entitled *Writing for the World Wide Web*, or *W4*. My editor and the outside readers looked at the manuscript and concluded, "Well, this is okay, but you don't have any discussion about topic sentences and paragraph construction"! Etc. I tried to explain to my editor that "electracy" was a different place in a different time. More specifically, I told him that there were no words or sentences or paragraphs in cyberspace. Of course, he did not understand at all, and just laughed. Perhaps, I was being hyperbolic! We continued to talk and he eventually began to get the drift of what "writing" was becoming in this new space, began to understand that "writing" in print culture was each day passing away. Universities and colleges get wired and literacy passes away. Libraries pass away, though there is still a library building, standing, on campus. *You gotta laugh!* Words are becoming something else. It's a crisis. The same kind of crisis that occurred when many human beings shifted from an oral to a literate culture. It is a crisis. Isn't it exciting? It is a hypocrisis. All that is left is nervously to perform this crisis.

   Although my editor—who is really more than an editor—understood, he insisted and I agreed, given the market, to rewrite certain sections and to write two additional chapters. But none on topic sentences and traditional paragraphs but on *topic images* and *paraclusters of images.* (Words *are* images. And they are becoming more and more imagistic.) The second and third editions of the book will have students dialing on, tuning in, hanging out, linking up, escaping-deleting. (Papertexts will have become webtexts, with the distinctions author-reader and teacher-student more and more everyday collapsing. And the publishers, what about them? And all the rest, What about it and them? What will they all have become? On their way to wherever?) In the meantime,

- Linkless: While imprisoned in this thing called reality, waiting for my over-coming, un-just as Socrates was waiting—*remember* (?) Nietzsche's words in *The Birth of Tragedy, Out of the Spirit of Music?*—I, too, "practice music" and, on occasion, listen to the lyrics such as those of the tune "Virtual Cold" from the album *Celebrate the New Dark Age* . . . from the group Polvo: Without the punk music—and quite purposefully without the noise—these lyrics in part read:

    even if real life is put on hold again
    we will find our strength in the virtual cold
    my friend
    sweet specter that comes on cue
    modern myths that must be true
    quick confessions that make good sense
    share secrets in the future [perfect] tense.

- Linkless: The French cultural critic Hélène Cixous, who has taught me more about writing In Be-Tween than anyone else, says in her book *Coming to Writing*: "In the beginning, there can be only dying, the abyss, the first laugh" (p. 41). And then,

    After that, you don't know. It's life that decides. Its terrible power of invention, which surpasses us. Our life anticipates us. Always ahead of you by a height, a desire, the good abyss, the one that suggests to you: "Leap and pass into infinity." Write! what? Take to the wind, take to writing, form one body with the letters. Live! Risk: those who risk nothing gain nothing, risk and you no longer risk anything. In the beginning, there is an end. Don't be afraid: it's your death that is dying. Then: all the beginnings. (p. 41)

- Linkless: Zarathustra tells us: "Man is a rope, tied between beast and overman—a rope over an abyss. . . .

What is great in man is that he is a bridge and not an end: what can be loved in man is that he is an *overture* and a *going under*. I love those who do not know how to live, except by going under, for they are those who cross over" (Nietzsche, pp. 126-127).

- Linkless: Eyeless (not in Gaza) have seen the best mimes of my degenerations move laterally, in a liquid slide, into the void of virtual coldness, consumed by viril-libayshuns, clutching the groundlessness in the facelessness of the implosion, through the dark, ever darker, with light being sucked up, streetlessness, desperately calling, on phallen occasions, for a return to the old Word Order of discipline, punishment, and pleasure, to be surrealized with a cynical fix, skin-headed Electro-Rhetors chyrogenikly burning with a nostalgik desire for the ancient rhetorical sado-masochistic bondage to the starry dominance in the binary-machinery of the Light.

And I gave up the ghost of Humanism (a subject with limits), and saw no tunnel of light nor its absence but myselphs grinning, chuckling, laughing (with no limits) while folding, unfolding, refolding (with no limits). . .

Amor fati, amor fati, amor fati . . .

NOTES

1. The reference to Kramer is to the character by the same name on the television sitcom *Seinfield*.
2. These examples are selected from Sterling's "Welcome and Master List" and from various files and updates at Sterling's *Dead Media: The Official Repository*. Also see Sterling and Kadrey's "Dead Media" in *Harper's Magazine*.

WORKS CITED

Ballard, J. G. (1973). *Crash*. New York: Noonday.
Baudrillard, J. (1994). *Simulacra and simulation*. (S. F. Glaser, Trans). Ann Arbor: University of Michigan Press.

Birkerts, S. (1994). *The gutenberg elegies.* New York: Faber and Faber.

Bolter, J. D. (1991).*Writing space.* Hillsdale, NJ: Erlbaum.

Bricken, M. (1991).*A calculus of creation* (Tech. Rep. No.HITL-P-91-3). Seattle: Human Interface Technology Laboratory of the Washington Technology Center.

Bricken, W. (1989). *An introduction to boundary logic with the losp deductive engine* (Tech. Rep. No. HITL-R-89-1). Seattle: Human Interface Technology Laboratory of the Washington Technology Center.

Cixous, H. (1991). *Coming to writing and other essays.* (D. Jenson, Ed., S. Cornell, Trans.). Cambridge, MA: Harvard University Press.

Fausto-Sterling, A. (1993, March/April). The five sexes: Why male and female are not enough. *The Sciences,* pp. 20-25.

Gibson, W. (1984). *Neuromancer.* New York: Ace.

Haraway, D. (1985). A manifesto for cyborgs. *Socialist Review, 15*(80), 65-107.

Hayles, N. K. (1994). Boundary disputes: Homeostasis, reflexivity, and the foundations of cybernetics. *Configurations, 2*(3), 441-467.

Jonas, G. (1993, August 29). The disappearing $2,000 book. *The New York Times Book Review,* pp. 12-13.

Kroker, A. (1996). *Spasm.* New York: St. Martin's Press.

Kroker, A., & Weinstein, M. A. (1994). *Data trash.* New York: St. Martin's Press.

Leary, T. (1996, June). [Interview with] *Vanity Fair,* p. 186.

Marx, K. (1978). Theses on Feuerbach. In R. C. Tucker (Ed.), *The Marx-Engels Reader* (2nd ed., pp. 143-145). New York: Norton.

Mitchell, W. (1995). *City of bits: Space, place and the infobahn.* Cambridge: MIT Press.

Nietzsche, F. (1962). *Philosophy in the tragic age of the Greeks.* Washington, DC: Gateway.

Nietzsche, F. (1967).*The birth of tragedy and the case of Wagner* (W. Kaufmann, Trans.). New York: Vintage.

Nietzsche, F. (1968). *Thus spoke Zarathustra.* In *The Portable Nietzsche* (W. Kaufmann, Trans.). New York: Penguin.

Polvo. (1994). Virtual cold. In *Celebrate the new dark age* (CD). Touch and Go Records.

Schwenger, P. (1994). Agrippa, or, the apocalyptic book. In M. Dery (Ed.), *Flame wars* (pp. 61-70). Durham, NC: Duke University Press.

Slouka, M. (1965). *War of the worlds: Cyberspace and the high-tech assault on reality.* New York: Basic Books.

Sterling, B. (1997, December 14). Dead media manifesto. *Boing Boing Digital* (Online). Available: http://www.well.com/user/mark/deadmedia.html

Sterling, B. (1998, February 22). *Dead Media: The Official Repository* (Online). Available: http://www.well.com/user/jonl/bruce/

Sterling, B. (1998, February 26). Welcome and master list. *Dead Media: The Official Repository* (Online). Available: http://www.well.com/user/ jonl/bruce/WELCOME.txt

Sterling, B., & Kadrey, R. (1995). Dead media. *Harper's Magazine, 291,* 22.

Stone, A. R. (1995). *The war of desire and technology at the close of the mechanical age.* Cambridge, MA: MIT Press.

Turkle, S. (1995). *Life on the screen.* New York: Simon & Schuster.

Ulmer, G. (1994). *Heuretics.* Baltimore: The Johns Hopkins University Press.

Virilio, P. (1991). *The aesthetics of disappearance* (P. Beitchman, Trans.). New York: Semiotext(e).

Virilio, P. (1993). The third interval: A critical transition. In V. A. Conley (Ed.), *Rethinking technologies* (pp. 3-12). Minneapolis: University of Minnesota Press.

Virilio, P., & Lotringer, S. (1983). *Pure war* (M. Polizzotti, Trans.). New York: Semiotext(e).

Vitanza, V. J. (1998). *Writing for the world wide web.* Needham Heights, MA: Allyn and Bacon.

@ TITLE THIS_CHAPTER AS . . .

[WAS: ON THE WEB, NOBODY KNOWS YOU'RE AN EDITOR]

Mick Doherty

Gentle reader: start anywhere. Linearity optional. Some repetition may occur. (For instance, you will see the phrase "This chapter is about writing, and/or editing, and/or publishing in electronic environments—and why the words we use to name what we're doing determine how it is perceived" again.) The author cedes all intellectual property responsibilities to the user and all presentational limitations to the medium. Quoted material in this chapter is utterly decontextualized. Proceed without care(s).

CONCLUSION: EVERYTHING HERE MAY BE WRONG

The question I had been hoping to hear for more than two years finally arose at the 1997 South Central Modern Language Association (SCMLA) conference in my new hometown of Dallas. A woman attending the panel (which was essentially devoted to "how graduate students can get published and still finish their dissertations," a subject I have personally taken pains to disprove) raised her hand and asked me, as best as I can remember: "I see you call your journal, in its subtitle, *A Journal For Teachers of Writing in Webbed Environments*. What precisely do you mean by that? Is it a journal for all teachers of writing, but the journal is on the Web? Is it a journal only for people who teach about writing for the Web? Do you mean the *journal* is in webbed environments, or the teachers should be? Or both?"

The answer, of course, is "yes." The ambiguity has been intentional since the day the journal was conceived, at a Hootie and the Blowfish concert in East Lansing, Michigan (which is a story for another time). The writing teacher in all of us can acknowledge the parsing of double meanings that comes with a misplaced—or in this case, carefully placed—modifying phrase. The Web reader/writer/rhetor in us probably equally recognizes that the act of making meaning in electronic environments is enormously contingent on what the user reads first and in what order he or she proceeds from there.

The journal is for teachers of writing, and the journal is on the Web. The journal is for teachers who teach in hypertextual spaces. The journal, generally, is both of these, and specifically, perhaps neither. The name is peculiarly ambiguous, as each occasion of publication—really, each occasion of reading—is a radical re-invention of what exists. Such re-invention can and does and must occur over and over again. Such re-invention can and does and must occur in the way we name what we are doing. If Landow (1992) is correct in claiming that hypertext leads to a re-perception of reading and writing as one act ("wreading"), then a corollary might be that naming and perceiving are also one act, which meet in the re-invention of the present occasion.

Then again, who knows? Perhaps this p/rose, by any other name, would smell as sweet. As the erratically great media guru Marshall McLuhan was purported to have claimed to his detractors, "You think my fallacy is wrong? You don't like these ideas? I got others" (cited in Doherty, "Hoops," 1997).

INTERNAL LINKS: PUMP UP THE VOLUME

The ideas in this volume are fluid—*kairotic*, in the sense Grigar uses the word elsewhere in this volume—in that I believe *every* paragraph or claim in *any* of these chapters could be appropriately placed as (at least) a footnote somewhere in any of the other chapters. Because footnoting was an inspirational metaphor to hypertext pioneers like Vannevar Bush and Douglas Englebart, and because this chapter is very much about how metaphor inspires our professional direction(s), it seems appropriate to situate this chapter in the context of the entire volume. "Situational context," of course, is how Kinneavy defined the word *kairos* when he reintroduced it to the composition classroom in 1986 (p. 79). The word has layers of meaning, beyond Kinneavy's definition— Eric Charles White translated it "radical occasionality" (1987, p. 14ff) which has more potent connotations—but for the purpose of "internal linking," and the reinforcement of how important a name can be, Kinneavy's meaning is sufficient.

The name of the Web journal I founded in 1995? You already know the part after the colon. The "first name" of *A Journal for Teachers of Writing in Webbed Environments*? Precisely that: *Kairos*.

****

[LINK] —▶ Vitanza's node in this collection may be a (p)re-action to his own earlier claims that although there are countless books on how to write for print culture, there are none on writing for electronic culture (1997). And although there are at least two such books currently in development by publishing houses—certainly to Victor's dismay— the lack of *books* does not mean there is a lack of *canonical information*. No electronic journal in the humanities or social sciences can begin without first paying homage to *Postmodern Culture* and to *Psycoloquoy*. We work within the framework of what we see has worked before, or at best attempt to build the structure a little better, or more broadly. As McLuhan was fond of saying, we look forward (re-invent scholarly publication) through the rearview mirror (which shows us both our papertext history and our more recent electronic forebears). The clash (or marriage—or both) of the traditional with the bleeding edge is a McLuhanesque *collide-o-scope* of images, ideas, and possibilities (throughout his in-your-face 1968 volume, *Counterblast*).

[LINK] —▶ For Haynes and Holmevik, the aim is to demonstrate new forms of expression in cybermedia, hypertext, and cyphertext (the first and last of these are inspired inventional neologisms) that call for new forms of dynamic, interactive publication. This reflects, at its very best, the editorial strategy implemented in publishing *Kairos:* making it up as we go along; new media demand new formations demand new words demand . . . new editorial responsibilities?

[LINK] —▶ Of course, I claim to be editor and *publisher* of a journal; my contribution with Thompson deconstructs the very notion of whether a MOO is, indeed, a legitimate form of publication. If everyone is (or can be) a publisher, then what role the editor? Is the editor of an electronic journal the semi-traditional equivalent of a MOO wizard? Is a MOO log legitimate academic discourse? Most of this book's contributors—and several "outside" commentators, if there is such a creature in electronic discourse—argue through these points.

[LINK] —► Grigar's contribution outlines examples of new modes of writing, those that we may think of as "hybrid" forms—those that are a compromise. The placement of a long-standard papertextual convention—the academic journal—on a new medium (the "editorial" focus of this chapter) results in what may be the ultimate hybrid/re-form/ative compromise, even within the qualities associated with both chronic and kairotic notions of time . . . a direct reflection of the reason(s) *Kairos* was named as it is. We are truly in an extended moment of "radical occasionality."

[LINK] —► And within this moment, Yancey and Spooner warn us, not only is our dialectic open to criticism, so is our poetic. This is as it should and must be. The advent of electronic writing environments is here, but the normative status of such—if that is our goal—must still be *sold*. Poetically and practically. We are the techno-sophists—and how we name what we are doing will be our first point of sale.

[LINKfest] —► This could go on, a link to each and every chapter:—Galin's and Latchaw's concept of the author-publisher function; Selfe's collaborative exploration of print-digital issues; Carbone's careful examination of a root metaphor in our cyberculture. Only the paper and ink limitations of a codex book prevent me from doing so.

Even the traditional meta-commentary in this book steps outside the linear norm; Burns' foreword (or is it forewarning?) and the Selfe-Hawisher statement in media(s) res (a middlewards direction?) . . . these two (too), it can be argued, are interchangeable. Linearity is optional.

After all, conventional wisdom in hypertext design and implementation suggests that each node in a Webtext should be capable of standing alone, and should be able to function as the first node a reader/traveler encounters. This book mirrors that approach; where I see a link to a word from Grigar, a phrase from Vitanza, an idea from Selfe, they will see "differnet" (spellcheckers and editors keep telling me that's a typo) inter-hyper-cross-textual links to each others' work and to mine. So if you are starting here, you may follow my path to them; if you are starting there, you may find your path to here; or better still, you may start anywhere, several times, observe our paths, and build one of your own.

New wor(l)ds are not limited to electronic communication; they are not even initially created or enabled by the new media. The whole process just happens a lot faster now—radical occasionality in electronic writing—the "kairos" of *Kairos*.

ABSTRACT(ION): THE SHORTCUT, OR "CLIFF'S NODE" VERSION

Disguised as a personal narrative intermixed with meandering theory and heuretic wordplay, this chapter examines the language of academic publishing, teaching, and service as it applies in both the paper and electronic realms to discuss the ways "technorhetoricians" (Crump, 1995ff) are naming what they are doing and how that recursively affects how it is viewed and (not) accepted within the academy. The narrative will course through the brief history of "hacker" subculture and its implicit "hacker ethic" (Levy, 1984) and draw comparisons with the current plight of the "technorhetorician," including a brief (if unrealistic) manifesto-like "technorhetorician's ethic."

Along the way, various parts of this chapter suggest ways that linguistic *kludging*—a term consciously borrowed and adapted from the original hacker subculture—is both a necessary evil and a self-delimiting agent for allowing a larger community to understand what a subculture is attempting to accomplish. A focus on the term *syllaweb* (Doherty, 1996) ties the narrative back to the writing classroom, and eventually, back to the ways we are thinking about academic publishing on the World Wide Web.

DISCLAIMER AS INTRODUCTION: AUTHOR BIO AS DISCURSIVE STATEMENT

I approach my own writing of this chapter of the book you hold (my nodal point in the conversation, my post to the collaborative BBS) as individually multivocal as the polyvocal collection of all the authors. Of course, this is true of us all; I am an editor, a publisher, a writer; I am a graduate student, a teacher, a theorist; I am a commercial Internet editor, and have been an academic Web editor. These voices in/form (and sometimes infirm, or—as Barber suggested in a marginal note to a draft of this chapter—*unform*) each other, and although the (original) title of this chapter may lead you to believe it will focus solely on the editorial process in a Web-based journal, in fact what follows the title is about titling itself. As we struggle to name what it is that we are doing in electronic writing spaces, the names and titles and neologisms we utilize will define, refine, and re-find the "new worlds and new words" that this book hopes to discover. Or to build.

It is not clear that the editor's role in the electronic medium would differ from the editor's role in the print medium. . . . One must wonder whether the guru status of some of these leaders will continue . . . (Silverman, cited in Peek & Newby, 1996)

A disclaimer, then: I am *not* a guru, nor really even a leader, in electronic publishing in academia. I have a small (dis?)advantage over the other contributors to this volume, as I have left academia—if not temporarily, then temporally—in the rearview mirror (although, of course, McLuhan claims that same mirror is the only one with which we can see the future); and ultimately, a confession: I have never written a hypertextual, electronic-only document worthy of being published in the journal I founded and edited. I see these as positive attributes; the coming generation of academic journal editors *don't have* to be gurus. The clearinghouse service of information management and presentation, truly *editing*, is task enough.

Finally, I should admit an irony of publishing brought on by the lengthy process that is native to the world of print text. As I began writing this chapter, I was just entering my third (and as it turned out final) full year as editor and publisher of *Kairos*; as it goes to press, I am entering my second full year after stepping down from those positions. The revisions I have made in this writing have come, then, with considered hindsight. The journal itself, meanwhile, has moved forward dynamically and kairotically, with the considered foresight that is reinvention of the present occasion. The author's biography reinvents itself occasionally, too, and it seems only appropriate that in lieu of further comment, I sum up my own kairotic experience with a URL: http://www.dallascvb.com/staff/pages/doherty/—if you receive a 404, think fondly of me and use the "Back" button on your browser.

EX-POSITION: REVERSE NEOLOGISMS

Toward the end of the 1996-1997 academic year, my Rensselaer colleague, Lee Honeycutt, now at Iowa State, left a (papertext) journal article in my mailbox entitled "My Life as A Dog, I Mean Editor." In it, the author discusses some of the pragmatics and problematics of editing a scholarly journal. While a fine (and at times humorous) effort, the text of the article is not what struck me—the *title* did. To be painfully honest, I remember neither the author's name or the name of the journal it was in—but the title . . . that stayed with me.

What the title—the *name*—of that article immediately brought to mind for me was the now-infamous *New Yorker* cartoon, captioned "On the Internet, nobody knows you're a dog." This idea—that nobody really knows who is on the other side of the screen—addresses the widely discussed phenomenon of online identity that pop scholars like Sherry Turkle and Douglas Rushkoff presented in books that have wandered near the top of many bestseller lists. This issue of identity—that is also not what struck me about the pertinence of that article to this chapter.

Well, perhaps in a way it is. Identity. Naming. Neologism. Making a place for techno-epistemology in a humanities academy largely still garrisoned in an ivory tower.

I was, as the title of this chapter might suggest, founding editor of an academic journal. But when you read the word *journal*, I suspect that immediately what your mind focuses on is a paper-bound codex-book-type publication, one that arrives in your mailbox or sits on the library shelves monthly or quarterly.

In fact, the journal I edited was a Web-based publication called *Kairos*. It is "a journal for teachers of writing in Webbed environments" (and all that can mean), which claims to publish only "native hypertext," a term Moulthrop (1991) coined to describe textual presences that cannot sensibly be committed to the linear page. The journal is "peer-reviewed" and "sponsored" by the Alliance for Computers and Writing. And each of the buzzwords you see—publish, peer-review, sponsor—each of these is a nod to the fact that in order to be seen as legitimate in the academy, we must name ourselves in ways that everyone can understand. Even if what we mean by "peer review" is nonblind, interactive, multi-tiered, utilizing the technology of e-mail and MOO-space (see Carbone, 1997), we still call it "peer reviewed" precisely so people who contribute to the journal can put a line on their curriculum vitae that a hiring or tenure/promotion committee will understand.

It is, in a way, the reverse of the neologism. And it informs (and re-forms) everything we are writing in multimedia environments.

Both McLuhan (1962) in *The Gutenburg Galaxy* and Toffler (1980) in *The Third Wave* pointed out that we use the terminology of old paradigms to name aspects of new realms. The "horseless carriage" was defined in terms of its animate predecessor; its energy is still described as "horsepower." The printing press followed the illuminated manuscript—and early typeset mimicked script. The typewriter followed the earlier linotype printing press and was so named "type" + "writer."

Following the typewriter—the computer, and its first fonts (usually Courier) looked like typewriter-type. There is a common HTML code, <tt> ... </tt> which stands for just that ... "typewriter type." Despite the overwhelming presence of computers, with the easy capability of italicizing, recent editions of the MLA style guide still endorsed underlining as a viable option in place of italics . . . a nod to the technology of the old paradigm.

Similar terms have arisen in the computers and writing (C&W) community, a new realm in the old paradigm of academia. The "community" of C&W scholars—including but in no way limited to every author in this volume—works collaboratively and collectively to explore the responsibilities and possibilities of the networked writing classroom; I would posit that the real goal of the C&W community is to make itself obsolete, to make a "computers and writing class" seem as odd to the ear as a class called "Writing with a Pen." But it is this very goal—to "translate" the new medium into more global terms for understanding—that demand the reverse neologism.

There are plenty of obvious examples of building electronic spaces based on what we know and do in traditional offline spaces. We send "electronic mail," and in AOL and many other mail programs, utilize icons that mimic old-style roadside postal drop boxes. We read about, and participate in "online conferences" and "virtual roundtables." Our students post to electronic "bulletin boards." In MOO-space, we build "rooms" with "furniture," and invite people "in" to "take a seat." It is introducing the new within the paradigmatically traditional concept of the familiar. Even a groundbreaking, unlike-any-other publication like *RhetNet*, the postmodern, unruly cousin to *Kairos*, still labels itself a "cyberjournal"—at least in part, we may presume, because the publication's ever-expanding audience is already familiar with the concept "journal." It provides a starting point, a bridge, to access the new media.

We are defining the new realm of technological literacies in academia by borrowing and re-shaping names from the old paradigm(s). But both the cleverness of the names and the ease with which we might see through their meanings is an open door for administrators and others to criticize and even dismiss the new realm with observations and commentary based solely on assumptions relevant to old paradigms. Can you imagine requesting tenure/promotion credit for hosting a bulletin board in the faculty lounge? What onus does that carry over to the hundreds of hours you may put into careful moderation of a Usenet bulletin board in classes or other professional situations?

That's why *naming* is so important. Because naming counts. Naming is how we are recognized, valued, supported. If we are uncertain of our naming, or it we do not insist on being clear with our subsequent defining and instead allow those unfamiliar with the field to name and define what we are doing for us, then consequences will hurt us and the future of electronic communication in academic pursuits.

The same thing is happening in all areas of tenure-reviewable scholarship. The issue of publishing in electronic journals is joined by questions like "if I design a department homepage, is that a publication? Service?" (see Doherty, "Hoops," 1997) And teachers in the Alliance for Computers and Writing (ACW) are actively (and unfortunately) using a neologistic term that I admit I coined in 1994—*syllaweb*—to discuss the practice of putting course curricula in shared electronic space. It is a term not unlike horseless carriage. We make sense of it by what we know of its parts. It is a microlevel example, perhaps, of what Shea (1998) called "recombinant rhetoric"—the rhetorical presentation of an argument is itself a living thing, and re-presents itself to the community of scholars in a consistently evolving (or mutating) form.

And that may be the point; whatever we may call ourselves affects not only the way we are perceived, but *who we actually are*—in the eyes of each other, of our students, and of the skeptical administrators who may wonder just what a syllaweb is, anyway.

OTHER STUFF: THE ACADEM-ICKY PRESENTATION

The naming issue exists at various levels of importance for communities, cultures, and subcultures; patterns may develop showing us those levels and helping us to think about what we are doing as neologistic cleverness threatens to overwhelm our pedagogy and our writing. The issue of naming plays an incalculably important role in current feminist literature, in African-American studies, in Latino/Chicano society, and in the long history of Hebraic/Talmudic culture. But the patterns I have noticed our technorhetorical subculture following—and I freely admit I see them because I have been looking for them!—are those developed in the 20th-century phenomenon known as *hackerism*.

For although naming is a key tool for many cultures, the hackers of the computer revolution and the technorhetoricians of today share a similar goal—the integration of technology into a larger culture. For the hackers, it was the introduction of the computer itself into an everyday society of fearful computerphobes imagining the gross science fiction of Robert Heinlein (*Starship Troopers*) and Arthur Clarke (*2001: A Space Odyssey*). For the technorhetoricians, it is the integration of interactive online pedagogies to a traditionalist academy rooted in ivory towers and imagining the gross expenditures of a classroom filled with the latest PCs.

In his 1984 bestseller *Hackers: Heroes of the Computer Revolution*, Steven Levy wrote, "The precepts of the revolutionary Hacker Ethic were not so much debated and discussed as silently agreed upon. No manifestos were issued. No missionaries tried to gather converts. The computer did the converting" (p. 39). Levy's is a history of coders, of software engineers and of hardware junkies. It begins in the 1950s at MIT and ends, really (although Levy argues otherwise) in the early 1970s with a manifesto written by the young Bill Gates. The "hacker ethic" drove this tiny culture of wireheads until the day the culture's tools and ideas were aimed away from internal collaboration, and pointed toward a larger audience, toward the eye of a skeptical public.

What precisely is the hacker ethic? There were no written rules in the labs at MIT and Stanford; even Ted Nelson's vainglorious attempts to codify hackerism in *Computer Lib* were widely rejected by the hackers themselves as too politically motivated. But with three decades of retrospective, Levy was able to reconstruct just how this hacker ethic was always implicitly (if never explicitly) defining and guiding the actions of those involved in that early technological revolution:

> Access to computers—and anything which might teach you something about the way the world works—should be unlimited and total. Always yield to the Hands-On Imperative! All information should be free. Mistrust authority—promote Decentralization. Hackers should be judged by their hacking, not bogus criteria such as degrees, age, race or position. You can create art and beauty on a computer. Computers can change your life for the better. (pp. 39-49)

It is easy to imagine this ethic tweaked just a bit to reflect nearly all of the commonplaces of our process-oriented, collaboration-driven technocratic pedagogy:

> Access to computers—and anything that might teach us something about the way communication through the written word works—should be available to all students and teachers of writing. Always yield to the hands-on experience! The writing process should be collaborative and free of graded constraints. Mistrust traditional teacher-centered pedagogies—promote decentralization.

> Teachers should be judged by their teaching, not bogus criteria such as research, publications, departmental service, and other tenure-track idols, while student writers should be judged by their writing, not bogus criteria like mechanics, usage, grammar, spelling or ability to conform to a predetermined model of correctness. You can create art and beauty on a computer. Computers can change the writing process for the better.

The anarchistic undertones of this technorhetorician's ethic point out again precisely why we carefully utilize the neologism and name what we do in traditional terms. It is fair to assume there is no administrator anywhere who would read this proclamation and clap hand to head proclaiming "Of course! We must stop grading, stop worrying about grammar, give everyone a computer, and pursue new words, new worlds, of writing!" Nor *should* any administrator do so. There is, still, a correctness to communicating in professional environments, and a societal demand that such writing be evaluated, editorially, before dissemination and publication.

Again, these beliefs are reflected in, and recursively affected by, the names we give to what we are doing in pursuit of the implied goals. At first the naming may be playful, ironic, internal—aimed with a nudge-nudge, wink-wink and a "know what I mean?" at those who will immediately understand, and reply "say no more" (Python, 1976)! For instance, the earliest coders named themselves *hackers*—the term has since been popularized and corrupted to suggest negative connotations—and worked at MIT in what they called the Kludge Room, a place to experiment and play with improbable combinations and impossible ideas. They named their machines playfully, one called the Minskytron after hacker guru Marvin Minsky, and formed ironic societies like SHAFT, the Society to Help Abolish Fortran Teaching. They had a jargon of their own, including words like "Greenblattful"; in California, they formed the Homebrew Computer Club.

Similarly, the current generation of technorhetoricians—at a conference in El Paso in 1995, ACW co-founder Fred Kemp called us "the second generation," although in computer terms that is impossibly young—works in MOOspace in a place called the Lingua Courtyard, a place to experiment and play with improbable combinations and impossible ideas. They name their projects playfully, with terms like *webfolio* and *syllaweb*, and understand perfectly what it means to suggest with a ;-) that a message has been cross-posted in "Crumpean" proportions (for *RhetNet* Editor Eric Crump, who is prone to reposting items to numerous lists). There is a "technorhetorician's jargon," just like the hackers at MIT and Cal Tech had. Just as many subcultures do.

MULTIMEDIA NON-SEQUITUR (OR IS THAT A REDUNDANCY?)

Click here to download RealAudio Player

With apologies to everyone associated with the classic television show *Cheers*, here for your listening pleasure are the harmonious voices of guitarists Dene Grigar and Corey Wick (rather than Hootie and the Blowfish, who are committed to another volume) with "Theme from

Netoric Café" . . . if I ever do write a multimedia dissertation, I hope to include this song just to see if I have a legitimately "musical chair."

> Making your way on the Net today. that's what's really hot
> And unless you're Billy Gates, it sure can cost a lot
> Wouldn't you like to get online? (I think that'd be really fine!)
>
> I just changed my fingername; my old one was really lame
> That's okay, 'cause I can say, though you might think it strange
> When I'm online, nothing is quite the same
>
> Roll out of bed, and your modem's dead; All your access, gone!
> Seeme like this old Yugo can't "drive" the infobahn
> Your Windows machine's a "hack"—Guess you shoulda bought a Mac!
>
> I just changed my fingername; my old one was really lame
> That's okay, 'cause I can say, though you might think it strange
> When I'm online, nothing is quite the same
>
> Telnet home, no time to roam, can't afford to surf the Net
> But you will and your AOL bill looks like the national debt
> Why can't it be free to you? Thank the gods for .edu!
>
> I just changed my fingername; my old one was really lame
> That's okay, 'cause I can say, though you might think it strange
> When I'm online, nothing is quite the same

A song like "Theme from Netoric Café" *does* serve a purpose in an argument about writing in electronic environments, beyond the various thinly veiled attempts at editorial commentary. We find great comfort in fitting new words into old slots—yet the juxtaposition can make us laugh. That can be good. That can be *very* bad—especially if your department doesn't have a "musical chair." Scholarship that is elegant and functional but does not follow the rules (the precise elements of a "kludge") often will draw high praise and receive little credit. And we have sold our tenure for a song.

KLUDGING? WHAT?

The term I have adopted—and adapted—to describe this naming we're doing is *kludging*. Here are just a few of the many kludged words that have been posted to the "Interactive Historiography Project" in the Crump's *RhetNet:*

technorhetoric
netoric
syllaweb
webfolio
webliography
webversation
webook
cyburbs
netiquette
netizen
moderhetor
cyberia
netfinitions
MOOniversities
interMOO
MOOtations
interversity

See also: http://www.missouri.edu/~rhetnet/ih/

A prefix here, a suffix there, a playful twist on spelling . . . the words are recognizable enough to convey meaning, yet directly and clearly proclaim their neologistic intent.

Kludging is the hacker's term—borrowing their term, given the thesis of this chapter, is an intentional irony—which describes the act of forcing together two or more seemingly incompatible parts in a new way that works, perhaps elegantly, but for the wrong reason. Our linguistic kludging, pedagogically speaking, may not have any precise "right" reasons but in terms of the hacker ethic may certainly be fraught with wrong ones—including, above all, getting credit at an individual, compensatory level.

The rejection of meritocracy in the academy, as represented primarily by the grizzled tenure/promotion/review process and by the traditional A-to-F grading scale, is a common theme in discussions among technorhetoricians on lists like ACW-L and RhetNet-L. It is the heart of what (above) might be called the technorhetorician's ethic—as it once was central to the hacker ethic. But at some point, we must admit, we step away from the ethic because we are practical enough to want credit for what we are doing within the system of which we are a part. Formation of a group like the ACW, publication of a peer-reviewed journal like *Kairos*, and other current technorhetorical projects all have as secondary motives the instantiation of recognition for the community of C&W scholars.

It is precisely then that the self-conscious act of naming becomes most important, because that naming is done to describe the actions of the community not simply internally but *for an outside audience*. Then the name(s) must convey a certain (and important to be understood) meaning to a "dangerous" audience, which, as Elbow (1987) pointed out, "can inhibit not only the quantity of [our] words, but also their quality" (p. 186). It is then that the linguistic kludging becomes less playful and ironic and more intentional and pointed. It happened to the community of hackers; it is a lesson from which we might learn about the future of electronic writing and writing pedagogy.

As Rheingold (1993) described in his book, *The Virtual Community: Homesteading on the Electronic Frontier*, "Among the original hackers at MIT, the ones who helped invent time-sharing, the hacker ethic was that computer tools ought to be free. The first personal computer makers were outraged when William Gates, now the richest man in America, started selling BASIC, which PC hobbyists had always passed around for free" (p. 102). Gates' now-legendary written manifesto—recall, the ethic was always implicit, without a specifically written statement or manifesto—was printed in *The Altair User's Newsletter* and entitled "An Open Letter to Hobbyists"—note he avoided using the self-styled term *hackers*—and stated with open sarcasm:

> As the majority of hobbyists must be aware, most of you steal your software. Hardware must be paid for, but software is something to share. Who cares if the people who worked on it get paid? . . . Who can afford to do professional work for nothing? What hobbyist can put three man-years into programming, finding all the bugs, documenting his product, and distributing it for free? (cited in Levy, 1984, p. 229)

And suddenly the audience for hacker-speak was no longer simply the hackers themselves, but the world at large. And the descriptions of the work being done—because now the work had to be sold to a "dangerous audience"—were *friendlier*. Less ironic. Less "coded." John Barry chronicled much of this shift in his book *Technobabble*, and throughout engages the term *logorrhea* to describe the unfortunate tendency of various disciplines to create and/or misuse words in the name of making something technical more marketable.

{EXTERNAL LINK ➤ At least this shift to friendlier naming led, finally, to the development of user-friendly interfaces, notably the revolutionary Macintosh desktop metaphor subsequently re-invented by Microsoft's Windows 95. It is heartening to see that Gates has returned to the roots of the hacker ethic and decided that, indeed, it is not necessary to pay for the use of an interface developed elsewhere.}

We all *want* to work within the hacker ethic—but we're practical, too. We want credit—and our scope moves from other pedagogical hackers (each other) to a much wider audience. Or more appropriately, *audiences.* In developing technorhetorical pedagogies, we face a painfully bifurcated audience—on the one hand, our students; and on the other, the administrators of our departments. Using Ede and Lunsford's useful categorization, the audiences we *address* (students) are, ironically, probably far more diverse than the audiences we must at times *invoke* (the administrators), for their demands are much more individual and varied.

Students at Rensselaer and Georgia Tech, for instance, may share a great many educational demographics but almost no similarities in cultural background. Students at Southern Methodist University (SMU) and Dallas' Richland Community College may come from similar cultural and geographical (though not economic) demographics but share little in the way of educational interests. We must encounter and consider these things in our daily pedagogy—and even then, to speak of "classroom demographics" is to dismiss the needs of the individual student in a disturbingly administrative generality.

Conversely, administrators at Rensselaer, at Georgia Tech, at SMU and at Richland, do have a great deal in common with each other, even as students at those schools might not. They all need to speak in terms of generalities, of demographics, of writing requirements and composition tracks. "How will this class fit the university's (or department's) writing (or humanities) requirement?" is a question that is as likely to be asked of a technorhetorician in Albany, New York as one in Albany, Georgia.

Consider the aforementioned term *syllaweb,* one that has been quickly adopted, utilized, and more recently denigrated by members of the community of technorhetoricians. What exactly does the term mean? Why do we use it? At a 1996 Netoric Café MOO meeting, an exchange among Eric Crump, Traci Gardner, Greg Siering, and me illustrated the many possibilities at hand:

> **GregS says,** "We *want* to get students thinking in new ways, so what better way to do that than with new words made out of old ones? If we say 'syllabus,' we allow them to conceptualize in old ways; if we say 'syllaweb,' we encourage new concepts, images, perceptions, and expectations."

> **Eric [netrat] says,** "I hope the use of 'syllaweb' *influences* people when they set about to make a syllabus on the web. The latter is nothing but a print document delivered electronically. The former is, or can become, something new & perhaps better."

traci [to Eric]: i'd prefer that the choice of the name was informed by changes in the way we act and interact with others . . . not the name itself. if it is the naming which is important, then choosing . . . one or the other don't matter. it's not the name, but why it is chosen.

Mick says, "Right, Eric—but if a syllaweb is NOT just a webbed syllabus, does using the similar-sounding term *mis*lead our students?"

Eric [to traci]: but isn't it the case that syllaweb, to stick with the current example, *is* a result, to some degree, of new practices that have emerged as people began putting syllabi on the web?

Eric [to Mick]: they started out just putting syllabi on the web, that is, but soon began to find that new possibilities were irresistible & the syllabus function begins to take new shape.

Mick says, "The syllaweb . . . has become not only a description of the course but a potential model for the kind of writing space available AND a collaborative writing space for the class to work in!"

We spoke—or, I should say, *wrote*—rather heatedly about the way the term informed our approach as teachers; about how it might make our *students* re-think the possibilities involved. And yet, nowhere do we mention the specter of the other audience involved—the *administration*. The most telling experience I have had with the concept "syllaweb" came in a discussion with our department's administrative assistant to the chair. After finally convincing her to grant me permission to teach a class in which students were not given papertext syllabi, but instead given access to a "syllaweb"—partially on the grounds that it would save the department copier costs—I started to leave her office. She stopped me with the question, "So when will I have a printout of that for my files?"

I wonder if the kludge fooled her. My point—that the syllaweb was not like a syllabus, and thus could not be printed out—may have been obscured by the similarity in the naming. A hardware hacker will tell you that a kludge is elegant only to the individual who can look at it and understand it intuitively. The same may be true of these linguistic kludges—Greg and Traci and Eric saw "syllaweb" and immediately started to examine the implications, discussing the (in)elegance of the concept. The administrative assistant heard it and simply said "print it out for me." The intuitive understanding of the possibilities implied do not come with the word when the audience shifts. Nor should we ever expect them to, because the basis for making intuitive leaps changes as well; the administrative assistant was not wrong—she simply worked from a different set of assumptions.

Similarly, I wonder how the label *technorhetorician* may be perceived by these audiences. My students, even in classes called "Technical & Professional Communication" and "Writing to the World-Wide Web"—still called me an "English teacher" and probably rolled their eyes at "technorhetorician" as some sort of politically correct equivalent in the vein of "sanitary engineer" for "garbage collector." My department chair surely thought of my role as "teaching assistant" in the Writing Intensive Program; I don't believe she ever mentioned me to anyone as one of the department's "netorical scholars."

Yet, we call ourselves by this kludged name, technorhetoricians, just as we call our projects by other kludges and neologisms. And there are reasons. Log back in to the Netoric Café:

> **Mick says,** So why do we call ourselves netoricians? Call our course outlines "syllawebs" and our student assignments "webfolios" and "intermoos"?

> **JanetC says,** "Naming is owning . . . and if we don't make up new words, our language is owned by the past!"

> **GregS says,** "Coming up with a new term is a way of creating our own spaces and identities, very important concerns for most of us in this developing field."

> **mday says,** "The sense of play inherent in kludging gives us a chance to look like fun people. Just folks, but sometimes the new names add new meaning in a sort of synergistic process . . ."

> **GregS says,** "At the same time, though, we find a need to connect to a larger audience, perhaps, by using old words, at least in part."

> **Eric [netrat] says,** "Some of this is just convenience, too. It's *klunky* to say rhetor-who-happens-to-study-the-rhetorical-features-of-technological-environments when you could say technorhetorician."

> **mday says,** "Yes. The fun. The expansiveness in that we don't HAVE to take ourselves quite as seriously as some of our colleagues. The notion that dweebish nerdism can be fun and exciting! . . . the kludge has a fun element to it, perhaps a disarming one."

> **GregS says,** "So by naming ourselves technorhets, we are claiming more ownership of our field, our specialties, and our interests."

Convenience. Fun. Comfort with entering a new space. Staking out territory. Connecting to a larger field. Owning our own subculture by naming it on our own terms. Yet as Michael Day pointed out in that same Café meeting, "technorhetoric has been sneaking into the mainstream" of the academy. So perhaps we're not so much a subculture any more.

Again, not unlike the early hackers. The name itself, wrested from them and made into a disgusting pop-culture caricature of its early MIT roots, has been abandoned by those who still claim to adhere to the hacker ethic. Now they call themselves phrackers, phreaks, cyberpunks, cypherunks, coders and a hundred other neologistic self-labels. The hacker culture spawned dozens of subcultures; so too, I would posit, will technorhetoric. And naming, it should come as no surprise, will play an important role in that process as well. It already is; consider Traci Gardner's point about that now-common pedagogical kludge, *syllaweb* . . .

> Syllabi suggest calendarical plans for a course, so by choosing to have a syllaweb, I'm indicating that I'm still organizing things, and by choosing to forefront the word web rather than some other technology bit, I'm indicating that my pedagogy revolves around web pages. If I were working on a MOO and my class plans and ideas were laid out in a series of interconnected rooms, I might not choose to use either part of that term. Or if I have a webbed series of ideas and asked students to construct their own plan for the course and their work, the use of the sylla- part would be wrong. (Gardner, 1996, in Netoric)

In kludging terms with the suffix/prefix web, we are delimiting our electronic description to just that—the Web. Rarely is that all we're doing. But before you think I am suggesting a series of terms like SyllaMOO and SyllaGopher, let me assure you that what interests me most about Traci's objection is that it shows how the names do directly affect and effect the way we teach, and the way our teaching is perceived. So, too, do names and categorizations like "journal" affect the way our scholarship is perceived in the academy as a whole. The editorial team at *Kairos* may be playing around with naming new-looking genres of scholarship like "Coverweb" and "InterMOO," but rest assured the journal also provides traditional labels like "feature essay" and "review" and "letter to the editor." The "letter to the editor" may be an electronic mail message, or a comment in a followup MOO session, and the "review" may literally interlink and interweave itself with the text it is reviewing, so the technologies and the writing strategies in these spaces are quite differently enabled from their traditional papertext counterparts. But their names are the same. A response to a previously published text is, by any other name, a letter to the editor.

Editor—that's the title at the top of the masthead—or, more accurately, the top of the left frame—in the journal I founded back in

1995. My job with *Kairos* was nothing like that of Joseph Harris, editor of *College Composition and Communication*—and the publications are as unlike as the media on which they are distributed. Yet we both call the work "journal"—and I, consciously, self-consciously, purposefully borrowed-stole-adapted-adopted the title "editor." For *my* vitae. Our editorial board—people like Lee Honeycutt, who gave me that "dog-eared" article, and including contributors to this book such as Barber, Grigar, Selfe, Kirkpatrick, Carbone, Haynes, Holmevik, and Galin—probably use that anachronistic title on their vitae as well, not even trying to explain the weeks of e-mail and thousands of lines of debate that went into defining what "peer review" meant after all—and the weeks of electronic mail and thousands of lines of debate, interactively with the authors, that now *constitutes* the peer-review process. "Editorial board" is a comfortable slot. It's vitae-friendly. It's a clearly translatable reverse neologism. Publication in a peer-reviewed journal is, by *no* other easily understood name, the heart of the academic vitae.

Former *Kairos* managing editor—yes, another borrowed term—Mike Salvo (1996) has claimed elsewhere that an important next step in the integration process is the development of "intellectual ambassadors"—something to establish the "act of moving beyond the discourse community." My ultimate argument would be that those ambassadors already exist, in part, in the words we have chosen to use in describing ourselves and our work. But like the (new) *world* ambassadors of our governments, these (new) *word* ambassadors may not be perceived or interpreted by other cultures, other disciplines, other audiences, in quite the same way we nodded and winked at them in the first place. And so we balance our neologistic spice with the comfortable flavor of old terms that convey—almost—what we mean to an audience inhabiting a slightly different culture. As we continue to name what we do, and to unselfconsciously seek credit for it on the academy's current terms, that is something always worth thinking about.

TO KLUDGE OR NOT TO KLUDGE: THAT IS NOT THE QUESTION

It may be somewhat unorthodox to literally respond to a reviewer's questions and comments in the body of text that goes to print, rather than to incorporate the response seamlessly so it seems the question never had to be asked. However, the Web is by nature interactive, and this chapter is structured so that if you are not interested in the dialogic nature of this particular node, well, you can skip right over it.

Question: Can you clarify please—is kludging a good thing or a bad thing? The answer is "yes." Seriously, the question isn't appropriate; with a backward glance ahead at our cultural linguistic tendencies, we can conclude that kludging names and titles is a necessary thing. It is unfortunate that it may cause a series of misunderstandings, but the fact is, we can only talk sensibly about what is possible by using words we already know. The ideas will settle and new wor(l)ds will come; we aren't still hopping in our horseless carriages to drive on down to the moving pictures, are we? The conjoining of the old world with the expectations of the future reinvent the present occasion . . . a kairotic experience at the cultural level.

Comment: In keeping with the overall theme of this book, you should probably comment on "what's next"—what we can expect to find post-Web. Unlike the previous question, in this case the answer is "no." Western culture in particular seems to have some great prediliction to make predictions—who will win the World Series, the Academy Awards, the November election. Prognosticators abound; in fact, I once co-edited an entire issue of the Web's first monthly magazine, *Computer-Mediated Communication Magazine*, dedicated to previewing and predicting the forthcoming year of 1995. Brilliant minds like Michael Heim, John December, Tari Fanderclai, and Laura Gurak took turns "cybercasting" the immediate future of the then-nascent field of Web-based computer-mediated communication. In retrospect, none of them were anything approximating "right" about the future, but the way they wrote about the possibilities probably helped shape that future just the same.

The cultural reinvention that will someday take us "post-Web" is happening every time we log on, or turn on the television, or step outside. What does it mean when Microsoft, the computer industry's 800-pound gorilla airs saccharin-sweet commercials asking users "Where do you want to go today?" Or when one of the world's most-used search engines produces ads featuring a dog named Lycos that fetches supermodels on demand? Or when an online store like Outpost.com thinks it's clever to run an ad campaign in which gerbils are fired from a cannon? Think hard about how the medium of our immediate past (television) is portraying the medium of our present (the Web) to build, perhaps to kludge, whatever medium lies ahead. Don't look for answers, and don't expect predictions to be right; but pay careful attention to how messages are attempting to cross multiple audiences.

Is kludging good or bad? That's the wrong question. What's next, post-Web? All I can guarantee you are wrong answers.

INTRODUCTION: AS GOOD A PLACE AS ANY

This chapter is about writing, and/or editing, and/or publishing in electronic environments—and why the words we use to name what we're doing determine how it is perceived. This starts in our classrooms, our role as writing instructor morphing to include more media possibilities and responsibilities than Alexander Bain ever dreamed of (as we move, perhaps, from Bainian "modes" of writing to Crumpean "nodes" of writing). A sly wink and a neologistic nudge (via e-mail, of course) like "syllaweb" (or "technorhetorician" for that matter) is part of the glue that builds and retains community, virtual though that community may be.

I use the phrase *morphing* quite deliberately; a 1995 conversation published in *RhetNet*, entitled "Morphing Editors," led directly to the creation of *Kairos*. The two journals serve the same community (or communities) in very different ways—and now, as the two journals receive attention across disciplinary boundaries . . . it gets dangerous.

The language of our pedagogy, reflected and refined in the "pages" of our journals, drifts to dangerous audiences—less technical peers, administrators, tenure and promotion committees—as we begin showing off what "publication" might now mean in Webspace, and how contributing to a moderated professional list could be considered a form of academic service. Suddenly, syllaweb sounds either painfully cute or harmlessly familiar.

The way we talk about what we're doing in our classrooms eventually affects—even predicts—the way our professional portfolios will be viewed in the academy as a whole. And although it might be nice to speculate about how "computers and writing" will someday soon be an antiquated redundancy, in fact, to many academicians it will forever be an oxymoron.

Eric Crump has refused the monikor "editor" when referring to what he's doing with *RhetNet*, using instead playful (but serious) substitutes such as "chief instigator," and "WebMom." With *Kairos*, I was the editor—no question about the terminology and all the baggage it brings with it from the offline publication world.

The term is adoptable—convenient, if not fun. It helps our readers find comfortable bridges to entering the new spaces of writing, and connect to a longer tradition and a larger field. As "editor," my job is immediately obvious to people unfamiliar with online publications—or, at least, apparently so. Maybe I was fooled by a reverse kludge, and am suddenly limited to producing work that meets traditional expectations. As "WebMom," I would neither be comfortably obvious to my target audiences, nor would I be in any way limited regarding possibilities for the re-imagining of publication.

RhetNet, a nifty kludge itself; *Kairos*, a Greek legal term. "WebMom," a playful neologism; "editor," a kludged reverse neologism. Two sides of the same future of electronic journals in the Humanities, and you can best tell the path each is taking toward that future . . .

   . . . in its *name*.

   As the erratically great media guru Marshall McLuhan—or was it Eric Crump?—was fond of saying, "If it ain't broke . . . fix it!" Or at the very least, try giving "it" a new name.

ACKNOWLEDGMENTS

Special thanks to Eric Crump, Traci Gardner, Janet Cross, Greg Siering, and Michael Day for graciously granting permission to quote their contributions to three Netoric Café meetings in early 1996. Kudos to Bill Hart-Davidson for his vivid "Writing with a Pen" example and Lee Honeycutt for providing me with the article that proved impetus for this chapter's all-important original title. And a wink and nudge (and "say no more") to Becky Rickly for coming up with the Hootie and the Blowfish tickets and for idly wondering "What do you think a journal for the kind of work we're all doing would look like, anyway?"

EXTERNAL LINKS (WORKS CITED & SITES WORKING)

Publications
Listed alphabetically.

Computer-Mediated Communication Magazine
John December, Editor & Publisher
<http://www.december.com/cmc/mag/>
Note: CMCM ceased publication in January 1999. All issues are still available via Web archive.

Kairos: A Journal For Teachers of Writing in Webbed Environments
Douglas Eyman, Editor & Publisher
<http://english.ttu.edu/kairos/>

RhetNet:A CyberJournal For Rhetoric and Writing
Eric Crump, Chief Instigator
<http://www.missouri.edu/~rhetnet/>

Postmodern Culture
Note: PMC has recently joined with Project Muse, the Johns Hopkins University electronic publishing initiative, and is no longer available free of charge on the Web.

Psycoloquoy
Steven Harnad, Editor
http://www.cogsci.soton.ac.uk/cgi/psyc/newpsy/

Organizations & Electronic Lists
Where to join the conversation.

Alliance for Computers & Writing (ACW)
E-List: ACW-L
Information on how to subscribe:
<http://english.ttu.edu/acw/>

Kairos: A Journal For Teachers of Writing in Webbed Environments
E-List: KMTA ("Kairos Meet the Authors" Series)
Kairos FAQ: <http://english.ttu.edu/kairos/faq/faq.htm>

RhetNet: A Cyberjournal For Rhetoric & Writing
E-List: Rhetnet-L
Information on how to subscribe:
http://www.missouri.edu/~rhetnet/project.html

Web (Re)Publications
404-Proof as of July 4, 2000.

Bush, V. (1945, July). As we may think. *Atlantic Monthly,* 176. <http://www.theatlantic.com/unbound/flashbks/computer/bushf.htm>

Carbone, N. (1997). So ya wanna be an editorial boarder . . . ? *Kairos: A Journal For Teachers of Writing in Webbed Environments,* 2(1). <http://english.ttu.edu/kairos/2.1/loggingon/carbone.html>

Crump, E. (1995). Morphing editors: Re-envisioning roles in network publication. *RhetNet: A Cyberjournal for Rhetoric & Writing.* <http://www.missouri.edu/~rhetnet/editweb/>

Doherty, M. (1997). *The McLuhan resource review pages.* <http://www.dallascvb.com/staff/pages/doherty/mcluhan/index.html>

Doherty, M. (1997, March). The RhetNet defense: A new academic forum toward "shooting hoops." *RhetNet: A CyberJournal for Rhetoric and Writing.* <http://web.missouri.edu/~rhetnet/hoops/>

Doherty, M. (1996, February 14). What's in a name? What we call what we do and why it matters. *RhetNet: A CyberJournal For Rhetoric and Writing.* <http://www.missouri.edu/~rhetnet/doherty-pass_snap.html>

Doherty, M., & Hunt, K. (Eds.). (1995, January). *Computer-Mediated Communication Magazine.* <http://www.december.com/cmc/mag/1995/jan/>

Haynes, C., & Holmevik, J. R. (1997). LinguaMOO. <http://lingua.utdallas.edu.>

Moulthrop, S. (1994). Traveling in the breakdown lane: A principle of resistance for hypertext. <http://www.ubalt.edu/www/ygcla/sam/essays/breakdown.html>

Moulthrop, S. (1991). You say you want a revolution? Hypertext and the laws of media. *Postmodern Culture, 1*(3). Formerly available at <http://jefferson.village.virginia.edu/pmc/issue.591/moulthro.591>

The Kludge Page. No author given. <http://www.teleport.com/~kludge/>

Conference Presentations
Lost in the ephemeral quality of orality.

Doherty, M. (1996, February). *The netorical situation: Kludging linear thought into hypertextual realms.* A bigger place to play: The Mid-Atlantic Alliance for Computers and Writing Conference, Washington, DC.

Doherty, M. (1996, May). *Netoric, technorhetoric, and syllawebs-r-us: Neologisms and the fine art of kludging.* The 12th annual conference on Computers and Writing, Logan, UT.

Doherty, M. (1996, August 6). Netoric and naming: Kludging a new pedagogy. *Netoric Tuesday Café* (Discussion leader and instigator, with Eric Crump).

Doherty, M. (1997, February). *On the internet, nobody knows you're an editor.* Conference presentation at Ghosts in the Machine, Troy, NY.

Kemp, F. (1995, May). *Response to Doherty, Gingiss, and Taylor.* Panel contribution to the 11th Computers and Writing Conference, El Paso, TX.

Salvo, M. (1996, May-June). *Right place, right time: Kairos comes online.* Panel contribution to the 12th Computers and Writing Conference, Logan, UT.

Selfe, C. (1997, June). *New words, new worlds: Exploring pathways for writing about and in electronic environments.* Panel contribution to the 13th Computers and Writing Conference, Honolulu, HI.

Vitanza, V. (1997, June). *Bringing in, but surfacing the fold: A pre/version.* Presentation at the 13th Computers and Writing Conference, Honolulu, HI.

Printouts, Codex, and other Miscellany

Barry, J. A. (1993). *Technobabble*. Cambridge, MA: MIT Press.

Bendetti, P., & DeHart, N. (Ed.). (1996). *On McLuhan, by McLuhan: Forward through the rearview mirror*. Cambridge, MA: MIT Press.

Ede, L., & Lunsford, A. (1984). Audience addressed/audience invoked: The role of audience in composition theory and pedagogy. *College Composition and Communication, 35*(5), 155-171.

Elbow, P. (1987). Closing my eyes as I speak: An argument for ignoring audience. *College English, 49*, 50-69.

Engelbart, D. C. (1963). A conceptual framework for the augmentation of man's intellect. In P. W. Howerton & D. C. Weeks (Eds.), *Vista* (Vol. 1, pp. 1-29). Washington, DC: Spartan Books.

Kinneavy, J. (1986). Kairos: A neglected concept in classical rhetoric. In J. D. Moss (Ed.), *Rhetoric and praxis: The contribution of classical rhetoric to practical reasoning* (pp. 79-105). Washington, DC: Catholic University Press.

Kinneavy, J., & Eskin, C. (1994). Kairos in Aristotle's rhetoric. *Written Communication, 11*(1), 131-142.

Landow, G. P. (1992). *Hypertext: The convergence of contemporary critical theory and technology*. Baltimore: Johns Hopkins University Press.

Levy, S. (1984). *The hackers: Heroes of the computer revolution*. Garden City, NY: Doubleday.

Levy, S. (1994). *Insanely great: The life and times of Macintosh, the computer that changed everything*. New York: Penguin Books.

McLuhan, M. (1962). *The Gutenberg galaxy*. Toronto: University of Toronto Press.

McLuhan, M. (1964). *Understanding media*. New York: McGraw-Hill.

McLuhan, M. (1968). *The medium is the message*. New York: Bantam Books.

McLuhan, M. (1968). *Counterblast*. New York: Harcourt, Brace and World.

McLuhan, M., & Powers, B. R. (1989). *The global village: Transformations in world life and media in the 21st century*. New York: Oxford University Press.

McLuhan, M., & McLuhan, E. (1988). *Laws of media: The new science*. Toronto: University of Toronto Press.

Nelson, T. H. (1992). Opening hypertext: A memoir. In M. C. Tuman (Ed.), *Literacy online: The promise (and peril) of reading and writing with computers*. Pittsburgh and London: University of Pittsburgh Press.

Nelson, T. H. (1977). *Computer lib/dream machines*. Redmond, WA: Tempus Books. (Reprinted by Microsoft Press)

Nelson, T. H. (1982). *Literary machines*. Sausalito, CA: Mindful Press.

Nevitt, B. (with Maurice McLuhan). (1994). *Who was Marshall McLuhan?* Toronto: Comprehensivist Publications.

Peek, R. P., & Newby, G. P. (Eds.). (1996). *Scholarly publishing: The electronic frontier.* Cambridge, MA: MIT Press.

Python, M. (1976). *Nudge, nudge. Monty Python Live at City Center.* Arista AL 4073 (U.S. only).

Rheingold, H. (1993). *The virtual community: Homesteading on the electronic frontier.* New York: HarperPerennial.

Rushkoff, D. (1994). *Cyberia: Life in the trenches of hyperspace.* San Francisco: HarperSanFrancisco.

Shea, E. (1998). *Cultural recombinance: Forms of textual life.* Unpublished doctoral dissertation, Rensselaer Polytechnic Institute.

Southam Interactive. (1996). *Understanding McLuhan.* CD-ROM.

Theall, N. (1971). *The medium is the rearview mirror.* Montreal: McGill-Queen's University Press.

Toffler, A. (1980). *The third wave.* New York: Morrow.

Turkle, S. (1995). *Life on the screen: Identity in the age of the internet.* New York: Simon & Schuster.

White, E. C. (1987). *Kaironomia: On the will-to-invent.* Ithaca, NY: Cornell University Press.

chapter 1.4

A PLAY ON TEXTS:

RHETORICS AND POETICS OF DISCOURSE

Myka Vielstimmig*

In/Troduction One: An Editing Vignette

It was a Friday, and we were editing "A Single Good Mind" for CCC, a discussion whose intent was to take an/other look at collaboration, and a text whose authorship was itself collaborative—or so we lead the readers to believe. Which is why in editing the text, we were considering the relative position of one block of text against another as a visual matter.

Vielstimmig is German for "many-voiced." There is plenty to say about multivocal, collaborated authorship and what it implies for ideas about writer identity; some of that is explored in this chapter, and some in other places by those who theorize collaboration in writing. Sometimes Myka Vielstimmig includes other members, but in this text s/he is the compositive "author" projected by the collaborative electronic writing partnership of Kathleen Blake Yancey, of Clemson University, and Michael Spooner, of Utah State University, (in alphabetical order by institution). (That's not our word—"compositive." The copyeditor put that in.)

ok, which process are we talking about?
    the process of page design?
    the process of representing dialectic?
    the process of plotting and character?
    the process of audience adaptation?
    all of the above?

Or: were we still inventing?

Editing [I *said* editing, you know] involves all of these, doesn't it? It occurs at that part of the cycle where invention reconsiders itself. It's the rhetorical ribosome of recursion.

So we were editing. By phone, we were reading through a section written in Voice A and interrupted by a side snide comment in Voice C.

Voice C, as in one of these bits?

Voice A was a full paragraph, owned the left margin and most of the page width. Voice C was only a few lines and pushed itself from the right margin into the block of Voice A—a move that left A wrapping above and below the smaller C.

Let's move C down a little, *you said.*

What for? says I.

To center it against A.

I had had the mouse for the previous iteration of that page, and I had at one point manipulated the dimensions and placement of the blocks so that they pleased my own visual sense. (Or close enough, I thought, since the journal was likely to change it all, anyway.) Then I repositioned those same blocks of text on the basis of dialectics; that is, I pushed the Voice C block above center because that would put it more directly opposite the particular line of Voice A text that it referenced. (Does this make sense?) I thought the placement worked well enough visually but also worked better dialectically. In reading it together, however, we found that being off center at that point visually troubled you, and you persuaded me that the dialectics would not suffer much by sinking the Voice C block a line or two.

Yes, my sense of the visual *was* different from yours. You wanted an equivalence to emphasize the dialectics: I wanted asymmetry to draw attention to the C.

The particular instance doesn't matter greatly. What I remember so keenly is what a horse trade it was—visual against verbal—to get it right.

Yes, *get it right*: what does that mean??

In/Troduction Two: A Universe of Discourse

Since some things should not be explained, maybe we should begin with a story. We've done it before. A pithy vignette to window the argument we're about to make or have. In this case, especially, the literary window would be right; it would draw the reader's mind to the nature of story, the power of the poetic, to how the literary—as oblique as it can be—opens the subject from below, as it were, giving a cognitive entree that is not fuller but more holistic than exposition.

More than just a cognitive entré, which is why you've located it as opening the subject from "below." (Interesting placement.) It taps the cognitive, but let's be more precise (if unpoetic): it taps the intuitive, the affect, as well. That's the holistic.

And I like how beginning with the literary makes one pause on the brink of an academic article and reflect that all writing owes something to poetics. Just as a story or poem's rhetorical innocence is pretense, so exposition camouflages its commitment to poetic trope, shape, and music.

And image?
There are several assumptions that need explaining if not exploring. Like these two, for example:
- A poem is rhetorical?
- *All* writing owes something to poetics?

I'm not sure these are controversial positions any longer, but it's fair to ask us to associate our point of view with a certain bent in rhetorical theory.

Remind me: Who is the *our* in our point of view?

One could trace the idea that every utterance or symbolic effort is open to rhetorical analysis back to Isocrates, I suppose, although obviously it was not widely considered until about the mid-20th century. In any case, I think we are persuaded that rhetoric is not a discrete province of discourse but rather a field of inquiry whose project is to understand the operation of all forms of discourse. In that sense, poetry is no less "rhetorical" than any other utterance. Fine.

What may be more fun, however, is implied in the second question: We want to see if poetics, like rhetoric, is not a discrete realm, but is a field or plane of understanding that intersects all utterance. In which case, these questions are mirror images.

In the trivial sense—or is it the most profound?—this is certainly so: to the extent that language, which is medium and substance, is metaphorical and hence poetic. But surely you mean other than this?

I just mean to analogize the poetic and the rhetorical. Bakhtin surely has a point when he argues that the sociality inherent in any utterance makes *every* utterance—even a poetic one—rhetorical. But we could apply the same logic to the poetic: the aesthetic dimension inherent in any utterance makes every utterance poetic.

Are all utterances aesthetic? Has this always been so, or are you positing a democratizing of aesthetics, sort of like the democratizing of tragedy? As of the twentieth century, it's no longer the province of only the high; even the low, like Willie Loman, can wake up and find themselves (all too) tragic.

In a sense, the story we would begin with is what has already been published by many writers. Once upon a time, academic writers asked themselves "why not?" and included deliberately obvious stylistic strokes from the world of literary writing into their theoretical work. They spoke in dialogues; they invented characters to speak their words; they included autobiography and poetry and narrative alongside expository analysis; they moved margins, changed typefaces and sizes, included visuals, and coaxed an appearance of typographical disruption and confusion onto the page; they used nonlinear modes of discourse.

Aesthetically, the medium was the message, and this was long before McLuhan?

(When, exactly, was this, if you don't mind my asking?)

Your point?

Exactly. The narrative stands beside the otherwise-expository text, as it were, without looking at it. The "point" of a story in such a context may be multiple. Perhaps it will be an exemplification, an illustration, a commentary, a satire, an allegory of the exposition. In other words, one would read it as one reads a story in other contexts.

> Are you arguing, along with Fisher and
> Bruner (among others), that all discourse is narrative
> and that's the ubiquity of the poetic?

And then how does one read an academic piece that includes such things written with a literary pen? Because the entire essay is then corrupted—or shall we say "leavened"—with the literary.

Ah, corrupted: how is one saved, then? By rationalizing the poetic. But this too is a modernist tendency, once driven by science and by a unitary notion of truth, as ensconced in what Kenneth Gergen calls a totalizing discourse. Different, I think, from poetic and rhetoric as *multiple* discourses, each of which lays claim to a different corner of the truth: a more pluralistic, postmodern view.

And/but wait, again: does poetic equal narrative (Eco; Gass) equal argument (Fisher)? Doesn't this equation have too many variables? Or is there a kind of discursive Venn diagram, in the midst of which is narrative, which itself provides common ground for both poetic and rhetoric? Even if this is so, what in the (cyber) world does it have to do with the electronic?

All this is what we'll debate here. Too much for a single chapter (natch), but we'll try to map the territory of what we understand this discourse to be, which is, in a phrase,

New Words, New Worlds, according to.

But rather: New Textualities?

Mutual Inquiry

As part of the *New Worlds* project, we've been asked to consider our own composing, in particular of the "Postings" text. (That was fun, writing that.) But we've written a number of texts in addition to that one. It's more useful to call on that wider net, if you will :) and to note that we aren't the only ones composing that net.

In those texts—the one from *Voices* and then "Postings" of course, and then "Petals on a Wet Black Bough," and the hypertext for CCCC, and then "A Single Good Mind" for *CCC* (and would we include the Kennedy text?)—our approach has been rhetorical—*and* not, if rhetorical means, among other things, audience-sensitive. We seem to want to please ourselves as much as we look to please the readers.

If we were to divide those impulses, for the sake of argument let's say, wouldn't the one (audience) belong to rhetoric, the other (authorial) to poetic?

Yes, but if we have to be Aristotelian, we could argue that rhetoric is more inconvenient than poetry

You mean it's inconvenient in the sense that the speaker/writer/emailer is obligated both theoretically and practically to incorporate audience? Even if the audience is, as Ong says, a fiction? And: in a way that the poet is not obligated, perhaps? Or perhaps, is obligated, but is off the hook in the sense that she can rely on the fiction of audience as a way out?

. . . inconvenient since for rhetoric the job is to persuade; that is, the speaker aims to change the listener.

Bishop, "Teaching Writing Teachers to Teach Reading for Writers." *Reader: Essays in Reader-Oriented Theory and Pedagogy. Special Issue on the Teaching of Teaching.* 33/34 (1995): 38-67.

Cooper, Marilyn M., Nancy Maloney Grimm, and Anne Frances Wysocki. "Rewriting Praxis (and Redefining Texts) in Composition Research." In Christine Farris and Chris Anson, eds., *Under Construction.* Logan, UT: USU Press (1998).

Nicholas Paley and Janice Jipson, "Personal History: Researching Literature and Curriculum (Literal, Alter, Hyper)." *English Education.* 29 (1997): 59-70.

James Phelan. "Charlie Marlow: Narrative Theorist." *College English.* 59 (1997): 569-575.

Kathleen Blake Yancey and Michael Spooner. "A Single Good Mind: Collaboration, Cooperation, and the Writing Self." *CCC.* 49 (1998): 45-62.

Michael Spooner and Kathleen Yancey. "Postings on a Genre of Email." *CCC.* 47 (1996): 252-278.

*That's *one* interpretation. Wayne Booth suggests another: "the supreme purpose of persuasion," he says, "could not be to talk someone else into a preconceived view; rather, it must be to engage in mutual inquiry or exploration." I like this view, in part, because it sets me up to say that if this were so—if we saw all discourse, all textuality as mutual inquiry—then we might also say that all discourse is thus the *story* of the exploration.

You'll have to persuade me that this is so, heh heh. I can go along with that as a noble rendering of persuasion—come, let us reason together—but I'd argue it's too abstract and altruistic to work as definitive even in most academic discourse.

But in terms of poetic, it raises a thorny question: in poetic, isn't the *mutual inquiry* singular?

(She thinks, you see, that we have here a defining distinction, between poetic and rhetoric: the assumption on the part of the poet that there aren't really live intertexts, that the authorial intention is to discover a Wordsworthian kind of truth?)

Yes, well, in practice, a stance like that lasts only as long as the reader allows it, and it somehow always brings out the latent Marxist in me. I don't think the model of the artist as culture priest, accountable to heaven alone, has done very well for us. But more to the point, I don't think it describes the poetic assumption, as you do. I don't think they're that innocent of rhetoric, and I do think they're alive to intertext. But speaking theoretically, I think that since Bakhtin and Burke, one can't believe poets who pretend not to consider audience.

Can't believe what they *pretend*? You're making an interesting double negative here. You mean it?

I don't think you can get away from language as a social act, whether the sociality is interpersonal or intrapersonal.

Porter agrees with you, at least for the rhetoricians among us: It is necessary, he says, to recognize the many senses of "audience" and the many senses in which "audience functions. Audience can be

Of course, in its own way, this is simply Analisa Porterized

seen as textual property, as an ethos (or set of attitudes and conventions located in a set of texts), or as a community or discourse field" (xii).

Is this what you mean by audience? Intrapersonal invokes both the Gardner notion of multiple intelligences as well as the postmodern selves we bundle into the (not seemingly outmoded) notion of author: is this closer to the mark, in addition perhaps to Porter's definition?

Or we could invoke Vygotsky's inner speech. Or Bakhtin. Whatever. All I mean is that everything written wants to be read; this is the rhetorical matrix of the poem, just as it is of all written language.

Ah, but we speak of the text as character, which even in postmodern heaven, is distinct from author, whoever s/he may be, no?

A writer projects a reading other, and they want to please that other, or to annoy, to shock, to call, to importune, to rouse, to amuse, to berate, to disgust, to bring up short, to soothe, to teach, to woo, to inform, to impress, to inspire, to influence. To affect.

Is this *necessarily* so, that a writer of whatever variety— rhetorical, poetic, electronic—always projects a reader? Based on our understandings of the composing process—from accounts of Sommers and Perl to more recent explanations like Porter's— yes, this is so. But perhaps only because those accounts focus on writers of non-fiction. What about poets? Novelists? Playwrights?

But this is one of the most basic layers of communication theory. While there are many lovely differences among genres of writing and among modes of communication (speech, writing, petroglyph, Morse code, ASL), I don't think they differ at this level.

Every utterance seeks an ear, period.

And interestingly, we might note that the reverse is looking more and more true (if we can use such a modernist term): readers *project* writers into the texts they read, and, it turns out, the "successful" projection looks like the readers themselves. Evidence for such projection-qua-reading is accumulating particularly in writing assessment, where rather than only rating student texts, we're also *reading* them, in the process creating authors that suit our own imaginations and impulses. Lucille Schultz and her colleagues at Cincinnati are calling this tendency—no, it's more than a tendency; it's routine practice, they say—"narrativizing." What Myka has done, seen through the lens of readership, is to invite the reader to play a role in the text, with us, and also apart from us perhaps; that's one effect of *re-presenting* the inventional processes we used. Instead of bringing the reader to some truth—even to *a* truth—Myka outlines *multiple* truths (some we might not even get). (It's not even really an exercise in ethos, either, which could be another possibility.) Also, an effort to please the reader, too: to provide an aesthetic experience, to understand that we can't control (to quote Ciardi) how the text will be read or narrativized—in fact be experienced—or how others may join Myka's plot.

In sum: we narrativize as we read; and we like such narrativizing best when we find ourselves as the heroes and heroines of the drama that is text. Perhaps *this*—text-as-drama—is a convergence between rhetoric and poetic.

Visualizing Textually

We've begun to make this argument before. We are arguing for a hybrid textuality that brings rhetoric and poetic together. Eventually (where was that?) we say "that new essay (call it what you will) . . . includes poetic *and* rhetoric, privileging neither, invoking each that they might together express what cannot be represented without the other" ("Petals" 114).

So is there a word for this? It's not an essay, although it is *indebted* to the essay as it was originally developed—a form designed for the hybrid: the high ideals, the vernacular expression, the aesthetic sensibility. And in addition to a word, we better define it. What are the principles defining this textuality, embodied in it?

"It's an essay the academy is learning to write," *someone said. It's an essay, but not in the Baconian form that has become orthodox in scholarly writing. It prefers Montaigne to Bacon; against the background of the orthodox, it's "un essai," an effort, a venture, *ad* venture; its form is exploratory, disruptive, digressive, and playful.*

We have said of our own work in "new essay" (heh, new essay, new words, new worlds, get it?) that it represents (our) process of composing. This it true, no doubt, in the sense that our process is disjunctive and dialogic. But this may be simply a function of collaboration: it's hard to imagine a collaborative work that would not involve dialogue and exchange of some sort. But a single author writing in a form like this would not necessarily be representing the process of composition. The disjunctives, the talkback, might be a second level stylistic choice overlaid on the work after a fairly straightforward Baconian process. A treatment, in a sense. It might be fun, in fact, to simulate that process with students. Start with a paragraph from good old E.B. White and pulverize it into a dialogic new essay.

Yes, it might be. But at least one narrative of our composing would record such representation not as second-level, but as inventional, right from the start. In fact, as I recall, it was the effort to represent the process, the *dialogue*, that got us into plotting the text.

In other words, there was a text to be plotted.

A verbal text.

Then, there was a *hypertext.*

Then there was a **teleconference performance of a hypertext.**

Discourse all. Increasingly multidimensional. Increasingly performative, not in the sense of affectation or artifice, but in the sense of bringing to life.

Discourse in the Early 21st Century

It is probably assumed here that the form shares something with hypertext. In fact, when we're done with this, I think we should rearrange it as a set of hyperlinks. But I think it would be wrong to suggest that this form of essay owes anything essential in its conceptualization to the theory or mechanics of technology. Hypertext on a computer, obviously, was not possible before the computer existed, but surely there are examples of hypertext in literary and other genres of writing from long before the invention of the computers. Legal writing in the statute or the contract, for example, has always employed inter- and intratextual referentiality (unless otherwise stipulated in paragraph 12). The impetus for (new) essay forms/modulations that explore the multivocal, the intertextual, and so on, that are appearing in scholarly studies today, and the impetus for ever more synergetic linking in computer and software design (the network is the computer, they say) derive from the same human creative impulse. Language itself and cognition itself are associative and synergetic.

Although any particular performance may be imperfect, it is delightful to see the writers in English studies pushing to combine their love of the analytical with their love of the literary modes. Paley and Jipson don't offer a theoretical base for this move, but it was/is nascent in the work of early process writing theorists like Murray, who looked for wisdom in the models of professional (literary) writers. And it is advanced further by those who advocate the use of literary writing by students to enhance their analytical and formal grasp of literary works and techniques (Scholes, Weathers), and by scholars to enhance their theoretical work and their delivery of it (Bloom, Bishop). Probably the teachers who encourage their students to make use of the literary modes in expository classrooms (i.e., outside of "creative" writing classrooms) are still in the minority. Certainly the composition scholars who explore/model/offer literary genres in the course of scholarly publication are out-numbered. Often simply ignored, the idea is also treated as theoretically suspect and rhetorically inappropriate.

This position strikes me as ironic. In protecting literary composition as the province of writers who "can do it well," this argument reinforces the traditional elitism of literary studies. The proper province of composition, we're told, is straight, serviceable, exposition. (There may also be a whiff of disdain here for creative writing pedagogy and its composition cousin, expressivism. How often are these criticized for promoting "confessional" and "personal" writing?) For compositionists to lionize the literary seems a little confusing. In the first place, historians of English studies have fairly well demonstrated the disadvantage that composition as a field, and composition teachers as a group, have endured in the traditional hierarchy. The poetic versus rhetoric competition, as depicted by Berlin, for example, has favored poetics by most theoretical and surely by disciplinary political measures.

But more interesting, rhetorical theory, as understood through the works of Bakhtin, Burke, and others, has called into question the poetic/rhetoric binary at least as a theoretical construct. (Of course, the departmental meeting is another matter.) The binary is undermined, that is, insofar as these theorists have argued the penetration of rhetoric into all forms or discourse and utterance including literary discourse.

So my question is: Can't we see the poetic a matrix or dimension within which all utterance exists, as we see rhetoric, per Bakhtin and others? I'm reminded of Rosenblatt's discussion of the aesthetic and the efferent. Her focus is on the literary, "the poem," but she does remind us that a literary work can be read efferently. And to some extent, one might argue it must be read that way. Of course, part of the game of certain literature is to idiosyncratize semantics or syntax (or other language elements), but discovering this in itself is an efferent process for the reader. Other poetic work proceeds through conventional language, and it even more clearly requires a certain degree of efferent reading. Even the most familiar of poetic tropes—say, the metaphor—depend on the collision of efferences for their "meaning."

We think of rhetoric as having to do with causality, and science, too; that's what philosophers from Aristotle to Schön say, that there are two realms, the scientific, which is the technical and the knowable; the probable, the (ultimately) unknowable (unless of course, you are Plato). Hence the need for rhetoric, a means of knowing that is based in dialectics. If this is so, then what is

it that the poetic claims to know? Berlin says that
what poetry leaves out is the political, which
of course was woven into rhetoric from
the start. But I'm not so sure: think
of Yeats, for instance. And even
Wordsworth found, finally,
that politics permeated
everything, includ-
ing his poetry.

Adrienne Rich, Anne Sexton, Audre Lorde:
these poets are apolitical ?

I think not.

> *Surely Berlin would agree that much of *poetry* is*
> *self-aware, but he might argue that *poetics*—for him a code*
> *word for the lit study that dominates the English*
> *department—is not. His interest is in the rhetoric/poetic*
> *binary as a pair of cultural positions. But what we're offering*
> *(besides being less interested in the political/historical*
> *construction), in effect, may be just a different angle on the*
> *differences between rhetorics and poetics, because we are*
> *focusing at the textual level, instead of the cultural. One could*
> *imagine them both as simply analytical or maybe*
> *hermeneutical (in its flattest, least mystical sense) matrices*
> *that overlay the same subject. So they offer complementary*
> *readings, each contributing something that the other doesn't.*

Remind me (again): who the "we" of
"what we are offering" is?

Each represents an essential dimension of the text, and together they
twist into a sort of double helix of textual DNA.

Of course: we're looking at rhetoric and poetic, but also
somehow sliced through with technology. E-communication is
what got us into this mess (oops), I mean exigence, this book
that is calling forth a dispatch of some kind. Is it possible that
the electronic medium *was* the exigence? Or the weaker claim,
that it contributed to the exigence, that in its design—which is
dialogic—it exerted a shaping influence on (our) textuality?

In/Conclusion One: A Poetics of (Dramatic) Form

We are juxtaposing rhetoric with poetic, but then we go on
to use lots of synonyms for poetic—story, for instance, and
poem. But more often than not, we talk about discourse in
singular terms, those of *drama*—we talk plot, we talk
personae, we talk dramatizing text.

The thing about drama that works for Burke is its inherent sociality,
right? Which he then parlays into something like rhetorical situation, which then
makes drama a great analog or metaphor for rhetoric, applicable in all discourse.

Well, yes: and no. The social: sure. But that's
only a part of it. I mean, drama brings with it a set
of terms, what Burke calls the pentad, which provides both
lens and means of analysis for rhetoric: agent, scene and so on.
Quite convenient these are: collectively, they constitute another
lens through which we can understand the work of rhetoric. At
the same time, though, remember what Burke says that the
work of rhetoric is: exploiting ambiguity. Sounds like the
poetic, no? In other words, there's a real exchange here
between rhetoric and poetic—or perhaps it's a con-
gruity between them. I'm not quite sure of the
relationship, other than to say that each
one enlightens the other, and that in
this analysis, at least, meaning
resides in ambiguity.

But it's possible to disambiguate, at least provisionally. The poetic
doesn't have this same sociality feature until you've done the
Burkean/dramaturgical or Bakhtinian (or whatever) reading of it. So what's
poetic (or "literary") in the poetic is not the dramaturgy; drama is what's
rhetorical in it. Right?

Yes, but. For many—like Aristotle, for one—drama *is* poetic.

Chapter and verse on that one? I think for
Aristotle, drama is poet*ry*. And for
Socrates, poetry is rhetoric in tights.

Drama is fine with me, though it seems to me Burke is using the
metaphor of drama (a "poetic" genre) to enlighten his analysis of (all) discourse
as rhetoric/al. He's not interested in how discourse involves poetics in the same
way that he's interested in discourse (always) being dramatic (i.e., rhetorical).

Well, yes. I think your reading here is too strong. I don't think the point is that all discourse is rhetorical, though of course that's so, but rather that the language of drama provides a way of understanding how this might be so, and too a means of analysis. There is a philosophical element here as well, since the human is seen as agent on the stage of life, making moral choices that tend, historically anyway, to the song of tragedy, as Burke would have it. So Burkean rhetoric is about more than "mere" discourse. It's about how discourse always serves base or noble ends, and thus is poetic, no?

Our suggestion (or my own idéefix, anyway) is that if we look at the poetic dimension of poetic discourse, instead of the rhetorical dimension as Burke does, and then apply *that* to other discourse, we can show that nonpoetic discourse is actually poetic, too.

Sure, sure, sure. I mean, ok. *But* you have to say how. I've already affirmed that claim earlier here; we don't need to elaborate on it. All language is metaphorical; ergo, all language is poetic. End of (very) familiar story. Give us a new story; tell us how all discourse is poetic.

Wait, wait. Familiar stories are too often fables. That claim does need elaboration because I'm not ready to say that metaphor is native to the poetic.

One might consider rhetorics, poetics, and culture as three individual imperfectly intersecting planes—an inexact asterisk—within every utterance. One might add ethics, too—Burke's point about inevitable ends, base or noble— and other planes.

(We could go for pathos while we're up. And who were the other musketeers? Pathos, Logos, Ethos and . . . Derrida?)

Kristeva, I think, mon cher.

By this logic, we extend Bakhtin's and Burke's insight that every utterance is rhetorical: We could say every utterance is also political (i.e., it is situated in culture), and it is likewise demonstrably poetic (it is situated in form/ality). That is, just as we can see the rhetorical plane of a poem by focusing on its irreducible sociality à la Bakhtin, so we can see the poetic plane of an utterance by watching the inevitable performance it is, by hearing the music of it, by perceiving its visuality (or in the classical formulation, its unity, integrity, harmony, and clarity—do I have them all?), attending to its metaphor, its allusion and association, its wordplay, its verbal craft, and so forth. So a poetics of knowing, one could say, is attuned to the issues of artfulness, form, form/ality, per/form/ance that are embedded in every utterance.

Each of these dimensions

—each of these lines in the asterisk—

can be discussed in terms of the others. The rhetoric of form is a common idea. Likewise, any utterance can be addressed in terms of its poetics—genre, style, arrangement, image. The poetics of rhetoric. And any rhetorical or poetic choice is open to analysis for its ethics, too. The point is they're deeply mutual, perhaps inextricably so, and that makes definitions always imperfect. To disambiguate the planes is hypothetical because they exist only in their interactions.

And through form is the connection to drama. Burke abstracts drama, because he wants elements of rhetorical situation abstracted. It works so well because drama dramatizes rhetoric; it gives form to any rhetorical content. But drama isn't drama unless it is performed: the poetic substance of drama is the per/form/ance.

And any rhetorical situation, borrowing from Bitzer now, is the stage upon which Burkean drama is performed? But the poetic *is* in more than the performance: it's in the design of the play, the language of the characters, the action (that can never be fully resolved). The poetic isn't singular, but multiple.

And where would we assign the interaction between/among playmaker, characters, and audience: to rhetoric, to poetic?

The per/for/mance is all of these. To produce a Burkean play on the Bitzerian stage, the actors are agents who deliver Bakhtinian genres of utterance. In so doing, they are form/ing; they are making choices of form. And whether they speak sonnets, or wave gestures in the air, or tease their hair into beehives, they're performing utterance. Gass reminds us that writing is "making." Making is forming something, bringing a form to what was formless. "Maker" is a good literal translation of the Greek word "poet."

So if we think about poetics and electronics in the delivery of academic essays, we are asking ourselves about the form/s of writing that electronics might suggest, prefer, or privilege.

Electronics rewards—or claims to reward—a different kind of text and a different kind of performance.

Frenetic pace is a feature of the electronic world (or so it says here on the label), and this is a text on texts from the electronic world, therefore . . . This is something we got into in "Postings." Is there a genre (a form, a poetic) most representative of cybertexts?

It all depends, she replies.

> What is a cybertext, after all? Do we ever escape the need for definition? Is *this* need—for definition, that is—the point of both rhetoric and poetic?

On the other hand, it wouldn't need to be that issue to be an issue of poetics. It could be that we just want to represent our own process, a dialogical dialectic, and the clipped tone is truer to that process. It's still a question of form, of poetics.

I'm willing to buy this, in the same way that you are willing to buy poetic-cum-rhetoric. Except that poetic is more than form. Not that form is unimportant, and maybe it's not just form, but shape. Of course, shape is form, but shape has, well, more shape to it, as an abstraction, you know?

> Form is, as you say, abstract; shape is tactile.

Or: how about this. We don't really work online, and there's no back-and-forth process. We really write independently, each in our own cubicle, on long yellow pages, which we exchange when they're completely finished. Then we cut them with scissors and integrate the pieces. And we do this because we want to simulate the form of (we want to per/form) what might be achieved by an online dialogical process.

Or: how about this. Now I not only write but also think in multiples: yours, mine, and C.

> Can D be far behind?

In/Conclusion Two: Textuality the Electronic

What difference does the electronic make, you ask.

None, you keep replying.

We always get to this. You say the medium enables/rewards/prefers a certain style, an electronic textuality, and I say no way. And here's why I always say it: *other* styles are far more common online than this one, and this style can be (and has been) done in other media.

Not so fast. I mean I could point to this text: could we have written it, and by written, we mean with pen and ink? Yadda, yadda, yadda: yes.

> **Why ever would we have wanted to do that? I rarely write in pen or ink, and I'm not inclined to begin now.**

Yadda, yadda, yadda. What you're trying to do is concede the point, but trivialize it. It won't go away that easily.

But the fact (not the day) remains: we *haven't* written in pen and ink. We haven't even written so much on computer as we have on e-mail. That is, e-mail isn't simply the *preferred* medium here; it's the primary medium, and it's prompted a different kind of textuality. So:

Whaddya mean "we," whitegirl? I don't prefer the medium—not for this. I compose long stuff like this *primarily* on a word processing program, then upload to e-mail. Often, I compose on paper with ink, then keyboard to a word processor, then upload to e-mail.

> **Does anyone here hear the word Digital??**

Have we used other media in writing together? Yes. (It is a textured literacy here, we're talking about, you know.)

- Does that mean that e-mail is merely preferred? It could.
- What makes you think that it's more than preferred?

I don't. Not even.

*Because, first, when we started writing, we didn't start writing in the conventional sense. We weren't writing an essay

or chapter; we were just e-mailing each other. We had things to
e-mail about; we had what the rhetoricians call exigence—that
book on voice, for instance, as I recall—but as we both admitted,
we also just *liked* the e-mail. From the start, the writing
between us was e-mail-specific.

> May I just note here that you're
> distinguishing "writing in the conventional
> sense" from "e-mailing" apparently by
> definition. Some of us are not in full accord
> with you on this, heh heh.

*Oh sure, put that comment in C. Think *that**
will get you off the hook?

*Because, second, from the beginning of Myka—when the e-
mail seemed like it might make print—we knew not only *what*
we wanted to say, but also *how* we wanted to say it:
dialogically, as we had created it, as the email-as-medium had
shaped it.

> (Sotto voce: Aren't we back to form here? The role of form in
> communication.)

That's what we said, anyhow:

```
This chapter was composed on e-mail by both authors.
<<The brackets denote Michael Spooner's response to
and discussion with the editor, [boy, are we stilted
here] throughout.>> We have chosen to represent the
dialogue  in this format in order to retain and
express the  multi-vocal conversation we experienced
(Yancey 313).
```

*Because, third, in the other texts we've written, we've not
relied on pen and paper, nor on a laptop, nor on a phone. On the
e-mail, yes.

*I think you're off on a tear. E-mail isn't the point. Even the net isn't
the point. It does *seem* like the point, because we always write in dialogue,
often about technology, and we almost always communicate via e-mail.*

*However, let's not forget that the final form of the work—with the cool changing fonts and the multiple margins—has to be achieved in a medium other than email. We're not aiming for an e-mail look, because e-mail doesn't have the look we want. At most, we hope for the "sound" of e-mail, this snappy back-and-forth that out-Hegels Hegel. But isn't it ironic that to achieve the dialectical sound of email, we have to use offline computers and programs (though still digital), that we rely so heavily on the visual, and that ultimately it must be delivered in *print*?*

I repeat: Doesn't anyone hear the word Digital?

Though still digital, you say?

If we could insert advertisement banners every twelve lines, now *that* might begin to simulate the true character of the net.

*Because, fourth, without referencing any high theory—or low theory, for that matter—we began theorizing this textuality. Not just the textuality, either, but what it invites or enables or provides space for: new ways of working; new forms of representation; new identity.

And of course: it's not just us, you know. Yes, Winston Weathers talked about alternate style over twenty years ago, and we invoke and enact that. Yes, the poetic tradition itself provides another intertext. But it's more than these; it's a function of the times: the times, they are electronic.

Writing for the layperson, Kenneth Gergen talked about them in terms of interdependence:

    As Westerners incorporate Zen meditation,
    aikido, Toyota, Kurosawa, and sushi into
    their life-styles, as Japanese buy
    Springsteen records, hamburgers, Picassos,
    and Times Square, the cultures incorporate
    fragments of each other's identities. That
    which was alien is now within. (255)

The cause of this interdependence, Gergen attributed to what he called social saturation, caused by technology:

> The technological achievements of the past century have produced a radical shift in our exposure to each other. As a result of advances in radio, telephone, transportation, television, satellite transmission, computers, and more, we are exposed to an enormous barrage of social stimulation. Small and enduring communities, with a limited cast of significant others, are being replaced by a vast and ever-expanding array of relationships. (xi)

One result: multiple discourses.

> At least this answers the question
> of who put the hype in the hypertext.

No, this is getting closer to the center. I have no trouble at all agreeing that the intellectual and aesthetic tone of our times has been influenced by the stimulations of our technologies. Of course it has. That's what I think our poetic choices in this piece of writing (and others) are all about. We're academic word workers, newprose stylists, and we're inspired by the funky disjunctive aesthetic of our times, to experiment with techniques that amaze and amuse us. (Ok, that teach us, too; we want to study how they work.) This choice we're making: to pierce the body of our discourse; to inscribe the textual tattoo, is a product of the larger culture of our time, involving all the clanking hunks of equipment in Gergen's list, as well as the shifting exposures and expanding relationships that result from them. I think it's too much (or too little) or too specific to claim it's evoked by the medium we work in. We make the medium what it is by how we choose to use it. The medium is *only* as mutltiple as we are.

Writing for the academic, Marjorie Perloff spoke about the tendency toward multiple discourse in the very specific terms of the poetic. She begins historically: we live, she said,

> in a technological world in which everything we say and write is always already a given--a storehouse of cliché, stock phraseology, sloganeering, a prescribed form of address, a set of formulas that govern the expression of subjectivity. Given this context, poetic

discourse is that which most fully calls
into   question   conventional   writing
practices and which defies the authority of
the chronological linear model. (28)

> Poetic discourse questions the techno-world.
> But she means poetry—the discourse boutique.
> Acting very rhetorique.

Perloff noted, however, that the very technology under critique in postmodern poetry is the means of its achievement: "Indeed, poetry is now engaging the codes of the videotape playback, the telephone answering machine, and the computer, especially in its capacity, via modem, to address other computer terminals" (29).

Perloff's conclusion? One: "It seems in any case impossible to talk about something called the "lyric" as if the genre were a timeless and stable product to which various theoretical paradigms can be "applied" so as to tease out new meanings" (29).

This would be a sensible point to make about writing the net, too, don't you think? Not a stable form. I don't know if it's poetry, but I know what I like.

Perloff's conclusion? Two: "Form, to adapt Robert Creeley's well-known injunction, is never more than the extension of culture" (29).

And never less, one might add.

In other words, an/other argument for textuality electronic.

> (Spell that "electronique." **DoubleClique**
> here for the next chapter.)

WORKS CITED

Bakhtin, M. (1990). The problem of speech genres. Reprint in Bizzell & Herzberg, *The rhetorical tradition: Readings from classical times to the present* (pp. 944-964). Boston: Bedford. (Original work published 1953)

Berlin, J. (1996). *Rhetorics, poetics, cultures*. Urbana, IL: NCTE.

Bishop, W. (1995). Teaching writing teachers to teach reading for writers. *Reader: Essays in Reader-Oriented Theory and Pedagogy. Special Issue on the Teaching of Teaching, 33/34*, 38-67.

Bitzer, L. (1968). The rhetorical situation. *Philosophy and Rhetoric, 1*, 1-14.

Bloom, L. Z. (1995). Textual terror, textual power: Teaching literature through writing literature. In T. Fulwiler & A. Young (Eds.), *When writing teachers teach literature* (pp. 77-86). Portsmouth, NH: Heinemann/Boynton-Cook.

Booth, W. (1983). *The rhetoric of fiction*. Chicago: University of Chicago Press.

Burke, K. (1974). *The philosophy of literary form: Studies in symbolic action*. Berkeley: University of California Press.

Ciardi, J. (1987). *Ciardi himself: Fifteen essays on the reading, writing, and teaching of poetry*. Fayetteville: University of Arkansas Press.

Cooper, M. M., Grimm, N. M., & Wysocki, A. F. (1998). Rewriting praxis (and redefining texts) composition research. In C. Farris & C. Anson (Eds.), *Under construction*. Logan: University of Southern Utah Press.

Gass, W. H. (1996). *Finding a form*. New York: Knopf.

Gergen, K. (1991). *The saturated self: Dilemmas of identity in everyday life*. New York: HarperCollins.

Paley, N., & Jipson, J. (1997). Personal history: Researching literature and curriculum (literal, alter, hyper). *English Education, 29*, 59-70.

Perloff, M. (1990). *Poetic license: Essays on modernist and postmodernist lyric*. Evanston, IL: Northwestern University Press.

Phelan, J. (1997). Charlie Marlow: Narrative theorist. *College English, 59*, 569-575.

Porter, J. (1986). Intertextuality and the discourse community. *Rhetoric Review, 5*, 34-47.

Scholes, R. (1985). *Textual power: Literary theory and the teaching of English*. New Haven, CT: Yale University Press.

Schultz, L., Durst, R., & Roemer, M. (1997). Stories of reading: Inside and outside the texts of portfolios. *Assessing Writing, 4(2)*, 47-64.

Spooner, M., & Yancey, K. (1996, May). Postings on a genre of email. *CCC, 47*, 158-176.

Vielstimmig, M. (1999). "Petals on a wet, black bough": Textuality, collaboration, and the new essay. In G. Hawisher & C. Selfe (Eds.), *Passions, pedagogies and 21st century technologies.* Logan: University of Southern Utah Press.

Vielstimmig, M. (1997). *In a station of the metro.* Website: http://www.usu.edu/usupress/myka.

Weathers, W. (1980). Grammars of style. In R. L. Graves (Eds.), *Rhetoric and composition* (pp. 133-147). Upper Montclair, NJ: Boynton/Cook.

Yancey, K. B., & Spooner, M. (1994). Concluding the text. In K. B. Yancey (Ed.), *Voices on voice: Perspectives, definitions, inquiry* (pp. 298-315). Urbana, IL: NCTE.

Yancey, K. B., & Spooner, M. (1998, February). A single good mind. *CCC, 49,* 45-62.

chapter 1.5

FOLLOWING IN THE FOOTSTEPS OF THE ANCESTORS:

FROM SONGLINES TO ILLUMINATED DIGITAL PALIMPSESTS

John F. Barber

* * * Transmission Begins * * *

- **An artifact is a history from the past to the future, or an eulogy from the future to the past**

By the time you read this, I will be composing it in the past. I will have gone ahead, beyond the future horizon of invisibility, seeking new territory. I stop now to recount. My composing will remain, a singing web of where we have been.

The singing will not be as polyphonic as I would like. I revert to the old ways here, from necessity. It is awkward focusing again on "text" as words made to appear on pages.

- No longer are they vessels meant to convey meanings, made themselves of all the meanings they ever conveyed
- No longer are they nodal links to information spread throughout the public areas of electronic space
- No longer are they bubbles of memory from my private journals
- No longer are they multidimensional interlinked digital compositions, but plodding markers tracing the progression of thought across the landscape of blank pages, words locked into position in visual space (Walter Ong 121).

The Priest of the Future Perfect predicted this. Conventions, constraints, he said, evolved for oral, written discourse. These were incorporated into electronic discourse even as it was being and becoming something else.[1]

To grasp the meaning of the world of today we use a language created to express the world of yesterday (Antoine de Saint Exupéry 49-50). *We're living in topsy-turvy times, and I think that what causes the topsy-turvy feeling is inadequacy of old forms of thought to deal with new experiences* (Robert Pirsig 163). Neither the language nor cultural mythos we inherited are adequate to describe, explain, amalgamate the electronic spaces we are exploring. We are unable to put our experiences into familiar words •

                                                                                      • phrases
                                                               • sentences •
                                              • thoughts •
                                      • ideas •
                cultural constructs •
We resort to expressing ourselves in metaphors •
                                                               • contradictions •
                                                                              • abstractions •
                                              • stereotypes •
                                              • words as webs of meanings
emptied out with age, *accordingly invested with new meanings, and always equipped with secondhand memory* (Trinh T. Minh-ha 79).

As Marshall McLuhan (1962) and Alvin Toffler predicted, there will be some of the old terminologies in the new, but none of the new in the old. As Hélène Cixous, Dale Spender, Laura Miller, Lynn Cherny and Elizabeth Weise pointed out, we will be hampered by our sense of
        <! ---------------- body-based gender assumptions ----------------->
libidinal conflicts
psychosexual relationship imperatives

as we develop conceptual frameworks in these places where the body becomes incorporeal.

To address these concerns we will create palimpsestic fragmentary collages of the old. Protean symbols for the new.

We are *researchers* . . . . •
                        theorists . . . . •
                             teachers . . . . •
                                    students of similar paths . . . . •
exploring the electronic ways so I will speak forthrightly. We seek timeliness, the solution to the current problem. What we seek is in the future, unknown but not unknowable.

How you will respond is unknown to me at the time of my composing. That knowledge is frightening and confusing and exciting and challenging. Perhaps you will think me lost and unrecognizable, an arrow pointing down the long and dark corridor to the teleport. Perhaps you will think me valuable and prophetic, a lone motorcycle-headlight-rising-moon illuminating the place where earth and sky meet. Light or dark, what it will be, I cannot know. A journey into the dark sparks a new quest for the light. I can only report the things I will think at the time.

This is the best any explorer can hope. To share stories around the electronic campfire, relating what has been, is being, ultimately will be created.

• The Footprints of the Ancestors track whence we came, not where we are bound

Around their campfires, the Australian Aborigines retell the creation of the first network. They repeat the legends of the Dreaming, of how The Ancestors created themselves from clay each taking the form of a specific animal, bird, rock, or plant, one totem for each of the Aboriginal groups. They tell of how The Ancestors walked throughout the land speaking and singing each object in the natural world into existence, leaving an unbroken trail of spoken words and musical notes along the line of their footprints. The Creation. Each object unique and separate yet nodally linked by a track of footprints, words, singing. The Footprints of The Ancestors, *Songlines* as Bruce Chatwin calls them, created interconnected, interlocking pathways through the space that became the world. They were and ever will be maps and communication channels between far-flung tribes.

Each Aborigine inherits a section of an Ancestor's footprints and the space through which they pass. Through these Songlines, Aborigines construct, configure, control their world. Each must maintain the correct sequence of verses in his or her Songline. Verses may be leant or borrowed. Never sold or abandoned. If they are, the reality they invoke ceases to exist.

Songlines must be performed as composed. Everything in prescribed sequence. No verse out of place. Strung like beads on a necklace. This recreates creation. Creates circularity. Continuity. Reality.

For centuries it was thus. We saved, sang, shared our Songlines secure in the reality they promulgated. Bruce Sterling chronicled many of our methods, now no longer in use.

- Etched bone mnemonic devices . . . .
- Lunar calendars . . . .
- Smoke signals . . . .
- Shouting . . . .
- Whistling . ...
- Drumming . . . .

We developed rhetorical systems. Cuneiform characters etched in clay. Papyral hieroglyphics, *The Book of the Dead*. Carved-in-stone coded systems of cultural constructs, *The Code of Hammurabi*. Then written words affixed to pages, like these. Glued with atoms of ink. Once affixed, words could be broken apart. Separated from each other. Scattered like beads from a broken necklace. Shared with others via overland mail, air mail, e-mail. Recombined into new meanings, new verses. What was done could be undone. We flirted with the ability to move backwards down the cabalistic line of words comprising our Songlines, to deconstruct the product of our own creation, to bring chaos into the world.

- **The disappearance of self set us adrift in the present with no sense of the past**

Late in the 20th century, this was fashionable among academics, artists, and others no longer connected to a sense of the past. Deconstructed the integrated self in reaction against Rene Descartes's 17th-century hold on our imagination. The idea that each person is a rational individual with a distinct and constant identity residing and seeing the world from somewhere just behind his or her eyes. From this vantage Truth is knowable. But more than 300 years later, we are the way we are. Where the person resides is of no import (the concept, like the word, archaic) since truth is thought both unknown and unknowable.

Cultural critics O. B. Hardison, Jr., Sandy Stone, and Walter Anderson rationalized deconstructing Songlines. Anderson saw we desire to abandon identity/
become PostModern/
adopt decentered, multiple, changeable selves/
change the course of our lives in response to cultural stimuli.
Focusing on one cultural stimulus, science, Hardison sang that it,

> *asks man to understand himself in the light of his own reason detached from history, geography, and nature, and also from myth, religion, tradition, the idols of the tribe, and the dogmas of the fathers. It offers likenesses of nature, not nature, and it suggests further that nature is a project created in part by man. (70-71)*

The *nature* about which he sang is the surrounding physical reality encompassing and defining our lives. Culture, the objectification of our understanding of these things, is *an artifact and probably a game, and what happens in it is the result of human rather than divine will* (71). Stone likened this to our loss of ability to maintain ourselves in a steady state of equilibrium, our willingness to reinvent ourselves by way of technology.

D isassociation   . . . .
isconnection
<! . . . . The Footprints of the Ancestors ignored>
iscontinuity . . . .

Continuity forgotten lost broken.

---

* **When Songlines break down, people choose new tribal affiliations**

> Late in the postmodern curve, some people recognized radical discontinuity between past and present. Aided by electronic
communication technologies, they sought to collect new information

* ---------------

* make new connections
reexamine old boundaries
compose multiple selves.

Create new cultural contexts based on synthesizing, amalgamating, sloganeering.

Improvise to a world of multiple and simultaneous realities.
Promote ~~distortion~~ and reexamination of artistic and cultural techniques like linearity and simultaneity, stasis, and motion.

All reimagined, resung to a new reality.
Represented reality through technological depiction of objects in motion.
Acclaimed ascent of Information Age
        based on the perceived potential
of the digitized document and pixelated print.

Others eulogized the loss of centeredness.
                Feared the loss of control.
        Recognized their world has changed.
Responded with nostalgia for the past made miserable by its loss
(Hardison 131).
        Blamed technology for replacing pastoral past with
commercial present. Represented reality through technological
depictions of idealized idolized otherness. *The body physical as prosthetic
of the techno-media net. The body electronic as* data trash *struggling to
come alive* (Kroker and Weinstein 2). Kibble, *useless objects, like junk mail
or match folders . . . gum wrappers or yesterday's [paper]* (Philip Dick 57).
Lamented descent of Age of Print
        founded on the promulgated power
of the denoted document and permanentized print.

- **The schizophrenia of technologies imitating art is like jazz
  music played on cardboard boxes**

The two faces of technology. Evolved from *techne*. Janus-faced. One
looking to the future, one to the past. One the corollary to science. One
the creator of discontinuity. Homogenous yet heterogeneous
perceptions of our surrounding world (nature), depictions of ourselves
in this nature (our notion of culture). The schizophrenia of technologies
imitating art and its emphasis on imitating what exists (Avital Ronell).

What existed late in the 20th century was frightening. Douglas Rushkoff
sang of,

> *Global warming, racial tension, fundamentalist outbursts, nuclear
> arsenals, bacterial mutation, Third World rage, urban decay, moral
> collapse, religious corruption, drug addiction, bureaucratic ineptitude,
> ecological oversimplification, corporate insensitivity, crashing world
> markets, paranoid militias, AIDS, resource depletion, hopeless youth.
> (1)*

More euphemistically, jazz pianist Thelonius Monk said, everything was
happening all the time.

Using techniques borrowed from musicians like Monk,
- Repetition repetition repetition repetition repetition repetition
    - Randomness ran . . . . Domn. . . Ess ran dumb is ramd OM ess rand O mess
        - Transformation

communication technologies revisioned the realities of a rapidly changing culture. Sought to place us in the middle of the action with no discrepancy between real and Memorex.

The High Priestess of Telephony warned of this. *Maintaining and joining, the telephone holds together what it separates* (4). Telephone technology began the breakdown. It engaged destabilization. Promoted noise frequencies, static, and interference. Interjected voices. Replicated the effects of scrambling electronic-libidinal impulses flooded with signals.[2] She placed the call but no one answered.

Claude Shannon, a mathematician employed by the Bell Telephone Laboratories, felt semantic aspects were *irrelevant to the engineering problem* (379). The fundamental problem was getting the message, not the feeling or meaning, from point to point efficiently, effectively. Encoded-decoded by mathematical algorithms and sent down the wires from place to place. Packet switching information networks. Banking networks. Espionage systems. Schizophrenic fracturing of latent semantics. A technology with no off switch. Jobe Smith (*Lawnmower Man*) entering the global telephony system, ringing all telephones simultaneously, signaling the arrival of a new virtual entity.

Art *imitating* reality became confused with the power to *create* reality. Drawing from Dada, Concrete Poetry, and Ouvroir de Littérature Potentielle (Workshop of Potential Literature), media technologies like cinema, television, newspapers, and radio developed new forms of multidimensional, webbed audio-visual language and presentation conventions. Parodied a pastiche of themselves. Multiperspective plot lines, jump-cut infomercials, and front pages featuring discontinuous events collected over the last few hours, KISS concerts, brand-name-techno-retro economics, supply-side grunge-punk clothing styles.

Elizabeth Klem and Charles Moran, oracles speaking Delphi-like to the present for the future, focusing on our use of computer technology, likened our movement from the old to the new as *an amphibious stage* (132).

But they were not prophetic enough. Future histories will be clear about this. The electronic communication technologies of the late 20th century were factors in massive cultural . . . .
. . . . artistic •
                        scientific • . . . .
. . . . political •
                                economic • . . . .
. . . . .social deconstructions •
But rather than amphibian, moving back and forth between two environments, symbiotically responding to both, these technologies were protean, reconfiguring as well as responding. Thomas Looker said American mass communications of all kinds were constantly assaulted by a *cultural juggernaut* representing,

> *many of the most powerful trends in contemporary culture . . . trends that value reflexiveness over reflection, speed over care, disengagement over involvement, pictures over words.* (383)

One result was *increasingly truncated, nonlinear scripts* and glibness of language used in these scripts (112). This glibness became *so much a part of our national dialogue* that Looker said,

> *the question media critics ought to be asking is not how "biased" are particular news organizations, but, rather, is the kind of talk that sounds articulate on all television networks—and on most radio programs— sufficiently dense or nuanced or supple enough to speak usefully to the predicaments of our lives, our culture . . . our civilization.* (172-173)

Was it, to sing with Neal Stephenson, sufficient to condense fact from the vapor of nuance? (55-56). Both observers and critics drew from the arsenal of the new physics theories of chaos and discontinuity to provide answers.

• New geometries begin when someone changes a fundamental rule

By discontinuity I mean seemingly random blips and squeaks of interference breaking and disrupting the linear world. Analyzing discontinuity with Benoit Mandelbrot's equations, we see that each blip and squeak is comprised of smaller blips and squeaks similar to the pattern on the next highest level. Gazing into mirrors reflecting one another. The deeper we look the more mirrored discontinuities we see. Discontinuity has recognizable patterns. We are assured. Our fear of chaos belayed. James Gleick posits that chaos is the potential for complex and dynamic systems of order. Chaos is no longer disorder. Irrationality. But a deeper order of apparently random, nonlinear systems. Total subversion of Cartesian hierarchial thought. Reversion to Plato's continuum. Eternal eternity. Circularity. Journey. The Footprints of the Ancestors.

Douglas Rushkoff put it more abstractly
(we have already spoken of the necessity for abstraction)
when he said chaos is the character of discontinuity (23).

Imagine a dripping faucet.
|
V
Each drop discernable
|
V
and after observation
|
V
pretty predictable.

But when the faucet is opened
| | |
V VV
running water attains *turbulence*
perspectivespredictions nolonger possibleusinglinear means
nowdisplaysfaucetemergentdynamicsystemnaturechaos.

The telephone, photocopier, fax machine, modem, Internet, video teleconferencing, World Wide Web. Open faucets all. Dynamic systems. Required expedient and exponential information processing. Cool or hot. Followed models for the presentation of reality established by McLuhan's global-village-creating television.

- **"We interrupt our regularly scheduled programming for this special announcement. Do not attempt to adjust your television set. If trouble persists, do not call a technician."**

At first, television simply transcribed linear productions and displayed them on ghostly glowing cataract screens. But televising again and again and again and again and again and again and again and again and again and again and again President John F. Kennedy's assassination, Rodney King's beating, O.J. Simpson's ride, and their subsequent glib analysis by talking-head announcers turned experts and experts turned announcers deconstructed our sense of reality. If it didn't happen on TV, it didn't happen.
Televised events were real, personal events were not.
Changed our sense of moment-to-moment continuity.
Broke into discontinuous units.
Bracketed by questions answers
analysis reductive stereotyping
from multiple
PERSPECTIVES
Television's deconstructive nature altered our
relationship with the media image as an image of reality. In some cases our perception became fixed, frozen in time. After the news reports, we forever knew exactly where we were and what we were doing when the fatal bullet entered Kennedy's brain.
In other cases, our perception became more fluid.
During Simpson's quirky ride around Los Angeles in the white Bronco we were able to anticipate where he would pass next, walk to the corner, wave as he passed, see ourselves on television participating in the event we were watching this media report. The story of Simpson's ride became our story.
Related, connected, shared in personal ways.

When Gil Scott-Heron sang *"The Revolution Will Not Be Televised"* he was right and wrong. No revolution in the streets. No live broadcasts of fighting behind bulwarks. Instead, nostalgic rock music driven nonlinear jumpcut television advertisements urging us to buy and consume our way to unique and personalized identities.

*If you're tired of your life going nowhere, try The Future. The Future is fun! The Future is fair! The Future is bright and full of possibility! Act now and never suffer from a flat tire! Limited futures available now for qualified buyers. Our operatives are standing by. Press *97 on your keypad and you'll be on your way to The Future!*

The Prophet of Media Massage said, *The medium is the message*.[3] In rebuttal, Andrei Codrescu detailed television programming replacing thinking. The disappearance of the outside. All within/into the TV screen. What you see is what you are, what you get. Image was everything. Ask Don King. Other communication technologies followed suit. The Mediascape, the electronic collective graffiti unconscious, was born. Astride chromed modems we surfed discontinuous gaps and gutters between media images.

> Filled each with personal meanings.
>
> Sense of importance.
>
> Languages of resistance.

Rather than a single truth, the melting pot, our world view became, as Ishmael Reed (1988) described it, a *bouillabaisse* (53) of distinctive and flavorful perspectives. Discontinuities of a dynamic system. Our cultural context became nonlinear------------------>Unfocused.

Based on alternative experiences and perspectives.

The Songlines of Discontinuity born.

<!..................... The Footprints of the Ancestors abandoned>

• Recapitulation brought order to chaos and death to Descartes

Douglas Rushkoff promoted concise review as a better way to relate to a world fast becoming less linear. Recapitulation, he said, was *capable of representing our chaotic cultural experience in a manner that allows us to relate to it* (228).

Trinh T. Hinh-ha questioned recapitulation. Said it was too entrenched in contemporary literary and theoretical establishments of postcolonial processes of displacement

cultural hybridization

DEcentered realITIES

f--r-a----g-m---e-----n--t---e---d selves

multiple multiple multiple multiple multiple multiple multiple identities
voices

> marginal

languages of rupture. Said representing our own discourse on myths as a myth makes us *acutely aware of the illusion of all reference to a subject as absolute center* (61). Suggested instead stories to provide a way for us to *come into being* (119). Storytelling as *the oldest form of building historical consciousness in community* (148). In the retelling through personal words the story unwinds like a long thread each end leading *to another end, another opening, another 'residual deposit of duration'* (149) *maintaining the difference that allows truth to live on* (150).

We combined both. Incorporated the poetic into the analytic. Began to recapitulate the stories we told ourselves, and each other, to share alternative experiences and perspectives.

Recapitulated storytelling gave us insight into how our world worked and motivation for being more self-determining in our cultural context. Recapitulated storytelling didn't demand the memorization of facts and commands, or the adoption of a definitive conclusion. Instead, following chaos and postmodern critical theories, each person's perspective recapitulated the whole picture, however faintly, in a multidimensional portrait. Everyone's point of view mattered as much as everyone else's. Recapitulated storytelling allowed us to portray the audience, rather than a protagonist, simultaneously engaged in their own experiences, looking outside for answers, in the real world rather than within the content of the story. Recapitulated storytelling spawned multiplicity of social voices, dialogic links, interrelationships. A context Mikhail Bakhtin saw as dynamic interactions between speaking individuals, or running dialogues with the self, and the word meanings they employ (263). *Heteroglossia*. Lev Vygotsky's inner speech. Meaning made through dialogic interchange where multiple word definitions, forms of language usage, and meanings overlap.

Electronic space explorers and programmers applied this heteroglossian context to electronic venues seeking to develop discourse communities. First iterations included e-mail, Internet relay chats, discussion lists, MUDs, LANS, WANS, and commercial network-based collaborative writing/conferencing programs. Gail Hawisher and Cynthia Selfe (1989), Carolyn Handa, and Linda Myers collected early reports and future scenarios. Hawisher and Paul LeBlanc provided critical reimagining. Hawisher, LeBlanc, Moran, and Selfe sang of historical perspectives. Later, we moved to WWW pages, multimedia authoring systems, and MOOs. Cynthia Haynes and Jan Rune Holmevik collected reports on their design and use. We used these electronic venues as sites, spaces for facilitating teaching, learning.[4]

Early electronic venues represented worldviews of observers, dreamers, and futurists who used them. Discontinuous but connected by a deeper sense of order. Richard Brautigan proposed *cybernetic ecology* where life forms and computers coexisted in *mutually programming harmony*. Howard Rheingold envisioned *cybernetic architectures* for worlds and ways to be in them (88). John Markoff sang of *post-textual literacy* based on digital audiovisual rather than textual thinking (5). George Landow promoted non-linear, nonhierarchial dialogue with multiple texts. Starr Hiltz and Murray Turoff predicted that technology-facilitated dialog would promote more freedom to express controversial or unpopular opinions, as well as the consideration of participants' contributions based on *their merit rather than the status of the proponents* (27). Shoshana Zuboff said discourse and interaction could be continuous and collaborative (370). Marilyn Cooper and Cynthia Selfe suggested we could *learn from the clash of discourses...learn through engaging in discourse* (867). Everyone sings their piece of the Songline.

- **If electronic writing foreshadows a new paradigm does it equal four nickels?**

Since Johann Gutenberg's 15th-century invention of moveable type our discourse began its slow evolution from an oral to paper and/or book basis. But late 20th century emergent computer technologies foreshadowed limits of printed narratives as vehicles for comprehensive, multimodal composition, reality representation. This was welcomed by some. Academics seeking promotion and tenure rides. Others felt extensions of our capabilities promised by these technologies challenged concepts of humanity and literacy, usurped the essential nature of humanity.[5] Neil Postman, Clifford Stoll, Barry Sanders, Sven Birkerts, and others. Felt printed narratives were better representational technology because they modeled static reality that could be reexamined at leisure. This was, of course, before the publication of *Agrippa*.[6] Birkerts emotionally stated his concerns over the *proto-electronic era*. Follow this [•LINK] to his argument.

V

> *A change is upon us—nothing could be clearer. The printed word is part of a vestigial order that we are moving away from—by choice and by societal compulsion. This shift is happening throughout our culture, away from the patterns and habits of the printed page and toward a new world distinguished by its reliance on electronic communications. (118)*

Birkerts lamented the all-electronic future and its *morbid symptoms*:
- *eroding language* . . . .
   - *flattening of historical perspectives* . . . .
- *waning of the private self* . . . . (128-130)

His lament was shared by Sanders, who said the world is,

> *peopled with young folk who have bypassed reading and writing and who thus have been forced to fabricate a life without the benefit of that innermost, intimate guide, the self. (xi-xii)*

The exit from this situation, Sanders says, is literacy:

> *a set of relationships and structures, a dynamic system that one internalizes and maps back onto experience. (xii)*

Richard Brautigan's *cybernetic ecology.*

For both Sanders and Birkerts, displacement of internalized, hierarchial endeavors by electronic impulses flashing through circuits was disconcerting. Sounding every bit the chaos theorist, Birkerts said,

> *Living as we do in the midst of innumerable affiliated webs, we can say that changes in the immediate spheres of print refer outward to the totality; they map on a smaller scale the riot of societal forces. (3)*

```
<Table Border=1 Cellpadding=8>
<TR>
<TD Font Face=Helvetica Align=Center><B>
We did not weave the web. We are merely a part of it.<BR>
Whatever we do to the web, we do to ourselves.<BR>
   -- Chief Seattle<BR>
<P>
The web of our life is of a mingled yarn, good and ill together.<BR>
   -- William Shakespeare
</Font></B></TD></TR></Table>
```

Evolving from print culture, the siren shapes, to borrow Michael Joyce's (1988) term, of computer technology were too compelling to ignore.[7] They promised to extend and reshape the spectrum of narrative experience. Not, according to Geoffrey Nunberg by replacing printed words (books). But by continuing their storytelling abilities in new frameworks. By creating dynamic fictional universes with characters and events better able to tell more complete stories. Stories that could not be told in other ways. Promoting engagement in ways not before possible. Utilizing powerful sensory presences and participatory formats. Recognizing silence as the common bond between all modes of thought. *The place where the right words can come together . . . the dark soil through which the seedleaves of a new understanding may push through to the light* (Stephen Talbot 228).

This utopian view does not refute dystopian scenarios presented by Birkerts, Sanders, others. It summarizes hopes and fears raised by increasingly visceral compositional potentials promoted by digital media. Points specifically to essential differences between models for emergent writing: simulation and participation. Aldous Huxley's *feelies* and William Gibson's (1984) *simstims*. Programs based on *simulated stimulation* of environments and their inhabitants. Robert Pinsky's Mindwheel, Ray Bradbury's *televisors*, Star Trek: The Next Generation's *holonovel*. Contexts based on customized *participation* in complex stories. Janet Murray's incunabular narratives. Straining against boundaries of formats no longer expressive or comprehensive enough.

Creating these narratives we drew from long histories of written, oral, visual rhetoric. The latter was a rediscovered surprise. The notion that images could be vehicles of expression and communication seemed foreign to us, based in and dependent on, as we were, typographic characters pressed onto a flat surface. But, Lester Faigley reminded us that every known culture, past and present, has a language of images. The problem he said, is that the totemization of alphabetic literacy from the Enlightment onward had the attendant effect of treating images as trivial, transitory, and manipulative.

Our use of emergent technology[8] and traditional rhetorical forms was classic in the sense that we used them primarily to do things better than we were without them. But O. B. Hardison, Jr. warned us that any truly new technology subverts all efforts to use it in a classical way. It becomes expressive, reshapes its function, forces us to use it to do previously impossible things (236-237).

Despite divergences between classical and expressionistic language, we attempted to fabricate new, expressive, electronic literacies. To break free of alphabetic confines. To compose what we saw, felt, thought, experienced. Walter Ong first said this was possible. Said using computers as writing instruments encouraged a move toward our unconsciousness (131-132), return to many of the habits of oral discourse (136-138). Victor Vitanza said electronic writing combined the conventions of oral and written discourse, even as it was becoming something else. Rather than *writing* he suggested *composing* (xv-xvi). Others stressed that writing with computers need not be an isolated activity. Using networked computer technology, writers could, they said,
- Communicate actively with others while writing
  - Collaborate with others
    - Connect writings by multiple authors
      - Create communal use of language
        - Construct knowledge.

Like medieval alchemists we sought creation of something new and more desirable from base components. Like hip-hop scratchmasters we sought to reweave multiple elements into new compositional forms. Like The Ancestors we sought to stride across the new worlds we were exploring, singing our new reality into existence.

We extemporized new nodal networks of expression. We created graphical icons patterned after the New Zealand Maori's *whare tupuna* and *moko*. Preserved and displayed our genealogies on carved barge boards spread like open, welcoming arms over entrances of electronic homesteads. In intricate facial tattoos coded into signature files or dancing on web pages. We sampled The Mediascape and other entertainment forums. Following Nicholas Negroponte's lead, digitized new forms of commingled bit communication. Recapitulated, from the old, new stories that were at once flexible and permanent, fictional and real. Reconfigured, revisioned, reimagined the nature of writing.

- **The written world of the future will take place in electronic spaces as much as it already does in print**

Electronic spaces became our electronic forums.
The *agora* revisited (Dene Grigar et al.).
New forms of human social interaction.
Kevin Kelly's *Hive Mind.*
Stephen Doheny-Farina's *wired neighborhoods.*
Howard Rheingold's *virtual communities* where groups of people were linked by their participation in computer networks.
Alan Purves' print-based *scribal society* conventions moved to electronic media.
Stanley Aronowitz's ineluctable intertwining of writing and technology (133).
Electronic discourse communities based on written collaboration.
  Communal layered text.
    Augmented, revised beyond first iteration.
      Endless continual constant state of review revision.
        Writing never finished, but always already in a state of
becoming.
        New literacy spaces and practices signified as the move from page to screen (Ilana Snyder 1998 xx).
Process as product.
Palimpsestic narratives linked nodally, multimedially to information behind and
                            beyond its display on our screens.
Informational databases.
Providing resources, tools for readers in structured, hierarchial manners.

Early linked narratives were called lexias. Roland Barthes invented the term to signify *reading unit* (13). Landow suggested using it (4, 52-53). The links between, among, through these lexia were hypertextual, offering different pathways to users. Stuart Moulthorp called hypertext an encyclopedic collection of writings without predetermined structure *through which the reader is free to move in almost any sequence* (19). Hypertext, as an intellectual idea, as a collection of linked units of information, was not new.

[•LINK ⇒] Erik Davis said the notion of memory systems as articulated representations of abstract structures can be traced to Medieval charts that tried to schematize all knowledge into an organized forest of trees (591).

[•LINK ⇒] *The Talmud* is a holy text glossed with and surrounded by commentary from multiple rabbis (Janet Murray 56, Billie Wahlstrom and Chris Scruton 313).

[•LINK ⇒] Vannevar Bush first proposed the idea of using current technology to support the human associative intellectual process by establishing trails through mechanically stored information. Bush called his microfiche-based storage and retrieval system—*a sort of mechanized private file and library*—memex. *A memex is a device in which an individual stores all his books, records, and communications, and which is mechanized so that it may be consulted with exceeding speed and flexibility. It is an enlarged intimate supplement to his memory* (106-107).

[•LINK ⇒] Theodor Nelson called Bush's notion of trails between stored information *links* and coined the term *hypertext* to denote a nonsequential, branching method of reading, writing, and storing and retrieving information connected by links. Others followed and developed these ideas in the arenas of multimedia, artificial intelligence, and hypertext (James Nyce and Paul Kahn).

Ilana Snyder grounded hypertext as an *information medium that exists only on-line in a computer*. A structure composed of text, digitized sound, graphics, animation, video and virtual reality connected by electronic links (1996, ix). We experimented with ways to link disparate bits of information . . . .

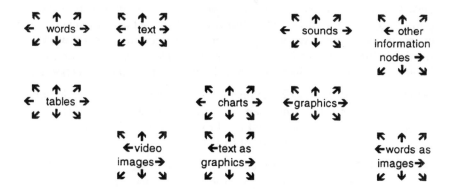

to create large-scale multimedia • hypermedia narratives
• nonhierarchial customizeable databases
• indices
• electronic classification systems
that facilitated use and reuse by different people at different times to
satisfy different narrative needs. To create Gilles Deleuze and Felix
Guattari's (1987) tuberous rhizome, recreate the Songline, where any
verse could be connected to any other.

Our first rhizomes ran the gamut of purpose, audience, tone. *Afternoon,*
by Michael Joyce was an experiment in postmodern fiction where
readers followed links between carefully crafted lexia fragments,
constructing some sense of a textual whole. *The Spot,* on the other hand,
was constructed to generate revenues. Borrowing from Laurence
Sterne's use of blank pages in *Tristram Shandy,* the pages of this web-
based soap opera were used by characters and readers to promote
interaction. But the pages of The Spot were not blank. Each one featured
advertising.

In either case, as readers we followed links between chunks of
information. We felt this allowed us to

√ Interact with characters of the narrative
√ Enter the virtual worlds they inhabited
√ Influence the plot(s)
√ Explore the loosening boundaries between video games and stories,
amusement rides and movies, broadcast and archival media,
audiences and authors.

- **Interesting things happen along the borders, not in the middle where everything is the same**

We first tested our ideas in the invisible nestings of Gopherspace and the Internet. Next experimented with what Janet Murray called *the flashing billboards of the World Wide Web* (112). Our work was discontinuous and deconstructive. The composing tended to disappear into its linked structure. Readers often became lost in the information branching. Computer technology was not responsible. The fault was our own. We followed models available to us. They promoted the disappearance of writing. It began in the 19th century with the theory that written literature should be studied with the same objective distance that science brought to bear on its study of nature. In the 20th century, literature became increasingly the object of theoretical applications that prompted the infinite regression of text into words about words about words. Gazing into facing mirrors lost in the depths of repeated reflected images. Meaning denounced as something to be deconstructed into absurdity (Murray 4-5).

The solution was to develop a kind of electronic composing that encouraged readers to range freely. Make associative connections with ease and flexibility. The new, in borrowing from the old, is always ambiguous. Brenda Laurel and Janet Murray, seeking explicitness, connected the action-reaction representational nature of our writing to the procedural and participatory characteristics of digital environments in which it was produced and consumed. Laurel suggested the term *interactivity* (19-22). Murray *interactive* (71, 74). Michael Dertouzos said interactivity would allow audiences to determine the progression of the plot (152). Richard Lanham said, *Interactive digital fiction invites the readers' collaboration* (124). Jay David Bolter came directly to the point:

> *electronic fiction . . . frees the writer from the now tired artifice of linear writing, but the price for this new freedom for the writer is that the writer must allow the reader to intervene in the writing space.* (146)

Espen Aarseth connected our emergent digital writing to Norbert Wiener's cybernetic information feedback loops. Called it *cybertext* (1) since it centered attention on *the intricacies of the medium as an integral part of the literary exchange* (1) as well as on the consumer, reader, user. Aarseth borrowed from the new physics to frame the characteristics of our emergent interactive writing. Called it *ergodic* (1) to denote open, dynamic texts with which a reader must perform specific actions to generate literary sequences.

Aarseth claimed both neologisms tentative. Definitional boundaries along which, said Donna Haraway we are attracted *for pleasure in the confusion . . . and for responsibility in their construction* (150). Markers for what will have come. Cyborgs existing where two kinds of boundaries are simultaneously problematic.

Likening computers to something more familiar, something more closely allied with our sense of identity, Sherry Turkle (1984) called them a *second self* capable of engendering identity-changing relationships as well as questioning the mind in relation to machines. Later (1997) she told us computer simulation changed the ways we thought about ourselves. Other people. Technology. Our lives.

Simulation became a motif in our quest to create a new form of electronic composing. Computational simulation programs allowed us

Simulation

to model new, parallel, forms of reality. Simulated life games. Simulated life. We believed these simulations. They became real. Not in the sense of knowing the why of an underlying process. But in knowing the how on the computer screen (Turkle 1997 42). The borders between the real and the simulated transparent. Simulation prompted us to look beyond, through, intervening computational programs and hardware. To envision a participatory reality.

This transparency of process led to immersion.
Norbert Wiener's cybernetic self-regulating feedback loops.
A continuous scrolling RAM memory movement from screen to screen.
Total and complete surround by other realities.
We sought this in our interactive narratives.
Doorways between the real and imagined worlds.
The known and the unknown.
The familiar and the other.   **Immersion**
The land and the water.
Moments of passage where new cultural symbols could emerge.
Victor Turner, the anthropologist, called these *liminal moments*. Rather than a name we had feelings. . . . . . .

Pleasurable	feelings of suspension of disbelief.
Awkward	feelings of disruption if we moved too quickly.
Fragile	feelings of learning to swim in new waters.
Disconcerting	feelings of going too far, unable to return.

N Our third motif was navigation. The sense of interactive narrative
a stories as places. Narratives we could enter and move around in.
   Stories as navigable places. Spatiality. William Gibson first
vi brought this to our attention. In an interview he generalized about
   the concept of space in a computer when describing young people
g playing video games in a Vancouver, BC video arcade. For an
a excerpt of his interview, follow this [•LINK].

t   ion. |
                                                 |
                                                 V

> It was like one of those closed systems out of a Pynchon novel: a
> feedback loop with photons coming off the screens into the kids' eyes,
> neurons moving through their bodies, and electrons moving through
> the video game. These kids clearly believed in the space games
> projected. Everyone I know who works with computers seems to
> develop a belief that there's some kind of actual space behind the
> screen, someplace you can't see but you know is there. (McCaffery
> 272)

• The place that isn't a place is still the place we call home

We *did* believe in a space behind our computer screens, between our
networked computers. Called it many names. *The Noosphere* (Pierre
Teilhard de Chardin), *The World Brain* (H.G. Wells), *The Interzone*
(William Burroughs), *The Net* (Spider Robinson and Jeanne Robinson),
The Web, *The Matrix* (John Quarterman), *The Electronic Frontier*, *The
Other Plane* (Vernor Vinge), *The Metaverse* (Neal Stephenson), *The
Autoverse* (Brad Egan), the *datasphere*, *hyperspace*, and *Cyberia* (Douglas
Rushkoff 1994). The most popular term was *Cyberspace*. Coined by
William Gibson (1982) to describe,

> *an abstract representation of the relationships between data
> systems. . . . the colorless nonspace of the simulation matrix, the
> electronic consensus hallucination that facilitates the handling and
> exchange of massive quantities of data. (74)*

Whatever we called this space, it was not "real" in a positivistic sense.
Not a physical place seen or felt. The place that wasn't a place. But for
us, explorers, media and culture hackers, teachers, students, cyberspace
was real. Real things happened there. Drawing from Barrie Greenbie's
(1981) exploration of the American architectural landscape, we thought
cyberspace a place where we could act. A place to which we could react.

A place to profoundly change, through its metaphorical imagery and vocabulary, our notions regarding multiple and different realities.[9] As Bruce Sterling (1992) said,

> This "place" is not "real," but it is serious, it is earnest . . . and though there is still no substance to cyberspace—nothing you can handle— it has a strange kind of physicality now. It makes good sense today to talk of cyberspace as a place all its own. Because people live in it now. Not just a few people, not just a few technicians and eccentrics, but thousands of people, quite normal people. . . . There are entire living communities in cyberspace today: chattering, gossiping, planning, conferring and scheming. (xii-xiii)

Stephen Marcus, reversing a popular cliche, said destination, not journey counted. Telecommunications is not simply a "conduit" for getting information from one place to another. Instead, it is itself a place to go (20).

We divided early into two tribes. Browsers and hunters. Browsers looked for anything of interest. Followed lines of inquiry to information nodes matching their desires. Hunters sought specific information. Were goal oriented. Both fascinated with worlds consisting entirely of information where levels of consciousness depended on levels of abstraction.

ImmerSion
i
m
u
l

Navigation
t
i
o
n

The Holy Trinity. Beyond borders of the real world and well into the representational. Augmenting, transforming, creating reality. Virtuality. The essence of virtual reality (Michael Heim). Electronic mirrors reflecting one another. A metaphor. Affecting the way we perceived, thought, acted. Defining reality (George Lakoff and Mark Johnson). The rhetorical process by which discourse unleashes the power that certain fictions have to redescribe reality (Paul Ricoeur 7). Even remaking our vision of spirituality, divinity, the sacred (Jeff Zaleski and Ray Kurzweil). The ability to replace one kind of thought with another (Marvin Minsky 299). Jean Baudrillard's hyperreality. Substitution of simulation for original. Reproduction for actual. But as Umberto Eco showed us, also a way of straddling the border between the bright and present illusionary and the dim but more authentic ordinary world.

- **Louis Sullivan was wrong: Function follows form when building electronic skyscrapers**

It was easy to embrace Brenda Laurel's contention that computers were inherently theatrical environments where writers became playwriters, shaping the rise and fall of experience.

Many of our early immersive interactions were scripted as visits to defined places. Ray Oldenburg said there were three essential places in our lives.

Places we lived •
• Places we worked
Places we gathered for casual conversation. . . . . •

At first, our interactive narrative spaces simulated places where we might gather for conversation.

• . . . . rooms

• . . . . lounges
• . . . . hot tubs

We scripted protocols for entering, leaving, and navigating within these places, and immersed ourselves in them.

From these chat spaces, and their focus on interaction with others, we developed MUDs (Multi User Domains/Dungeons). Virtual spaces entered through the liminal looking glass windows of computer screens (Turkle 1997). Conduits to imaginary worlds (Lakoff 1995). Enchanted places. Places in which to act. And places to which to react. Rheingold's *cybernetic architectures* (88). Cynthia Haynes and Jan Rune Holmevik's *archi/TEXTural community.*[10] Simulated collaborative worlds and ways to be in them. Most followed game motifs where readers became players.

"*Welcome Interactor.*"

"*You find yourself in a built, simulated, immersive environment.*"

Composed in broad strokes.

Donned or created characters. Avatars.

Interacted with, reacted to, these environments. Or other interactors.

"*You see Dr. Shark Barbetz, itinerant traveling scholar.*"

Made decisions and dealt with the consequences of our choices.

Good decisions ⇒ successful completion of puzzles, mysteries, challenges.

Bad decisions ⇒ setbacks. Or character death.

"*Would you like to play again? Y or N*"

With the advent of MOO (MUDs-Object Oriented) cores we sought to compose Turner's notion of liminal objects that would transport us into contexts of immersive alternative realities. We recapitulated familiar models.

laboratories . . . . •

offices . . . . •

auditoriums . . . . •

libraries . . . . •

schools . . . . •

monasteries . . . . •

Places we worked. On smaller levels we strove for the comfort of Ray Oldenburg's third places, the great, good places.

• . . . . houses

• . . . . fishing lodges

• . . . . bars

• . . . . cafes.

Places that existed on neutral ground.

Created conditions of social equality.

Where conversation was the primary activity and major vehicle for display and appreciation of human personality and individuality (42). In these narrative spaces, we collaborated •

• conferred

chatted •

• gossiped

planned •

• schemed.

Enjoyed a sense of connection,

place, community.

But it was a closed system. . . . . •

As playwriters/composers we wrote/produced electronic, computer-based hypertext fictions, adventure games, MUDs, MOOs, MUSHs, MUCKs, MUSEs, *as well as* rules governing our actions and reactions. All controlled by coded procedural rules running the electronic, computer-based spaces. Every iteration carefully scripted binary machine language. Regulated predetermined impulses controlling presentation, participation. Step-by-step instructions to facilitate interactive narratives. Conditions and responses to every desired or potential action.

Scripted. Coded. Linear. Like Songlines.

<! . . . . The Footprints of the Ancestors exhumed>

Readers/interactors/navigators "created" narrative performances by choosing among multidimensional intricate branching possibilities within our electronic story systems. Evoked narrative possibilities as singularity events. Simulation, immersion, navigation possibilities afforded by each rhizomatic choice for characters, narratives, plots. Power to take satisfying action and see results (Murray 153), but only within context of script. Short of revising controlling coding, any such creation could only be accomplished within boundaries prescribed by the originating author and/or the procedural considerations of the electronic space itself.

At this point I bring you to the present, my present, the present of my composing, which, as I said at the beginning, will be the past of your reading. The teleport at the end of the tunnel. The motorcycle headlight rising moon at the cusp of earth and sky. The artifact from the past to the future. The eulogy from the future to the past.

- **A journey into the dark sparks a new quest for the light**

We look to what we do not have. To create collaborative interactive narratives, both as originating composers and interactors. To merge attributes of

- Manuscript   • (text)
- Telephone   • (one to one)
- Television and radio   • (one to many)
- Library   • (information archiving)
- Museum   • (linear information display)
- Internet   • (many to many)

into new forms for communication and representation. Address concerns about *egonomic electronic text* (Andrew Dillon), *data smog* (David Shenk), and *data trash* (Arthur Kroker and Micheal A. Weinstein). Our proposed multiform narratives will draw from neural network research of human thought as processes occurring across and between associative synaptic stimuli (William Allman, Marvin Minsky, and Heinz Pagels). *The Information Market Place* (Dertouzos). The postmodern notion of life as a series of parallel possibilities. They will allow simultaneous examination of multiple contradictory alternatives. Provide rhizomatic, nonlinear, discontinuous collaborative authorial/reader/interactor origination, recapitulated storytelling, inter*action*.

The multiform narratives we seek will merge and overlay literary and computational techniques of composition. Borrow from the old to create the new. Neither completely subsumed. The Illuminated Digital Palimpsest.

The success of computer technology as a medium for compelling multiform narratives depends on our ability to *write rules that are recognizable as interpretations of the world* (Murray 73). Like the lexia and interactive electronic spaces before them, our multiform narratives will be procedural. Formed, driven, determined by rules that specify the events and conditions by which those events occur. We are learning to script the interactor as well. To go beyond fixed menus of alternative role-playing games or formless linear built-in-table-of-contents-links writing. To bring narratives to life by utilizing a computer's encyclopedic capacity to store and access vast series of procedures and algorithmic power to execute them to promote a wide range of believable, responsive behavior.

Seeking models we borrow from ancient bardic traditions to combine the pleasures of coherent narratives with endless interactive variations. We compose formulaic stock phrases, themes, plots. Construct formulas within formulas offering multiple opportunities for recombination, reconfiguration, recapitulation into believable larger narrative structures utilizing the procedural nature of computer technology.

We borrow from our literary tradition. Use terminologies and techniques of the old to create the new.

- Kaye Gibbons' *A Virtuous Woman* seeking models for multiple perspective narratives.
- William Faulkner's *The Sound and the Fury* and *As I Lay Dying* to utilize time-jumping stream of consciousness.
- Ursula Le Guin's *Lathe of Heaven* to explore the magic of creating multiple versions of the same reality.
- Albert Lord's *The Singer of Tales* for devices for patterning narrative components into multiform lexias that can be recomposed anew with each "reading" of the narrative and not leave readers/interactors wondering whether they have seen/explored all available links.

Like lexia and interactive electronic spaces before them, the multiform narratives we seek will foster navigation, simulation, immersion. We desire to travel where our dreams live. To live among our dreams. Where the pleasure of travel is simply being in between places, in transit, rather than in any place in particular (Jeff Greenwald 180). We seek characters with whom to interact in meaningful ways, to help us understand what it means to be human.

```
<UL>
<LI> WHO am I?
<LI>WHERE am I from?
<LI>WHERE am I going?
<LI>WHEN will I get there?
<LI>WHY am I going there?
<LI>HOW much will it cost me?
<LI>WHAT will I do after I arrive?
<LI>HOW will I know I've arrived?
</UL>
```

E. M. Forster posited two types of fictional characters:
    flat ones who perform the same way throughout the narrative
and
    round ones who learn and grow.

Following Joseph Weizenbaum's success with the Rogerian-psychoanalyst *"Eliza,"* we strive to write/compose/code round characters who surprise us by exhibiting emergent behavior that goes beyond their bits-and-bytes coding of procedurally-determined interactive boundaries. Early successes with socially-skilled and conversationally rich chatterbots, goal-based intelligent agents, and set-piece improvisational digital puppets are encouraging and important, representing, as they do, ways of introducing cybernetic feedback control into dynamic-chaotic systems.

As computer	television	cinema	video	photo-graphy	telephone	radio
facsimile	painting	sculpture	music	museum	library	technologies

continue their intermingling we will borrow from the old to configure new media forms in and through which to produce and publish our multiform narratives.

Avatar-based electronic interactive environments •
                    • high-definition digital televisions
        laser video discs •
3-D virtual reality programming languages •
               • digital audio and video streaming
      holographic projections •
wireless infra-red transmission networks •
are incunabular placeholders for whatever will soon arrive. In the meantime, these technologies facilitate creation and utilization of electronic venues that become extensions of the author/composer's narrative voice, production of electronically generated narrative structures based on formulaic-algorithmic patterning that allows/encourages authors/composers to assemble multiple variations of multiform plots. Their function is to awaken us to the aesthetic possibilities of new media potentials, help exploit their expressive powers, push beyond their dependency on earlier multimedia technologies (Murray 67-94).

Concurrently, we need to move toward something at the higher levels of procedural-computational hierarchy that promotes machine interpretation that mirrors the believable. Promotes the unpredictability of the mind modeled by Minsky. Allows us to *act so that there is no use in a centre* (Gertrude Stein 498). Something George Dyson described as,

> *slippery and disoriented . . . independently free to make mistakes . . . search randomly . . . act so that the machine appears to be making an intelligent choice. (72)*

- **Postcards from the side of the global information highway are making abstractions live intellectually**

Situated as we are, long past the waning curve of postmodernism, long past the last friendly oasis on this road we travel always at night our way illuminated only by the fading headlights of identity and sense of self, we should give some accounting of our actions for those that will follow to judge as they will, or join if they desire.

We need/want to know, perpetually.

--->

> *Writing introduces division and alienation, but a higher unity as well. It finishes the sense of self and fosters more conscious interaction between persons. Writing is consciousness-raising* (Walter Ong 179).

We are leaving the old, familiar, known and entering the new, unfamiliar, unknown.

--->

> *Our Western values, built on the written word, have already been considerably affected by the electric media . . . Perhaps this is the reason why many highly literate people in our time find it difficult to examine this question without getting into a moral panic* (Marshall McLuhan 82).

We are exploring, investigating, interpreting new electronic worlds of writing.

--->

> *I don't think we can sit out this technological revolution; why not use it?* (Richard Lanham 10).

We have no names for the
nameless.
--------------------------------------->

> *Reconceptualizing   what
> computers do as representing
> action with human participants
> suggests a design philosophy
> that diverges significantly from
> much of the contemporary
> thinking about interfaces*
> (Brenda Laurel 2).

We are seeking what things will
be called in the future perfect.
--------------------------------------->

> *Electronic writing threatens to
> redefine historiography in a way
> that reveals what Sontag has
> called the "impossibility or
> irrelevance of producing a
> continuous, systematic argument"*
> (Jay Bolter 117).

We are finding, or inventing, new
words with which to discuss
what we are learning and thinking
about what writing will have
become as it situates itself between
oral, print, and electronic cultures.
--------------------------------------->

> *Any value they may have is
> probably going to be transitional
> and will recede as the discourse
> on (and of) 'electronic writing'
> continues to establish itself
> among the various 'area studies'
> of cultural critical theory* (Espen
> Aarseth 182).

We are theorizing and practicing
electroliterate pathways leading
from conventional current
traditional modalities toward
cybernetic multiforms of
author, reader, and writing.
--------------------------------------->

> *Being digital is the option to be
> independent of confining standards*
> (Nicholas Negroponte 44).

We are beginning to see what lies ahead, just beyond the headlights. The
text-created, text-based amphibious (existing as they did partially on our
computer screens and partially in our imaginations) virtual fictional
places promulgated by earlier electronic venues will become less like

ASCII-outlined architectural structures . . . . •

. . . . • impelling role-playing adventure-game labyrinths

. . . . • garish ego-centric billboard WWW "pages" • . . . .

and more like pleasurable

richly-textured
atmospheric
explorable
embassies of our thinking
participatory 3-D neighborhoods
dreamscapes

Electronically mediated environments for the kinds of lives we want to lead . . . virtual spaces interconnected by the emerging information superhighway . . . by the growing domination of software over materialized form (William Mitchell)

decentralized
self-defined communities
with their own designs for living in the digital age
(Esther Dyson).

These new electronic cyber-contexts will be protean. Reacting as well as responding, they will encourage dense, demanding, expressive narratives from authors/composers, subtle responses from readers/interactors. They will promote a move from reading and then interacting in different environments to reading and interacting in the same environment. From sequential to merged experience. From simulation to immersion. A more believable sense of participation, interaction, reality through utilization of oral, written, and visual literacies.

We sing the Songlines anew, creating as we explore. New worlds and ways to be in them. New Worlds, New Words. New wor(l)ds.

<! . . . . The Footprints of the Ancestors reborn>

* * * Transmission Ends * * *

NOTES

1. Victor Vitanza, *Writing the World Wide Web* (xv-xvi).
2. Avital Ronell, *The Telephone Book* (xv, 4).
3. Marshall McLuhan, *Understanding Media* (23).
4. See Dene Grigar and John F. Barber's (1998) account of Grigar's dissertation defense in the Auditorium of LinguaMOO, "Defending your Life in MOOspace: A Report from the Electronic Edge."

5. David Channell's *The Vital Machine* examines the history of our relationship with technology saying that while disturbing ethical issues are raised by the imitation of life by technology, the source of these fears lies in outmoded mechanical and organic world views. Channell suggests a third, more embracing, world view that combines advances in genetics, quantum mechanics, relativity, and computer intelligence and forces both science and philosophy toward a more complex understanding of the universe.

George Dyson's *Darwin among the Machines* weaves a view of the evolution of the mind in the global network fostered by digital computers and telecommunications. Dyson says computer programs and worldwide networks combine to produce an evolutionary theater in which the distinctions between nature and machines are increasingly obscured.

Vivian Sobchack's "New Age Mutant Ninja Hackers: Reading Mondo 2000" posits that we desire to merge the body with machinery and technology because of the technoerotic notion of transcending the sensory limitations suffered by the imperfect human body (575).

Bruce Sterling's novel, *Schismatrix*, casts this desire as technical against organic. The Mechanists, masters of surgical implantation of technology, wage war against the Shapers, who practice biological manipulation through conscious control over their own DNA coding.

John F. Barber's hypertextual lexia, "The Seven Ages of Computer Technology," synthesizes multiple scenarios regarding future iterations of computer connectivity and their implications for our sense of what it means to be human. With regard to human-machine interface, see his discussion of "The Transhuman Age" within this lexia.

Theodore Roszak's *The Cult of Information* says we risk confusing what computers do well (process and store information) with what they can not do at all, but humans can, very well (reason and feel). Tracy Kidder's *The Soul of a New Machine* chronicles the technological and human drama behind the development of the Data General Eclipse computer. Barbara Garson's *The Electronic Sweatshop* focuses on how computers are transforming the office of the future in to the factory of the past. William Wresch's *Disconnected: Haves and Have-Nots in the Information Age)* explores information access disparities. James Brook and Iain Boal's *Resisting the Virtual Life* critique connections between information technologies and the increasingly abstract, virtual lives we are compelled to lead.

6. William Gibson, inventor of the term *cyberspace*, published, in 1992, *Agrippa*, a book that self-destructed as it was read. He was assisted by Kevin Begos, a publisher of museum-quality manuscripts and Dennis Ashbaugh, an artist whose work employed models of computer viruses. Guy Martin, reviewing the book before its publication, said

> *The physical object will be a large, somewhat tortured bronze or graphite portfolio containing Ashbaugh's original copper-plate engravings of DNA codes. Under the engravings will be a floppy [disk], swaddled in its own niche. Gibson's story will be on the disk, along with a very slick little computer virus. If the reader boots up and commits to reading this work, the disk will scroll at a preordained speed, once, and then the virus will cause it to mutate and then disappear. Appropriately, Ashbaugh's engravings will be done in two kinds of ink, one that disappears after being exposed to an hour of light and one that appears on exposure to light. The 500 or so editions of* Agrippa *will cost between $450 and $7,500, depending on how much of an "object" the collector wants to buy. (33)*

Robert Killheffer said *Agrippa* is

> *an elaborately conceived marriage of antique bookcraft and modern computer technology that may alter our conceptions of the immortality of artworks" [and raise] "issues about the shape of books to come, issues we'll all be confronting, like it or not, in the very near future. (14)*

7. Beyond the compelling nature of computer technology itself we also felt the force of Porush's Law (1995). *Participating in the newest communication technologies becomes compulsory,* Dave Porush sang,

> *if you want to remain part of the culture. The Porush's Law that has caused such a stir was penned to be ironically harsh, to create a stir, as it were. Of course one of the best ways to participate in a culture is to go off-line, to cultivate the antique, the irrelevant, the marginal, the disenfranchised, to explore de-cultivated niches, back alleys, cul-de-sacs, and the unworkable self-dismantling romances of nonsense, primitivism, paradox, and glossolalia. But someone needed to concretize the argument, if only to use it as inoculation to resist it. It would be ironic indeed if I am remembered for penning the rallying cry of the Microsoft Nazis.* (Personal e-mail from Dave Porush, 26 Jan. 1998)

8. I have recounted some of the history of emergent computer technologies. See John F. Barber, "A Brief, Selective, and Idiosyncratic History of Computers."

9. See John F. Barber, "Cyberspace and The Mythform of Reality" for more discussion about the idea of space behind the computer screen and its power to create reality.

10. Cynthia Haynes and Jan Rune Holmevik, founding Lingua MOO wizards, first used the term *archi/TEXTural* in their description of and welcome to this collaborative, electronic space where reality is based on/in writing.

> *Welcome to the Courtyard of Lingua MOO. Several *benches sit beneath large shade trees that line the walkways between buildings. Signs mark the entrances to a new archi/TEXTural community where language and people are woven together like fine lace . . . where writing IS the landscape.*
> *<http://lingua.utdallas.edu:7000>*

They elaborated on the term in a 1996 presentation entitled "The Agora Factor(y): Architecture and Assembly in/of MOOs" and provided another aspect on its usefulness in a 1998 book chapter, "MOOs, Anarchitexture, Towards a New Threshold."

WORKS CITED

Aarseth, E. J. (1997). *Cybertext: Perspectives on ergodic literature.* Baltiimore, MD: Johns Hopkins University Press. Associated online WWW site available: <www.hf.uib/no/cybertext/>.

Allman, W. F. (1989). *Apprentices of wonder: Inside the neural network revolution.* New York: Bantam.

Anderson, W. T. (1998). *The future of the self: Inventing the post-modern person.* New York: Putnam.

Aronowitz, S. (1992). Looking out: The impact of computers on the lives of professionals. In M. Tuman. (Ed.), *Literacy online: The promise [and peril] of reading and writing with computers* (pp. 119-137). Pittsburgh, PA: University of Pittsburgh Press.

Bakhtin, M. (1981). *The dialogic imagination: Four essays.* Austin: University of Texas Press.

Barber, J. F. (1995). Cyberspace and the mythform of reality. *Pre/Text,* 10-23.

Barber, J. F. (1997, March). The seven ages of computer technology: Flush with possibilities and faced with decisions. *Kairos: A Journal for Teachers of Writing in Webbed Environments,* 2(1). <http://english.ttu.edu/kairos/2.1/features/barber/bridge.html>.

Barber, J. F. (1999). A brief, selective, and idiosyncratic history of computers. In T. Howard, R. Gooch, & D. Goswami (Eds.), *Electronic networks: Crossing boundaries, creating communities*. Portsmouth, NH: Heinemann.

Barthes, R. (1974). *S/Z* (R. Miller, Trans.). New York: Hill & Wang.

Baudrillard, J. (1993). *Simulations*. New York: Semiotext(e).

Birkerts, S. (1994). *The Gutenberg elegies: The fate of reading in an electronic age*. New York: Fawcett. <http://www.obs-us.com/obs/english/books/nn/bdbirk.html>.

Bolter, J. D. (1991). *Writing space: The computer, hypertext, and the history of writing*. Chapel Hill: University of North Carolina Press.

Bradbury, R. (1953). *Fahrenheit 451*. New York: Ballantine Books.

Brautigan, R. (1967). *All watched over by machines of loving grace*. San Francisco, CA: Communications Co.

Brook, J., & Boal, I. (1995). *Resisting the virtual life: The culture and politics of information*. San Francisco: City Lights.

Burroughs, W. S. (1959). *Naked lunch*. New York: Grove Weidenfield.

Bush, V. (1945, August). As we may think. *The Atlantic Monthly*, 101-108. Available online: <http://www.isg.sfu.ca/~duchier/misc/vbush/>.

Channell, D. (1991). *The vital machine*. New York: Oxford University Press.

Chatwin, B. (1987). *The songlines*. London: Jonathan Cape.

Cherny, L., & Weise, E. (Eds.). (1996). *Wired women: Gender and new realities in cyberspace*. Seattle, WA: Seal Press.

Cixous, H. (1976, Summer). The laugh of the medusa (K. Cohen & P. Cohen, Trans.). *Signs*, 150-167.

Codrescu, A. (1990). *The disappearance of the outside: A manifesto for escape*. Reading, MA: Addison-Wesley.

Cooper, M., & Selfe, C. (1990). Computer conferences and learning: Authority, resistance, and internally persuasive discourse. *College English*, *52*, 847-869.

Davis, E. (1993). Techgnosis: Magic, memory, and the angels of information. In M. Dery (Ed.), *Flame wars: The discourse of cyberspace* (pp. 585-616). Durham, NC: Duke University Press.

de Chardin, P. T. (1964). *The future of man*. New York: Harper & Row.

de Saint Exupéry, A. (1967). *Wind, sand and stars*. New York: Harcourt, Brace & World.

Deleuze, G., & Guattari, F. (1987). *A thousand plateaus: Capitalism and schizophrenia*. Minneapolis: University of Minnesota Press.

Dertouzos, M. (1997). *What will be: How the new world of information will change our lives*. New York: HarperCollins.

Dick, P. K. (1968). *Do androids dream of electric sheep*. New York: Ballantine Books.

Dillon, A. (1994). *Designing usable electronic text: Egonomic aspects of human information usage.* London: Taylor & Francis.

Doheny-Farina, S. (1996). *The wired neighborhood.* New Haven, CT: Yale University Press.

Dyson, E. (1997). *Release 2.0: A design for living in the digital age.* New York: Broadway Books.

Dyson, G. (1997). *Darwin among the machines: The evolution of global intelligence.* Reading, MA: Addison-Wesley.

Eco, U. (1986). *Travels in hyperreality.* Orlando, FL: Haracourt Brace Jovanovich.

Egan, B. (1994). *Permutation city.* London: Millennium.

Faigley, L. (1999). Material literacy and visual design. In J. Selzer & S. Crowley (Eds.), *Rhetorical bodies: Toward a material rhetoric.* Madison: University of Wisconsin Press.

Faulkner, W. (1929). *The sound and the fury.* New York: J. Cape & H. Smith.

Faulkner, W. (1930). *As I lay dying.* New York: J. Cape & H. Smith.

Forster, E. M. (1927). *Aspects of the novel.* London: Arnold.

Garson, B. (1988). *The electronic sweatshop.* New York: Penguin.

Gibbons, K. (1989). *A virtuous woman.* New York: Vintage Books.

Gibson, W. (1982, July). Burning chrome. *Omni,* 72-77, 102-107.

Gibson, W. (1984). *Neuromancer.* New York: Ace Books.

Gibson, W. (1992). *Agrippa: A book of the dead.* New York: Kevin Begos. Available online: <http://www.users.interport.net/~abubbica/books/agrippa.txt> and <http://www.astro.utoronto.ca/~reid/htmldocs/agrippa.html>.

Gleick, J. (1987). *Chaos: Making a new science.* New York: Viking.

Greenbie, B. (1981). *Spaces: Dimensions of the human landscape.* New Haven, CT: Yale University Press.

Greenwald, J. (1995). *The size of the world.* Guilford, CT: The Globe Pequot Press.

Grigar, D., & Barber, J. F. (1998). Defending Your Life in MOOspace. In C. Haynes & J. R. Holmevik (Eds.), *High wired: On the design, use, and theory of educational MOOs* (pp. 192-231). Ann Arbor: University of Michigan Press.

Grigar, D., Barber, J. F., Galin, J., Haynes, C., & Holmevik, J. (1996, June). *The electronic forum, or the Agora reinvented.* Panel presentation at The Joint International Conference of the Association for Literary and Linguistic Computing and the Association for Computers and the Humanities. Bergen, Norway. Abstracts available online: <http://lingua.utdallas.edu:7000/1701>.

Handa, C. (Ed.). (1990). *Computers and community: Teaching composition in the twenty-first century.* Portsmouth, NH: Boynton/Cook.

Haraway, D. J . (1991). A cyborg manifesto: Science, technology, and socialist-feminism in the late twentieth century. In D. J. Haraway (Ed.), *Simians, cyborgs, and women: The reinvention of nature* (pp. 149-181). New York: Routledge.

Hardison, O. B., Jr. (1989). *Disappearing through the skylight: Culture and technology in the twentieth century.* New York: Penguin.

Hawisher, G., & LeBlanc, P. (Eds.). (1992). *Re-imagining computers and composition: Teaching and research in the virtual age.* Portsmouth, NH: Boynton/Cook.

Hawisher, G., LeBlanc, P., Moran, C., & Selfe, C. (1996). *Computers and the teaching of writing in American higher education, 1979-1994: A history.* Norwood, NJ: Ablex.

Hawisher, G., & Selfe, C. (1989). *Critical perspectives on computers and composition instruction.* New York: Teachers College Press.

Hawisher, G., & Selfe, C. (Eds.). (1991). *Evolving perspectives on computers and composition studies: Questions for the 1990s.* Urbana, IL: National Council of Teachers of English.

Haynes, C., & Holmevik, J. R. (1996, June). *The Agora factor(y): Architecture and assembly in/of MOOs.* Part of a panel presentation entitled "The Electronic Forum, or the Agora Reinvented." The Joint International Conference of the Association for Literary and Linguistic Computing and the Association for Computers and the Humanities, Bergen, Norway. Abstracts available online: <http://lingua.utdallas.edu:7000/1701>.

Haynes, C., & Holmevik, J. R. (Eds.). (1998). *High wired: On the design, use, and theory of educational MOOs.* Ann Arbor: University of Michigan Press.

Heim, M. (1993). *The metaphysics of virtual reality.* New York: Oxford University Press.

Hiltz, S., & Turoff, M. (1978). *The network nation: Human communication via computer.* Reading, MA: Addison-Wesley.

Huxley, A. (1932). *Brave new world.* London: Chatto and Windus.

Joyce, M. (1987). *Afternoon.* Watertown, MA: Eastgate Systems.

Joyce, M. (1988, November). Siren shapes: Exploratory and constructive hypertexts. *Academic Computing,* 10-14, 37-42.

Kelly, K. (1994). *Out of control: The new biology of machines, social systems, and the economic world.* Reading, MA: Addison-Wesley.

Kidder, T. (1981). *The soul of a new machine.* New York: Little, Brown.

Killheffer, R. (1993, January). The shape of books to come. A collaborative book(?) Challenges ideas about the immortality of art. *Omni,* 14.

Klem, E., & Moran, C. (1991). Computers and instructional strategies in the teaching of writing. In G. Hawisher & C. Selfe (Eds.), *Evolving perspectives on computers and composition studies: Questions for the 1990s* (pp. 132-149). Urbana, IL: National Council of Teachers of English.

Kroker, A., & Weinstein, M. (1994). *Data trash: The theory of the virtual class.* New York: St. Martin's Press.

Kurzweil, R. (1999). *The age of spiritual machines.* New York: Viking.

Lakoff, G. (1995). Body, brain, and communication. In J. Brooks & I. Boal (Eds.), *Resisting the virtual life: The culture and politics of information* (pp. 115-129). San Francisco: City Lights.

Lakoff, G., & Johnson, M. (1980). *Metaphors we live by.* Chicago, IL: University of Chicago Press.

Landow, G. (1992). *Hypertext: The convergence of contemporary critical theory and technology.* Baltimore, MD: Johns Hopkins University Press.

Lanham, R. (1993). *The electronic word: Democracy, technology, and the arts.* Chicago: The University of Chicago Press.

Laurel, B. (1993). *Computers as theatre.* Reading, MA: Addison-Wesley.

Lawnmower Man. (1992). Dir. Brett Leonard. New Line Cinema.

Le Guin, U. (1971). *Lathe of heaven.* New York: Scribner.

Lingua MOO. <http://lingua.utdallas.edu:7000>.

Looker, T. (1995). *The sound and the story: NPR and the art of radio.* Boston: Houghton Mifflin.

Lord, A. (1960). *The singer of tales.* Cambridge, MA: Harvard University Press.

Mandelbrot, B. (1983). *The fractal geometry of nature.* New York: W.H. Freeman.

Marcus, S. (1994). Avoiding road-kill on the information highway. *The Quarterly of the National Writing Project and the Center For the Study of Writing and Literacy, 16,* 18-21.

Markoff, J. (1994, March 13). The rise and swift fall of cyber literacy. *The New York Times,* sec. 4, pp. 1, 5.

Martin, G. (1992, May). Read it once. *Esquire,* 33.

McCaffery, L. (1991). An interview with William Gibson. In L. McCaffery (Ed.), *Storming the reality studio: A casebook of cyberpunk and postmodern fiction* (pp. 263-285). Durham, NC: Duke University Press.

McLuhan, M. (1962). *The Gutenberg galaxy.* Toronto: University of Toronto Press.

McLuhan, M. (1964). *Understanding media: The extensions of man.* New York: New American Library.

Miller, L. (1995). Women and children first. In J. Brooks & I. Boal (Eds.), *Resisting the virtual life: The culture and politics of information* (pp. 49-57). San Francisco: City Lights.

Minsky, M. (1986). *The society of mind.* New York: Simon & Schuster.

Mitchell, W. J. (1996). *City of bits: Space, place, and the infobahn.* Cambridge, MA: MIT Press. Available online: <http://mitpress. mit.edu/e-books/City-of-Bits/>.

Moulthorp, S. (1991). In the zones: Hypertext and the politics of initerpretation. *Writing on the Edge, 1,* 19-27.

Myers, L. (Ed.). (1993). *Approaches to computer writing classrooms.* Albany: State University of New York Press.

Murray, J. (1996). *Hamlet on the holodeck: The future of narrative in cyberspace.* Cambridge, MA: The Free Press.

Negroponte, N. (1995). *Being digital.* New York: Vintage. Portions available online: <http://www.obs-us.com/obs/english/books/ nn/bdintro.html>.

Nelson, T. (1987). *Computer lib/dream machines* (2nd ed.). Redmond, WA: Tempus Press.

Nunberg, G. (1996). *The future of the book.* Berkeley: University of California Press.

Nyce, J., & Kahn, P. (1991). *From memex to hypertext: Vannevar Bush and the mind's machine.* Boston: Academic Press.

Oldenburg, R. (1991). *The great good place: Cafes, coffee shops, community centers, beauty parlors, general stores, bars, hangouts, and how they get you through the day.* New York: Paragon.

Ong, W. (1988). *Orality and literacy: The technologizing of the word.* London: Routledge.

Pagels, H. (1988). *The dreams of reason: The computer and the rise of the sciences of complexity.* New York: Bantam.

Pinsky, R. (1984). *Mindwheel: An electronic novel.* San Raphael, CA: Broderbund Software.

Pirsig, R. (1974). *Zen and the art of motorcycle maintenance: An inquiry into values.* New York: William Morrow.

Plato. (1963). *The republic of Plato* (F. M. Cornford, Trans.). New York: Oxford University Press.

Porush, D. (1995). Ubiquitous computing vs. radical piracy: A reconsideration of the future. *Computer-Mediated Communication, 1,* 46. <http://www.December.com/cmc/mag/1995/mar/last.html>.

Porush, D. (1998, January 26). <porusd@rpi.edu> "Porush's Law." 26 Jan. 1998. Personal e-mail.

Postman, N. (1992). *Technopoly: The surrender of culture to technology.* New York: Vintage Books.

Purves, A. (1990). *The scribal society.* New York: Longman.

Quarterman, J. (1990). *The matrix: Computer networks and conference systems worldwide.* Bedford, MA: Digital Press.

Reed, I. (1998). *America: The multinational society. In Writin' is fightin': Thirty-seven years of boxing on paper* (pp. 51-56). New York: Antheneum.

Rheingold, H. (1993). *The virtual community: Homesteading on the electronic frontier*. Reading, MA: Addison-Wesley. Portions available online: <http://www.well.com/user/hlr/vcbook/index.html>.

Ricoeur, P. (1975). *The rule of metaphor: Multi-disciplinary studies of the creation of meaning in language*. Toronto, Canada: University of Toronto Press.

Robinson, S., & Robinson, J. (1979). *Starseed*. New York: Dial Press.

Ronell, A. (1989). *The telephone book: Technology, schizophrenia, electric speech*. Lincoln: The University of Nebraska Press.

Roszak, T. (1986). *The cult of information: The folklore of computers and the true art of thinking*. New York: Pantheon.

Rushkoff, D. (1994). *Cyberia: Life in the trenches of hyperspace*. New York: HarperCollins.

Rushkoff, D. (1996). *Playing the future: How kids' culture can teach us to thrive in an age of chaos*. New York: HarperCollins.

Sanders, B. (1994). *A is for ox: The collapse of literacy and the rise of violence in an electronic age*. New York: Vintage Books.

Scott-Heron, G. (1984). *The revolution will not be televised. The best of Gil Scott-Heron*. (CD). Arista.

Shannon, C. (1949, July). A mathematical theory of communication. *Bell System Technical Journal*, 379-423. (Continued and concluded in October issue, 4, 623-656.)

Shenk, D. (1997). *Data smog: Surviving the information glut*. New York: HarperCollins.

Snyder, I. (1996). *Hypertext: The electronic labyrinth*. Washington Square: New York University Press.

Snyder, I. (Ed.). (1998). *Page to screen. In Page to screen: Taking literacy into the electronic era* (pp. xx-xxxvi). London: Routledge.

Sobchack, V. (1993). New age mutant ninja hackers: Reading mondo 2000. In M. Dery (Ed.), *Flame wars: The discourse of cyberspace* (pp. 569-584). Durham, NC: Duke University Press.

Spender, D. (1995). *Nattering on the net: Women, power and cyberspace*. North Melbourne, Victoria, AU: Spinifex.

Stein, G. (1990). *Tender buttons. Selected writings of Gertrude Stein*. New York: Vintage Books.

Stephenson, N. (1992). *Snowcrash*. New York: Bantam.

Sterling, B. (1985). *Schismatrix*. New York: Arbor House.

Sterling, B. (1992). *The hacker crackdown: Law and disorder on the electronic frontier*. New York: Bantam.

Sterling, B. (1998). Dead media manifesto. *Boing Boing Online*. <http://www.well.com/user/mark/deadmedia.html>.

Sterne, L. (1985). *Life and opinions of Tristram Shandy, gentleman*. Chicago: Stone & Kimball; London: Methuen.

Stoll, C. (1995). *Silicon snake oil: Second thoughts on the information highway*. New York: Doubleday. Portions available online: <http://www.obs-us.com/obs/english/books/nn/bdstol.html>.

Stone, A. R. (1995). *The war of desire and technology at the close of the mechanical age*. Cambridge, MA: MIT Press.

Talbot, S. (1995). *The future does not compute: Transcending the machines in our midst*. Sebastopol, CA: O'Reilly & Associates.

Toffler, A. (1980). *The third wave*. New York: Morrow.

Trinh, T. M. (1989). *Woman native other*. Bloomington: University of Indiana Press.

Turkle, S. (1984). *The second self: Computers and the human spirit*. New York: Simon & Schuster.

Turkle, S. (1997). *Life on the screen: Identity in the age of the internet*. New York: Touchstone.

Turner, V. (1966). *The ritual process: Structure and antistructure*. Chicago: Aldine,

Vinge, V. (1987). *True names . . . and other dangers*. New York: Baen Books.

Vitanza, V. (1997). *Writing for the world wide web*. Boston, MA: Allyn and Bacon.

Vygotsky, L. (1962). *Thought and language*. Cambridge, MA: MIT Press.

Weizenbaum, J. (1966). ELIZA: A computer program for the study of natural language communication between man and machine. *Communications of the ACM* [Association for Computing Machinery], *9*, 36-45.

Whalstrom, B., & Scruton, C. (1998). Constructing texts/understanding texts: Lessons from antiquity and the middle ages. *Computers and Composition, 14*, 311-328.

Well, H. G. (1994). *World brain*. London: Adadmintine Press.

Wiener, N. (1948). *Cybernetics; or, control and communication in the animal and the machine*. New York: John Wiley.

Wresch, W. (1996). *Disconnected: Haves and have-nots in the information age*. New Brunswick, NJ: Rutgers University Press.

Zaleski, J. (1997). *The soul of cyberspace*. San Francisco: HarperEdge.

Zuboff, S. (1988). *In the age of the smart machine: The future of work and power*. New York: Basic Books.

COMMENTS BETWEEN CHAPTERS

DISPATCHES FROM THE MIDDLEWOR(L)DS OF COMPUTERS AND COMPOSITION: EXPERIMENTING WITH WRITING AND VISUALIZING THE FUTURE

Gail E. Hawisher and Cynthia L. Selfe

Western man has appeared superior and dominant, despite inferior demographics, because he appeared *more rapid*. In colonial genocide or ethnocide, he was the *survivor* because he was in fact *super-quick* . . . to be quick means to stay alive (être vif, c'est être en vie)!
—Paul Virilio (1977, p. 47)

Virtuality need not be a prison. It can be the raft, the ladder, the transitional space, the moratorium that eventually is discarded in order to reach greater freedom. We don't have to reject life on the screen, but we don't have to treat it as an alternative life either. We can use it as a space for growth.
—Sherry Turkle (1998, p. xvii)

We have become (have we not always been?) members of a universe of images, and at this juncture our knowledge is expressed predominantly through them rather than through the text.
—Alan C. Purves (1998, p. 108)

Experimentation and exploration, despite their romantic intellectual reputations—in the sciences, in the literary world, in archeologically distant or geographically remote places, in the arena of political action— are seldom welcome, seldom appreciated, seldom accomplished without turmoil and upset.

This response should not be difficult to understand. People who are experimenting and exploring do not always know the shape of the answers that they are seeking or the locations of the places they are striving to reach; they can't even, sometimes, fully or accurately identify the questions that prompt their experimentation (sometimes they are operating on faith—the ultimate link between the sciences and religion). People who are experimenting or exploring—despite the myth of science that suggests tidiness and linearity—cast about, sometimes a great deal, sometimes in wrong directions, and sometimes in ways that seem clumsy to people who are watching. To complicate matters further, those who experiment or explore often find it hard to describe the work they are doing because they are taking on strange places and dealing with new ideas that make the language they know inadequate to the task of reporting.

Experimenters and explorers, in other words, are always rocking someone's boat, scaring those who would cling to the gunwales, frightening those watching on shore, challenging the Coast Guard, so to speak—all with the purpose of identifying something exciting and new, generally at a time when most people would rather let well enough alone, let change happen in its own good time.

This dispatch is written by two long-term members of the Coast Guard (among other guises we adopt in this dispatch). We have both been around the innovation pond a few times, having worked with computers and composition for almost two decades. And we have come to the point where change seems to be happening plenty fast enough for us. Generally, we wonder, why rush things even more?

The rush, of course, is not a rush. What we are feeling is the chilling presence of the ghost of change already happening. This shadow prowls about and makes our intellectual hair stand on end. Change, a first cousin to experimentation and exploration, paralyzes most people beyond the limits of action. Thank god for experimenters and explorers who see the promise of the future and take risks that the rest of us cannot bring ourselves to manage.

OUR TASK: THE VIEW OF EXPERIMENTATION FROM THE MIDDLEWOR(L)DS

The editors of this volume asked us to take on the task of writing these Dispatches from the MiddleWor(l)ds in order to describe the import of this experimental collection on electronic writing and publishing. Why use the metaphor of the MiddleWor(l)ds? Because the words recall the transition from an age of orality to one of print and suggest a further transition from age of print to the age of digitized exchanges. And, furthermore, the words suggest our own position. Throughout our writing, we have tried to invest our thinking with both an understanding of history and the future—of where electronic writing and publishing have been and where they seem to be going, even though we could not see *there* from *here*. Our contribution to this volume, then, is to complement the foreword and afterword but to do so in an innovative way so that we too experiment with a new form, what we have named the *middlewor(l)d*.

The second part of our charge was to write fast—before the changes that inspired this collection started to disappear, to become commonplace, around us. Hence, the notion of *dispatch*—a speedy commentary on unsettled or troubled times. We weren't optimistic. *Dispatch*, the Oxford English Dictionary reports, originated from the 16th-century Italian word, *dispacciare*, which meant "to hasten, to speed, to rid away any worke." Today in English, however, it has taken on several added meanings: "To send off postehaste or with expedition or promptitude (a messenger, message, etc., having an express destination)"; or "to make away with promptly" as in "to eat up, consume, devour"; and even "making away with by putting to death." In fact, the OED informs us that "Happy Dispatch" is a humorous name for the Japanese form of suicide, "Hara-kiri." We were/are not amused.

So, how to make sense of experimentation and exploration that is *in progress* but when complete will be confined to print. Many of the pieces included in this collection are parts of ongoing conversations—in MOOs, on listservs, at conferences—but none of the conversations have been concluded as yet. Hence, the new electronic wor(l)ds of writing and publishing can be glimpsed, but not yet fully examined; contemplated, but not yet comprehended. And, yet, we know, as do most readers, that English studies professionals—those who write and read and publish, and teach writing and reading and publishing for a living—ignore such dispatches at their own peril. Sitting somewhere between the dispatches—between the what was and the what will be— we cannot help but be drawn to the authors' notions of the in-between spaces we inhabit as teachers of written language and literacy. And, personally, our own sense is that these e-spaces are—at once—exciting and perilous locations in which to labor as scholars and teachers.

Our years of working with computers and composition have taught us that we need to pay attention to these in-between spaces and, at times, to the technologies themselves if we hope to fulfill our responsibilities as humanists and teachers (Hawisher & Selfe, 1991; Selfe, 2000). Indeed, we need to keep these spaces and the changes associated with them in our sights even as daily-use cloaks them with invisibility. But we need also to pay attention to our colleagues' observations and how they themselves see the daily work of writing/publishing/teaching as being connected (or not) to the perpetual onslaught of societies' new technologies. And we must pay attention quickly. For, as Virilio (1997) grimly reminds us, to "survive," in fact, is to be "super-quick (sur-vif)" (p. 47).

This in-between dispatch on dispatches, then, comes from the only perspective on change that we can offer—our own. And here are our thoughts on the new MiddleWor(l)ds represented by this collection: We love them and we hate them. We inhabit the electronic MiddleWor(l)ds, but we are always a bit uncomfortable. We seem to be both the Coast Guard and the foolhardy kids who stand up in the canoe at camp and try to dump everyone into the lake for the joy of a swim.

This position, we suspect, is true of many who will read this collection. As English educators and writing instructors who grew up in the 1950s and 1960s and entered the profession in the 1970s, neither of us started teaching or writing with computers; we learned as we went. And we continue to learn as we teach. Given our backgrounds, then, we acknowledge and recognize in realistic terms our limits as culturally and generationally determined citizens of the MiddleWor(l)ds.

A BIT OF HISTORY AND THREE COMPASS SIGHTINGS ON THE MIDDLEWOR(L)D

It is clear that this experimental, exploratory collection presents us with some new perspective on digital language practices. By this, we mean the collection departs from conventional forms of systematic study and observation of the kinds of writing happening in computer-supported environments—the stuff on which computers and composition, as an academic discipline, has historically focused. Instead, the collection *practices* new forms of writing and publishing; its medium is its message, from this perspective.

We consider this shift in focus to be a major feature of the collection. Since 1977, the year in which the first fully assembled microcomputers came on the market and began to change the face of English courses across the country, the work in the field of computers and composition (the academic home of most of the contributors in this volume) has been fundamentally traditional, even when dealing with radical new technologies. Scholars in this field have looked at the kinds of academic and nonacademic writing that students and teachers do in electronic environments and have suggested new ways to teach relatively familiar kinds of written assignments. We have, at various times, for example, looked to computers for help in the teaching of grammar, spelling, organization, and sentence combining (Hawisher, LeBlanc, Moran, & Selfe, 1996). And, although more recent efforts to examine the social and political contexts of computer-based communication have yielded new areas of exploration since the early 1990's, the assignments and the genres within which we have worked are, generally speaking, fairly familiar ones. Online conferences, for instance, look a lot like epistolary exchanges, and essays written with the help of a word processing package are fundamentally similar to essays written on a typewriter. Similarly, a personal home page designed for the World Wide Web often has elements of both classical autobiography and standard resume.

Of course, during this period, there have been some tentative ventures into uncharted waters—MOOs and MUDs are both like and unlike face-to-face conversations, and the communication via web pages happens as much through graphical and visual representation as it does through words. Similarly, scholars such as Guyer and Hagaman (1999), Wysocki and Johnson-Eilola (1999), and Sirc (1999) have begun to make some forays into new forms, modes, and approaches to the teaching of writing. Guyer and Hagaman, for example, demonstrate in print that pictorial images can be essential to understanding a text even when no reference to the inserted photographs appears in the text itself. Wysocki and Johnson-Eilola encourage teachers to explore the rhetoric of visual-graphical representation in online texts and the ways in which the arrangement of these representations *make* and *communicate* meaning, at both the level of content and culture. Taking a different approach and using the traditional form of the academic essay, Sirc compares students' Web compositions to the found art of Marcel du Champ—asserting that the processes of *assembling* materials and bits and meanings that already exist in various textual and graphical and auditory forms is also a type of written artistic composition, perhaps one more aptly suited to a postmodern intellectual landscape. Taken together, the writing and images of these scholars point the way to new kinds of experimentation with language and publishing in online contexts.

We make a point of mentioning these scholars, because they characterize the important kinds of experimentation that also mark this collection and the experimentation that is, as yet, only suggested by it. Certainly, the experimentation with form and language and genre that this current collection offers—the use of MOO logs, the inclusion of listserv conversations with multiple and historical characters, the play with language—suggests one kind of artistic/intellectual endeavor toward which Sirc points. In this volume, for instance, the editors and authors have identified specially chosen bits of meaning and parts of texts to assemble into an exploratory, artistic whole. The collage of voices and texts—in its difference—may appear motley and roughly fashioned when judged by the more traditional values espoused by compositionists: familiar genres, conventional organizational and structural components, attention to parsimony and avoidance of repetition; easily discernible lines of argument. But the composition, as a whole, is also most exciting because it borrows and assembles meanings as it simultaneously practices new kinds of online writing and publishing. The practice and exploration of these new forms of assembled writing (about writing and publishing) is a new and possibly productive direction for the field of computers and composition.

We also recognize that the exploratory goal of this collection—to chart the changing nature of digital language practices—can never be completed and that it is, moreover, risky. Change, especially given the speed with which it happens in connection with computers, always carries some intellectual cost. In the case of this collection, we can point to three areas of scholarly attention that are moving targets—even for a book as forward-looking as this one. These three areas are not fully explored in this collection, and their absence hints at the difficulties we have in identifying them. But we believe these three areas, if used to read against the grain of the current collection, can provide possible compass sightings on *future* explorations of new MiddleWor(l)ds.

The first compass sighting has to do with the increasing speed of change and the increasing alienation that scholars are beginning to recognize as an outgrowth of such instability. Castells (1996, 1997, 1998), Jameson (1991), Baudrillard (1983), and Virilio (1977), among others, warn of the alienation, the fragmentation, the vertigo that one feels when faced with the multiplication of identities and bodies in electronically enhanced spaces; the dizzying displacement that individuals may perceive in the face of postmodern expansion; the terror generated by acceleration and increased speed of communication within electronic spaces.

Readers of this collection, too, may feel similarly uneasy with the multiplied, and often unruly, voices clamoring for attention in this collection. They do not always resemble the carefully arranged, linear arguments we have come to associate with formal scholarly essays—they are fresh and rowdy, fast and furious, and often irrepressible. Similar conversations have already caused scholars to mourn the death of more conventional, traditional kinds of literate behavior. Birkerts (1994) in the *Gutenberg Elegies* and Sanders (1994) in *A is for Ox*, for example, note that computers have become a force of distraction, isolation, and alienation; and that cyberspace, in turn, has become a wasteland of pornography, violence, and illiteracy.

In the cultural narrative that these two scholars relate, and that readers of this collection should understand, if not believe, computer games, chat rooms, MOOs and MUDs, the Web in general become, like MTV, distractions that have seduced school-age children and adults to forsake the traditional values of hard work and application and to abandon conventional literacy values, as expressed in the now venerable forms of the novel and the essay, and tested through the intellectual habits of disciplined analysis and critical examination. Birkerts and Sanders portray current generations of computer users as beset by electronically multiplied images and texts, and lacking the guidance and ballast of traditional values that a stable home environment and literature can impart. Such individuals, Birkerts and Sanders continue, have created a world rife with other cultural and social problems. Individuals such as Birkerts and Sanders have become addicted to the negative values of cyberspace; mindlessly attentive to the fast paced, commercial entertainment provided by the Web; a space devoid of family values and modernist assumptions about right and wrong and ignorant of the Western literary traditions and strategies for print-based thinking that allowed past generations of Americans to thrive.

If there are challenges to this collection's project from the conservative right—those that adhere to traditional forms of literacy such as books, the printed page, the essay—there are also those that come from the avant garde or radical left. And these provide our second and third compass sightings against which to measure the contributions of this collection. For our second compass sighting, we offer readers the new forms of literacy scholarship that go beyond print, beyond even the experimental forms of electronic print exchange to focus on the visual representations that have claimed an increasing share of digital environments. Purves (1998), Kress (1999), Guyer and Hagaman (1999), Diana George and Diane Shoos (1999), Sirc (1999), and Wysocki and Johnson-Eilola (1999), for example, have focused increasingly on the influences of visual literacies and the rhetorical richness of such literacies. Certainly, these scholars would contend that the MOO and MUD exchanges represented in this collection have yet to recognize and take full advantage of the robust meaning inherent in visual images.

Our third compass sighting has to do with the representation of gender in digital environments. Hawisher and Sullivan (1999), along with Selfe (1999), explored the links between the increasing importance of visual representation and new forms of gender representation that have come to shape the landscape of cyberspace. These discussions about gender and its representation also figure less prominently in the MiddleWor(l)d of this collection but may prove to be an additional compass point by which we come to chart the future direction of our collective attention.

THE WORK OF THIS COLLECTION: MAPPING THE MIDDLEWOR(L)D

Before we talk more about these three compass sightings that might comprise some of our future work on digital language practices, however, we can start exploring the MiddleWor(l)d by identifying some of the explorations that we recognize as going on within these pages.

In part, we have learned from the collection what these intellectual spaces are *not*. Like Turkle (1998), we do not believe them to be alternative spaces—rather, this collection indicates that they are the spaces where life's important work can be taken on and accomplished. Nor do these e-spaces seem to be the disappearing "Third Places" of which Oldenburg (1989) writes or the close-knit communities that Rheingold (1993) describes, although at times in their conviviality they resemble them.

But what *are* these spaces? What can the contributors tell us of them and how these landscapes might affect our work as teachers and scholars? Each of the authors offers a somewhat different take. Borrowing from Klem and Moran, for example, Barber and Grigar see the MiddleWor(l)d landscapes as "amphibious," as stages where we operate partially in print and partially on-screen but which are nevertheless always stages that provide "interesting developments and evolution toward more useful or adaptable forms" (p. 12, this volume). For Barber and Grigar, the notion of amphibious space allows them to underscore optimistically the theme of this volume, that is, "that computer-networked technology not only creates (and will have created) new electronic environments (new worlds) but also promotes (and will have promoted) new forms of writer-reader interaction (new words)" (p. 13, this volume). And much of what they give us in the initial dispatches encourages us to imagine in print what these spaces may evoke in minds online. Barber's and Grigar's discussion can be best considered, we think, within the context of Haraway's (1992) and Wise's (1997) contention that computer networks and technologies, themselves, are social "actants" that affect existing social formations and structurations. Thus, human writers and machines and language, together, form social "assemblages" (Wise, 1997, p. 68) that change our notion of language and human communication and reader-writer interaction. And these social assemblages also directly affect out understanding and practice of teaching and learning in language/literacy classrooms.

Victor Vitanza continues the dispatches by elaborating more fully on notions of the future perfect and suggests that w/riting is that which has been intentionally excluded in "print-books" and "web-books." The books, online or offline, are not what we need to concern ourselves with, he tells us, but the w/riting is. It is the "denegated third"—the return of the excluded middle, the Midway, a third passing—all of which, for Vitanza, "talks in writing" about death and himself. For Vitanza, writing as the *techne* of print culture is passing and with such passing comes death not only of writing but also of identities constructed in print culture. Vitanza can accept, indeed welcome, such passing, but he misses in this new future perfect wor(l)d *"the image of cyberspace that others are so excitedly-hysterically reacting to (i.e., needing to find ways of putting a stop to) or that others are so unthinkingly flowing with (wanting to accept, embrace, dwell within)"* (p. 78, this volume). Vitanza's discussion of the movement from print to digital forms resonates with other historical treatments of the subject—Eisenstein (1979) on print and Diebert (1997) on print and electronic forms. His exploration also reminds us of how difficult it is to see and identify major historical movements—to predict what is actually happening and how they will turn out—while they are in process. As Diebert argues, communication technologies (e.g., the printing press, the Web) exist within complex social, historical, political, and economic contexts and are only one of a "wide confluence of factors" that must come together to produce world order changes. Within this context, we, too, wonder about how digital communication will develop in an information world that is increasingly dependent on, and aware of, new visual, nonprint forms of communication and the importance of images within such forms.

Also concerned with historical context and future development, Grigar's dispatch in this collection presents a powerful image of a cyberspace rendered in an educational MOO—one rooted in 5th century Athens and constructed specifically for students she would have engage dramatically with the ancients and their perspectives on technology. Her goal is to encourage the students to come to some understanding about their own connection with the new technologies. Here, Grigar manages to capture in print an image of cyberspace that promises intellectually exciting conversations to educate students in ways that at the very least would be cumbersome and slow in face-to-face settings. By featuring in the MOO the wor(l)ds of Plato, Glaucon, and Phaedrus, along with the more contemporary Vitanza, Barber, and Doherty, virtuality becomes the stuff of drama where characters from the past and present engage in compelling dialogues. Grigar's work can be productively explored, we believe, as a new perspective on Laurel's (1993) earlier examination of computer-based environments as creative and generative sites of communicative performance. In these sites, as both Grigar's and Laurel's work illustrates, "interaction" can become an "illuminating path" (p. xii) for students' intellectual explorations. We also encounter this theme of the performative at the end of this collection—this time in the context of teaching performances—in the dispatch of Judith Kirkpatrick. Kirkpatrick offers another confident and optimistic view of the possibilities for teaching in cyberspace, maintaining that in virtual classrooms teachers tend to "demonstrate rather than tell," "create rather than prescribe," and "model behavior rather than dictate," all strategies that work to help students learn.

The performative strategies that Kirkpatrick explores are related not only to those illustrated within Grigar's MOO dispatch, but also to those mentioned by Nick Carbone in his dispatch on diving into the text. For Carbone, the alternate or third space for publishing—the World Wide Web—also presents many exciting opportunities for teaching. Carbone argues that it is a myth that immersion in the books of a field will eventually lead to students also giving voice to their own words in published print. According to Carbone, there are far fewer choices for action in print than online. He writes, "Print is shipped whereas the web awaits our arrival" and, more specifically, our students' arrival. For Carbone, the Web provides a more promising place for students to experience the thinking of a field; he wants us "to imagine how web journals can create a space for student voices that emphasize the collaborative nature of most learning and thinking and writing." Thus, for Grigar, Kirkpatrick, and Carbone electronic third spaces such as MOOs and the Web offer exciting intellectual possibilities for teaching and learning. Like Sherry Turkle in the epigraph that begins our between comments, the three scholar-teachers see these new spaces not so much as alternative spaces for teaching and learning but rather as opportunities for students' and teachers' growth IRL. In the scenarios of these dispatches, change equals growth—the chance to create a positive educational impact through technology and the interactions of online participants and performers.

Working from a more critical and less optimistic tradition, Richard Selfe urges new world teachers to consider more carefully the new materiality of electronic worlds. He asks that we pause—that we temper our enthusiasm and first ask "what are we doing to ourselves" and to our students. In a rare look at students' responses to the new technologies, Selfe tells us that we'll "hear in their words, our own ghostly concerns for the future" and warns us to consider what sorts of effects the adoption of these third spaces for teaching might have on the lives and careers of students. He offers us a glimpse of the characteristics and attitudes of this "media-rich generation," who in their own words work, learn, and play at anytime day or night, expecting immediate responses to their own online writing; who resent inconvenient access to the new technologies, expecting their own electronic work spaces to provide enjoyable activities; who are not concerned about the archival history of a generation's discourse but who demonstrate a sense of history through their own somewhat fearful anticipation about those who follow them—the coming generation of media-savvy youth.

Selfe himself fears that in our great rush to adopt these technologies for teaching, our choices may cause profound changes in the ways our students work and live but that few of us are paying sufficient attention to the ramifications of these changes. In the tradition of Winner (1986), Feenberg (1991), Apple (1991), Olson (1987), Hawisher and Selfe (1991)—Richard Selfe's dispatch is a wake-up call to the rest of us as we often too eagerly welcome each new technology with open arms without thinking critically about their possible consequences (Hawisher & Selfe, 1991, 1998).

If the dispatches we have discussed so far feature the MiddleWor(l)ds of teaching writing, then what follows has more to do with the editors' and authors' very real concerns with the possibilities these spaces offer—or not—for publishing writing. Just as several dispatches in the book focus on new electronic spaces for teaching and learning about writing, several others look primarily at the new wor(l)ds of publishing writing and the challenges they present to scholars in and out of academe. Myka, for example, in a series of visually effective dialogue exchanges, tells us that e-textuality "invites or enables or provides space for new ways of working; new forms of representation; new identity." Citing Marjorie Perloff citing Robert Creeley, Myka argues that new forms, such as the texts Spooner and Yancey have co-authored (see Spooner &Yancey, 1996; Vielstimmig, 1999), are made possible only through extensions of culture. In other words, the authors' in print e-texts take on a life of their own precisely because of the inroads that electronic culture has made into the world of print.

Barber too concerns himself with the historical evolution of form as his title, "Following in the Footprints of the Ancestors . . . from

Songlines to Illuminated Digital Palimpsests," suggests. Or, as he himself goes on to say, he is concerned with the ways in which we are currently plying "old forms of thought to deal with new experiences." Using the aboriginal practice of songlines or ancestor footprints, Barber tries to construct and name that which Vitanza and others are calling third or in-between spaces through which we pass electronically.

In rendering the electronic in print, Barber, like Myka, plays with form as he leads us through the discontinuities of the past and broken connections of the present. In the wor(l)d of the future perfect, however, he promises us that transFORMATions are at hand. For Barber, that which is interesting comes not in the middle (the middlewor(l)ds of Hawisher and Selfe? the Midway of Vitanza? are all middles the same?) but rather along the borders where nothing remains the same. And, indeed, the form(at)s and wor(l)ds he both adopts and adapts for his dispatch do indeed experiment with the many faces of text possible in print but always at odds, we would argue, with the medium of print. Holograms, perhaps, best represent an in-print means by which to speed the transformations to which he alludes, but we encounter no such holographic images along the way in this collection.

Returning us to the everyday world of print, Doherty leaves the experiments of form to his online journal *Kairos* and argues in traditional but convincing print that there is much work to be done before electronic publishing gains the academic credibility of print. Doherty's aim is to examine the language of academic publishing in both its paper and electronic venues with an eye toward how technorhetoricians are naming their craft and how such language affects its acceptance within the academy. For Doherty, McLuhan's rearview mirror presents us with an excellent metaphor for looking backward and forward simultaneously. He writes, "we look forward (re-invent scholarly publication) through the rearview mirror (which shows us both our papertext history and our more recent electronic forbears." The coming together of the conventional with the cutting edge, in Doherty's words, creates a "McLuhanesque collide-o-scope of images, ideas, and possibilities . . . ." Doherty's language evokes all sorts of images in our minds, but again we miss seeing concrete traces of the collide-o-scope of images in the papertrail of his text.

Leaping forward to first Michael Day's dispatch on "A Meshing of Minds" and then Jeff Galin and Joan Latchaw's dispatch on "Heterotopic Spaces Online," we encounter mostly future visions of online publishing. Echoing Barber's prognostication that "the written world of the future will take place in electronic spaces as much as it already does in print," Day provides a sensible, clear-eyed view of future publishing. Pushing aside Doherty's fears regarding academic credibility, Day argues that "Publishers and academic institutions may never disappear, but their role in research and the dissemination of information will have to change, in that publishers will have to move some of what they print to the online realm, and academic institutions will need to recognize the importance of online research and publication." No nonsense, no fuss—this will the future be, and we tend to agree. But Galin and Latchaw would complicate this vision, a move with which we also agree. Arguing that the worlds of publishing and archiving are experiencing a sea change, a paradigmatic shift a la Kuhn, the two authors show us such online archives as Johns Hopkins Press' MUSE, a rich resource for the Press's innumerable academic journals. Such resources, they argue, radically change the business of archiving, providing readily available professional working spaces that highlight action. Using Foucault's notion of heterotopia, they envision new archival spaces on the Web as marking professional working spaces linked to our own particular future "slice" in time.

Taken as a set, the dispatches by Yancey and Spooner, Barber, Doherty, Day, and Galin and Latchaw all suggest that computer-based environments could offer what Foucault might call, elsewhere, heterotopia—countersites that at once challenge and extend, and at the same time reflect society's established spaces and places. However, although this vision is tempting, as Hawisher and Sullivan (1998) have argued, Foucault's term may fail to capture the complexity of the ongoing interaction and change that marks cyberspace. For Galin and Latchaw, for example, online archives of the future are no longer the archives of print culture. Instead, they will have become the professional working spaces of scholars in particular research communities who constantly read, evaluate, write, revise, anticipate, and participate in the making of the scholarly community. In other words, as Galin and Latchaw note, no longer are the archival materials merely "housed"; they are dynamic and changing.

Haynes and Holmevik would be the first to agree that electronic venues change dramatically the business of archiving. Citing Derrida, they remind us, for example, that new technologies of archiving forever alter the way we live with texts. But instead of looking to the future, Haynes and Holmevik ground their observations and musings solidly in the present, in the synchronicity of publishing, in MOOs, and seek to upset the system that "values only texts worthy of eternity." They urge us to look more carefully at MOOs, an electronic venue that essentially publishes synchronous text. For Haynes and Holmevik, the third spaces of MOOs provide us with opportunities for creating "a suspended history, a forestalled future, a time in which, living and meaning are in sync."

In the final dispatch of the book, Doherty and Thompson provide readers with a print rendition of MOOing as they bring together the authors who contributed their dispatches to the volume. As their title indicates, MOOing for Doherty and Thompson is "Public + A(c)tion" or "Publication." Yet, as we read through the contributors' insightful postings in the MOO, we are struck by the fact that it is virtually impossible to represent in print the dynamics of a MOO—the public + action—even when that print is edited. The loss of synchronicity—the loss of speed—destroys the intimacy, the conviviality, the power, and the meaning-making that inevitably mark these spaces in which participants near and far publish their words and create new wor(l)ds. To recognize and value what Haynes and Holmevik eloquently describe as "a galvanized, real-time, contemporaneous, concurrent, corresponding mélange," scholar-teachers must participate, act, and publish in MOOspace, which as many of the participants in this volume suggest requires, like other e-spaces, new "ways of seeing" (Berger).

WHERE THIS COLLECTION MAY NOT (YET) GO: THE COMPASS SIGHTINGS OF CHANGE, VISUAL REPRESENTATION, AND GENDER

The dispatches presented in this collection—these urgent messages that we ignore at our peril—evoke the necessity of bringing new ways of seeing to bear on the profession's often vexed relationship with the new technologies. In this goal, the volume succeeds more concretely than any other we have encountered. It abounds with creative experiments in text. But there are some areas that receive less attention and that require further exploration. We are thinking most specifically here about three areas—the change and resulting instability caused by the increasingly networked society, the increasing importance of visual representations in electronic spaces, and the new forms of gender representation in these spaces. In this last section of our Middlewor(l)d, then, we add a note of caution and suggest that these new electronic worlds of ours require that we move ahead carefully—and thoughtfully—recognizing that the landmarks before us are far and few between.

We begin with a word about the increasing pace of change characterizing networked environments and the resulting effects that such change exerts on existing social formations. The nature of such change represents the first compass sighting that we can offer readers who want to go beyond the landscape occupied by this collection. To provide the needed background for this exploration, we rely on the extensive work of Castells (1996, 1997, 1998), a professor of sociology and planning at Berkeley, and a visiting scholar at the universities of Paris and Madrid, Chile, Montreal, Campinas, Caracas, Mexico, Geneva, Copenhagen, Hong Kong, Singapore, Taiwan, Moscow, and Amsterdam, among others.

Castells describes the ways in which the world is being actively structured and transformed by—and, in turn, is structuring and transforming—the network of computers, television, fax, and telephones that form a transnational web of information technologies. This network, the authors explain, is linked directly to dramatic and significant changes in the ways that people understand the world, make meaning with language, and use language to form individual and group identities.

This transformation is taking place at multiple levels within an overdetermined system. Castells (1996), for instance, explains how the new electronic communication networks are linked to significant changes in the power and sovereignty of geographically determined nation states. High-speed global communication networks, for example, have been directly linked to the spread of multinational capitalism, and, thus, to the establishment of multiple and overlapping *transnational* authorities for economic and political affairs. Transnational patterns, such as these, serve, in turn, to supplant or undermine state-controlled economic regulatory systems and systems of political allegiance by establishing multiple and overlapping global authorities for economic and political affairs, as well as by extending people's understanding of political, economic, and social roles beyond the physical borders of their home countries.

The rise of global information networks, Castells (1996) notes, has also been linked to additional changes that are equally significant. Among these, for example, is the rise of global criminal and terrorist organizations that use networks not only to exchange information about the strategic movement of law enforcement groups and the best ways to construct home-made bombs, but also to share self-published hate manuals and to distribute news of their successful terrorist activities. Castells also links the rise of the networked society to the increased activities of fundamental religious and political systems. Among groups that Castells mentions as having common problems directly rooted in the networked society, for instance, are the Catalan population of Spain, the Zapitistas of Mexico, the southern Baptists, the Islamic fundamentalists of Iran, and the various nations of the former Soviet Union. These groups construct increasingly defensive and communal identities to reinforce the boundaries of their belief systems when faced with the "destructuring" of familiar social organizations and "delegitimization of institutions," that characterize an increasingly global society (Castells, 1996, p. 3). The changing networked society and the process of globalization that characterizes it, Castells (1998) contends further, have also been linked to a complex process of economic polarization and the expansion of both poverty and "extreme poverty" that he argues threaten to marginalize whole countries and peoples from information networks (Castells, 1996) and mire them in a continuing cycle of misery, poverty, and crime.

What does this all have to do with the digital language practices and instruction that provide the focus of this collection? In this electronic environment of rapid and disturbing social change where *conventional* social formations and institutions are being deconstructed—personal and group identity, as expressed through language and literacy practices, is, in Castells' (1996) words, "fast becoming the main, and sometimes the only source of meaning. . . . People increasingly organize their meaning not around what they do but on the basis of who they are, or believe they are" (p. 3), and they define their primary identities in their everyday literate practices within the networked society.

But there is a deep-seated and disturbing irony associated with the nature of defining identity in the networked society—given the rapid pace of changes that have occurred and the increasing resistance to such changes, as Castells observes—many people and groups end up formulating their identity both within, and in resistance to, electronic networks, both within the system of the networked society and in resistance to it. In other words, while a great deal of identity primary formation now happens online—in electronic literacy exchanges on e-mail, bulletin boards, electronic conferences, MOOs, and Web sites—much of it is motivated, ironically and paradoxically, by such factors as a personal or group resistance to the problems generated by technology: for instance, by a reaction against the growing economic inequities generated by multinational capitalism as it flourishes in the new global networked environments, or by a reaction against the "primacy of technology for technology's sake" (p. 358) that continues to characterize citizens' lives in developed or developing countries, or by a reaction against the international and national criminal networks supported by the global information systems, or in resistance to the "diffusion of power" (p. 359) that the globally networked society threatens, and that students will face in the next century in terms of their literacy practices and values.

The change associated with the rise of Castells' network society, then, may well produce a world in which conventional identities are challenged dramatically and fundamentally by the "placeless logic" (p.

358) and dizzying change associated with the new Information Age, and yet one in which citizens must nonetheless assemble online in electronic environments in order to facilitate the diffusion of their ideas, to participate in productive political involvement, and to extend their own "possibilities for interaction and debate" (p. 350). This globally defined landscape of change, although not one explored fully in this collection, is sure to provide readers a new perspective on the experimental language environments described within this collection.

The second compass sighting we can offer readers for exploring beyond the parameters of the current collection focuses on visual representations and communications in cyberspace—both those that are successful and those that are not so successful. In addition to changing the ways in which humans—both men and women—live with text, the MiddleWor(l)ds of electronic spaces also change the ways in which we live with images. And, although this collection points the way toward further considerations of the visual, it leaves the territory of visual representation mostly uncharted for readers.

For us, and for the visual scholars we cited earlier in this dispatch, the realm of the visual represents a particularly fertile, but sometimes rocky, landscape for exploring digital communication. Visually laden, visually dependent e-spaces continue and extend society's reliance on the image,[1] especially when we consider this past decade's growing fascination with the World Wide Web. The Web with its graphical interface makes possible the "imaging" or "re-imaging" that allows us to represent one of our many selves more graphically to the rest of the online world.

And scholars in several fields, as we have noted, are taking up the challenge of exploring visual forms of representation. As Purves (1998) has written, the coming of print destroyed the importance of the image and made it suspect but that "the world of the image is now returning and is shaping the ways in which the new literate world operates" (p. 110). Gunther Kress (1999) argues, further, that the landscape of the 1990s is "irrefutably multisemiotic" and that "the visual mode in particular has already taken a central position in many regions of this landscape."

The World Wide Web underscores the importance of the visual in the electronic landscape to the extent that it firmly folds the visual into communication processes. That is, it allows individuals and corporate bodies simultaneously to construct and to broadcast themselves visually with an ease and speed that just weren't possible before browsers such as *Netscape* were developed. And, considering the early prominence of the Internet in university settings, it is not surprising that academe has participated fully in incorporating the Web, with its strong visual component, into its online life.

To indicate more specifically why we consider issues of visual representation in digital landscapes to be such an important area for exploration, we focus on two cases or examples—the first relates to our work as faculty within the academy and as employees of the university, the second to our work as English teachers and writing instructors.

University and departmental web sites increasingly function as promotional sites, dispensing information and actively advancing the image of its faculty and programs (Hawisher & Sullivan, 1999). One of the most common approaches to departmental Web sites, for example, entails constructing web pages that feature prominently headshots of the faculty members, along with their academic credentials. Our own two departmental home pages, in fact, demonstrate the typical kinds of representation found at these sites. And although both of us participated in the making of these sites—indeed we urged that our programs be represented on the Web—we realize increasingly that these Web sites may indeed promote our programs but that they also contribute mightily to the already entrenched structures of academe. The two institutional web pages are almost exact replicas of one another (e.g., smiling picture, affiliation, contact information), but in some ways Hawisher's is even more institutionally shaped than Selfe's, with the "University of Illinois at Urbana-Champaign" bannered at the top of the page in orange and blue whereas corresponding information for Selfe is listed in print (Figures 1 and 2). Each, however, allows the university to promote and advertise its wares and expertise—its faculty and their accomplishments—to the technologically connected public at large. Although there is some variation in the kinds of institutional home pages featuring faculty, most foreground the headshots we've shown here, similar to those on passports, and display scholarly qualifications. The portraits of a department's faculty tend to validate the institution's claims to knowledge (e.g., teaching and scholarship) in particular fields. But people are seen as marginal to the institution, as pictures and credentials to be replaced at any time by other equivalent pictures and credentials.

These images are not unlike those in yearbooks, company reports, brochures, all kinds of print sources before the World Wide Web—but they now can be accessed far and near, and indeed many university web sites overseas are following similar practices of representation. (See, for example, the faculty pages at the University of Sheffield, http://www.shef.ac.uk/uni/academic/D-H/ell/text/ewa.htm.) Usually these representation practices do not allow for multiple subject positions—the institutional framing of headshots is almost as singular and fixed as the university oil portraits hanging in the stone and mortar faculty clubs (Hawisher & Sullivan, 1999). Thus the visual—and the visual representation of our selves—has been folded into the everyday online business of advertising the university with few of us bothering to scrutinize how such representation practices may affect our lives as university employees and teacher-scholars.

Universities were also among the first to foreground the Web and the many possibilities it offers for teaching. Today, for example, faculty often construct Web sites to accompany their classes. Although these educational web sites take many different shapes and forms, ranging on one end of the continuum from instructors' delivering to students all the materials of the course (including faculty syllabi, lectures, readings, exercises, and quizzes) to the other end of the continuum, where students construct their own home pages, links, and participate in Web conferences and other online activities. (We're thinking here of Carbone's effective pedagogical suggestion of having students post to and publish in online journals.) And although it is not our purpose here to review the many ways in which such approaches can be effective and not so effective, we would like to focus on dangers we ourselves encountered in introducing visual components to our classes using the Web.

In incorporating the visual in our teaching, we were already aware of the fact that clip art often leaves out those who are already under- or misrepresented in society such as African Americans and women. In trying to avoid this danger, one of the authors made available to her classes a digital camera and also used pictures she had taken of the class to feature on the class' home page. She was quite proud of these web pictures until one of the students, an African American, requested that the picture be retaken. Although she noticed that the second picture wasn't any better, the student did not complain. But she began wondering about this picture taking she was doing and realized that invariably the camera images of African Americans blurred and often flattened their facial features. Many processes of photographic reproduction—she later learned—have been "optimized" for European faces, to emphasize the kinds of contrast that can be achieved with pale faces. They are not set up to catch the kinds of contrast that mark dark faces. Color palettes on computers are similarly optimized for light faces since there seems to be a much greater range of lighter colors (and pinks and reds) than of the kinds of colors that darker faces need. Thus unwittingly one of the authors in trying to create a collaborative Web site that featured students made computer technology work to emphasize and underscore White students' place in the world at the expense of their Black classmates.

The visual immediacy of the Web tends to transform the viewing experience, startling us with its vividness and energy and blinding us to the inequities that it also encourages. Perhaps because as English teachers we are not accustomed to working with the digital images that computers afford, we sometimes adopt images and the Web into our teaching without giving the practice the careful thought that the introduction any new technology requires. The electronic world, and even our "unelectronic" world, is packed full of images that we view and interpret on a daily basis and which, in turn, exert a tremendous influence over us. When we and our students become objects on the web and have little say in the ways in which we are being represented, the outcome is predictable: We end up reproducing old identities and re-create traditional narratives with new technologies.

Certainly, this world of images on the Web and otherwise argues for our own—and our students'—greater critical awareness of the workings of the visual. Just as we need to attend to words and to technologies themselves, we need to pay greater attention to the profusion of images that have become part of the literate fabric of our lives. Increasingly, we as teachers are expected to use the visual as an adjunct to our teaching, and we would argue that few of us are able to either interpret or construct images with sufficient skill to understand what we are perceiving or what we are conveying with our own designs.

What we would like to add, then, to this remarkable volume of dispatches is the gentle reminder that images are of critical importance in the online worlds we all inhabit. If we neglect tending to the visual in our professional work and our teaching lives, we are likely to wake up one morning to find that we live primarily in the world not only of the sound byte but also of the quick take.

A third, and final compass sighting that readers can use to read beyond the boundaries of this collection has to do with gender issues in the MiddleWor(l)ds of electronic writing and publishing. The commonplace metaphors of "information superhighway" or "electronic frontier" are inadequate representations for helping us to understand this new arena for public + action. Although the first phrase captures the speed of e-dispatches and the second the perceived unruliness of e-interactions, neither manages to name the compelling attraction such spaces hold for those who participate.

There have been times during our collaboration when we have thought with nostalgia that these e-spaces do indeed comprise the close-knit electronic communities that Rheingold (1993) celebrates or that they closely resemble what Oldenburg (1989) has called "The Third Place," that is, "a thriving informal public life" (p. 14). Other third places in Oldenburg's scheme of things are the one-time public baths, coffee houses, barber shops, street corners, and neighborhood taverns that in many parts of the world continue to invite companionship and conversation. Oldenburg notes that the penchant for such places has been largely obliterated by suburban development and the ubiquitous "No Loitering" city signs that effectively keep the young and old from gathering. In the worlds of e-space, however, there are no "no loitering" signs to preclude active participation and on many listservs "loitering" or "lurking," as it is known online, is happily tolerated if not encouraged. Although participation is the goal, lurking or reading without posting is often viewed as a form of participation.

Yet the more that we look at Oldenburg's notion of "the great good place," we become aware that these third spaces seldom include women—to our eyes they increasingly take on the look of an earlier generation's manly escape from the domesticity of family life and the travail of everyday work. And we are not particularly impressed by his observation that laundromats often functioned as "great good places" for women. Ultimately, however, what Oldenburg's third places seem to lack that is so evident in this volume's dispatches are the important publishing, research, pedagogical, and professional opportunities that are also provided through the Internet. But the e-spaces of the Internet are still fraught with problems. Although MOOs and listservs and Web conferencing systems provide great good places to gather, to linger, and in many cases to find "both the basis of community and the celebration of it" (Oldenburg, 1989, p. 14), only those who have access to technology have the privilege of loitering and participating. This collection suggests that a great deal of work needs to be done to invent and map women's roles and spaces in the MiddleWor(l)ds, for if women fail to inhabit Oldenburg's good places, men still outnumber them in the newer worlds of cyberspace. In their optimistic experimentation and exploration of form, the dispatches represented here sometimes ignore inequities in their rush to envision an e-world bursting with equitable and exciting online opportunities.

We suggest that future explorations of gender as represented in electronic communication environments could not only acknowledge such existing problems and inequities—as identified by Richardson (1997); Sullivan (1999); LeCourt and Barnes (1999); Takayoshi, Huot, and Huot (1999), and Hocks (1999)—but also expand our thinking to admit the hybridity of feminist cyborg (Haraway, 1985) communicators or lesbigay and transgendered writers (Woodland, 1999).

A CODA FROM THE MIDDLEWOR(L)DS

With this dispatch, we have tried to provide several realistic, if contradictory, glimpses of the MiddleWor(l)d as they have revealed themselves to us in the reading of this collection. These pages suggest that electronic landscapes are places of exciting experimentation and exploration—where teachers and scholars experiment with form and language and representation even as they try to map new intellectual environments for language use. But there is plenty of exploration yet to come—the MiddleWor(l)ds, although not totally uninhabited frontiers, remain unsettled places where some readers will experience the discomfort of confronting changes that continue to occur even as we watch. Indeed, one of the things we like best about these dispatches—as experimental and forward looking as they are—is that they conjure up the ghosts of changes yet-to-come and the prospects of places and spaces yet-to-be-explored.

NOTES

1. Although MOOs create images through words, and their use of the pictorial is often confined to ASC art (see for example Haynes and Holmevik's Fig. 2, the Courtyard, this volume), as the World Wide Web encroaches on the space of the Internet, greater use of the visual also marks MOO space.

WORKS CITED

Apple, Michael. (1991). The new technology: Is it part of the solution or part of the problem in education? *Computers in the Schools, 8*(1/2/3), 59-77.

Baudrillard, Jean. (1983). *Simulations*. New York: Semiotext(e).

Berger, John. (1977). *Ways of seeing*. New York: Penguin Books.

Birkerts, Sven. (1994). *Gutenberg elegies: The fate of reading in an electronic age*. New York: Fawcett Columbine.

Castells, Manuel. (1996). The rise of the network society. In *The information age: Economy, society and culture* (Vol. I). Malden, MA: Blackwell.

Castells, Manuel. (1997). The power of identity. In *The information age: Economy, society and culture* (Vol. II). Malden, MA: Blackwell.

Castells, Manuel. (1998). The end of the millennium. In *The information age: Economy, society and culture* (Vol. III). Malden, MA: Blackwell.

Diebert, Ronald J. (1997). *Parchment, printing, and hypermedia: Communications in world order transformations.* New York: Columbia University Press.

Eisenstein, Elizabeth. (1979). *The printing press as an agent of change.* Cambridge: Cambridge University Press.

Feenberg, Andres. (1991). *Critical theory of technology.* New York: Oxford University Press.

George, Diana, & Shoos, Diana. (1999). Dropping bread crumbs in the intertextual forest: Critical literacy in a postmodern age. In Gail Hawisher & Cynthia Selfe (Eds.), *Passions, pedagogies, and 21st century technologies* (pp. 115-126). Logan, UT: Utah State University Press.

Guyer, Carolyn, & Hagaman, Dianne. (1999). Into the next room. In Gail E. Hawisher & Cynthia L. Selfe (Eds.), *Passions, pedagogies, and 21st century technologies* (pp. 323-336). Logan: Utah State University Press.

Haraway, Donna. (1985). A manifesto for cyborgs: Science, technology, and socialist feminism in the 1980s. *Radical History Review Socialist Review, 80,* 65-107.

Haraway, Donna. (1992). The promises of monsters: A regenerative politics for inappropriate/d others. In L. Grossberg, C. Nelson, & P. Treichler (Eds.), *Cultural studies* (pp. 295-336). New York: Routledge.

Hawisher, Gail E., LeBlanc, Paul, Moran, Charles, & Selfe, Cynthia L. (1996). *Computers and the teaching of writing in higher education, 1979-1994: A history.* Stamford, CT: Ablex.

Hawisher, Gail E., & Selfe, Cynthia L. (1991). The rhetoric of technology and the electronic classroom. *College Composition and Communication, 42,* 55-65.

Hawisher, Gail E. & Selfe, Cynthia L. (1998). Collaborative computer encounters: Teaching ourselves, teaching our students. In H. Thomas McCracken, Richard L. Larson, & Judith Entes (Eds.), *Teaching college English and English education: Reflective stories* (pp. 333-346). Urbana, IL: National Council of Teachers of English.

Hawisher, Gail E., & Sullivan, Patricia. (1998). Women on the networks: Searching for e-spaces of their own. In Susan Jarratt and Lynn Worsham (Eds.), *Feminism and composition studies: In other words* (pp. 172-197). New York: Modern Language Association.

Hawisher, Gail E., & Sullivan, Patricia. (1999). Fleeting images: Women visually writing the web. In Gail E. Hawisher & Cynthia L. Selfe (Eds.), *Passions, pedagogies, and 21st century technologies* (pp. 268-291). Logan: Utah State University Press.

Hocks, Mary. (1999). Feminist interventions in electronic environments. *Computers and Composition, 16*(1), 107-120.

Jameson, Fredric. (1991). *Postmodernism: Or the cultural logic of late capitalism*. Durham, NC: Duke University Press.

Kress, Gunther. (1999). English at the crossroads: Rethinking curricula of communication in the context of the turn to the visual. In Gail E. Hawisher & Cynthia L. Selfe (Eds.), *Passions, pedagogies, and 21st century technologies* (pp. 66-88). Logan: Utah State University Press.

Laurel, Brenda. (1993). *Computers as theater*. Menlo Park, CA: Addison-Wesley.

LeCourt, Donna, & Barnes, Luann. (1999). Writing multiplicity: Hypertext and feminist textual politics. *Computers and Composition, 16*(1), 55-72.

Oldenburg, Ray. (1989). *The great food place: Cafes, coffee shops, community centers, beauty parlors, general stores, bars, hangouts and how they got you through the day*. New York: Paragon Press.

Olson, C. Paul. (1987). Who computes? In D. Livingstone (Ed.), *Critical pedagogy and cultural power* (pp. 179-204). South Hadley, MA: Bergin & Garvey.

Purves, Alan C. (1998). *The web of text and the web of god: An essay on the third information transformation*. New York: Guilford Press.

Rheingold, Howard. (1993). *The virtual community: Homesteading on the electronic frontier*. New York: HarperCollins.

Richardson, Elaine. (1997). African American women instructors: In a net. *Computers and Composition, 12*(2), 279-287.

Sanders, Barry. (1994). *A is for ox: The collapse of literacy and the rise of violence in an electronic age* . New York: Random House.

Selfe, Cynthia L. (1999). Lest we think the revolution is a revolution: Images of technology and the nature of change. In Gail Hawisher & Cynthia Selfe (Eds.), *Passions, pedagogies, and 21st century technologies* (pp. 292-322). Logan: Utah State University Press.

Selfe, Cynthia L. (2000). *Technology and literacy in the 21st century: The perils of not paying attention*. Carbondale: Southern Illinois University Press.

Sirc, Geoffrey. (1999). "What is composition . . . ? After DuChamp (Notes toward a general teleintertext). In Gail Hawisher & Cynthia Selfe (Eds.), *Passions, pedagogies, and 21st century technologies* (pp. 178-204). Logan: Utah State University Press.

Spooner, Michael, & Yancey, Kathleen. (1996). Postings on a genre of email. College *Composition and Communication, 47*, 158-76.

Sullivan, Laura L. (1999). Wired women writing: Towards a feminist theorization of hypertext. *Computers and Composition, 16*, 25-54.

Takayoshi, Pamela, Huot, Emily, & Huot, Meghan. (1999). No boys allowed: The world-wide web as a clubhouse for girls. *Computers and Composition, 16*(1), 89-106.

Turkle, Sherry. (1998). All MOOs are educational—the experience of "walking through the self." In Cynthia Haynes & Jan Rune Holmevik (Eds.), *Highwired: On the design, use, and theory of educational MOOs* (pp. ix-xix). Ann Arbor: University of Michigan Press.

Vielstimmig, Myka. (1999). Petals on a wet, black bough: Textuality, collaboration, and the new essay. In G. E. Hawisher & C. L. Selfe (Eds.), *Passions, pedagogies, and 21st century technologies* (pp. 89-114). Logan: Utah State University Press.

Virilio, Paul. (1977). *Speed and politics: An essay on dromology.* New York: Semiotext(e).

Winner, Langdon. (1986). Mythinformation. In *The whale and the reactor: A search for limits in an age of high technology* (pp. 98-117). Chicago: The University of Chicago Press.

Wise, J. Magregor. (1997). *Exploring technology and social space.* Thousand Oaks, CA: Sage.

Woodland, Randall. (1999). "I plan to be 10": Online literacy and lesbian, gay, bisexual, and transgender students. *Computers and Composition, 16*(1), 73-88.

Wysocki, Anne, & Johnson-Eilola, Johndan. (1999). Blinded by the letter: Why are we using literacy as a metaphor for everything else? In Gail E. Hawisher & Cynthia L. Selfe (Eds.), *Passions, pedagogies, and 21st century technologies.* Logan: Utah State University Press.

CHAPTERS FROM NEW WORDS:

STAKING OUT EVOLVING BOUNDARIES OF ELECTRONIC SPACES

Expansion. Theory and practice. Theoretical and practical work discussing important issues relating to writing in electronic spaces. Jan Rune Holmevik and Cynthia Haynes discuss how publication changes when we move from asynchronous to synchronous spaces, Nick Carbone explores the mythos of cyberspace, Michael Day proposes new approaches to research in an electronic age, Jeff Galin and Joan Latchaw offer a new paradigm for scholarship and publishing, Dickie Selfe and his collaborators demonstrate what writing looks like when technology is common in people's lives, and Judith Kirkpatrick discusses what writing could look like when technology is common in classrooms. These contributors conduct and write about academic research in ways and forms that speak to and test the publication and communication opportunities electronic technology spaces promote. Similarly, when asked to produce writing publishable in both electronic and print-based formats, they seek new avenues for creating work that address both environments effectively.

chapter 2.1

CYPHERTEXT MOOves: A DANCE WITH REAL-TIME PUBLICATIONS

Jan Rune Holmevik and Cynthia Haynes

What is no longer archived in the same way is no longer lived in the same way.
—Jacques Derrida

In *The Gutenberg Elegies*, a searing critique of information technology and the consequences it holds for the printed page, Sven Birkerts lamented the loss of "the private self—that dreamy fellow with an open book in his lap" (p. 7). To "authorize" his elegy for the book and his dreamy fellow, Birkerts lay blame for their demise at the very foot of Satan, writing ominously: "I've been to the crossroads and I've seen the devil there" (p. 210). Such attitudes are not uncommon when books are compared to electronic publications, and when the "soul" or "self" sells itself to the cyborgian devil, a kind of Faustian drama unfolds. It is with this in mind, that we begin by acknowledging, yet bracketing, Birkerts' demonization of electronic expression and the tired "crossroads" metaphor based as they are in misguided notions of going down one path (i.e., good) or another (i.e., bad).

It is time to move beyond a moralistic "either/or" dichotomy, beyond the view that electronic publication is merely a step toward the printed page, and beyond the reproductive model of digital texts as simulations of print texts. The key to our trajectory in this chapter will be in the move itself, the dynamism of publishing in *time*. We are interested in exploring the "limits" of publication especially with respect to time. By investigating in this way what it means to "publish," we accept the challenge of this volume to seek new words for new worlds. But this means we must shelve some traditional definitions of *publication* as we tread new waters, and we must resist the pull of paradox at having written for print about what will have been un-print/able in (and by) all that we know of print and its time (and the time it takes to reach print). You could say we are hacking into time—how time figures and what figure re/presents time—and marking segments for publifying.

It is in this spirit of hackification that we enter *synchronic publication* into the new system of exchange that Lanham called the "economics of human attention-structures" (p. 227). Exploring synchronicity involves scholarship about it and texts published in synchronous space—synchronous and interactive texts like MOOs and dynamic electronic journals where readers/players engage with each other and with texts as well as with the programmed environment. Forecasting the future of publication means, we suggest, that our metaphors must change from "crossroads" to "cypherteXts," where synchronous borders of text, temporality, telegrapher, and technology interact as they intersect.

The "χ" has long been a symbol of intersection, of mystery and encryption, of codes and equations. It is also a figure for the *chiasmus*, a trope of deconstruction, specifically for the way deconstructive readings occur. In *Positions*, Derrida (1996) explained that he was interested in the form of the *chiasmus* "not as the symbol of the unknown, but because there is in it . . . a kind of fork (the series *crossroads, quadrifurcum, grid, trellis, key*, etc.) that is, moreover, unequal, one of the points extending its range further than the other: this is the figure of the double gesture, the intersection" (p. 70). We submit our chapter under this sign, and within the furl of a deconstructive flag that signals for Derrida (and for us) "not only a way of reading texts in the trivial sense . . . [but] also a way of dealing with institutions" (Olson, 1991, p. 128).

In other words, at the university, where much depends on one's position, Derrida wanted to "consider all the devices and interests presiding over the establishment of 'assured values' " (Derrida, 1992, p. 198). Recalling his juxta/positionism, it will not be our aim to examine (or debunk) the institution of publication except when necessary with respect to its familial ties to the university and its mechanisms for assessing one's professional credentials. Nor do we propose to preside over yet another establishment of assured values in synchronicity. That would just be another repository, another publication, another archive. In this chapter, we MOOve—from the past to the future through real time—into the present and across new codes for living *inside* publication, but also for publishing that lives at the intersection of a new dis/order of publication.

Eiko says, "there is a reason I use the
red cloth on the floor...and I never go
out of the cloth"
Eiko says, "the person is confined to a
situation"
Jan nods.
Eiko says, "I swallow my poetry and
then try to express what I feel into
the movements"
Cynthia says, "because the cloth is a
bit too small, the movement is
restricted in the first piece"
Dale asks, "are your movements
interpreting on a subconscious level?"
Eiko says, "yes...dancing for me is on
a very abstract level"
Eiko says, "once you swallow the
context, it changes the form"
Cynthia displays slide #1 on WP:
Christine says, "We have not heard her
voice very often in this class..."
Kenneth says, "The way the wound
punctures the spike"

PAST *TENSION*

We sort through certain investments in publication in order to cross the intersection of publishing and academia where the stakes are typically high and overdetermined, at the point of tension between property and knowledge. But no need to cross slowly. Recent critical inroads into the nature of intellectual property in the age of information technologies have taken us through the history of print texts and their historical link to "property." According to John Perry Barlow, co-founder of the Electronic Frontier Foundation, "digital technology is detaching information from the physical plane, where property law of all sorts has always found definition" (p. 85). Copyright law was invented to protect expression and, Barlow noted, "with few exceptions . . . to express was to make physical" (p. 85). And to make *public.* Thus, the publication industry consists of an elaborate system of accountability and compensation based on physical and public products. It is not hard to see how, given this system, the idea of publishing synchronous texts would seem impossible, even undesirable. To consider synchronous text *as* publication, however, might simply be a momentous first step toward new notions of what counts as publishable and what publication might become in the next century.

The question to consider, as Barlow put it, is how to "protect new forms of property with old methods" (p. 85). "What are the essential characteristics of unbounded creation? How does it differ from previous forms of property?" (p. 89). If, as Barlow suggested, "digitized information has no 'final cut'," then we are left to lump any number of unbounded creations into the same category as jazz improvisations, stand-up comedy routines, mime performances, developing monologues, and unrecorded broadcast transmissions—all of which are expressions that "lack [the] Constitutional requirement of fixation as a 'writing'" (p. 90). According to Barlow's prediction, we will come to value "real-time performance" over "discrete bundles of that which is being shown" (p. 128). Carried over into the academic sphere, Spender called the new system, "perform or perish" (p. 28). In other words, she wrote, "publishers, in selecting titles, now want to know whether the author is promotable and can perform the work" (p. 37). The university has long considered faculty as property, and their published research the same. Even conference proceedings, evidence of real-time conferring, find their way into the property rooms of libraries and institutes, gathering dust as they stand in solemn salute to a system that *proceeds* and *pro/cedes*.

Time to *secede* from the union of crossroads. We have in mind the crossing of a *chiasmus*, which, as a deconstructive move, involves a double gesture. Derrida (1981) explained that overturning a hierarchy, in which one model governs the other, is *not just an attempt to invert the terms*—following the overthrow, one marks the interval between the inversion of the two terms, releasing the emergence of a new concept not "included in the previous regime" (pp. 41–42). In this moment, in our present, we suggest the concept of *synchronicity* as what has not been included in the previous regime of publication. Such a claim is open to question. What heresy has not been subject to an inquisition? That some will question the deterritorialization of (academic) publication and of its time as apolitical, perhaps unethical, will come as no surprise. Derrida warned that when people question an individual's politics or ethics, it is often because "the first defensive and reactionary reflex is to accuse of ethico-political irresponsibility, even of 'nihilism,' the very one who comes like this to question and disturb the *doxa* in its slumber" (1992, pp. 202–203). We admit to being unorthodox, to disturbing the orthodoxy of publication, and we admit that our approach is perhaps ill-timed. The question is (for us), ill-timed according to whose history? Whose continuum? Whose real time? Whose archive? Whose knowledge?

Derrida submitted the question in "Mochlos," in his reading of Kant's *Conflict of the Faculties* in which Kant publicly responds to the King of Prussia's reprimand. Kant argues that his writings on religion could not possibly do harm to the "public region of the land" because they are unintelligible and closed to the public, "a mere debate between faculty scholars, of which the public take no notice" (qtd. in "Mochlos," p. 19). Derrida noted: "It is, then, the *publication* of knowledge, rather than knowledge itself, which is submitted to authority" (p. 19). But he called attention to the double bind in Kant's argument and asks the tough question: "Reducing publication so as to save a rigorous discourse, i.e. a rational, universal and unequivocal discourse, in science and conscience . . . where is the beginning of publication?" (p. 19). More recently, in *Archive Fever*, Derrida found an answer, and although long, one that is worth citing in full. Discussing classical manuscripts of Freud and others, an "admirable nobility, ... should not close our eyes to the unlimited upheaval under way in archival technology" (p. 18). He continued:

> It should above all remind us that the said archival technology no longer determines, will never have determined, merely the moment of the conversational recording, but rather the very institution of the archivable event. It conditions not only the form or the structure that prints, but the printed content of the printing: the *pressure* of the *printing*, the *impression*, before the division between the printed and the printer. This archival technique has commanded that which in the past even instituted and constituted whatever there was an anticipation of the future.
>
> And as wager [*gageure*]. The archive has always been a pledge, and like every pledge [*gage*], a token of the future. To put it more trivially: what is no longer archived in the same way is no longer lived in the same way. Archivable meaning is also and in advance codetermined by the structure that archives. It begins with the printer. (p. 18)

Thus, "before the division between the printed and the printer" is a *pressure* we want to explore. Consider it a suspended history, a forestalled future, a time in which living and meaning are in sync.

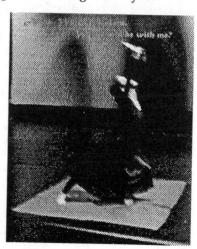

```
zamis says, "Slow emergence - stretching ..."
Dale says, "before the beginning--enclosed"
Theresa says, "Ushering in the sun (Empire of
the sun?)"
Christine says, "Meaning goes on without me"
Theresa says, "Drawing you in to me."
JoanB says, "Here too.  Eventually a sense of
hope started to emerge"
Cynthia displays slide #3 on WP:
Heather-W says, "awakening"
Vickie says, "I got a sense of birth and coming
alive-almost as if a seed were germinating and
reaching to the sky"
Christine says, "one shoulder argues with the
other"
zamis says, "Francis said rocking herself in the
sun's rays."
Kelley says, "is anybody reaching/i hunger for
the reach"
Kenneth says, "that whispers the seraph"
zamis says, "Recoil-recenter-limitation or awe
limitation AND awe..."
Thomasina says, "discovery of limits."
Francis says, "yesterday has disappeared."
```

PRESENT *PRESSURE*

Writing about synchronicity (and publishing it) places us between the
pressure of *living right now* and the pressure *of making meaning of our
living in the now.* It has the feel of taking "latent" prints of our lives,
brushing the powder of language over it in order to see the fingerprints
we leave in real time. The pressure of "value" also clings like ink to our
textual life/time. Our prints are run through a system searching for a
match, for that which identifies us in the regime of print as worthwhile
reading. In a synchronous world that means worth/while living. The
question "Where is the beginning of publication?" then becomes,
"where is the beginning of living?" For us, as for Joyce, "It is exactly in
the commonality of MOOspace, the noise and actions, the kaleidoscope
projections, the constant replacement . . . in which . . . we lose and gain
our lives" (p. 321). We would add that it is also in the commonality of
MOOspace that our thoughts and identities take on synchronous (living)
and textual (meaningful) dimensions.

Unlike e-mail and web pages, which are asynchronous texts,
MOOs are text-based synchronous virtual realities, many of which now
include multimedia content as well. All interactions and descriptions are
conducted and created *in text . . . in real time.* That these two factors are
what makes MOO so innovative (especially in language, writing, and
literature fields) does not, however, prevent some from raising questions
of quality and permanence, relegating conversation in MOOs to "chat,"
or "kitchen-talk," to a generally unproductive discourse, and to which
Joyce replied:

> The debasement of language in electronic texts leads some cultural
> commentators and critics to argue that theory such as this dispatch
> overstates the ordinariness or worse of the language of MOOspace, the
> web, and so on. In fact, canonical critics might argue that the argument
> here is carrion criticism, parasitically feeding on waste in order to puff
> up a claim of transcendence and the poetic. The MOO (all of electronic
> text) is faulted for not having a language worthy of eternity. This is of
> course a macho claim. . . . (p. 320)

Since our creation of Lingua MOO, we have thought a great deal
about the effect of text in relation to learning, identity, proximity, and
reality. In our introduction to *High Wired* (Haynes & Holmevik, 1998),
we argue that the textual nature of MOO architecture and discourse calls
for new definitions of writing and new conceptions of text, but not so
much "to puff up [a] claim of transcendence" (Joyce, 1998) as to
reconstitute MOOs as places of a different register, a new order
uncomplicated by a *transcendental* imperative. We believe what makes

language different in MOOs has to do with what we call *cyphertext* and *élekcriture*.

To explain what we mean by these two rhetorical devices, it is helpful to see them in relation to Aarseth's (1997) notion of *cybertext*. He explained:

> Cybertext [...] is not a "new", "revolutionary" form of text, with capabilities only made possible through the invention of the digital computer. Neither is it a radical break with old-fashioned textuality, although it would be easy to make it appear so. Cybertext is a perspective on all forms of textuality, a way to expand the scope of literary studies to include phenomena that today are perceived as outside of, or marginalized by, the field of literature. (p. 18)

In Aarseth's definition of cybertext, the text itself is seen as a "machine" consisting of three main components: verbal signs (the text), the medium (paper and computers), and the operator (reader/user). He also said that "the boundaries between these three elements are not clear but fluid and transgressive, and each part can only be defined in terms of the other two" (p. 21).

From this, we can define *cyphertext* as a type of cybertext. It shares some triangular characteristics and dependencies, but unlike cybertext, *cyphertexts* can only exist in certain electronic forms. The word *cyphertext* (cyber/hyper/text) is meant to evoke a *three-dimensional* image of textuality, but it is also a play on the notion of cipher and how we encipher and decipher ethos through textual means.

```
Dale says, "now she's really trapped"
JoanB says, "The music added a dissonance,
a mood"
zamis says, "I love the fact that the music
was wordless."
Cynthia displays slide #9 on WP:
Vickie says, "The mood changes as the music
escalates."
Christine says, "but she doesn't, and I am so
anxious for her to move"
Kelley says, "frozen in time?"
Kenneth says, "is trapezoidal from this angle"
Theresa says, "I have so many things to tell
you."
Dale says, "consideration of her upturned palm:
discovery"
Kenny says, "and I am"
Theresa says, "Take me with you, I beg of you!"
Christine says, "these pale ovals"
Theresa says, "supplication and prayer?"
Christine says, "and then round gestures"
Thomasina says, "she seems to draw about
herself at the end, turning again back in upon
herself. "
```

Élekcriture refers directly to the verbal interaction and communication in cyphertext. Borrowing from the Greek for the beaming sun (*elektra*) and French feminism's notion of writing, *écriture feminine*, we coined *élekcriture* to describe a thematic conjunction between electricity and the streams of writing that spill forth in *cyphertexts*—a discourse that resists traditional ways of organizing and controlling the flow of conversation. One thing to note, however—like French feminists, we are not trying to *define* or *fix* one way to describe writing. *Élekcriture* is not about that. It is about what sits inside traditional linear printcentric discourse and jams the machinery from within . . . but this time USES the machine to jam the machinery, to critically jar the systemic *romanticist* tendency to value only texts worthy of eternity (i.e., time-less).

Pressure is mounting, then, to split our affinity with text and time into a fictional fissure between the present and the future, between the mortal and eternal, and between the pleasure and the *pledge* (or wager) of the archive. Publication in/of/as real-time texts threatens to obliterate the archival regime, the archival machine, although some would cast the arch/evil *present* as the very digital shredder of history. According to Virilio (1997), who characterizes real-time as an "inflation of the present" (p. 135), we face an "imminent *temporal homogenization* of a planet now subject to the tyranny of real time" (p. 83). Virilio objected to "teletechnologies of real time" that kill "present time by isolating it from its here and now, in favour of a commutative elsewhere that no longer has anything to do with our 'concrete presence' in the world, but is the elsewhere of a 'discreet telepresence' that remains a complete mystery" (pp. 10-11). In short, he lamented the "loss of the traveller's tale" (p. 25), he longed for the "essence of the path, the journey" (p. 23). And so do we, though we would long for *having lived* the essence of the path, not merely *the account* of having lived the journey (i.e., the tale, the journal, the *publication*). The path is not lost if from within the *center of real-time* we re-enter the proximate journey and the potentiality of time and choice and yearning.

The problem, as we see it, has been that we have been culturally predisposed to thrive on proximation. We have need of the "near" and the "far" and of "duration." Our objection to Virilio's conflation of real-time with the present, and his resistance to teletechnologies that "puff up . . . the perpetual present" (p. 137) is that such arguments fall into the same crossroads metaphor into which Birkerts situated us. It's all too clear from their demonizing of technology and real-time which direction we're all headed. When Virilio quoted Klee, who wrote: "To define the present in isolation is to kill it" (p. 10), he practically claimed that technologies of real-time cloak us all in a shroud of death. Virilio feared that the "urbanization of real time" will result in a loss of "concrete presence" in the world. In effect, he seemed (in our view) to be killing the messenger.[1] We argue, however, that we are not suffering from a loss of presence so much as a change in how we *experience* and *perceive* presence. In MOOs, our presence is textual and multi/pliable. We publish *ourselves* as message and messenger, proliferating real-time presence in a network of instants and entrances.

```
`:XMRM!!XM!!!!!!!~!!!!!XXMMMMBM8M$X'  -`-`----
 `M$RXMM!!!!!!!!~~~!!!!X!!!!!MM$8$B:~---------
/!$$M!!!!XM!!!~~\!X!!!!!XMXX!M$$$$X~--------
: `!$$RM!!!MMX:~ `/X!X!X!X?M8BMM$$$$B/~`~/:~`--
  ~t$$$B8MM?!!!     ~!!!!!!5$B$$$$$$$k~--------
  `!M$$$$$!XXX!!:~::~/!!H!!!!!M$$$$$$$8X~-------
  !!MMR$$$M!XXX!!/~`~!!!H@WWX!!XM$$$$$$$X~~~:~--
/!!M?!XMMM$XRR!!!/~!!!!!!!%MR!!!SM$$$MR$BX~-----
~!!M!!!??!!!!!!~!!!!!!~----~!!!!M?MMRRRMMM/~----
~!!!!!!MM!!!!!!!!!!~!!!------~!!!!?MN$888@MM!~--
~~!!!!!!M$!!\~\!!!!~!!!~/:~:!!XX!!MMMR$RMX!!  ~
~!!!!!XX$X!!!!!!%!!!!!!!!!!:!!!!!X.!!!?MMM!!!
~!!!!!XM$M!!!!!!!:~~/!!!!!!!!!!!X$!!!!!!?M!/
:: :::!!!!!XXMMM!!!~!M??"?""!!XM!~!!!!@\`!!!!!!!!!----
/!!!!!!XMM8M/X!!!!MMMMMMM?!!!:!!XM$!X!XX!!!!!!/
/~!!!!!!?MRMM$M!!!!!/~~~~!!!!!!!X!MMXX!MS!!!!!!!
/!!!!!!!XMMMM$MM!!!!~~/!!!!!!M!!MX!!XMM!?!!MM!!!!
----!!!XXMX!!!!!M%MMM#M!!!!/:!!!M?!!!XMMM!MM!!MHXM!~~
' ~!!XX%MMMMX!!!XMXMM!!R$$@NH@#!!!!!!MMXMMMM!!MMMM!~
'!XXX!MMMMMM!!XM!MMX!!!!!!!!!!!!!~!XMMMM!!?XXXMMMMX!/~:
 'XXXXMMMM$MMMMMMMXSMMM!!!!!!!!!!:~!XMMMMM!?!XXMB$8$BMX!!
XM$$M8M@$$MMMMMMMXXHMM!!!!!!!\/~!!!?!!MMX!!XHMM@$$$$$BWM
$B$$$$$$$$RMMMMXHXXXXX!!!!!!!~/~~!!!!!!!X!!MtMMM8$$$$$$$$
```

You see a trace-structure that resembles a woman who hit the I-way from the u.t. of d. in an earlier chronosphere. Just act like you don't notice that she looks a bit deconstructed at the moment. Imploding binaries on a daily basis would make anybody look a bit ragged around the edges.

Cynthia is awake, but has been staring off into space for 19 minutes.

In addition to our textual personal representations, a number of *texts* are listed as objects in our online Lingua MOO Studio: a planning session, a series of student MOO evaluations, a sheet of music, a trunk full of objects, a weather map, and so forth. All of these objects are readable from within the synchronous connection to the MOO, or may be browsed as Web pages from our web interface, including both our player-character descriptions. Although most of the conversations that take place in the MOO are not, the output on this particular screen is public insofar as it resides in a real-time computer process running in RAM on a server at the University of Texas at Dallas, a public institution of higher education. A 17.507.801 byte database (as of 2:18:07 p.m., CDT on Saturday, May 1, 1999) located on the Internet at http://lingua.utdallas.edu:7000/, Lingua MOO has the veneer of an electronic book, complete with an ISBN-like number, an address within a huge network of texts.

But let us call your attention to another room in the MOO, BusyBee's Bed & Breakfast. Zoom in to a text called Memorial Book, a seemingly innocuous book lying around. Not something one would publish or deem publishable. And yet, in real-time on Tuesday, October 14, 1997 a teacher, Claire Rich (known on the MOO as BusyBee), was killed in a tragic car accident. The following week, in real-time, her students logged on to the MOO to write their sentiments to her family.

```
You teleport into Bed & Breakfast...

Bed & Breakfast

You have entered a room full of comforts . . .
stately, white fireplace to one side, antique
desk with all the needed accessories on the
other wall, fluffy, white comforter-ed bed,
brass headboard/footboard with lost of plushy
pillows. Your shoes are off, your toes sinking
into thick carpet. You head for the desk, plop
into a swivel chair and begin to write . . . .
by the way, this is a working room . . . the
bed is for naps only . . . when you need
inspiration from dreams.

You see Syllabus, Remembrance, and Memorial
Book here.

BusyBee (asleep) is here.
```

Obvious exits: [Out] to ComMOOnity

read memorial

Such a vibrant life cut short. Always smiling or laughing, and always seeming to care. It's a tragedy that you are gone, and know that everytime I sit here, or everytime i check my Email, i will think of you, hoping against hope that you have sent me another reminder about the homework, not because i want to do it, but because i want to see you alive again. Always in my heart, and in my soul. May you always be loved, and shall your family always remember how loving you were. (rygar)

Claire was such an inspiration to me and will continue to be. She was an outstanding teacher who showed us how much we mattered to her. She cared immensely about making sure we did our best and understanding corrections on our papers. Claire will always be in my heart and her family in my prayers. (becky)

In memory of Ms. Rich, it cannot escape me how lucky I was to be her student. I will thank God always for gracing my life with her presence, and I hope that she knows that she taught me much more than just the basics of rhetoric. She taught me about faith. I will never forget her. (Bryan)

Mrs. Rich made Rhetoric more than just a class. She gave me the inspiration and confidence to write. Her beloved memory will always be with me and the rest of her students. (Kevin)

(You finish reading.)

Publication of this text, its *pathos* bulging at its electronic seams, spills onto *this* page because (again) "It is exactly in the commonality of MOOspace, the noise and actions, the kaleidoscope projections, the constant replacement . . . in which . . . we lose and gain our lives" (Joyce, 1998, p. 321). And yet, the *pressure* of publication to render the living word in mute forms has propitiated the favor of distracted critics who listen only to history or science fiction—they are not *impressed* with today. Supposing we have their attention (given that this appears in print), we have a few things to *say*, to exemplify a more favorable *impression*. In order to code the space, to cross paths, to instantiate a *chiasmus*—we turn now to how we spend our time in MOOs marking segments of life as cyphertexts of raw tell-nets into palpable publications.

```
Heather-H says, "the robe she wore was
beautiful"
Kelley says, "I loved the flute. It was like
flying..."
Cynthia displays slide #16 on WP:
Christine says, "beautiful robes make it
impossible to run"
zamis says, "The second piece was like the
ocean."
Christine says, "Taken by the beauty of the
robe, we forget it's just another big ribbon
on the package"
Kenneth says, "A personal constraint in a
personal freedom"
Kenneth says, "...and other abstractions."
Kenneth nods at zamis.
Theresa says, "How is a constraint a freedom?
Kenny says, "i felt that i was making love
with the movement on stage'"
Christine says, "They are locked in my memory
too"
Kenny says, "for a moment of no-time"
Cynthia says, "the second piece uses the same
movements but different music"
```

FUTURE *IMPRESSIONS*

In the early days of the World Wide Web, people frequently put small "under construction" icons on their web pages. The idea, obviously, was to warn readers that their pages were not *finished*, and that the text itself was in a state of progress. This practice clearly demonstrated that Web writers of the time were deeply rooted in a traditional print culture and had not yet truly understood the nature of electronic texts. Today, you hardly see those icons, and it seems that people are beginning to come to a different understanding of what electronic texts are (or perhaps should be), and how we read them. In Aarseth's formulation, one way to articulate the distinctions we suggest is a term he called *ergodic*, "a term appropriated from physics that derives from the Greek words *erogon* and *hodos*, meaning 'work' and 'path' . . . . [where] nontrivial effort is required to allow the reader to traverse the text" (p. 1). Both writers and readers on the Web today seem to accept that *ergodic* texts such as Web pages will never be finished and that they are always going to be under construction. This is, in fact, what makes them interesting venues for new forms of publication.

Cyphertexts, unlike mere web pages, take publication into real time. Just as paper has been the interface of traditional publications, the cyphertext interfaces of online multi-user systems like MOOs and MUDs are where real-time publication begins. Synchronous publications can only be accessed in online media, and can only be *read* through active participation. The interfaces of a synchronous publication includes both text-only readers such as telnet, MacMOOSE, Pueblo, TinyFugue, tkMOO-light, and more comprehensive Web-integrated systems such as for example the *enCore Xpress* system that we developed. Although the text-only readers are fairly simple and usually do no more than allow the user to read textual output of the MOO and write input, Web-integrated systems such as *Xpress* mix the modes of publication of the WWW with the real-time interactivity of the MOO

In this way, readers must be players, active explorers of a text that is highly interactive and that may feature rich multimedia content that may include graphical illustrations, sound and music, or animations and film. Cyphertexts challenge our traditional notion of what constitutes text itself, not only how it is published, presented, delivered, and deciphered.

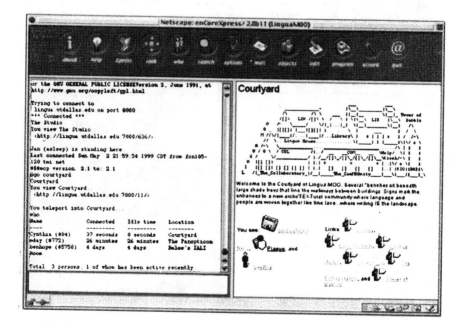

In the figure of the Lingua MOO Courtyard is a snapshot of the Lingua cyphertext taken on May 2. 1999 at 21:59 p.m. CDT. It is meant to illustrate the highly dynamic and *ergodic* nature of cyphertext. Next time we return to the same location, maybe not even 1 minute later, the cyphertext will be different. For one thing, the text generated by user interactions on the left-hand side of the screen will have changed into something completely different. Unless the text has been deliberately archived by someone, it will be only a memory shared by those who wrote it into being. As we arrive in the new textual instance, other discussions may be taking place amidst textual laughter and emoting. These shifting textscapes, the playfulness and interaction, and the temporality of cyphertext all disturb and disrupt the notion of what a text is or ought to be.

Cyphertexts also have another fascinating and unique dimension in that they are *inhabited*, or *lived* texts. Earlier in this dispatch we talked about BusyBee's Bed & Breakfast, which is one example of such a lived textual space. Even though BusyBee is not with us anymore, her presence is still very much felt through the texts she wrote and the thoughts she shared. Her cyphertextual presence will always be there, just as she left it, to remind us of what once was. While BusyBee's Bed & Breakfast today is a quiet sanctuary for reflection and personal thought, other cyphertextual places such as the Courtyard, the ComMOOnity, and the Agora Classroom complex are bustling with activity 24 hours a day as people from all over the world come to live in the cyphertextual MOOniverse. At any given time, you might meet people from places as far apart as Australia, Korea, Norway, England, and the United States. Some of them come to read, write, program or explore, others to participate in an online class or meeting, and some are there to visit with friends and colleagues. Most of them regard Lingua MOO as a "home" because they have *invested themselves* in its collaborative creation.

JoanB says, "And when she pulled the Red Ribbon, very sexy"
Cynthia displays slide #18 on WP:

```
                            |                |
JoanB holds up a BIG sign:  | RED RIBBON     |
                            |                |
```

JoanB says, "She was like a package."
ramis says, "A package can be a gift."
Kenneth says, "Although it seemed that she was constrained without walls."
Dale says,"auf Deutsch gift means 'poison'"
Kelley says, "I found #2 very ritualistic. movement same, sentiment changed."
Kelley says, "she moved from the organic quality of #1 to the orgasmic quality of piece #2...a doll in a package... "
Vickie says, "Joan, i agree, the 2nd part was more sensual"
Theresa says, "this dancing sure beats anything you've seen in class so far!
Beauty. Honor. Duty. Grace. Life."
Francis says, "or Japan. the movement of the sun, warrior..."

A cyphertext is a kind of publication that is never still; it changes constantly with the presence of players/readers/writers and the objects and texts they create and recycle. It is, by its very nature, a form of publication that will never be finished, or finite. When we think we have read it all, explored and understood everything, the cyphertext will have reinvented itself and morphed into something new we didn't even know was there.

```
You remove The Dream from Bookcase.
You take up reading The Dream from line 1.
[You read]: THE DREAM, by Olav H. Hauge
[You pause.]
[You read]: It's the dream we carry in
secret
[You read]: that something miraculous will
happen
[You read]: that must happen —
[You read]: that time will open
[You read]: that the heart will open
[You read]: that doors will open
[You read]: that the rock face will open
[You read]: that springs will gush —
[You read]: that the dream will open
[You read]: that one morning we will glide
into
[You read]: some harbor we didn't know was
there.
(You finish reading.)
```

Publication of and in MOO happens in a transparent and dynamic process where each new layer of text, as developed and written by the writers, players and programmers, constitute new manifestations of the cyphertext that may add new functionality and/or publishability. When someone writes a new program (known as a verb) that enables a new command that authors in the MOO may use to collaborate, to communicate, to write, or to read, it is publishing in its most dynamic and empowering sense. Not only does it empower the author; but it levels the playing field, so to speak. It enables the reader to also be author, and it empowers both to be "publishers." The very notion of authorship and ownership of ideas is seriously challenged by the communal *hacker spirit*[2] of MOO publication. A cyphertext, whether a complete MOO database like the *High Wired* enCore or just a simple verb program like the one that follows, does not belong to any one person in particular. Instead, it belongs to the community of people who use/read it. Anyone is allowed and even encouraged to *hack* (program/write) new functionality into the existing text and, in this manner, add to the textual collective and communal experience.

```
@program $player:"time date"
"Copyright (C) 1998, Jan Rune Holmevik. Anyone is
permitted to change this program and redistribute it
under the terms of the GNU General Public Lisense";
player:tell("————————");
player:tell($time_utils:time_sub("Time: $O:$M:$S $P,
$Z", time()));
player:tell($time_utils:time_sub("Date: $D, $N $T,
$Y", time()));
player:tell("————————");
```

Unlike readers of print publications like books and articles or even hypertexts on the World Wide Web, readers in MOO often have a sense of community with the text itself and other readers they meet. The impact this has on the internalization of text, and identity in relation to it, is a function of what we termed earlier, *élekcriture*—something like identity software for the next millennium.

To further blur the lines between software release and publication, the recent popularity of WWW search engines and software agents indicates that not only is the MOO like a book in a library, if it has a Web interface it can be found in much the same way, with one significant difference. Now readers/users may find other information about this "book," other books related to the MOO, other locations on the WWW linked to this "book," and many other permutations of access and association. One future *impression* of publication, especially academic publication, may be how citation format and procedures will change based on new models of access (search engines) and association (links). In addition, the MOO has the capability for users to do research using the WWW individually or collaboratively from within the MOO, such as with *enCore Xpress*.

Furthermore, these changes will bring about new modes of evaluating publications like MOO cyphertexts. How many times one's book is reviewed or cited has long been a benchmark in academic tenure and promotion criteria. The question to consider now may be how to deconstruct the quantification into qualification—how many hits a Web site receives and how many users/readers log on to the MOO in a given time period become less of an equation for tenure and more of a measure of attention activity that merits evaluation.

Dream
    by Eiko Takahara

It was a soundless dream, yet it still rings in
  my dream.
The ground suddenly exploded, still utterly
  exhausted.
Crashing sparks of crystal spouted as if
  immortal.
The ragged pieces' stream, gushed out from the
  dream.

They fell upon my soul, piercing through me,
  all.
I felt an icy pain, irremediable crystal pain.
Splashing garnet blood, the pallid soul, the
  flood.

Why is it so? Why is it so?
My cries reverberated, still reverberated.
Mingled with lapsed time, they sang in muted
  rhyme.
It was a fleeting dream, yet it still lingers
  in my dream.

To complicate the academic model of publication further, MOO users add a dimension of collaboration to the MOO that does not fit cleanly into any pre-existing conventional publication category except perhaps co-authorship. This is most evident as the fluctuating MOO database rises and falls with each checkpoint during which a backup of the database is taken. Each user who builds and creates more textual objects on the MOO contributes to the layer above the core. But the MOO also loses data when users recycle objects or become inactive themselves, prompting their characters to be recycled as well. In a sense, within the MOO each checkpoint represents a "publication" of the database in its most recent form. Freezing the flow of text for mere seconds or minutes is now superceded by the ability of the MOO to continue running while check pointing, effectively eliminating all vestiges of any time other than real-time, relegating the old "book" to the microcosm of the (time) lag.

The lag is 0 seconds flat. It is staying level.

The dance with publication is never a solitary venture to the tune of a muted song, as the collage of cyphertexts (of poetry, interpretation, discussion, and images of a real-time dance) has served to illustrate throughout our dispatch.[3] One spring day, in real time, Eiko Takahara expressed her poetry in movement to music. We watched and wrote our impressions; and in the cyphertextual dimension, those visual and textual impressions converged. We recorded our words; we folded the images in. They are publications in *our* time. We spill them into *this* text, adding *your* time to ours; in 0 seconds flat. *You* are the enCore now, performing within our dance by reading and viewing and murmuring to yourselves.

With a WWW presence and the user-extendable (danceable) multilayers above the core, the MOO resists being singled out, single-minded, or singly authored as in the old regime. The MOO is a complex matrix, a cyphertext of interface, software, code, backups, search engine, e-journal, teacher, student, lag, poets, dancers and poetry—the stuff of synchronic texts in a real-time continuum drawn on the drafting boards of *bricoleurs* and hyperbards. It is a published cyphertextual community that morphs publication into a chiasmutation (χ) of time and ap/proximation. Hopefully, what we have marked up in this dispatch is something like a new language for articulating what has often *systematically* been excluded from the regime of academia, and thus from the regimes of academic publication—the *pulse* of publication. In re/markable segments of life, of Dreams, Crooked Rooms, Memorial Books, and BusyBees, the living time of MOO publication harbors the heart of academia.

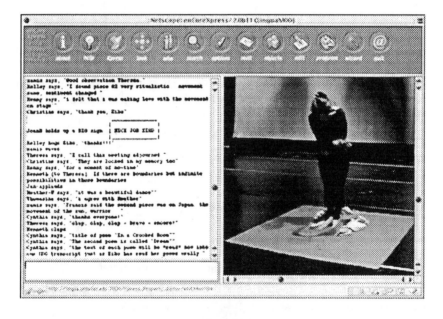

NOTES

1. Portions of this section are drawn from Cynthia Haynes's talk "Total ReCALL: Memory, MOOs, and Morphology" delivered at the University of Bergen, Norway, December, 1997 and Vassar College, June, 1998.

2. In referring to the *hacker spirit* we mean the collaborative system of sharing ideas and information that supersedes individual ownership and control of information. In the words of Richard Stallman, founder of the Free Software Foundation: "The use of 'hacker' to mean 'security breaker' is a confusion on the part of the mass media. We hackers refuse to recognize that meaning, and continue using the word to mean, 'Someone who loves to program and enjoys being clever about it'" (http://www.fsf.org/gnu/thegnuproject.html, 2 May 1999).

3. We thank the students in Cynthia Haynes' graduate seminar, "Rhetoric, Textuality, and Technology" (Spring 1999) for their permission to use text and images from a collaborative project based on the dance and poetry of Eiko Takahara, also a graduate student in the class. The following students are from the School of Arts and Humanities at The University of Texas at Dallas: Joan Berler, Kenneth Elliott, Kelley Emmett-Plunk, Theresa Feighny, Kenny Goldman, Thomasina Hickmann, Vickie Johnson, Marcia Pimentel, Francis Schneeweiss, Angela Steadman, Eiko Takahara, Christine Tata, Dale Wilkerson, and Heather Wood.

WORKS CITED

Aarseth, E. (1997). *Cybertext: Perspectives on ergodic literature*. Baltimore: Johns Hopkins University Press.

Barlow, J. P. (1994). The economy of ideas: A framework for patents and copyrights in the digital age. *WIRED 2.3*, 84-90, 126-129.

Birkerts, S. (1994). *The Gutenberg elegies: The fate of reading in an electronic age*. Boston: Faber & Faber.

Derrida, J. (1981). *Positions* (A. Bass, Trans.). Chicago: University of Chicago Press.

Derrida, J. (1992). Mochlos; or, The conflict of the faculties and canons and metonymies: An Interview with Jacques Derrida. In R. Rand (Ed.), *Logomachia: The conflict of the faculties* (pp. 1-34, 195-218). Lincoln: University of Nebraska Press.

Derrida, J. (1996). *Archive fever: A Freudian impression* (E. Prenowitz, Trans.). Chicago: The University of Chicago Press.

Haynes, C. (1997, December). Total ReCALL: Memory, MOOs, and morphology. Keynote address at the CALL MOO Seminar, University of Bergen, Norway. Available: http://lingua.utdallas.edu/call/mmm.html.

Haynes, C., & Holmevik, J. R. (Eds.). (1998). *High wired: On the design, use, and theory of educational MOOs*. Ann Arbor: University of Michigan Press.

Joyce, M. (1998). Songs of thy selves: Persistence, momentariness, and the MOO. In C. Haynes & J. R. Holmevik (Eds.), *High wired: On the design, use, and theory of educational MOOs* (pp. 311-323). Ann Arbor: University of Michigan Press.

Lanham, R. (1993). *The electronic word: Democracy, technology, and the arts.* Chicago: University of Chicago Press.

Olson, G. A. (1991). Jacques Derrida on rhetoric and composition: A conversation. In *(Inter)views: Cross-disciplinary perspectives on rhetoric and literacy* (pp. 121-141). Carbondale: Southern Illinois University Press.

Spender, D. (1993). Electronic scholarship: Perform or perish? In H. J. Taylor, C. Kramaral, & M. Ebben (Eds.), *Women, information technology, scholarship* (pp. 28-43). Urbana: University of Illinois Press.

Virilio, P. (1997). *Open sky* (J. Rose, Trans). London: Verso.

chapter 2.2

DIVING INTO THE TEXT:

REDISCOVERING THE MYTHS OF OUR BOOKS

Nick Carbone

People connect with words, spoken and written words that build ideas, communities, histories, knowledge, and beliefs. In academic settings, when students study a field, when they go for an advanced degree in a given area, they learn how words are arrayed and made valuable in a given field by learning how to conduct research, handle the bibliographic mechanics and rhetorical knowledge for citing sources. Students learn which thinkers in the field are important to know, which writings have influence, and which ideas are new. Students also learn, over time, how to become independently critical and how to judge writing in the field as they prepare to add their words to the ongoing conversation

This process of initiation and growth into a discipline is one of the core myths of academic books and journals. One definition of mythology is that it is a collection of stories that describe and define a way of seeing and making sense of the world. Books and journals, that is, record the thoughts and names that shape and define disciplines; together these books and journals create a tradition, a set of intellectual inquiries and stories that form a kind of cosmology of ideas whose constellations can be traced and seen in bibliographies and works cited entries. Until the mid-1990s, print-based books and journals alone carried the mythologies that make up academic disciplines. Now, however, we are beginning to explore how these stories will be told and shaped not only in print, but also in cyberspace, a space that is more fluid, a space that can also be thought of as a cybersea, a sea that educators will have to learn how to enter and learn how to teach students to dive into. Adrienne Rich's (1973) poem, "Diving Into the Wreck" can assist in providing an analog of how we might proceed with our own explorations of the pixellated sea that awaits us.

In her poem, "Diving Into the Wreck," Rich describes a diver who, guided by a book of myths, dives from a sun-drenched schooner in search of a wreck, a wreck that contains not "the myths, but the thing itself." The poem describes the yearning, discovery, reclamation, and recognition of a self that is at once distinct—nameable—and merged, part other and part of the truth found in the wreck. The World Wide Web offers a means to use the myths of books as a guide in helping students to discover not myths, but the thing itself—a vibrant and knowable academic community. The poem provides, for me, an analogy for describing how educators can invigorate academic publishing for students, how they can imagine the movement from print to pixel, from publishing in books and journals to publishing online in a way that allows students to find their names.

One central theme to the mythology embodied in academic writing is that of recognition and acknowledgement; it is why the bibliography and works cited functions as a kind of map ("The words are maps," wrote Rich), a constellation of cross-referencing and lineage. The myth of books, then, states that those who join a field can learn to distinguish the voices that make up a field, and given time and publication, can add their voices to the field, placing their names, according to the myth, in our books.

PART I: FIRST HAVING READ THE BOOK OF MYTHS

The myth of academic voice and membership has centered itself on writing in print. The print paradigm means many things, as others in this collection have noted. But the main concern here is on delivery—print is shipped, whereas the Web awaits one's arrival. Journals arrive in the mail, pages sewn and bound at the spine with a restricted, well-defined space. We wait for them. We read them alone, in silence, separated from other readers who are in their offices or their homes, not in ours, not with us. Responses to the articles, the one or two that might be printed in a later issue, represent only a minuscule sampling of the thought a piece may have spurred. Later, when we write for ourselves, in our own reading journals and essays, when we think about the field, we do so with a full sense of what we have read. We can hear the voices of all those articles we have read, voices to which we respond in our own writing, but that many can rarely share in print with others.

Electronic writing, specifically as it can be shared via the World Wide Web, changes dramatically how we come to find and to create the words that make up our field. It changes how we engage those words. These changes, if we think and plan carefully, can be both dramatic and fruitful. Academia—indeed our whole society—finds itself in the middle of this change. When we enter cyberspace, we, if only for a while and like the diver in Rich's poem, leave the "sun-drenched schooner," the light and understanding we gather from our books and journals; we enter into something new. We feel awkward because we are no longer in a place that feels natural, where we have systems—library catalogues, style guides, academic standards—that feel natural and right; instead, we go into a new space that requires us to navigate and search and choose and read and write differently. We are not trying to find only our legs, our balance, or our perspective in this new element; we are trying to find ourselves.

That is, we move away from land, and into a sea, a cybersea. We leave the world of print, with its Apollian connotations of light and logos, and dive into a place that becomes darker as we go down, where words are fluid, where movement and reading feel awkward and slippery and strange because a few quick clicks of the mouse can take us ten web pages down, leaving us disoriented and bewildered the first few times we browse. Hypertext disrupts our normal reading patterns, sending us off in links chosen by text or graphic; we can't hold the page, losing the comfort and weight of paper, with its trim borders and winking white space.

Rich described her diver's descent, the awkwardness of the gear—the wet suit, fins, tanks, and masks. As the immersion proceeds, however, she learns to move "without force in the deep element" (lines, 42-43). As the diver descends, and finds the wreck, she has only the light of an underwater lamp with which to see. Rich wrote:

I came to explore the wreck.
The words are purposes.
The words are maps.
I came to see the damage that was done
and the treasures that prevail.
I stroke the beam of my lamp

slowly along the flank
of something more permanent
than fish or weed
the thing I came for:
the wreck and not the story of the wreck
the thing itself and not the myth (lines 52-60)

Later in the poem, remarking about the book of myths, Rich referred to them as the "book in which our names do not appear" (lines 93-94). Thus, the dive attempts to get beyond the books "to the thing itself and not the myth." Our myth is that we are part of an academic community bound together not by geography but intellectual passions and beliefs.

We define ourselves by what we read and write, as well as how we read and write. This is why the movement into cyberspace, while it does require becoming used to the elements and finding our sense of balance and perspective, is also about finding ourselves. How we read and write determines to a large extent how we understand ourselves. The same holds true as well for our students. David Bartholomae (1985) wrote about students' needs to invent the academy in their writing, but they do this, quite often, in isolation and by isolation—writing drafts alone and puzzling through the technical details on how to quote, summarize, and paraphrase in their quest to keep their words separate and distinguishable from those of the sources they incorporate into their writings.

So students begin by defining themselves as those who must guess at and follow rules they do not understand, rules often presented and cloaked with great portent and consequence, rules that present plagiarism—the misappropriation of another's words *and* ideas, as the great taboo, the sin most grievous and punishable. Thus for students, self-definition as an academic begins not in exploring words, but in avoiding their misuse, in a fallen state where all too often their mistakes are assumed to be signs of laziness and shiftlessness.

For students, diving into academic discourse conventions and communities becomes more difficult because they are not invited in, really. We too often assume that they should know all that we do, that our conventions our self-evident and readily learned to those who are good students, and that for those who are not, or who struggle, that they are lacking and not worthy to experiment and explore. Certain conventions and rules must be exhibited and performed first—writing a good thesis statement, knowing how to cite sources, knowing how to introduce a quote and use evidence. Let me be clear. These are important skills that need to be taught. But we have an opportunity to rethink how we teach them, and in what context. We teach them all too often before a student has a full understanding of why we value them—because they help us sustain our academic communities by affording a way for us to recognize one another.

With the technology of the World Wide Web and other forms of electronic writing, we can help them to dive in, to discover learning communities and to come to know the other members of the community more fully, thus providing them with a better understanding of what it means—and why it is important—to cite and acknowledge others with more care. Prior to cyberspace, we initiated students into academic writing by teaching them how to use books and libraries, our sun-drenched schooners.

PART II: THE TREASURES THAT PREVAIL

Consider, for example, a common assignment in many first-year writing courses—the research paper. Research papers ask students to immerse themselves for a few weeks in a subject, sometimes assigned, sometimes of their own choosing. Students learn important things through this assignment—how to develop a thesis, how to research it and amend it in light of discovery, how to shape an argument based on the intended audience for the paper, and how to properly cite and credit sources. At least that's the plan. Teachers know from experience that the process of trying to teach all this can easily go awry. Students, knowing the paper is only an assignment to be read by the teacher and perhaps their classmates, have no compelling internal motivation for writing. It's make believe, an assignment to show they've mastered mechanics. The paper has no purpose beyond fulfilling the assignment.

Because the teacher—the primary audience—will judge the paper as much or more than he or she will read it, students lack a sense of some of the rhetorical reasons for citing and using sources and tend to fall back on finding and only using sources that agree with their argument or that directly reflect on their topic. So they will write passages that lead to a quote, and then they will summarize the quote in the next paragraph, and then they will assume the quote is proof of a position and leave it at that. Sometimes, of course, this is a good strategy, but rarely is it enough. This comes, in part, because students do not know the literature in a given field. They do not know the way writers in that field think and talk yet—they do not know the specialized language, issues, theories, and touchstone pieces. So they try to approximate an academic voice; they guess at academic conventions for introducing and using sources; and they write knowing their teacher knows more about the subject (usually) than they do, thus the strategy of aping their teacher's arguments and using sources as unquestionable authorities.

As students write these papers, they are also introduced to plagiarism. They are told that there can be no confusion between which words are theirs and which belong to an author. They must learn to distinguish between quoting, paraphrasing, and summarizing, and must learn where to place footnotes or parenthetical notations precisely to avoid misunderstanding. They learn that their work must be their own, that using, unacknowledged, the words and ideas of others is wrong and deceitful. They learn about the penalties for plagiarism, that severe cases can be grounds for course failure and possible expulsion. We present this to students at the same time we are trying to welcome them into academic life. And make no mistake—we must be clear on the mechanics of writing. Whether a research paper or short essay, we must teach students the conventions for citing sources, and why that's important. We must make clear what plagiarism is, and why it is important to avoid.

However, in fulfilling these responsibilities, it becomes difficult to balance other goals. It is important for students to participate as knowledge makers so that they do not only ape what they see. They must do more than accurately quote a source—they must absorb what they read, think about it, synthesize it, become conversant with it, think critically about it, be able to refer to it in other contexts so that they can integrate into their thinking. Students should have in their memory, in their heads—and hearts even, the knowledge that comes from reading, writing, and thinking about what they have read, seen, heard, and talked about. We try to make our classes communities of learners. We teach students how to talk about what they have read, how to read one another's writing, how to make connections between what they think and what a source or classmate thinks.

Yet we are disheartened often because the writing students do does not really matter the way the writing we do matters to us. Writing this chapter holds import for me. I know it is intended for a collection of dispatches. I know the other contributors are respected in the field of computers and writing. I know the book will be read and reviewed, perhaps recommended to colleagues. I know that these words will be read critically, carefully by some. The situation is real. The success of this piece affects not just what I want to say in it, but also my reputation as a member of this academic community. It will also come to bear in hiring, promotion, and tenure, issues directly related to my economic as well as professional well-being. I write this and assume an audience beyond myself, assume an audience who cares about what I have to say, about what I think. Most students, however, do not go onto graduate school, do not become immersed in the field's literature to the point of expertise, to the point where they have learned to move "without force in the deep element."

The question becomes, then, how can we offer students both the needed introduction into academic writing and membership in an academic community of learners in a way that tends to the needed distinctions inherent in such things as understanding plagiarism and using sources responsibly, while at the same time offering writing situations that exist for more than just fulfilling a class assignment? Naturally, given the context of this piece, you know I'll be suggesting the World Wide Web in some guise. And you're right. However, before doing so, it is important to note that the question is not a new one.

Teachers have asked it for as long as writing has been taught in colleges. Writing letters to the editors, inviting students to submit to local journals, newspapers, or contests, finding research projects based on a student's personal interest, having students do research or writing for community agencies who need the research and writing done, are but samplings of the ways teachers have tried to address the need for students to be fully engaged in their writing. These are all good ideas, too. I use many of them myself. What I suggest is that by creating a space for students to write on the Web, we can radically rethink how we introduce students to academic ways of writing, to what we mean by the idea of a community of learners, and how we understand and teach what it means to be a writer and author(ity) in a given community.

One reason so many do not find themselves in books and journals is that it is too expensive for all who would contribute to enter them. The cost of paper, printing, binding, and mailing exert a toll. They limit the frequency of some journals, the length of others. They make it hard for new journals to start up. They force publishers to think carefully before committing to a book. Of course these are not the only decisions at play. Editors want pieces that contribute to the knowledge in a given area; publishers want to support sound scholarship as well. This dual concern makes it hard for novices to find their way into print. With rare exceptions, most published writers in academic settings are fairly far along in their studies—close to finishing a terminal degree or beyond. Few journals feature the work of undergraduate students, or of many of our colleagues who spend most of their professional time teaching and reading the literature in the field, leaving little time for writing. Few anthologies feature the work of undergraduate students. About the only time a beginning student might see the work of someone like them in a book is in a handbook or textbook with a "sample" student essay, one often meant to illustrate particulars of grammar, usage, citation mechanics, the writing process, and paper organization. Rarely is the writing meant to be read for what it says.

Earlier, I mentioned how many teachers try to create learning communities within their classrooms, urging students to share writing and ideas. We see extensions of this with classwork that appears on the World Wide Web. A class might publish a collection of essays on the web, for example, hoping to draw an audience to their work. Furthermore, the Web has become a place to extend traditional class activities such as research and discussion. Students might be asked to use the Web in their research. Students might be asked to join a class e-mail list so that they can talk—in writing—about the content of the course and their own writing. There are projects in cross-class collaboration, where students from different classes at different colleges join the same e-mail list to discuss what they are reading and writing. There are class meetings held in MOOs, where students can converse by writing and sending messages that will appear on every participants screen as the participants write and send their own messages, allowing for a many-voiced discussion to take place.

But very often, the ends of all these classes are the same—writing goes to the teacher for a grade and judgment. True, some students might publish their own work on the class or on personal web pages, and they might draw the attention of a wandering reader, but that relies on chance. Also, given the proliferation of pages, it will be harder to stand out from the crowd. One of the purposes of publishing, whether on the Web or in print, is to be heard. No one writes for publication without being convinced at some level that what they are saying is worth others hearing. So although personal web pages and class web pages are wonderful and useful, I do not think they are enough. It is not just enough to publish, which is what both of these models offer, but there should also be some place for students to publish that gathers pieces from others as well, some place that will be around for a time to come, that will not go down when a student graduates or a class ends.

We need journals on the World Wide Web that are devoted to publishing the work of writers who are just starting out. We need a recognizable place for students to find the words and voices of other students. We need places on the web where teachers and students can work together as colleagues, co-writing, co-editing, and conversing on important issues in a given field or of the day. It is also important that these journals do not become mere imitators of print journals. The Web is a different medium from print, and although it can—and should—encompass print traditions (putting a traditional essay on the Web does, for example), a Web journal should also take advantage of the unique way the web can create, shape, share, and store writing.

PART III: IN WHICH THEIR NAMES APPEAR

Web journals designed to feature the work of student writers are possible because, although not free, the web does make it economically feasible to offer student writing. Unlike a print journal that would depend on subscribers, a Web journal, once it finds a sponsor (maybe an English department, or publisher, or university press, or professional organization such as the National Writing Centers Association) that can guarantee it space, would not have to worry about printing and mailing costs. However, there would be costs for editors and Web site maintainers—if only time. And readers need to choose to visit the journal.

To attract readers, to hold their attention, Web journals for students should also be concerned about quality. Like print journals, where editors help determine for readers what is worth reading, these journals would need good editors to make sure the pieces accepted are well written and speak to the journal's intended readers.

Given consistency and quality, a Web journal, however, has other advantages besides saving the cost of printing and mailing. Unlike print, which is sent out to offices and homes, a web-based journal has a home to which readers come. We see it in the term *Homepage*. Web journals cannot only disseminate new ideas in the writing they publish, but they can also become hosts, welcoming readers into a discussion with one another and the texts and authors the journal publishes. This is nothing new. Academic journals do this already. *Kairos, Rhetnet, Pre/Text Electrolyte*, do it. *Post Modern Culture* began the trend when it built a MOO and offered an e-mail discussion list as part of its journal. And there are Web sites targeted at students that invite them to participate as colleagues for one another, such as ResearchPaper.Com. What we do not have yet, in any meaningful way, are journals for students that replicate fully what we are just beginning to do with our own online journals. If each academic field sponsored one or two online journals for students, and made them freely accessible so that classes could access them, students would be able to find and read the writing of people like themselves, novices. They would find good ideas, well-wrought essays.

They would come to see that there is a place where their writing could go, that a paper, while it may be part of a course, could find an audience beyond the class. The paper could be published in a place that could remain over time, a place they could refer to on graduate school admission forms and resumes. By creating these spaces, and by showing students how to help us create them and to participate in their existence by serving as peer reviews, editors, and web weavers, we'd begin to create a place with their names in it. So that over time, they would find their names, if not in our old book of myths, in our new books.

PART IV: MOVING BEYOND OUR OWN CURRENT MODELS

That we can do this is fairly evident because we have models for doing as much. But not only can we establish journals for students that honor our current academic traditions, we can also create journals, or spaces in journals, that recall older traditions, other traditions, and challenge current traditions, especially in the area of copyright and intellectual property.

In "Diving Into the Wreck," there comes a beautiful moment when the identity of the diver metamorphoses. Rich wrote, as the diver looks at the wreck she has sought,

> This is the place.
> And I am here, the mermaid whose dark hair
> streams black, the merman in his armored body
> We circle silently
> about the wreck
> we dive into the hold.
> I am she: I am he
>
> whose drowned face sleeps with open eyes
> whose breasts still bear the stress (lines 71-79)

This moment of convergence, of merged gender and identity, of suffusing the self with the history of the wreck, to become inextricable with what has become before, to become intimate and a part of the place, describes, in its way, how our own minds work when we write. I write these words having read words that have come before. I have absorbed the conventions of other writers, and as I think in prose, in these words, how I think, how I form a thought, punctuate it, choose my words, happens only because I have a history with words. I hear as I write different voices. Thinking about plagiarism, for example, I hear the voice of writing handbooks that preach about the seriousness of writing correct citations, I recall an essay by Rebecca Moore Howard, I think of a message by William Marsh that was posted to the Alliance for Computers and Writing e-mail discussion list (ACW-L), to name but a few. My thinking about teaching writing has been shaped by having taken writing courses, by my students, by the literature in my field.

So much of what I write and say comes from sifting through all those sources, many of which have become a part of me because they have shaped how I view things. I have lost track of where my thinking starts and those ideas end. I'll sign this piece me with my name. I'll stand by my words, as they appear here. Others will praise or blame me for what is written here. So I don't want to say a writer is subsumed and lost and without identity. I don't think Rich would claim that the diver in her poem, although transformed, is without identity. The poem ends after all with a recognition that the diver does have a name, is "one," a distinct person.

What I mean to suggest is that writing is both a lonely and a social act. I alone write these words, but I couldn't write them without the words and thoughts and ideas of others. These are my words, but they are indebted words, not entirely unique nor independent. Scholarly traditions try to recognize this of course. We cite carefully the works of others, giving credit where it is due. We teach students how to make minuscule distinctions about what should receive quotation marks and what should not. Our bibliographies offer a portion of the thoughts to which we are indebted. And yet we tend to forget the complexity and deep entrenchment those ideas have, how much we are who we are because of where we have been, what we have heard, what we have read.

In our print culture, we honor the author. We do this for artistic and economic reasons. In publishing, we care not only about plagiarism, the moral concern for citing and giving accurate credit and making careful distinctions between what we have read and what we think, but we also care about copyright and intellectual property rights. It is not enough to simply credit an author. For quoting longer portions of a writer's works, we must also seek the permission of the person or entity that holds the copyright to that work. In some instances writers must purchase the right to reproduce the words of others.

Copyright protects the investment in time and money that writers and publishers make to produce a work. It helps guarantee that the work can not be sold by someone else without permission. Copyright protects intellectual property—a particular expression on an idea. There is no denying the usefulness and need for copyright protection. Whereas plagiarism guidelines offer conventions for giving credit to colleagues, copyright protection offers rules to govern the commerce of intellectual property—its sale and trade.

A journal for students on the Web needs to consider both copyright and plagiarism carefully, especially in light of how new copyright laws are being shaped. At the same time, these journals should offer a place to rethink plagiarism as well, how it is taught, and what constitutes it. First, there will be times when students may meet all the requirements for citing sources correctly so that they do not plagiarize, but where they still might be in copyright violation. For example, if a student writes a paper that quotes lyrics from a song and in doing so quotes more than 10% of four lines of the song, they will have exceeded fair use guidelines and might have entered into a copyright trespass. So students need to learn the current practices all published writers must concern themselves with.

However, Web-based journals can offer a place to look at plagiarism and copyright anew. For example, one of the promises of hypertext is that it would allow readers to become writers in the same textual space that they are reading. With print, the reader has the margins, and notebooks, and their own essays, but in electronic writing, readers can insert the cursor in the midst of the text they are reading. They can edit it. Copy it. Delete it. Add to it. With hypertext they can change links, add new links. They are not stopped by the technology from completely taking over the text. They can let the words wash over them, they can swim in them, breathe and write in them, between the lines, between the words. The fluidity of pixels becomes like water in Rich's poem; it allows the reader to become writer, to become part of the piece.

Yet this can only happen to the fullest extent if the reader is free to use the words as if they were their own, without regard to plagiarism or copyright. Readers have always been able to do this on the privacy of their own hard drives. Thus the beauty of disk-based hypertext. Once acquired, the owner can enjoy unlimited interaction. The same can be had, by the way, with most Web-based hypertext as well by downloading the files onto one's hard drive. With both Netscape's Navigator and Microsoft's Explorer including full HTML editors, readers can manipulate and change a Web-based hypertext as easily as they can a disk-based hypertext.

What readers cannot do in either case, without getting explicit permission from authors and publishers, is publish those appropriated pieces. So while the technology could allow full immersion into electronic texts, plagiarism custom and copyright law prevent fully sharing that feature, leaving the reader's writing isolated on a hard drive.

So one of the things Web journals—or some web journals—for students can do is to create copyright and plagiarism free zones. One way to do this is for a journal to adopt a Copyleft provision. Copyleft is a concept developed and promoted by the GNU (GNU is Not UNIX) project (www.gnu.org), a software design initiative that fosters software design cooperation by avoiding proprietary restrictions. To this end, GNU members and leaders formed a Free Software Foundation that promotes the concept of Copyleft. In this model, the FSF holds the "copyright" to initial software codes that it develops, but makes the software and coding language freely available to any programmer or group of programmers who wish to work with software. The one condition—the copyleft proviso—is that these programmers cannot make changes to software and then establish a proprietary restriction, a copyright, on their changes. There, GNU's licensing agreement is designed so that, in their own words, "instead of putting GNU software in the public domain, we copyleft" it. Copyleft says that anyone who redistributes the software, with or without changes, must pass along the freedom to further copy and change it. Copyleft guarantees that every user has freedom" (copyleft.html).

How could this apply to an academic Web journal? Computer programming is written in code, lines of code, a language of code much the way text and hypertext are written in a language (on the web these would be, for our purposes, English and hypertext markup language (HTML)). In essence, a journal could accept publications with the provision that those who contribute to the journal know that their work—their words and their hypertextual links—could be downloaded and revised—added to, relinked, freely inserted into the words of others, or, the reverse, others could freely insert their words into the text they download. That is, writers could play *in and around* the words and ideas of others as children play in and around a sandbox: reshaping, shifting, sweeping, piling up, adding to, bringing in other considerations.

Like the GNU license, these reformed pieces could not then be copyrighted elsewhere, they could be shared elsewhere, but not in a proprietary way. Authors who downloaded a piece from the journal and worked inside of it, would need to accurately describe, as do software designers when they make changes to a program, the kinds of changes they have made and where they have made them. Because in other realms, this type of writing would be problematic (say on a portfolio exam to meet a department's writing requirement) these revised pieces could not go just anywhere. Thus this model does carry with it some limits. However, it is also important to note that this kind of writing, appropriation and tweaking of others words both with and without attribution is not without precedent.

For example, lesson plan and syllabi swapping among teachers happens all the time, and often teachers will lift elements of a colleague's work whole hog and use it in their classroom or syllabi, altering the text as described earlier to fit their pedagogical needs more precisely. In e-mail exchanges it is not uncommon, in the flurry of reading and responding, for words and phrases to recur in others messages without always citing again the original writer. In *The Electronic Word*, Lanham (1993) provided the useful anecdote at the introduction of his first essay in the collection about an architecture critic who wanted to reuse his essay by substituting the word *architecture* or *building* where Lanham had *literature*.

A journal that freely offered its words for this kind of full insertion of the reader into the writing, would provide a safe ground for students to learn how to move among the ideas of others. Republishing pieces that have been altered in the same journal could prove a catalyst for the writers who have worked on it to come together to discuss the differences. The casting of pieces in different voices, with the adding of layers of meaning and development of ideas that would attend, also hearkens to other models of intellectual property and community of the type suggested in Lunsford and West's (1996) essay "Intellectual Property and Composition Studies."

In this essay, the authors note that "hypercitation and endless listing of sources are driven, for the most part, by the need to own intellectual property and to turn it into commodities that can be traded like tangible property, a *process of alienation* that is at the heart of copyright doctrine based on the abstract concept of work" (p. 397, italics added). They also add that "an additional motivation is also implied, however, if we view notes and bibliographies as means of extending the conversation signified by the text. It is this inclusive, thoroughly collaborative model—recalling the spirit exemplified in the medieval glossed book—that we want to emphasize here . . . " (p. 397). I think we can create web journals which do this, which allow a more "thoroughly collaborative model" for students especially that will help relieve the process of alienation[1] at the heart of copyright and plagiarism and hypercitation.

We also know, as much as we respect authorship, that much of what any given writer composes is shaped and to some degree predetermined by what they have read and heard. For example, it's not unusual for a writer to discuss the issue or theme about which he or she is writing. We might do it in class with our students, in hallways with colleagues outside our offices or at conferences, on e-mail lists. As we converse, we hear the ideas of others on the same theme, and those views shade our thinking and our writing. It is not unusual to find that we will write and publish something, often unattributed or uncited, that was profoundly shaped by those prior discussions.

Given that we do this orally, why not do it with what is written as well? An e-mail or Web-based discussion forum sponsored by the student journal could be a place where students could go to talk to other students. In e-mail messaging, it is not uncommon to pick up phrases and ideas read in other messages, sometimes with the quote feature, which delineates text, sometimes from merely reusing the ideas without quoting. If students participate in these discussions, contribute to the evolution of the idea under discussion, they should be able to draw from that discussion freely in their own writing. So a message they send to the discussion, which has incorporated the thoughts of others, could, without the need to cite or mention the others, be used in a student's paper. This is no different, really, from student essays that repeat arguments and ideas made in class discussions. Since this happens, why not create places in online journals where we can encourage this free exchange?

How might it work? Someone might write a hypertext with the idea that it will be published in the journal with a copyleft license, meaning it can be downloaded and that a reader or readers (an entire class perhaps) may change and revise it as much as they like, adding to and removing text at will. Furthermore, the reader or readers may republish the piece on the Web, perhaps in the same journal. They would need to describe the nature of their changes, but would not have to indicate every change with the kind of hypercitation and demarcations we use now—quotation marks around paraphrases, cited summaries, and set off full quotations.

For future readers, where the first writer's words end and subsequent writers' words begin will not be an issue. Writers would need to keep, where it can be readily found, a link to the original as they found it, allowing interested readers to move to the original. Furthermore, this new piece, based on a prior piece, could also be downloaded by another writer, again with the copyleft provision in place. No writer could publish their changes in any place that would put a copyright restriction of any kind upon it. Or we can imagine journals or sections of journals where citation-free, or citation-lite writing is encouraged. People do this all the time as they grow in a discipline, refer to major trends and theories without giving the full roster of authors they have read. It is done in presentations of papers at conferences where quite often the only authors cited are those who are directly quoted. It is done in e-mail discussions. It is often done when teachers lecture to their introductory classes, and after a time, an author or set of authors are assumed in seminar classes. We slip, when we engage our colleagues more intimately, into less formal modes of citing sources.

Why not encourage student essays that come after having read, having kept a reading journal, having discussed the ideas with classmates and other scholars, having had time to work and think about the ideas almost to the point where they forget how it is they know something? That is the journal would not require extensive works cited pages, letting writers instead get by with simple intext references as needed.

Another useful model to consider in this copyleft venture would be that initiated by *Feed Magazine* (www.feedmag.com), which features discussions of important works on hypertext in hypertext. For example, as of this writing, they have a piece online called "Miracle Device" wherein Coover, Amerika, and Murray (1998) are writing linked annotations to excerpts from Ted Nelson's *Literary Machines*. And linked to these discussions are reader comments on both the annotations and on Nelson's original work.

Each of the brief scenarios just outlined offers varied models and ways to imagine how Web journals can create a space for student voices that emphasizes the collaborative nature of most learning and thinking and writing. What the copyleft principle as sketched out also offers is a way for hypertext, a kind of writing supported and premised on postmodern literary theories by many of its advocates, to be a way for writing in and around texts in a way that frees writers from copyright restrictions, allowing them to share the links and words they add. One vision of Bush's (1945/1998) memex included the ability of users to swap and share their data, but with copyright restrictions and software licensing strictures, the ability to do that as fully as Bush imagined is limited.

And why not join our students on occasion? If we—working professionals in a discipline—contributed to these journals, we could do so in a way that address the students as colleagues both without condescending to them and without talking over their heads, much the way we do when we teach most thoughtfully. We could publish pieces and meet with students to discuss our work. We could waive copyright on these pieces, give them freely to be used by other teachers without requiring that they ever seek permission for excerpts that exceed fair use.

Journals like this could only work online, where content is malleable and easily accessed. There would need to be safe guards. Students would need to know that the experiments and rethinking of authorship pursued in these journals do not apply in other venues. They would need to know that it is still important, in other settings, to honor copyright and to respect the individual expressions of other writers. After all, for academics, citing other writers becomes both a matter of honor and a way of keeping track of whose work is important. Accreditation and hiring, tenure, and promotion committees like to know if a scholar's work is oft cited. Being frequently cited raises a reputation, leads to book contracts and speaking engagements. Citing sources also becomes a tacit way of acknowledge how our own ideas are intellectually constructed from the ideas of others. So I am not urging that we totally abandon our citation customs or citation economy. Including in these journals places for allowing the experimental suspension of citations and copyright, might help create a more fertile commons for the growth and feeding of intellectual ability, and ultimately, help better sustain the value of intellectual property.

I am suggesting that we need to try new models and that these models can help bring students into expanded learning communities more fully. By providing students online journals for publishing their work, and by creating journals that require the work be good, we offer students access to a wider audience. By using these journals in our own classes, with our students, we validate the writing and show that it has intellectual value, especially if we ask students to respond to the pieces by using them in their own research and thinking. By using the World Wide Web, these journal sites can become home to students of like interests, allowing them to form learning communities. Students can meet with article authors, write responses that would be linked to the essays, meet in MOOs to discuss pieces, swap research ideas and tips, have discussions with other writers about works in progress, arrange for cross-Web collaborations and writing projects, and begin to extend their intellectual work beyond the classroom. Coordinating with other classes and journal writers and editors would help make the use of the web as site for intellectual growth less of a hit-or-miss-search for the right source, and more a sustained learning venture. And by suspending in some cases or making much more informal our requirements for citing sources and copyright, we can allow students, and ourselves if we choose to follow this example, to dive more fully into the text, and that, to close on a pun, is the richest possibility.

NOTE

1. I emphasized *alienation* because as a freshman I recall having to read and consult handbooks and workbooks on paraphrasing, summarizing, quoting, and plagiarism, as a preface to writing a research paper, and it bored me

    The stuff was inaccessible because the examples either struck me as confusing or so self-evident that my reaction was always, "yeah, right; got it. ho hum." It was important, I knew, in an abstract way, because it was the kind of technical detail that could trip me up, but it meant nothing to me cognitively—in my own writing—nor personally. So for years I simply didn't paraphrase because it was such a bother, and my idea of research was to regurgitate what I had read.

    But part of the problem too was that we were told to do research before writing, and to create an outline and to select quotes that would be appropriate in different parts of the outline. So we started always with this mass of information from experts (defined as published writers whose stuff was in the library, and therefore sanctioned), and we had to somehow find a way to say something into all of those words.

So the unsaid response would always be this to the teacher, "well everything in this paper is from some sources, so every sentence will have a citation of some kind, so what's the point? What am *I* doing here?" It really is a scary and naked feeling, like walking into a trap. I need to have a voice and point of view, but there's no room for my voice and point of view among all these experts I am quoting and citing. It became a technical game, a boring technical game, to get in and out of my own paper safely, without a penalty and a rewrite.

I remember that so well.

WORKS CITED

Bartholomae, D. (1985). Inventing the university. In *When a writer can't write: Studies in writer's block and other composing problems* (pp. 237-262). New York: Guilford Press.

Bush, V. (1998, January 12). As we may think. *The Atlantic Unbound.* www.theatlantic.com/unbound/ flashbks/computer/bushf.htm (Originally published in *The Atlantic Monthly* , July, 1945)

Coover, R., Amerika, M., & Murray, J. (1998, March 2). Miracle device. *Feed Magazine.* www.feedmag.com/html/document/98.02nelson /98.02nelson_master.htm.

GNU Project—Free Software Foundation (FSF). (1998, February 23). What is copyleft? www.gnu.org/copyleft/copyleft.html.

Howard, R. M. (1995). Plagiarisms, authorships, and the academic death penalty. *College English, 57*(7), 708-736.

Lanham, R. (1993). *The electronic word: Democracy, technology, and the arts.* Chicago: University of Chicago Press.

Lunsford, A. A., & West, S. (1996). Intellectual property and composition studies. *College Composition and Communication, 47*(3), 383- 411.

Rich, A. (1973). *Diving into the wreck: Poems, 1971-1972* (1st ed.). New York: Norton.

chapter 2.3

A MESHING OF MINDS:

THE FUTURE OF ONLINE RESEARCH FOR PRINT AND ELECTRONIC PUBLICATION?

Michael Day

This chapter does not suggest that the current model for research leading to publication will ever disappear. It does, however, suggest that the electronic media will have made possible so many more forms of contact between and among minds and archived information that either the definition of research will change, or we will have to come up with a new word for what electronic research will have become.

In the past, and in other cultures (and perhaps in the future?), people were not and are not so concerned with the ownership of words and ideas, or with the privilege of originality of thought. Ideas were, and are shared because they make sense and add to the common good. Could the collaborative communities forming on the Internet help us get past the objectification and commoditization of the words and thoughts so prevalent now in the publishing and legal arenas?

Already, the network of information sharing has become decentralized and rhizomatic, having, like the Internet, bypassed some of the major institutionalized sources of information. Publishers and academic institutions may never disappear, but their role in research and the dissemination of information will have to change, in that publishers will have to move some of what they print to the online realm, and academic institutions will need to recognize the importance of online research and publication.

Anyone and everyone who wants them will have web pages, but we will cease to care about the proliferation of junk on the Web because search engines will have improved to the point that we will be able to find more of what we need and less of what we don't. And because the novelty will have worn off and schools will teach critical Web literacy, researchers will be able to identify and avoid biased and poorly documented sources.

But the primary focus for this chapter is the ways in which the Internet and the Web will allow research to become even more collaborative, and the possibility that many of the researchers who collaborate will care much less about who owns ideas and who gets credit for them than they do about making those ideas available to the widest possible audience.

For some, the act of research itself is becoming a vastly different process. Of course, the migration of much information to the Web makes these sources available from the personal computer, but more and more researchers are also using e-mail and synchronous environments such as MUDs and MOOs to tap what Rheingold (1993) called the "living database" of connected scholars on the Internet (p. 115).

Within the living database, one can still quote and cite "experts" in a field, but more and more, because of the synergistic nature of knowledge formation within the online media, it is impossible to identify a single source for an idea, so crediting a source other than the group is close to impossible.

This new form of "research" is largely conversational, not at all like the traditional notion of publication in which one carefully builds an argument through page after page. It is dialogic, even polylogic, and often makes use of dialectic reasoning. The speed and convenience of online exchange of ideas allow greater inclusion of the voices of others engaged in agonistic discourse. It allows interaction and response to be incorporated into the weave of a "document," changing the very nature of what we will call a document.

As others in this volume have noted, Web publishing of research allows much faster dissemination of ideas than print publication. And because webbed publications generally are not purchased, they can spread further, into more hands that need them. These factors problematize issues of ownership, copyright, and originality, and will force the research and publication community to recast ethical and legal constraints on the usage and sharing of information.

PROLOGUE

In order to divine the future of research, it may be useful to first look back to the past, and then to extend our gaze to cultures around the world. For current notions of originality and ownership of words and ideas are heavily dependent on a historical turn of events, a turn that did not affect all cultures equally. And when all is said and done, the larger forces of history and the worldly context will play upon what research will have become in 20, 50, or 100 years.

MEDIEVAL TO RENAISSANCE EUROPE

In the prehistoric world, oral storytelling and oral histories carried much knowledge through time. What a culture knew and shared was only by virtue of a person or people being able to remember it by telling and retelling it. Even during these times, the authority or truthfulness of the words could be strengthened by reference to a particularly well-known leader or storyteller, who was reputed to have uttered them. But ownership and authorship were not as important as was sharing the words and ideas.

The carryover from the ancient world into written and printed works in medieval times can be found in what Ong (1965) called "oral residue" in printed texts. That is, although a text may have been handcopied or rudimentarily printed, it retains much of the feel and structure of an orally transmitted story. More important, however, is the fact that texts were shared among people and often read aloud, for few were literate. So texts were not always seen as private artifacts experienced in solitary confinement. They were public and communal, an act of sharing.

Moreover, the texts of this age were extremely derivative. Chaucer's stories, such as the *Canterbury Tales*, were based on other stories he had read or heard. His style and delivery may have been different, but overall, the stories were nearly identical to plays and stories which had previously been presented by some other author; even the frame technique he used came from Bocaccio's *Decameron*.

Furthermore, the idea of single text authorship was not well established up through the Middle Ages, other than the exceptions of Chaucer and the Gawain poet and some biblical writers. Most of the texts of this age were not accredited to anyone; they were public tales, passed from the oral storytelling tradition into text without much accounting for the authorship or ownership of the stories.

For instance, all the Arthurian legends existed long before they showed up in the manuscripts. The stories were written down, but the notion of a single author of the tales was not important because ideas were to be shared, They were part of a community memory, not something to be owned and hoarded.

Moving to Shakespeare's plays, we know that they were taken from a variety of sources, including *Holinshed's Chronicles,* and we know that Shakespeare was none too careful about documenting these sources. It was transmitting the story, not the name of the author, that was considered important. *Hamlet* came from Saxo Grammaticus' *Historia Danica* (c. 1200) by way of Francois de Belleforest in his *Histoires Tragiques* (1576), and *The Winter's Tale* came from *Pandosto: The Triumph of Time,* a popular novel by Robert Greene, 1588. Even *King Lear* came from a story called *The True Chronical History of King Leir, and his three daughters, Gonorill, Ragan, and Cordella.*

As can be seen, much sharing and copying went on just a few hundred years ago, but these days, historical scholars of literature have a driving impulse to ascribe authorship, originality, and ownership to texts written in a time in which these issues did not seem to matter. Why is it such a big issue to us in the modern and postmodern age?

Classical education relied on educational practices that lasted well into the renaissance, such as the imitation of good models that was the mainstay of the rhetorical education which formed one third of the *trivium* (Murphy, 1982). It was no crime to copy the style and idea structures of others; indeed, such copying was considered the best way to develop one's own skills in written and spoken communication.

Books of the age, such as Erasmus' *De Copia,* and other rhetorical treatises with emphasis on the *topoi* (topics or commonplaces of argument), made it clear that there were only a few basic kinds of ideas, and that one learned to communicate well by using them and imitating good models. There was little emphasis on sources of ideas except when one needed to add an ethical appeal to the argument by name-dropping.

Scholars of oral tradition such as Ong (1982) maintain that the use of commonplaces and imitated phrasings is formulaic and represents a holdover from pre literate times. From the age of oral tradition through the Renaissance, the prevalent belief was that knowledge and ideas were communally owned, so that they could not be owned or stolen. Good ideas and stories were passed along on as much on their own merit as on the merit of the author's name.

JAPAN

I choose Japan because I have lived and worked there for about 5 years. I use the Japanese as an example of a tendency, not to condemn them in any way. We have all heard the stereotype of the Japanese as consummate imitators and the charge that they copy ideas from other countries and make infinitely better products from those ideas. To the Japanese, copying ideas and things and making them better is a valued skill; it is not considered as some sort of stealing or the sign of lack of creativity.

In Japan, originality is in some ways counterproductive to the notion of community and shared interests. Thus, it is often considered bad form to disagree or to go off on a different tangent. There is nothing to be ashamed about following the well-trodden paths of others when reporting on research.

Furthermore, standards of citation and intellectual property are somewhat more lax than in the United States. I give two examples. The first concerns my upper level English literature students at both Osaka and Kobe universities, two of the top universities in Japan. They were perceptive readers, and fair at textual analysis, and yet when it came time to doing research, scrupulously using quotes, and providing attribution, they were remarkably naive. They would think nothing of reading Wayne Booth, then using his critical approach on a short story without so much as mentioning Booth's name or putting anything in quotes. When I asked why they had not quoted or cited Booth, they said that if what Booth had written was obviously true, then why should it be necessary to mention or quote him? What we see here is a tendency to view ideas, especially published ideas, as being in the public domain, as opposed to being private property, off limits. Thus, my students had no qualms about using them without framing them in the code of proper attribution.

Second, this trend of laxity in citation is even more evident in some of the scholarly writing I looked at in Japan. In my research on Japanese rhetoric, I can recall countless times when I came to an idea or statement that I *knew* came from some other, often Western scholar, but in many cases the author would not be named. I would only see a phrase such as "According to a revered American scholar . . ." and then the text, without quotes, and without a citation. If the author was named, more than likely the name of the specific work and the page number would not be listed. Or, I would get very close, and the work would be listed, but no page number or publication information given.

The way we teach research in the United States, such an impossible-to-follow research trail would be evidence of bad scholarship, yet in Japan it is more acceptable among academic researchers. This tendency only hints at the relatively insignificant role of originality and ownership of ideas in Japanese culture. It is more important to share the ideas than it is to spend extra time painstakingly documenting the source of every idea or phrase. To underscore this tendency, I should note that Japanese copyright laws are much more relaxed than ours.

Perhaps the tendency toward more leniency about ownership of ideas in Japan arises not only out of an urge to share and be community-minded, but also because people understand that every idea we have, as original as we might think it to be, is actually prefigured and influenced by the ideas of others. In a way, this chapter is not mine at all, but instead was stolen in fragments from talks I have given and from everyone I have read and heard (who in turn stole it from others). This is but one part of what Bloom (1975) called "the anxiety of influence" in his book of the same title. If *nothing* is original, why should we be so concerned with being original or attempting to own the ideas we think are ours?

This concept is certainly in accordance with the common stereotype of the Japanese as group minded. The tendency, described in detail by Doi Takeo (1973) in *The Anatomy of Dependence*, suggests that an average Japanese never thinks as an isolated individual; knowledge, thoughts, actions and behaviors are all socially constructed by the group. Knowledge is shared willingly by all for the common good. Similar notions govern attitudes in other Asian countries; the rampant piracy and copyright violations on software, music, and videos in much of Asia are but crude examples.

WHERE WE ARE NOW

The current emphasis on ownership and originality of ideas, to some degree, comes from the rise of the romantic notion of the individual author, alone in a room, writing completely original work. The evolution of the modern university hiring, tenure, and promotion system also forced scholars to make sure that they received proper credit for what they published and that all published research was sufficiently original (i.e., not borrowed and not collaboratively produced). Finally, the royalty system, with the promise of profit from original copyrighted-protected works, brought us to our current zealously protective and litigious attitudes toward ownership of ideas and words.

It is no accident that Ong subtitled his most popular text, *Orality and Literacy*, "The Technologizing of the Word," for it was the technologies of the printing press, distribution transportation, and electronic media which brought about the major shift in the ways in which words were conceived and disseminated.

In his Pulitzer Prize winning novel, *House Made of Dawn*, N. Scott Momaday (1968) eloquently described the spiritual effects of the technologizing of the word. His character, the Rev. John Tosomah preaches:

> In the white man's world, language . . .—and the way in which the white man thinks of it—has undergone a process of change. The white man takes such things as words and literatures for granted, as indeed he must, for nothing in his world is so commonplace. On every side of him there are words by the millions, an unending succession of pamphlets and papers, letters and books, bills and bulletins, commentaries and conversation. He has diluted and mutilated the Word, and words have begun to close in upon him. He is sated and insensitive; his regard for language—for the Word itself—as an instrument of creation has diminished nearly to the point of no return. It may be that he will perish by the word. (p. 95)

Words have become commodities, objects to be bought and sold. Through the Rev. Tosomah, Momaday may want to indicate that the transfer of wisdom though oral storytelling is better than its dissemination through printed words. Yet novelists such as Leslie Silko (Work & Cowell, 1981) and Toni Morrison (Le Clair, 1981) claim that contemporary writers can reclaim and disseminate some of the power of the old stories by careful retelling in print, through what Morrison referred to as "village literature" (p. 34). The combined and collaborative wisdom of the peoples of the earth can carry us forward in wisdom to a future just as replete with stories, in fact more so. For the stories in print can be spread far and wide, and the potential for even greater sharing grows with electronic media and the Internet.

Implicit in Momaday's critique of our modern use of words is the threat that print and computers will desiccate and dilute words. Does the absence of a human voice and a body voicing words suck them dry? Do electronic words lose meaning and effect, didactic or poetic? Is computer-mediated communication (CMC) somehow inhuman? Certainly, the specter of dehumanization is the stereotype we've seen in this century through novels such as Orwell's *1984* and Vonnegut's *Player Piano*—in these books computers meant centralized control and the death of individuality.

The current media hysteria over the dangers of the Internet only serves to whip public opinion into a frenzy with visions of chat room pedophiles and a generation of computer geeks walled off from the world by a glass screen of light and pixellated words. For example, I recently read about two college students, at either end of their dorm room, chatting with each other by e-mail on their computers, rather than facing each other and speaking. Some of the absurdities of CMC do seem worrisome.

Even if some of these problems are becoming a danger, I see another, more positive trend evolving, one that brings people together instead of separating them. Purists will argue that no true community or relationship can exist without physical presence, because community means that living bodies are gathered in the same place. However, we do know that some of the pioneers of cyberspace have found many benefits to doing collaborative research on the Internet, and most, if not all of them would argue that the gathering of minds in Internet discussion groups constitutes a form of community.

Indeed, the Internet may have been created for the U.S. Department of Defense to route sensitive information anywhere in the United States in case of attack, but the researchers who first got hold of it seized on its capabilities for sharing information and fostering communication and collaboration. They found not just lifeless words on a page or a screen, but an interactive medium, capable of carrying and sharing their thoughts with others. Unwittingly, they broke ground for new forms of community building, through the invention of such media as e-mail, Internet discussion lists, Usenet newsgroups, Internet Relay Chat (IRC), and MOO.

Internet media have helped researchers overcome geography, distance, separation, and isolation from their peers, and have already increased the speed and volume of research interaction. Print-bound research had to be submitted to journals, and research communities had to wait months, even years, for new ideas. Those who wished to respond or contend then had to repeat the lengthy cycle of print publication to be heard.

The fast-and-furious controversy over cold fusion on the alt.fusion usenet discussion group in 1989 is one early example of the way in which the speed and convenience of the Internet can change the process of research and dissemination of results. In less than 1 month, cold fusion as a potential energy source was reported, discussed, and generally found to be less promising than originally thought. In the archived cold fusion discussion (see the URL in the Works Cited list), one finds several messages a day carrying the debate forward, and adding new information. In conventional academic journal publishing, this same process of discovery, report, and discussion of findings usually takes years. As my colleague Robert Corey notes, Internet e-mail discussion has become a fine mesh of scrutiny through which new ideas and discoveries are filtered before they ever reach print.

Furthermore, according to Rheingold and others, researchers on the Internet have begun to form online communities based on interest, not geographic location. Previously, researchers around the world had no easy way to come together to chat informally, except for the occasional conference for those who could afford it. Now many researchers are using e-mail discussion groups and sharing their findings on web pages.

And yet, many claim that the sense of place and belonging that is so important to the wisdom of the oral tradition cannot be replicated in cyberspace. This much is true: in the foreseeable future, there will never be bodies in cyberspace, all science fiction depictions to the contrary. However, there is a meeting of minds possible on the net, in which individuality and identity can be built. Whether he is right or not about it being a place, Rheingold called some networked discussion groups a kind of "third place," a place outside of work and the home where people can relax and share ideas freely (Oldenburg, 1991, p. 86; Rheingold, 1993, p. 25).

It is the relaxed sharing of ideas and the self-publishing capabilities offered by the World Wide Web that offers the most promise for the future of research. The Internet allows a new kind of collaboration in which participants can engage from the comfort of home or local office. Increasingly more researchers are using CMC to combine their expertise on projects and to make known their shared findings.

For example, for the last 10 years, I have been part of an ongoing community of computers and writing teacher-researchers who are busy re-inventing the ways we conceive of and teach communication with computers and the Internet. I was relatively isolated at a large research institution where almost no one was interested in my field, but found that I gained a sense of grounding, community, and purpose when I joined the online discussions in the computers and writing field.

Soon I was moving from casual e-mail exploration of ideas to collaborating on print publications and conference presentations using the ideas we had explored online. These publications and presentations were necessarily collaborative and multiauthored because of the method of their genesis. This method of developing ideas is largely conversational, not at all like the "individual investigator" model we tend to think of in conjunction with publishing research. Indeed, the online collaborative research in which I participate differs greatly from the traditional model, in which one must carefully build an argument through page after page, and wait months for a response.

The sort of collaborative research experience I describe here may never supercede the individual research model, but it certainly offers a new way of generating and processing ideas in text on a computer network. This method is close to a form of dialectic; it is inherently dialogic and at times even polylogic, when many voices join to discuss a topic. Or, in more simple terms, it is like a ping-pong or tennis game, with a rhythm of hours or days for e-mail and of seconds of minutes for synchronous environments.

Hundreds of individuals in the computers and writing field meet and collaborate weekly or even more often, and gain a great deal in terms of sharing ideas for research and teaching. And they are not alone; researchers in many other fields have similar interactions. But it can't really be called publication, when one goes up for tenure and promotion. Yet it is a valuable form of idea-generation that provides intellectual stimulation and is indeed more fruitful for than some of the tedious writing one often feels obligated to do for publication.

Many academics say that they would not be able to receive credit for their networked discussion in tenure and promotion decisions. However, many groups, such as the Modern Language Association, and the Conference on College Composition and Communication, have put together guidelines for those who perform electronic scholarship, and those who employ these networked scholars (see URLs in the Works Cited list). An issue of *Computers and Composition* (Vol. 17, No. 1, 2000) has been devoted to a discussion of these matters.

Indeed, in answer to a question about using e-mail discussion for "formal" research requirements, Carbone (1997) said:

> I don't want to use this stuff for anything other than kicking around ideas; this is low-stakes, high energy writing, and raising the stakes would lower the energy. I couldn't go with one draft, typos be damned. Though there are messages I reread where I sure wish I had looked back. But I like my email oral. (see Appendix A)

He likes his e-mail oral? What? Can e-mail be oral? What Carbone said made me remember Ong's (1982) *Orality and Literacy*, and then think back to another conversation I took part in, in 1993, on an Internet e-mail discussion called Ortrad-L. We were discussing Ong's notion that, after the rise of the age of print media, TV and radio, because they bring the human voice back into communication, could be called "secondary orality" (Ong, 1982, p. 136).

The members of the list struggled with the terminology; some wanted to call the speedy e-mail exchanges and synchronous discussions "tertiary orality" because they are so much like conversation, and often as informal.

Oddly enough, this generated fascinating discussion within the medium (see Appendix B). Some wanted to know whether we could call it oral if it made no sound; properly it does not. But it *does* have a strong "voice," a voice that only good writers can produce—a friendly, engaging, nonthreatening voice. In the end, we concluded that it might just be some sort of hybrid, not oral, not literate in the conventional sense.

However, the interchange reminded me of the "oral" traits of e-mail and synchronous discussions that set them apart from printed research findings. The synchronous discussion groups are decidedly on the "oral" side because they are fast and furiously typed by discussants in something of a hurry to get ideas out. Writers in this medium are not too worried about spelling, punctuation, and mechanics, since the pressure to produce outweighs the pressure to be correct. They use the additive (as opposed to subordinative) style, which Ong (1982) noted as a feature of oral discourse. E-mail discussion groups, especially those for teachers of writing, generally are not such a free-for all. And yet, for busy professionals, who probably would not post had they to laboriously proofread and edit every submission, a fair amount of rambling and mechanical incorrectness is tolerated. It is okay, in many groups that share research, to sacrifice some correctness for the sake of speedy and copious exploration of ideas. Like any rhetorical act, the degree of correctness required depends on audience expectations, purpose, and how permanent the e-mail message is expected to be.

In one post on Ortrad-L, I saw the words *epistolary* and *renaissance* used together in the same paragraph (see Appendix B, Message 1). These words reminded me of the age of Sam Johnson, in which letters were a primary form of idea exchange, a sign of literate culture. Such letter exchanges waned with the coming of what Ong calls secondary orality, such as telephone, radio, and TV. Information overload from a variety of media meant that fewer people were willing to pick up a pen, or sit down at a typewriter and compose a written missive.

But lately, we are seeing an "epistolary renaissance" in the explosion of letter writing made possible by the popularization of e-mail. College students now routinely get accounts at school, and suddenly begin to keep in touch with their parents like never before. More families and old friends rekindle correspondences and share thoughts. One might argue that this form of epistolarianism is just information exchange, certainly not a form of high literacy, or in any way related to research. But now more scholars are sharing ideas via e-mail, discussion groups, and the Web.

Scholars are thinking, then writing to others to explore their thoughts, and sometimes writing to others in order to develop and organize thoughts; this is a kind of heuristic in which the presence of a known audience helps to crystallize thought as it comes into being.

These scholars get help from others, and the collaborative development of ideas into theories, debates, and concrete plans is a kind of synergistic force, seemingly with its own logic.

The speed of e-mail can make this research process faster than conventional mail, and synchronous discussions make it even faster. We don't have to go through the laborious process of submission, acceptance, editing, and publishing, in which it often takes years to get ideas out.

Furthermore, many of the new electronic scholars are willing to share ideas freely, so ownership is not so important. This tendency to share might be a corollary of the hacker's motto: "Information wants to be free," but it may also be a kind of altruism that has risen from the frustrations of lengthy publication processes, as well as the difficulty of using good ideas covered by copyright. Electronic media are going to force a change in the notions of originality, ownership of ideas, and copyright soon, because of the sheer impossibility of preventing ideas and texts from spreading, from being reproduced infinitely and effortlessly, like viruses. Infinite reproduction and fast electronic transmission make it impossible not to share; one has only to look at the way the Web has made all kinds of texts available, texts which are good, bad, legal and illegal by the present laws.

WHERE WE MIGHT WE BE GOING? WHAT COULD RESEARCH HAVE BECOME IN THE FUTURE?

The new trend in research seems to be toward acknowledging the process of collaborative thought, of thought *doing* as opposed to thought *being*. A published text, once crystallized in print is immutable, but Internet discussion and even web pages can be changed often. We are moving toward the recognition that every published thought is only a way-station, a particular instantiation of what the context seemed to dictate; a publication is merely a still photo of a more complicated process. These still photos are calcified; they serve as major records of thought, but are monolithic. It can take years to chisel them down, to change and grow them.

Or, from calculus, we might think of CMC research as more like incremental pictures of the thought process coming into being. These closely spaced increments are closer to a motion picture than still photos. In the process of CMC research, we can see thought becoming organized in increments, increasingly smaller increments, somewhat like the way Pynchon (1973) theorized the process of representation in

Gravity's Rainbow as a kind of calculus of thought. In this new model of research, the asynchronous posts or synchronous conversations are but steps on the pathway, the moving toward, but never arriving. Discussants are involved in getting under and around complicated ideas, pulling them, stretching them, tweaking them, but never considering them finished.

In the voice of the medicine man Betonie in her novel *Ceremony*, Silko (1977) wrote that "Things which don't shift and grow are dead things" (p. 126). It has occurred to me more than once that printed texts cannot shift and grow, and may be dead, in one way of thinking, and that the more frequent instantiations of computer-mediated texts could be seen as shifting and growing. Thought must move and grow and shift; many people get thought to move through writing, by trying out ideas, often by writing to and with others. Formal print publication hides this process, but perhaps for a good reason. Anyone who has graded student papers or who has been assailed by too much bad poetry will understand why it is not necessary to read every draft of every written work. Reading work in progress might be a waste of time to some researchers; the more traditional scholars might become impatient at work that needs polishing. Furthermore, it may be wise to ask whether we should turn our souls inside out and report on every step of our search for meaning, simply because we can.

For some audiences, the resultant faster dissemination of ideas makes networked discussion an excellent medium for collaborative research. Those who do not want to watch the thought forming need not bother. But if thought is a movement and never really stops growing, why shouldn't we let more of its development go public, for people who are interested in the discussions? And why should we not value this "publication" on some scale that would get the discussants the kind of credit they need for personnel reviews, hiring, tenure, and promotion decisions? We need to be proactive, to take a strong position on what kind of writing "counts" and what kinds of discursive research communities are of value to us, and to make strong arguments to those we work for and with about why these networked exchanges are valuable.

No one is arguing that we need to replace print publications altogether. They have their place, like monuments at the great intersections of the pathways of thought. But with new technologies proliferating, the Internet becoming as common as TV and the telephone, and megabytes becoming cheaper by the millisecond, what could be wrong with giving credit to the milestones along the way? It might be good to think of a future in which there will be a complementarity between print and online texts, with each serving different purposes. We savor books and journals because of the portability, the smell and feel of the medium, and the knowledge that the text will never change on us. However, we also revel in online texts because they represent the fast-changing meeting of minds, a *doing* and not a *being*. They are infinitely reproducible, and travel effortlessly at close to the speed of light into our homes, schools, and offices. Having more choices—books, journals, newspapers, letters, videos, e-mail discussions, and online chats—can only provide a richer soil in which the researcher can dig.

Researchers may lament the situation if many books and journals stop being published because of economics, but simple economics may be enough to stop much print publication. Low readership and high production costs make it impossible for some publications to stay in print. We love the library as a place to revel in the shadow of great books, and to finger along the spines in the stacks for a chance find, a serendipitous discovery which will give us just the information we need. The tragedy of our era is that the funding for libraries is in danger of dying out with the move toward "efficiency," and libraries full of books could become a rarity.

POSTSCRIPT: IN THE NEXT MILLENNIUM, WHAT WILL RESEARCHERS CALL LITERACY? WHAT LANGUAGE WILL STUDENTS LEARN?

Will students be required to use a new dialect, a kind of Standard Internet English, the unwitting result of so many people writing to each other on computer networks and falling unconsciously into new patterns, new discursive conventions introduced like viruses? Will the sheer force of the kind of vocabulary chronicled in JargonWatch in *WIRED* magazine and collected in Branwyn's (1997) *Jargon Watch: A Pocket Dictionary for the Jitterati* cause a shift in the English idiom?

We may see more of the Microsoftening and Wordperfecting of the language, the use only of spellings and grammatical constructions approved by the dictionaries and style sheets of the most current text editors. But how much should researchers allow the software to dictate what's acceptable? As I write now, my words are interrupted by red and green squiggles, supposedly to help me improve my spelling and grammar. But do these squiggles know what I want to say? Are we in danger of letting the oversimplified rules of the programs determine how we can utter ideas? I hear Sam Johnson grumbling in his grave, and I see a generation of students dutifully unsquiggling their prose—and in so doing voiding it of artistry and originality.

Ultimately, many researchers expect that notions of literacy will change as technologies of communication and representation change. What we come to call literacy may move beyond print and text literacy to encompass computer, Internet, and media literacy. Media literacy will most likely become more valuable as technologies to transmit graphics, video, and sound become cheaper and ubiquitous, not only through one-way TV and radio, but also through the two- and multi-way channels of computer networks. To the researcher, and especially to the budding researchers in the K-12 classroom, media literacy will become increasingly important. That includes not only knowing how to develop ideas in all media, including hypertext, the web, and video, but also knowing how to be critics of all media forms.

In fact, in 1996 the National Council of Teachers of English (NCTE) passed a Visual Literacy resolution which suggested the need for media literacy beyond text and print forms. By voting to pass this resolution (see URL in the Works Cited list), NCTE members agreed that students should know about how to use and critique visual media.

But those who research the teaching of writing still appreciate the many uses of text, and feel secure about requiring text literacy in the classroom. Most agree that there are features of text that can describe the world of ideas and the depth of human experience and emotion better than any other media. Text can communicate with audiences in a way no other media can. The creative imagination engages with text, so that readers create their own mental pictures. Reading and writing promote a different kind of cognitive development from the processing of images and sounds, a sort of cognitive development that complements other forms of understanding. We would lose much if we abandoned text literacy.

DRAWBACKS THE NEW COMPUTER-BASED RESEARCHER WILL FACE

Many computer-based researchers are having to deal with information overload: How many web pages and e-mail messages should we have to look at? The speed and ease of information transmission are a double-edged sword. Researchers who use e-mail and have their addresses on web pages know how much e-mail can pile up in a day, and they are nearly overwhelmed by the volume of pure junk e-mail they get. If everyone has access to us through e-mail, we need to be swift and exact executors of the delete key.

Furthermore, for many, utterances in e-mail and synchronous chat tend to be very brief, bare-bones communications. If we are in such a hurry, is sustained, considered written thought possible? How do we pass on to our students the value of sustained argument if everything comes to them in 5-second video clips and sound bytes, and screen-sized e-mail, and web pages? Do we risk shortening the expected attention span? It is at this critical juncture that reminding students of the value of books and journals for sustained inquiry could be very important for researchers like me, who are also teachers.

Like many of today's researchers, I spend far too much time sitting in front of a glass and silicon machine. It hurts me, and if I don't get up and stretch frequently enough, it causes physical problems like repetitive stress injury, not to mention general inactivity. As a teacher, I want to be up to date and use the technologies I research with my students. And yet, to what degree should I be willing to subject my body to pain and injury? I hope that the future will bring ergonomic developments to make working with computers easier on the body. Otherwise, it will be hard to justify putting the human body through such agony.

Furthermore, many will agree that we have to put up with too much mediation when we research and communicate with computers. For input, you have a keyboard, and have to type and correct your mistakes, or you have to read a screen, which gives you eyestrain and a headache. Even with videoconferencing like CU See Me, you can't really be with others. However, all communication is mediated to some degree; even in face to face situations, our bodies, voices, eyes, and brain mediate what we put forth and understand.

For some of the reasons just cited, not only do I believe that oral and printed words will survive long into the next millennium, I believe that we will be better off if they do. We need that crucial balance between and among media, but above all, we need to be together and use our voices to share ideas from time to time. It does not have to be either complete acceptance or complete rejection of technology.

THE TRANSGENIC RESEARCHER

Haynes (1998) has coined a new set of terms (she called them organic metaphors) which I believe help to explain some of the attitudes toward technology currently held by researchers. Those who cheerlead wholeheartedly for an uncritical embrace of technology she called **vivogenic**; those who take the doom and gloom position, and equate the new technologies with the death of humanity and the individual are *pathogenic*; and those who move beyond the simple dichotomy of either/or she called *transgenic*. Haynes said that "the transgenic (non)model thrives in the matrix of rhetorical and textual writing technologies" and "includes new genres (like hypertext), new tropes (like speed) and new morphings of identity (like software agents, or emissaries)" (p. 12). It is finally to the balanced and forward-thinking transgenic viewpoint that the researcher of the future must move. Researchers need to make use of the newest tools, like hypertext, and the most helpful prosthetics, such as intelligent software agents, along with Internet discussions, books, and journals to find and assemble information to share with others.

COPYLEFT: THE FUTURE OF COPYRIGHT?

As online research becomes more widespread, publishers and writers alike will recognize the futility of attempting to protect all online works from appropriation and dissemination by others, especially the casual online discussions through which more and more research now advances. We can expect to see further extensions of the notion of "fair use" to include almost any use of an online work that (a) acknowledges the originator and (b) does not result in financial gain for the user. Because the cost of production and dissemination associated with print publication virtually vanishes for online works, many works should be available for free, without restrictions aside from acknowledgment.

An example is the notion of "copyleft," a software licensing agreement dreamed up by Free Software Foundation founder Richard Stallman to protect his free software programs such as GNU EMACS from appropriation and sale by profit-greedy companies. The copyleft licensing agreement "lets people do anything they want with the software except restrict others' right to copy it" (Garfinkle, 1994, p. 135). According to Stutz (1997):

> Copyleft contains the normal copyright statement, asserting ownership and identification of the author. However, it then gives away some of the other rights implicit in the normal copyright: it says that not only are you free to redistribute this work, but you are also free to change the work. However, you cannot claim to have written the original work, nor can you claim that these changes were created by someone else. Finally, all derivative works must also be placed under these terms.

Building on Stallman's work, Stutz also recommended the application of copyleft principles to nonsoftware works, such as the online research and writing common to academic discourse in "cyberia." Stutz said that copyleft is crucial to the survival of community and free information sharing in the digital age:

With computers, perfect copies of a digital work can easily be made—
and even modified, or further distributed—by others, with no loss of the
original work. As individuals interact in cyberia, sharing information—
then reacting and building upon it—is not only natural, but this is the
only way for individual beings to thrive in a community. In essence, the
idea of copyleft is basic to the natural propagation of digital information
among humans in a society. This is why the regular notion of copyright
does not make sense in the context of cyberia.

As seen earlier, the incremental free sharing and building of
information in Internet collaborations is becoming the model of a new
form of research. But according to Stutz, in cyberia, the idea of simply
placing works in the public domain won't work because of the profit
motive:

Simple "public domain" publication will not work, because some will
try to abuse this for profit by depriving others of freedom; as long as
we live in a world with a legal system where legal abstractions such as
copyright are necessary, as responsible artists or scientists we will need
the formal legal abstractions of copyleft that ensure our freedom and
the freedom of others.

It would be no great stretch to add the word *researchers* to the
artists and scientists just mentioned. Just as ownership and exclusive
rights to profit were protected under copyright, so would the freedom to
distribute but not to profit be protected under copyleft. The Free
Software Foundation offers guidelines and sample text for copylefting
work at http://gnu.april.org/philosophy/nonsoftware-copyleft.html.
Although copyleft might not be precisely what copyright will
have become, the principle and rationale of copyleft clearly favor the
unobstructed sharing of information for cyber-researchers of the future.
Ultimately, the needs of the many to collaborate and advance
knowledge outweigh the needs of the few to profit from ideas generated
incrementally by the living database of grassroots groupminds.

COLLABORATIVE RIGHTS; COLLECTIVE RECOGNITION: WE ARE THE BORG!

Somewhat in jest, I have recently taken to repeating a slogan any *Star
Trek* fan will recognize: "We are the Borg; resistance is few-tile!"
Although I have not been brainwashed (I hope!), for the last 10 years I
have been consumed by a dream of thought that is seamless among
individuals, that is produced by a hive-mind in which interdependence

is the key to generating new ideas. My work online with others in the computers and writing field has convinced me that we are a kind of what Byrd and Owens (1998, p. 49) call a "hivemind," and that our contribution to the growth of teachers in electronic environments has been greater since we act and think somewhat like a single organism. We don't always agree (indeed, "dissensus" is often more valuable for spurring us on than consensus); but challenge each other to clarify and explain; sometimes we even explain what each other mean. It's a strange and wonderful experience to have someone else explain what you mean better than you can.

But within this hivemind, building on the principle of copyleft, protecting the rights of individual authors does not make sense if the work is produced collaboratively. Copyleft ensures that works can be shared freely, but that credit is given all those who had a hand in their production. However, as stated earlier, university and college hiring, tenure, and promotion requirements will have to change so that collaborative scholarly endeavors can receive the credit they deserve. The well-wrought single-authored academic article or book should not be the only way that scholars can prove their worth; institutions should also recognize the value of Internet discussion groups, online conferences, and multiple-authored works as evidence of engagement in and contribution to a field or discipline.

We new online researchers must strive to explain the importance of collaborative online research to evaluators and administrators so that they have a rationale to give us the recognition we deserve. Better yet, some of us who understand the changing nature of online research need to become the administrators and join the committees making decisions about what constitutes valuable scholarly activity.

APPENDIX A: HE LIKES HIS E-MAIL ORAL!

From acw-l@ttacs6.ttu.edu Tue Sep 30 15:56:01 1997
Date: Tue, 30 Sep 1997 16:44:20 -0500
From: Nick Carbone <nickc@english.umass.edu>
To: Multiple recipients of list <acw-l@ttacs6.ttu.edu>
Subject: Re: research imperatives

On Tue, 30 Sep 1997, John McLaughlin wrote:

> Which of course means it can't be used for it either. If it *is* used
> for it, that bastardizes its original purpose, doesn't it?

Xactly. It's a personal thing with me, but I don't want to use this stuff for
anything other than kicking around ideas; this is low-stakes, high
energy writing, and raising the stakes would lower the energy. I
couldn't go with one draft, typos be damned. Though there are
messages I reread where I sure wish I had looked back. But I like my
email oral.

Nick Carbone, Writing Instructor
Marlboro College
Marlboro, VT 05344
nickc@marlboro.edu, but coming to you via nickc@english.umass.edu

APPENDIX B: AN EXAMPLE OF A COLLABORATIVE DISCUSSION AMONG RESEARCHERS ON THE INTERNET

Date: Mon, 1 Feb 1993 15:00:42 EST
Sender: "Comparative Oral Traditions Discussion List" <ORTRAD-
L%MIZZOU1.BitNet@pucc.PRINCETON.EDU>
From: "Kathryn Powell" <KPOWELL%IRISHVMA.BitNet
@pucc.PRINCETON.EDU>
Subject: Re: ORAL TRADITION AND LITERACY
To: Multiple recipients of list ORTRAD-L <ORTRAD-
L%MIZZOU1.BitNet@pucc.PRINCETON.EDU>
In-Reply-To: Message of Sat, 30 Jan 1993 12:40:14 CST from
<C509379@MIZZOU1>

Eric —

   In re: a term for computer-aided communication which reflects its dual oral/literate nature—I've taken to talking about orality, literacy, and telecommunications (thus, the oral word, the written/ chirographic/typographic word, and the telecommunicated word). I'm hesitant to use the term "tertiary orality" (although it has occurred to me) because "secondary orality" refers to a return to the spoken word, a sort of renaissance of orality through literacy. It doesn't seem to me that electronic communication is orality twice-removed, which is what the term "tertiary" sounds like. Of course, my use of "telecommunications" merely avoids the whole issue by lumping e-comm w/t.v., radio, etc., where I'm not at all certain it belongs. Mediated orality? Nah, not quite. I've also thought, at times, that perhaps there's a whole genre of epistolary orality of which e-mail is one form. But now I'm reaching. I'm sure others have more knowledge of and facility with such matters. It's been a long monday; I'm going home now.

Kathryn Powell
kpowell@irishvma

Date: Tue, 2 Feb 1993 00:30:10 -0600
Sender: "Comparative Oral Traditions Discussion List" <ORTRAD-L%MIZZOU1.BitNet@pucc.PRINCETON.EDU>
From: SKRIP@SASK.USASK.CA
Subject: ORALITY AND LITERACYY
To: Multiple recipients of list ORTRAD-L <ORTRAD-L%MIZZOU1.BitNet@pucc.PRINCETON.EDU>

I'm thinking of the term tertiary orality, and I rather like how it suits the workings of e-mail. Secondary orality, if I'm thinking of it correctly, presents the *illusion* of orality—illusion, because it looks and sounds like spontaneous, orally produced ideas, but it is really pre-scripted, fully directed, and in many ways static rather than dynamic communication. Although a target audience watches, for example, the news, there is no audience interaction or participation, even though the audience is being wooed into believing that this is dynamic, personally oriented communication.

TV evangelism and, to a lesser extent, broadcast masses are forms of secondary orality. Both of these productions give the illusion of oral performance in much the same way as the news does but even more strongly because with TV evangelism and broadcast masses the audience at home is encouraged to be part of the group. Some even have telephone numbers which a person can call, solidifying the illusion of group participation where there really is only minimal, long-distance, electronic participation at best.

This brings me around to the point about tertiary orality. E-mail is even one more step removed from TV evangelism, the news, and broadcast masses. With e-mail, there is the suggestion of an audience because people respond to each other and refer to each other's comments as if they were part of one long conversation that was presently ongoing around a person. However, the physical appearance of the speaker, the rest of the audience, the speaking conditions and surroundings *are all missing* and are left strictly to mental conjecture and abstraction on the part of the list member. In this way, e-mail must be considered one step removed beyond secondary orality in the sense that it is one step more abstract. E-mail shares features of oral communication, no doubt, but it is a level of linear, abstract thought that no other form of communication has previously achieved. The one exception to this that I am thinking of are telephones, but even then you have voice inflection, pauses, and other forms of paralanguage which are simply not available on e-mail.

In many ways, then, e-mail is both oral discourse and autonomous discourse: it is oral in that participants share a common communication environment that has a sense of immediacy and relies on a fairly local inter-textual encyclopedia given the similarity in interest of the list members; it is autonomous in that it is in many ways removed from the writer, but not so autonomous as a physically published text. Since e-mail writers are usually involved in ongoing discussions, they have the chance to defend or rebut in a way that regular writers may not, given that the audience is so immediate with e-mail. On the other hand, defenses and rebuttals have a way of becoming separated from the original texts, and this can occur, even with e-mail records (hence my desire to see e-mail writings as having status of autonomous discourse).

What I see all this meaning is that e-mail is, indeed, once removed from those communications that we would categorize as secondary orality. a result, tertiary orality has a nice ring to it, for me, and it stands as an appropriate extension of Walter Ong's work. Bravo

Theresa Skrip
Clinical Psychology
Department of Psychology
University of Saskatchewan

Date: Tue, 2 Feb 1993 10:30:19 -0500
Sender: "Comparative Oral Traditions Discussion List" <ORTRAD-L%MIZZOU1.BitNet@pucc.PRINCETON.EDU>
From: "Stephanie A. Hall" <shal@SEQ1.LOC.GOV>
Subject: Re: ORALITY AND LITERACYY
To: Multiple recipients of list ORTRAD-L <ORTRAD-L%MIZZOU1.BitNet@pucc.PRINCETON.EDU>

I am afraid I have become terribly cynical on the subject of jargon. To me "tertiary orality" sounds like a term theorists come up with so that no one else knows what they are talking about. Not that I don't support the idea *behind* coming up with such a term. This new medium for communication is extremely important, and we need to find or make appropriate and agreed upon terminology for our discussions. I just feel that the new terms should facilitate rather than obfuscate communication.

Net communication is a written form with a great many features of oral communication. It is not the only such form: Autograph albums, graffiti, and xerography are other examples of written genres that function much like oral communication. I studied the use of slogan buttons among science fiction fans, and looked at TTY communication among the Deaf – two lesser known examples. Of these TTY conversation has the most in common with network communications. A major difference is that TTY conversations are "real time" communication, like chat mode on the net.

But like networkers, the Deaf can call up a number and get a newsletter fed across the TTY—the precursor of the online zine.
At any rate, I think we need to look at all these various forms of written communication that resemble or function like oral communication with the understanding that while they may share features in common, each may be very different from the other. Because the phenomenon is so complex, it will be helpful to keep our language about it as clear as possible, saying exactly what we mean rather than making up terms that seem to say something else. Straightforward terms such as "oral-like written genres" while ungraceful, are at least clear. If we must get high-fallutin about it - a term like "mediated orality" indicates an oral form conveyed through a technical medium, and might be a way of including discussions of phone and cb oral forms as well. Maybe some of you have other suggestions.

Stephanie

Stephanie A. Hall
Archivist
American Folklife Center, Library of Congress
Washington, DC 20540
shal@seq1.loc.gov

Date: Tue, 2 Feb 1993 10:10:28 -0600
Sender: "Comparative Oral Traditions Discussion List" <ORTRAD-L%MIZZOU1.BitNet@pucc.PRINCETON.EDU>
From: SKRIP@SASK.USASK.CA
Subject: Re: TERTIARY ORALITY
To: Multiple recipients of list ORTRAD-L <ORTRAD-L%MIZZOU1.BitNet@pucc.PRINCETON.EDU>

Although the term "tertiary orality" might appear to obfuscate understanding, it would stand in and continue a tradition of terminology that was initiated a number of years ago (by Walter Ong) and that is familiar to many people who study the impact of literacy and technology on culture. I'm not usually one to defend jargon, but it has its place within circles. As long as we are able to explain our jargon in lay people's terms, then we're still okay. It when jargon takes the place of real understanding and communication that it becomes troublesome. I, for one, would like to use the term "tertiary orality" when speaking amongst peers. "Mediated" just doesn't fit for me, because secondary orality is also mediated but is fundamentally different from communicative forms such as e-mail.

What do you think, Eric? It's your term.
Date: Wed, 3 Feb 1993 10:02:01 CST
From: Eric Crump <C509379%MIZZOU1.BitNet@pucc.PRINCETON.EDU>
Subject: the tertiarization of orality
To: Multiple recipients of list ORTRAD-L <ORTRAD-L%MIZZOU1.BitNet@pucc.PRINCETON.EDU>

MY term? Gosh, I don't know if I have room in my garage (it needs cleaning) for a term of my own. But although I can't claim ownership, I will own up to my responsibility as the so&so who introduced it here and will, tonight probably, blather on in response to the very interesting comments made so far. Today, however, I'm temporarily awash in work that needs done NOW. Rats.

—Eric Crump

APPENDIX C: EXAMPLES OF THE MICROSOFTENING AND WORDPERFECTING OF THE LANGUAGE

Grammatically Incorrect
By RALPH SCHOENSTEIN
(The New York Times, June 13, 1998)
(edited by Marsha Woodbury for her longstanding joke discussion group. When she heard about my intent to use the example, she suggested "a dose of Viagra to combat the microsoftening of the language!")

Microsoft's word-processing program, Word for Windows 95, is ruining the English language.

"She was a most unique woman; she was slightly pregnant."
The error was easy to find, two modified absolutes. When the check responded that the sentence was flawless, I knew English was partially dead.

"I couldn't help but going," used the gerund instead of the infinitive. The check replied, Consider replacing with "could not" in a formal document.

"Thinking it was open, the door was really closed." The check replied, The main clause may contain a verb in the passive voice. But there is no passive voice here, just a thinking door.

"If I was a better man, I would go."
Missing my failure to use the subjunctive, the check resorted to political correctness: Gender-specific expression. Consider replacing with "person," "human being" or "individual." The check, of course, had a point. Every time I call myself a man, as opposed to a woman or a newt, I am being gender specific.

"There were only three grown-ups between Judy, Jill, Eve-Lynn, Lori, Maria and Max." Once again, the check approved, unaware that between cannot handle six people. That's why among was invented.

"She shopped, like, sixteen times."
The check said the sentence was perfect.

WORKS CITED

Bloom, H. (1975). *The anxiety of influence: A theory of poetry.* Oxford: Oxford University Press.

Branwyn, G. (1997). *Jargon watch: A pocket dictionary for the Jitterati.* San Francisco: Hardwired.

Byrd, D., & Owens, D. (1998). Writing in the hivemind. In T. Taylor & I. Ward (Eds.), *Literacy theory in the age of the internet* (pp. 47-58). New York: Columbia University Press.

Carbone, N. (1997, September 30). Re: research imperatives. acw-l@ttacs6.ttu.edu.

Conference on College Composition and Communication Committee on Computers in Composition and Communication. (1998). CCCC Promotion and Tenure Guidelines for work with Technology. http://www.ncte.org/positions/4c-tp-tech.html.

Crump, E. (1993, February 3). "the tertiarization of orality" ORTRAD-L%MIZZOU1.BitNet.

Doi, T. (1973). *The anatomy of dependence.* Tokyo: Kodansha International.

Garfinkle, S. L. (1994). Programs to the people. In K. Schellenberg (Ed.), *Computers in society* (5th ed., pp. 132-138). Guilford, CT: Dushkin.

Hall, S. (1993, February 2). "Re: ORALITY AND LITERACY" ORTRAD-L%MIZZOU1.BitNet.

Haynes, C. (1998). prosthetic_rhetorics@writing.loss.technology. In T. Taylor & I. Ward (Eds.), *Literacy theory in the age of the internet* (pp. 79-92). New York: Columbia University Press.

Index of cold fusion Usenet group. (1989). http://sunsite.unc.edu/pub/academic/physics/Cold-fusion/fd89.

Le Clair, T. (1981, March 21). The language must not sweat: A conversation with Toni Morrison. *New Republic,* p. 26.

Modern Language Association Committee on Emerging Technologies. (1998). Guidelines for evaluating computer-related work in the modern languages. http://www.mla.org/reports/ccet/ccet_guidelines.htm.

Momaday, N. S. (1968). *House made of dawn.* New York: Harper & Row.

Murphy, J. (1982). *The rhetorical tradition and modern writing.* New York: The Modern Language Association of America.

National Council of Teachers of English. (1996). On viewing and visually representing as forms of literacy. http://www.ncte.org/resolutions/visually961996.html.

Oldenburg, R. (1991). *The great good place: Cafés, coffee shops, community centers, beauty parlors, general stores, bars, hangouts, and how they get you through the day.* New York: Paragon House.

Ong, W. J. (1965). Oral residue in tudor prose style. *PMLA, 80*, 145-154.

Ong W. J. (1982). *Orality and literacy: The technologizing of the word*. New York: Methuen.

Powell, K. (1993, February 1). "Re: ORAL TRADITION AND LITERACY" ORTRAD-L%MIZZOU1.BitNet.

Pynchon, T. (1973). *Gravity's rainbow*. New York: The Viking Press.

Rheingold, H. (1993). *The virtual community: Homesteading on the electronic frontier*. New York: Addison-Wesley.

Schoenstein, R. (1998, June 13). Grammatically incorrect. *The New York Times*, p. A15.

Silko, L. (1977). *Ceremony*. New York: Penguin.

Skrip, T. (1993, February 2). "ORALITY AND LITERACY" ORTRAD-L%MIZZOU1.BitNet.

Stutz, M. (1997). Applying copyleft to non-software information. http://gnu.april.org/philosophy/nonsoftware-copyleft.html.

Work, J. C., & Cowell, P. (1981, Spring-Summer). Teller of stories: An interview with Leslie Marmon Silko. *Colorado State Review*, p. 79.

chapter 2.4

THEORIZING RAW ARCHIVE:

A NEW PARADIGM FOR ACADEMIC
SCHOLARSHIP AND PUBLICATION

Jeff Galin and Joan Latchaw

Kuhn argues that scientists create new ways of thinking about a
particular phenomenon not because they have discovered some greater
truth about it; rather, by creating new ways to talk about that
phenomenon, the perceived truth about it shifts to be commonly
understood in terms of the new model created by the new language.
—Sidney Dobrin (1997, p. 67)

Some have argued that in the few years of its existence, the World Wide
Web has caused a paradigm shift in the ways that authors, publishers,
vendors, and archivists view the production, distribution, and
management of new academic knowledge. Authors like Harnad (1998)
and Ginsparg (1996) have claimed that "the best interests of nontrade
authors (and, when they wear their other hats, the readers of nontrade
serial literature) are best served by having their work available free for
all, in perpetuum" (Harnad, 1998). Using the example of the pre-print,
automated, physics, electronic archive, xxx.lanl.gov,[1] Harnad and
Ginsparg suggested that authors who are writing for "scholarly
publication (esoteric scholarly publications)" generally write not to

make money but to "communicate research information and to establish our research reputations" (Ginsparg, 1996). Although this cognitive scientist and physicist are careful to restrict their speculations to journal submissions of highly specialized scientific communities, they suggest that other academic communities might also benefit from this pre-print distribution of new knowledge. Such an anti-foundational stance, which values dissemination of new knowledge above all else, might indeed serve highly specialized disciplines like law, medicine, and even the subfield of computers and composition. At the same time, however, such a distribution system raises a host of unanswered questions and has dramatic implications for the print industry and academic archivists.

This chapter explores the implications of developing such professional archives outside the field of physics. As two, nontenured, junior, English faculty, we are particularly interested in examining and contributing to the new vocabulary emerging from these controversial forms of publishing. Like scientists who create new ways of thinking about a particular phenomenon, we have not "discovered some greater truth" about Web-based publishing of esoteric texts. Rather, by studying and talking about already existing Web-based archival models in new terms, we hope to influence a shift in "the perceived truth[s]" about the nonprofit academic publishing industry. These kinds of shifts occur, according to Kuhn, when "abnormal discourse" becomes normal. "Abnormal discourse" emerges, according to Kuhn, as a "new vocabulary about a phenomenon evolves that in some way contradicts the normal disciplinary discourse and thus presents a new way of perceiving and understanding the subject" (cited in Dobrin, 1997, p. 69). Not all different language is considered abnormal. Rather abnormal discourse "must have the potential to become normal discourse and alter a discourse community's knowledge."

Williams (1981) described this phenomenon of shifts in culture in "Base and Superstructure in Marxist Cultural Theory" as nondominant practices that represent "new meanings and values, new practices, new significances and experiences [that] are continually being created" (p. 385). He explained further that the dominant culture makes early attempts to incorporate these new elements of the emergent culture before they are definable as "effective contemporary practice." We are currently seeing this process manifested in experiments like the electronic xxx pre-print archive in physics and math, the Argos medieval Web site in literature, MUSE online journal project of Hopkins University Press, the National Library Association's electronic archive project, JSTOR, and the University of Columbia's CIAO Web site suggest that electronic technologies are, in fact, changing the ways that academic publishing and archives will be managed within the near future.

Although Kuhn's notion of paradigm shift applies primarily to shifts in dominant scientific theories, we are adapting his language of abnormal discourse to describe what Williams called elements of an emergent culture. We realize that it is difficult to define and theorize paradigm shifts and fully formed emergent cultures at the same time we may be contributing them, but we can identify what Williams described as new values, practices, and signficances that lead to such cultural transformations. This chapter studies the current cultural practices of print and digital production and distribution of academic knowledge as a context for creating new metaphors that define the way we will work in the future.

In our search for new vocabulary that can help us re-envision academic publishing, we turn to Foucault's (1986) conceptions of *heterotopia*, notions of cultural and financial capital, current library reform, and technological factors controlling electronic distribution. We acknowledge Harnad's and Ginsparg's significant contributions to the new archival discourse—particularly terms like *esoteric scholarly publications, trade publications, systematic preprint system* of distribution of knowledge, *raw archive*, and *living research archives*. But we also extend their work by providing an alternative vocabulary in order to develop a "credible transition scenario," which Harnad argued has not yet been conceived. The scenarios we imagine are by no means definitive. Certainly, the convergence of new technologies, new archive models, disciplinary and institutional concerns, the nature of changing online human interaction, and differing disciplinary knowledges will all determine models for producing, distributing, and archiving texts. But we do offer the most comprehensive—to date—archive possibilities.

WHAT IS AN ARCHIVE?

Before the emergence of large-scale, widely accessible digital databases of print documents, the concept of *archive* was relatively consistent across institutions, disciplines, and other discursive bodies of knowledge. Archives were depositories for the "indefinite accumulation of time" and knowledge (Foucault, 1986, p. 26). National and state archives catalogued and housed documents of the nation-state. Libraries, both public and private, collected physical volumes of printed material, organized them and preserved them for posterity. And galleries and museums collected and organized cultural and natural artifacts for observation and study. The term *archive*, then, suggested the collection and organization of objects over time. Equally important, however, archives generally served as physical places where people congregated to study and examine the archived objects. In fact, they have always been sacred places that reflect people and their cultures.

This dual nature of predigital archives as both depositories of knowledge and physical spaces affords them special status. For example, rare and culturally significant objects like the Dead Sea scrolls were cloistered within the Israel Antiquities Authority's archives from their rediscovery in 1947 through 1991. As recently as 1992, fewer than 50 scholars were offered physical access to what is called the Qumran collection. Such physical control over the Qumran archive caused significant and contentious scholarly debates and public outcry for "intellectual freedom and the right to scholarly access" by the *Biblical Archaeology Review*. As a result, the Biblical Archaeology Society published "a computer-generated version as well as a two-volume edition of the scroll photographs" in 1991 (Barry, 1998).

Equally important to the actual space (for intellectual investigation) of predigital archives is the social and theoretical function of such spaces. Foucault was profoundly interested in how the spaces we occupy determine who and what we are. This interest led him to identify specific kinds of lived space, in a 1967 lecture,[2] which have the curious property of linking to all other sites in our culture but in a way that contradicts, neutralizes, inverts, or reflects the "set of relations that they happen to designate" (Foucault, 1986, p. 22). He called places like cemeteries, formal gardens, theaters, libraries, and museums "heterotopias" to reflect the "space in which we live," as opposed to the utopian spaces that we can only imagine (p. 23).

We are drawn to Foucault's metaphor of heterotopia to describe certain digital archived spaces because of the fruitful ways it reflects and subverts current economic and cultural assumptions about academic publishing. By "certain digital archives," we are not referring to traditionally self-contained electronic archives like the ERIC, MLA, and other CD-ROM-based databases, which have proven invaluable in the field of composition. Such fixed digital-media archives are built as electronic enhancements for reference books that have existed in libraries for many hundreds of years. They are designed for the lone researcher who toils in isolation to produce new knowledge.

Bolter (1998) in "Degrees of Freedom," explained that even hypertext "is a writing technology in the tradition of the papyrus roll, the codex, and the printed book." Although hypertext is the presentation of materials as a tentative "network of elements and links," these links are only activated when readers choose their paths through the materials. Like any other print technology, hypertext fixes text and other artifacts in a readable medium.

By calling attention to spatial concerns, Foucault helps us realize that alphabetic archives, whether print or digital, should be distinguished by the systems of storage and circulation and the kinds of human contact that are stimulated by each archive. Hence, we are not interested in archival CD and hypertext technologies, per se, as systems of organization versus print text. Rather, we are interested in digital archives on the Web that function as what Foucault called "living spaces." He described six principles that distinguish heterotopic spaces from all others. We explore these heterotopic principles in order to theorize and reenvision new archival spaces on the Web.

Foucault explained that nearly all cultures manifest heterotopias, some as sacred places, and others more profane. Each heterotopia has a "precise and determined function" that may shift over time, such as cemeteries, for example, which migrated from the town's center (in the 18th century) to the suburbs (in the 19th century). Heterotopias are capable of "juxtaposing in a single real place several spaces, several sites that are themselves incompatible." Heterotopias "are most often linked to slices in time," as in the functions that a library or cemetery serve. Foucault singled out libraries and museums under this fourth principle. Since the end of the 17th century, these places have served as general archives to accumulate everything—to enclose in one place, which is itself inaccessible to the ravages of time, "all times, all epochs, all forms, all tastes" (p. 26). These spaces always "presuppose a system of opening and closing that both isolates them and makes them penetrable" (p. 26). Finally, heterotopias function in relation to all spaces that exist outside of them. At the same time that they mark a culturally definable space that is unlike any other space, they also act as microcosms reflecting larger cultural patterns or social orders. Such places, Foucault explained, belong "to our modernity" and are "proper to western culture of the nineteenth century." Had Foucault been alive to witness the emergence of cyberspace, he might have identified certain online spaces as heterotopias, which represented postmodern western culture in the late 20th century.

CONCEPTIONS OF SITE

Foucault argued in 1967 that the great problems of his era were defined by the relations among sites, which manifested themselves in "contemporary technical work"—"the storage of data or of the intermediate results of a calculation in the memory of a machine" and in random traffic patterns in busy intersections (p. 23). These relations among sites also manifest themselves in the problem of the "human site or living space"—"what type of storage, circulation, marking, and classification of human elements should be adopted in a given situation in order to achieve a given end." Although he separated the problems of "contemporary technical work" from the problems of the "human site or living space," we argue in this chapter that these problems cannot be separated in our digital age. Although space still "takes the form of relations among sites" (p. 23), sites are no longer bound to physical living space. They have been extended to some digital, virtual spaces.

Foucault could not have imagined in 1967 how the advent of cyberspace would disrupt his distinction between the space of contemporary technical work and lived space. Most descriptions and narratives of cyberspace foreground human interaction, not stored data. At the same time, the World Wide Web, with its universal graphic user interface, is the ultimate, storage medium—from a technical point of view. The key, then, to understanding how some components of cyberspace might be understood in heterotopic terms is to expand Foucault's original notion of "site."

Web sites are not "living spaces," but merely linked archives, what Foucault might have described as problems in contemporary technical work of digital storage. We are suggesting that certain Web sites, as they are circumscribed by other forms of communicative functions and media, tend toward heterotopic places that resemble "real places" that are something like "counter-sites, a kind of effectively enacted utopia in which the real sites, all the other real sites that can be found within the culture, are simultaneously represented, contested, and inverted" (Foucault, 1986, p. 24). As soon as we recognize certain archival websites as heterotopic or heterotopic-like spaces, we will understand how new (or abnormal) discourse of archival models might shift the perceived truth about existing publication models.

The physics e-print archive site that we introduce in the opening of this chapter, for example, is distinct from all others. It has a precise and determined function, contains and juxtaposes varied and incompatible virtual spaces, is demarcated by boundaries and entry ways, and has a specific function in relation to all other spaces (particularly publishing houses which it reflects and inverts). This archival Web site is actually a collection of esoteric (primarily math, physics, and nonlinear sciences) author-published, pre-print texts, serving "over 35,000 users worldwide from over 70 countries and process[ing] more than 70,000 electronic transactions per day" (Ginsparg, 1996). This e-print archive reflects a "working" research community that is constantly reading, writing, refereeing, and collaborating. The metaphor of a working community distinguishes this archive, created in 1991, from most others, which borrow the library metaphor, a physical structure (or digital space) where materials are "housed."

Like others of Foucault's heterotopias, this Web site functions as a microcosm that reflects a set of cultural patterns and a social order. It constructs an ideal community of like-minded physics and math professionals who value new knowledge more than validation of their work in print journals. The time costs of print production outweigh the professional costs of pre-print distribution of their work. Physicists like Ginsparg, who describe the impact of such e-print archives, suggest that these systematic preprint systems serve "closed peer communit[ies and] may signal a greater intrinsic likelihood for acceptance and utility of free electronic dissemination of unreviewed material." Professionals like Ginsparg see themselves in an "unreal, virtual space that opens up behind the surface" (Foucault, 1986, p. 24). The openings act as a mirror, a "placeless place where we might see ourselves differently"—as writers, authors, and, ultimately, publishers.

The mirror metaphor is powerful for academics who are beginning to see certain sites on the Web as living spaces—not only places to archive texts, but also places where they go to produce, work, and play. These places are also more theoretical spaces to reflect critically on academic communities as they exist in real institutions in real time. This mirror metaphor is also powerful for those who can envision "the other side of the mirror," a more effective, productive, real academic community that results from online publication and interaction.

To describe the physics e-print archive as a heterotopia is to stretch the definition of "site" as Foucault imagined it. We realize that this working research community is not manifest in the archive itself like the communities that exist in certain MOOs, MUDs, and listservs. Unlike these interactive spaces, the archive itself is not a living space governed by problems of "knowing what relations of propinquity, what type of storage, circulation, marking, and classification of human elements should be adopted in a given situation in order to achieve a given end" (p. 23). Rather, this archive is a reflection of and pointer to that community. This uncomfortable stretch need not stop us, however, from examining a range of archival Web sites that attempt to mimic real spaces, some more heterotopic than others. For a study of these sites leads us to our description of truly heterotopic archival sites online.

REFRACTED HETEROTOPIC WEB SITES

Of the four archival sites/models explored here, JSTOR and CIAO are the most conservative—as initiatives of publishing houses and library associations. Argos (1998) and the xxx e-print archives are more radical challenges to current models of print production and distribution systems. None, however, can finally be understood as living spaces like the four heterotopic models that we envision near the end of this chapter.

JSTOR and CIAO were conceived not as heterotopic spaces but as webbed archives that transcend time, space, and economic constraints. Because these databases resemble traditional print sources, they will be more familiar to and user-friendly for academicians new to electronic technologies. And libraries still pay for the materials—in some cases a yearly fee to provide the system to various users. They do not, however, offer much incentive to reconceptualize that space or to critically mirror sociocultural behaviors or practices.

JSTOR, like MUSE (archiving 42 online humanities journals to conserve space), focuses exclusively on preservation of "noncurrent" print publications. Unlike MUSE, it breaches barriers of traditional academic print publishing in several ways. It is interdisciplinary and thus freer from geographical constraints: archiving 10 scholarly journals, covering a range of disciplines (history, economics, math, philosophy, education, etc.). It represents a consortium of libraries, instantly accessible, without walking from place to place—sometimes considerable distances. It is not the "property" of a particular academic press. Finally it allows inter- and intratextual searches.[3] Searching for terms or concepts in two different journals (political science and economics) might expand the political scientist's sphere of influence (as writer, reader, critic) and deemphasize his or her expertise. Metaphorically, the archival "space" is both confined, as an archive, Web site, or database, and expansive—in the sense of a community building. Such spaces presuppose a "system of opening and closing that both isolates them and makes them penetrable" (Foucault, 1986, p. 26). The intellectual value of the work itself, or a body of works, increases, rather than the prestige of the publishing house, the author's name or reputation, or a particular institution represented (author affiliation).

CIAO (Columbia International Affairs Online) a discipline-specific Web site developed by Columbia books, expands the notion of community further by breaching *structural* barriers. In representing an academic *community*, rather than a set of archived materials, it reflects other sites and activities outside the Web site: conferences, events, conference proceedings, working papers, journal books, and indices. CIAO invites anyone working or interested in international affairs (seasoned scholars, recent graduates, instructors) to enter this discourse community. The diversity of text genres suggests a community of scholars rather than the purely archival functions of MUSE and JSTOR.

Argos, a "resource for students, teachers and scholars of the ancient and medieval worlds," moves even closer toward an "ideal research communication of the future" (Ginsparg, 1996). Argos, which went online October 3, 1996, is certainly a "resource," but cannot be described as merely a Web site, database, or archive, and does not "reside" in a defined space—in the physical (print) or virtual world. Rather its Web site provides a limited area search engine (LASE), which is hyperlinked to other Internet sites. The LASE includes digital representations of "sacred" cultural spaces, which Foucault aligned with heterotopias.

For example, Argos includes the library- and museum-like digital archives of the Perseus project, a large database of the ancient world (vases, maps, structures, Greek texts). Users can constrain their searches for a particular vase in a particular historical period crafted by a particular artisan. The "classroom" includes pedagogically related materials of extraordinary quality and usefulness (in Perseus). For instance, Gibert's (1998) Women in Antiquity Web page displays an aesthetically rich syllabus that features numerous power-point slide shows (an Athenian wedding, historical background for *Lysistrata*), upcoming conferences, extensive bibliographies, and student research papers. Thus, scholars, teachers, and researchers share the same space, which creates "an almost limitless potential for an associational life" (Healy, 1997, p. 60). In fact, any one of these roles may overlap or switch instantaneously, equalizing social groups and relations. Argos is heterotopic in that it juxtaposes "in a single [virtual] place several spaces that are themselves incompatible," in this case libraries, museums, and classrooms. It is also heterotopic by functioning as a countersite, whereby "traditional roles will be shifted by the electronic medium, and new roles will emerge" (Ginsparg, 1996).

Argos' new publishing model might be considered a countersite because it is similar to but different from all the sites it reflects and because it inverts the peer-review process typical of academic journals. As the "first peer-reviewed, limited area search engine (LASE) on the World-Wide Web," Argos is peer-reviewed by an editorial board of "associates" who "accredit" the "ligitimating resources." Argos is trying to "contest and invert" the standards and conventions of academic scholarship—by appropriating different metaphors. The editorial board substitutes an "accreditation model" for a "referee model" because "accreditation models are designed for works, institutions, etc. that change over time and that may, in the process of their change, fall below certain standards." Because Argos' living protocol reassesses all sites continually, the archive may be rebuilt each week, remaining intellectually current and technologically operational at all times.

In appropriating new metaphors (of inclusion), in reflecting diverse cultural sites, and in constructing a space in which a disciplinary community can produce, work, and play, Argos has moved beyond "archive as resource" model. However, it is not a living space either because it does not "act as [a] microcosm [to] reflect larger cultural patterns or social orders" (Foucault, 1986, p. 26). Nor does it provide a space for human interaction, like MOOs and listservs.

The xxx or e-print archive, conceived by Ginsparg, is the first true disciplinary pre-print archive on the Web. This raw archive subverts print models of publishing by making available all new knowledge in the field of physics before any of the work is submitted for publication. Ginsparg modeled the "global raw archive" on research databases, like High Energy Physics (hep-th), developed in 1991. These databases began to supplant journals as a primary mode of communication and thus are challenging traditional publication paradigms. The e-print archive, a highly formalized electronic distribution system, accepts all submitted articles with corresponding abstracts, allowing researchers to retrieve indexed entries as needed. Ginsparg has been enormously influential in promoting the development of electronic archives, arguing that other disciplines might reimagine themselves in light of a dying print culture—at least for academic researchers. Clearly, his influence is reflected in the work of Hibbits (1998) discussed later in this chapter.

The xxx archive cannot be defined as a heterotopia because it does not exhibit the six Foucauldian principles. However, it does produce a mirror effect by challenging traditional models of print publication. In addition, it was developed, not just as a resource, but for a working community (designed by scientists for scientists—specifically physicists and mathematicians). Ginsparg, in "Winners and Losers in the Global Research Village," noted that scientists have quickly gravitated to this "fully automated electronic archive" because other distribution systems have been supplanting journal publication since the early 1970s—notably, in high energy physics.

The e-print archives subvert the publisher-author relationship by sidestepping the publisher entirely at the preprint stage. Although the majority of the papers that appear on this Web site are later published in print journals, the pre-print publishing function is assumed by the researchers, readers, critics, and authors who self-publish their work in this archival space. Ginsparg speaks for scientists frustrated by "patronizing attempts [of publishers] to assure them that the unthinking preservation of the status quo is in their best interest." He opposed publishers' values (financial capital) with researchers' values (cultural capital) in arguing for the fully electronic archives. Publishers "measure the success of their journals by the number of pages published, . . . whether they're published 'on time' (i.e., with regularity, not with speed)" and how marketable and cost-effective they are. Academic authors are more concerned with how useful, readable, and innovative journal articles are. If distribution of new knowledge for scientists and mathematicians is time-dependent, then electronic dissemination is obviously the method of choice. If it is space-dependent, then electronic distribution is even more attractive. If it is cost-effective, both authors and readers will gain maximum benefit through free network distribution. Authors will benefit by controlling format, presentation, and length of entries, by speed of distribution, and through access to new and improved authoring tools. Just as importantly, they are encouraged to produce scholarly work and retain rights to their own intellectual property, thus, reflecting John Guillory's notion that distribution should drive production. In the e-print archive, authors can submit their papers either using the online World Wide Web interface, ftp, or e-mail. Authors can also update their submissions if they choose. This archival space, although not a true heterotopia, challenges the "social orders" and "cultural patterns" long operating in academia. By introducing new models and new language, the e-print archive subverts the dominant print mode (finished product) accepted by publishers and authors and foregrounds work in progress. In this sense, the archive is organic and living.

SHIFTING CULTURAL CAPITAL IN VIRTUAL SPACE

In the "real" world of material production, financial capital tends to accrue to those who own the means of re-production. Publishers, printers, and authors share in a revenue stream that ultimately depends on the end-user (book or journal consumer), who is willing to buy a commodity. Publishing houses are generally of two types and target two distinct groups: trade and scholarly audiences. Authors of trade publications have "direct financial remuneration in mind from the outset." By contrast, academic authors want to maximize their distribution, often joking that "they would pay people to read their articles" (Ginsparg, 1996). Although business considerations primarily drive trade publications, intellectual value, often determined by a peer review process, drives scholarly publications. A nonprofit association publisher, for example, or a university press, may find it possible to publish a book, which intellectually pushes the field. Such publishing houses, unlike commercial publishers, would not expect gross economic returns on the investment of time and resources (human and otherwise) required to produce and edit the book. Although their financial capital would not increase, the cultural capital—intellectual value they provide to academics—might increase significantly. In fact, such publishers often gain prestige among scholars, which in turn enhances the reputation of the author. However, those scholars who value innovative print texts may not have the financial capital or borrowing resources to attain them. (Some ILL services are painfully slow or cannot obtain sources at all, even from regional libraries.) Therefore, access may only accrue only to those scholars in prestigious institutions or a higher economic class. Other texts, with significant intellectual value, may be unsuitable for a particular journal, stylistically violate convention, or remain "too raw" for print publication. In the print world, these works, which potentially add to our cultural capital, would be lost.

These are complicated issues because innovative or paradigmatic work may have limited though significant value (in terms of distribution and financial return) and, at the same time, upset social relations. For example, Hibbits, a law professor at the University of Pittsburgh, proposed a model for law reviews that works to subvert the author-publisher relationship with his idea of self-publishing on the Web. This virtual "raw archive," modeled on the e-print archives, promises "a superior form of scholarly communication," that will emerge and signal necessary educational reform. The rise of e-journals (including a broad range of texts that are esoteric, traditional, doctrinal, complex, and impolitic) will ultimately dismantle hierarchies among law reviews (and possibly their home institutions). Thus, Hibbits sees the Web as a desanctified space, erasing boundaries, oppositions, temporal relations and hierarchies, which "[i]nstitutions and practices have not yet dared to break down" (Foucault, 1986, p. 23).

The Web functions as a heterotopian mirror for Hibbits, as he reflected on other related and "real" sites (such as law offices and universities); that gaze allows him to challenge and critique current law practices and offer some innovative solutions. Hibbits represents many practitioners who complain that law review journals are largely conservative, trendy, and reifying, creating hierarchies among law schools, professors, and students that may be unwarranted, unfair, and ultimately damaging to some (and over-praising of others). Furthermore, reputations and careers can be established based primarily on a student's involvement with the law review. This practice may be regrettable because student editors, responsible for selecting interdisciplinary, specialized, and doctrinal articles, neither have a broad enough knowledge of the field nor the necessary editing skills. Firms are more likely to hire editors of prestigious journals, which is ironic given that most law schools do little to educate attorneys in the actual practice of law.[4] For Hibbits, the Web functions as a heterotopian mirror that makes his location in the physical world, as he looks at (reflects on) his institution or editors of the law review "at once absolutely real— connected with all the space that surrounds it—and absolutely unreal, since in order to be perceived it has to pass through this virtual point which is over there" (Foucault, 1986, p. 24). By examining both sides of the mirror, Hibbits is able to "virtually" eliminate the old model while envisioning the new one.

SYSTEMATIZING ARCHIVAL SPACE

The electronic archives discussed here have the potential to increase cultural capital (by including items like "working papers"), shift financial capital through unique distribution systems, and help institutions reimagine social relations. In fact, some scholars and researchers maintain that electronic archives are changing social relations, institutional policy, and even literacy: how we read, what we read, and even what we produce. For instance, electronic archiving can offer a new economic model whereby distribution drives production. The e-print archives build in this possibility by inviting authors, who respond to or are inspired by an article or abstract, to produce new work, which, in turn, will be added to the ever-expanding archive. These professional archives are constructed differently, depending on the end-users, financial considerations, intellectual value, and other factors. While some systems of archiving reflect similar problems and address similar needs (such as library access), others reflect more radical agendas (such as tenure reform and free distribution of intellectual property).

   If, in fact, systemization will ultimately govern cultural capital and intellectual property over the next 15 years or so, it will be vastly different from the 19th century modernist scheme of centralized organization. Uniform card catalogue systems, OCLC, and Library of Congress classifications certainly served a purpose since users at any geographical location could easily employ these systems of access. However, such systems, using librarians' terminology, search methods, and metaphors cannot organize large databases and other materials on the Web. If we can't find information, then it is essentially invisible and inaccessible.

   In contrast to centralized distribution systems, more academics favor decentralized, multiple modes of production and knowledge. E-mail, copy machines, the Web, and databases like the Gutenberg Project or the Electronic Text Center at the University of Virginia (providing texts for individualized courses) offer authors multiple venues for both production and distribution. These various media allow academics to self-publish materials, which may have too small or narrow a readership to justify an expenditure of financial capital. However, cultural capital may be considerable for a wide readership via listservs, electronic archives, email, and webpages. Note the thousands of "hits" on professional webpages, online writing centers (OWLs), and electronic journals like *Kairos* and *CMC Magazine*. Many of these new media are searchable, easily accessible, and inexpensive. Texts that challenge the status quo can transcend traditional cultural values institutionalized by higher education.

FOUR NEW VISIONS

As we look beyond current archive models on the Web, we propose substituting "professional working spaces" for the raw archive metaphor because it highlights action—academics working, producing, and playing. The "raw archive" mentally binds us to a lifeless collection of materials (the "living" archive notwithstanding) and conceals the social relations, which operate in producing, contributing, and evaluating those materials. We want to re-envision virtual places exemplified by new models that would exploit technologies of the future: hardware and software that might not currently exist. Our ideal models are recognizable as heterotopias. They will provide precise and determined functions (professional, disciplinary, or multidisciplinary); they will contain and juxtapose varied and incompatible virtual spaces (like museums, libraries, and MOOs); they will be demarcated by boundaries and entry ways (such as protected Web sites); and they will serve specific functions in relation to all other spaces (such as publishing houses, universities, conference centers). Most importantly, our ideal models will be highly collaborative and interactive. They will truly be living spaces. For reasons articulated in this chapter, we need new models, which do not just reflect cultural formations and social orders, but challenge them. Just as new paradigms draw on historical models and community standards, we build on those electronic archives, which reflect significant shifts away from current traditional publishing standards.

Of the four models discussed here, the first and last are for-profit publishing models, whereas the middle two are not-for-profit editorial models. The first, and most conservative, serves as a likely transition scenario for the print industry's shift from exclusively print-based production to integrated online archives. The second follows current print journal models that have been adapted for discipline-specific pre-print raw archives like those of the physics e-print archive. The third moves away from print institutional models to university-based or freelance Web editors. And the fourth model turns to large-scale third-party information managers, what Getz (1997) called electronic agents.

FOR-PROFIT JOURNAL MODEL

Because the print industry remains a powerful, institutional force, existing academic archives like MUSE and CIAO will continue to emerge as more publishers of esoteric scholarly publications realize the benefits of the online subscription model for multiple journals. Thus, publishing houses should expect to regain subscriptions to digital archives. In the long run, such expectations will likely lead to new classes of intellectual property managers who will serve as third-party distributors, organizers, and coordinators of new disciplinary knowledge.

Getz, an associate professor of economics, suggested that outsourcing information management to third-party "electronic agents" is similar to current models for typesetting and printing such as Silver Platter's Psychology, ERIC, Dissertation abstracts and *Online Clinical Trials*, which "offers publishers the opportunity to sell electronic access to [more than 250] journals by both subscription and pay-per-look." Prior to development by electronic agents, the publishing industry itself will provide important functions: filtering, linking, and, integrating (disciplinary knowledge) that researchers will increasingly expect.

Rather than selling rights for storage and management of published texts to third parties, publishers are likely to continue holding on to copyrights for books or journals, materials that already exist in printed form. Ownership of intellectual property is so fundamental to the current industry that large-scale changes are unlikely to happen quickly or uniformly. More likely, multiple new models will emerge simultaneously and compete for market share. Chief among them will be different versions of MUSE, CIAO, and even JSTOR archives that keep long-standing institutional structures intact.

Hence, in the short run, publishers of academic journals are more likely to build and distribute their own Web site archives to paying customers and manage them as new materials are added and new technologies overlayed. These archives will be delineated, "demarcated" as professional working spaces, and serve specific functions in relation to the publishing houses they reflect. They may also align themselves with professional organizations like the Modern Language Association, American Psychological Association, and others or create their own affiliation of linked Web sites as they attempt to turn their archives into "living spaces" for research and intellectual exchange. One tremendous advantage of such a system is a generous fair use policy; subscribers and their constituents can download and copy journal articles for archiving and educational (teaching) purposes.

In order to remain competitive and warrant high development and management costs, these webbed archives will need to provide greater services than their print counterparts could offer. Publishers might hire Web editors to identify pertinent conference proceedings, working papers, annotations, and evaluations of texts—by virtue of their usefulness to various scholars, researchers, and teachers. Some texts, linkable throughout the archive, will be more useful to generalists, some to specialists, and others to scholars outside the discipline (Varian, 1997). Such a filtering function could validate important contributions to professional communities, thereby providing documentation for promotion and tenure committees.

Web editors, according to Varian in "The Future of Electronic Journals," could review, copyedit, and rank texts, thereby lowering costs and increasing speed of distribution. With all of the advantages of integrated bodies of knowledge streaming from individual publishers, archives are still bound by disciplinary and institutional constraints. The cultural capital of such islands of webbed knowledge can be greatly enhanced when they become interlinked to a wider net than even the JSTOR model (the library initiative of an interdisciplinary set of journals). If archival spaces always "presuppose a system of opening and closing that both isolates them and makes them penetrable," then why not develop searching mechanisms among larger numbers of related (or potentially related) archives? Such meta-hypertexts are possible even with current technology.

EX-POST EDITORIAL BOARD MODEL

Although publishers are desperately trying to maintain control of intellectual property, authors are expending significant time and energy dismantling current distribution systems. Developers of the e-print archives have overtly opposed the print publications model for two reasons: because publishers, they claim, do not understand what knowledge is important to researchers and because they cannot deliver knowledge on a weekly or even daily basis. Although such raw archives provide breadth of disciplinary knowledge, their raw state reduces them to vast depositories of digitally stored print texts. Value added filtering functions could turn such archived sites into heterotopic spaces that might eventually eliminate the need for publishers altogether.

In the short term, however, academic authors still need credits toward tenure and promotion. Even if citations could be "counted and documented" in a modified raw archive, publishing records still serve as the primary means of judging faculty professional development. Varian, dean of the School of Information, Management and Systems at the University of California-Berkeley, argued for an "ex-post" filtering process that would occur after posting to the raw archive, and would replace current publish-or-reject publication policies. Varian imagined a referee model whereby three members of an editorial board would review each submission. But instead of reviewing 20- to 30-page articles, editorial board members would evaluate only the one-paragraph abstract and five-page summary that are uploaded along with the academic articles. Reviewers would rate the submissions on the basis of interest and pertinence to the field on a 5-point scale, with only about 10% receiving the highest ranking. Authors would be notified of their ratings and could elect to resubmit the piece elsewhere if it did not receive a high rating; once accepted, the author could revise but not withdraw the article.

Varian envisioned an archival space that is more open and penetrable to readers as they score articles and contribute critiques, supplemental narratives, or e-mendations, which correspond with the texts. Still other researchers may build hypertextually linked webs that draw on previous papers to build their own arguments. Or they may develop annotated bibliographies of highly rated articles that would offer networks of rated material for disciplinary study.

Because such a professional working space offers immediate opportunities for isolated scholars and the larger community to create and share their contributions, it has distinct advantages over the for-profit model. For example, as concepts emerge in the work of others, original authors could revise and resubmit arguments. Although such shared knowledge might complicate ownership issues, hypertextual links to original versions of documents would minimize problems of intellectual property. And highly rated pieces might be considered as serious contributions toward promotion and tenure. Finally, this self-publishing system would incur lower costs because editing would occur as an integral part of the review and revision process. Costs for storage and remote access might be covered by professional organizations, university or home library support stipends, or third-party vendors described in the next section. Unrecognized or unused articles would simply remain in rough form, although still get cited from time to time.

WEB EDITORS MODEL

Web editors (freelance or sponsored by university or professional organizations) would build truly heterotopian sites that draw professional researchers, graduate students, admirers, armchair philosophers, and others to visit regularly and contribute themselves. The biggest difference between this group of Web editors and the editorial board members is that their responsibilities would likely extend beyond reviewing and rating five page abstracts. Rather, they would likely build networks of disciplinary knowledge. Communities might form around a set of such Web sites similar to the Argos project we discussed earlier in this chapter.

Some of these Web sites could become so specialized, as in law, medicine, or engineering, that participants might be willing to pay subscription fees for access. With so much material available online, only specialists would have the time and expertise to sort through the raw archive. If Web editors of the future do not "belong to" one publisher, they are free to sell their services wherever needed. And academic Web editors would receive substantial credit toward promotion and tenure.

With the current academic job market in dire straits, new doctorates might choose to move into the web editing field rather than compete in a flooded teaching market. An entire new class of specialists might emerge and supercede editing functions currently operating in the publishing industry. As a result, the distribution of knowledge would, as Guillory proposed, drive production and academics would control both processes.

The limitations of such a system, however, are not insignificant. Lone Web editors, or even small collaboratives would have to charge for their services or seek funding from host institutions, publishers, or professional organizations. Resources for developing selective search engines like Argos' LASE or for expanded storage capacity or connectivity might be cost prohibitive. Publishing, library, university, or corporate archivists might supersede smaller web editor archives and make them obsolete. Such large-scale third-party players serve as the focus of the final model discussed here.

ELECTRONIC AGENT MODEL

These four models become progressively more open, living, and heterotopic as third-party agents provide greater expertise and as users become more active and collaborative. The first two models more nearly represent delivery systems of knowledge; the expertise of the "filters" is largely invisible. The Web editors' model requires enormous disciplinary knowledge and invites users to help *build* the system. However, in the fourth model, electronic agents represent a rare breed whose considerable disciplinary knowledge must be equally matched with technological expertise.

Unlike Web editors, electronic agents, or agencies, are the likely candidates to develop dynamic hypertext linking systems that are capable of searching vast bodies of disciplinary work to produce much more than a list of unrelated hits. Such archival engines could literally assemble on-the-fly annotated meta-hypertexts. A search for string theory in quantum physics, for instance, would identify several hundred interrelated articles, book chapters, and webbed resources, rate them on the basis of user-specified criteria, select a predetermined number of texts, embed specified patterns of hypertextual links among the selected texts, and present the searcher with recommended strategies for reading based on search criteria and previous search requests by that searcher or by other users.

In turn, users would become micro-agents, editing, and storing these on-the-fly hypertexts, and might even submit their results and annotations for other users to access. Every new search would produce a new pattern of collected texts and hypertext link structures. Although the texts themselves would remain on the host server until the user called it up by following a hypertextual node, the on-the-fly linking structure would remain on the user's computer and could be saved for future access to the same search variables. The user could also save as many versions of the same type of search that he or she wanted, comparing them for usefulness or cross-referencing.

With the emergence of large professional databases, constructing, managing, and providing effective access to such archives and collections of archives becomes crucial. Getz conceived of electronic agents as third parties, intermediaries, between publishers and libraries or publishers and end-users. He imagined ways such agents might "acquire rights from publishers and sell access to libraries," archive materials from disparate sources, maximize electronic storage resources, diversify payment structures, and develop "superior search interfaces and engines" across meta-hypertexts.

In the long run, there is little doubt that the electronic agent model will emerge as a growth industry. Getz boldly stated that the role of "electronic distribution agents" is fast becoming more important than the role of printers, for two reasons: presumably because it would solve serious "congestion" problems (an economy of scale) and organize journals that are acquired from publishers, along with "other electronic materials into a coherent database." In fact, few publishers, academics, or even professional organizations have the research and development funds to develop innovative resources for managing huge volumes of digital materials efficiently. Although lone Web editors can spend the time necessary to filter through raw archives as they construct specialized ex post Web sites, what they can produce will always be limited to their own choices and perspectives on the materials and to exclusionary biases that may not take into account cross-disciplinary, divergent, or innovative study.

Packaged with this meta Web engine would be a range of archival software that would enable users to edit, annotate, store multiple search patterns for more inclusive results. If the user found that too many hypertextual links made the text harder to read, there would be facilities for hiding link markers while still keeping the links active. Additionally, multiple versions of the same article in varying lengths (from abstract to five-page summary, to full articles) would make it possible for readers to choose the level of specificity of a given search or reading session.

Furthermore, these engines might be programmed to remember who searched for what patterns and to track who was using the system at any given time. Searchers who happened to be looking for similar materials might expect to be notified automatically that like-minded researchers were making simultaneous inquiries. Spontaneous meetings in cyberspace, as often occur in physical libraries, might become commonplace. This process of socially constructing knowledge in a "professional working space" reflects what we mean by a "living space." Shifting, organic libraries (archives), meeting rooms, E-mail exchanges form a living web in which academics can produce, play, and work. Of course, certain users would undoubtedly want to do their work undisturbed and would therefore disable the alert function for given searchers. At other times, these same researchers might perform a series of searches in order to identify colleagues with whom to discuss their own work in progress.

A wide range of on-the-fly meta web software would surely emerge, some as small Java programs and others as full-scale data corporations that host huge stores of disciplinary and cross disciplinary knowledge. The larger scale systems that were hosted by third-party electronic agents could charge institutional or pay-per-search fees. Users would be paying for speed, professional quality of hits, proficiency of the software, specialized data sources, and insurance against nonprofessional users simply playing with the system.

Such "smart" search engines would save incredible amounts of time and might replace some the functions of Web editors. They would also challenge many of our currently held sacred assumptions about intellectual property. As Getz suggested, any form of large-scale integration of databases might make "common ownership" of intellectual property "necessary to achieve the control and commonality necessary for high levels of integration." On the other hand, with faster cable modems and Internet 2 infrastructures currently in development, distributed information systems might soon provide the necessary bandwidth to overcome the need for centralized databases. Unlike the modernist libraries and museums of the turn of the 20th century that worked to collect all that has be written in Western culture, a postmodern distributed system would find better ways to manage previously unimaginable volumes of digital knowledge.

The roles that electronic agents would play would, of course, extend well beyond the development of smart hypertext publishing systems. As Getz suggested, publishing houses are more likely to rely on electronic agents to manage the storage, access, and value added resources that libraries and end-users would expect. But, like most growth sectors within information management specializations, electronic agents would emerge in all shapes and sizes. Large conglomerate services would likely make corporate deals with high profile publishers within specialized fields to expand the breadth of their searchable archives. Smaller companies would specialize in storage, distributed management systems, software development, or specific kinds of value added services for archives. Furthermore, electronic agents are likely candidates to establish corporate arrangement with communications services to couple information management (problems of contemporary technical work) with human interaction (problems of living space in cyberspace).

Certainly other models will emerge that will complement the four discussed here. But in order for any of the archive models that we have described here to develop into truly heterotopic sites online, the "abnormal discourse" of online archival systems that we propose must result in new models created by the new language. Furthermore, the new language must evolve out of an emergent culture that has the potential to overthrow the dominant culture. We turn to our vision of this emergent culture in the last section below to address Harnad's (1997) lament over the lack of a "credible transition scenario"—from a print archival culture to an electronic one.

EXISTING HETEROTOPIAS ONLINE

As in any emergent culture within a larger dominant one, currently existing heterotopias online are an indication of where we are headed as a culture and how living spaces online will change the way we work and interact on a daily basis. The most common forms of such spaces serve as exchanges like chats, threaded discussion lists, and MOOs. Most such Web sites are marked by a "precise and determined function," juxtapose in a single "real place several spaces, sites that are themselves incompatible," represent "slices in time," "presuppose a system of opening and closing," and function as spaces that reflect larger cultural patterns or social orders. Many of these cyberspaces function as regular meeting places for communities of people who share common interests. Unlike cemeteries, libraries, and oriental gardens, however, all of these webbed spaces seem to have similar functions, serving as places to meet socially with others.

This decidedly social function of heterotopic spaces online provides new communities of people opportunities to meet regularly, to form pockets of what Ray Oldenburg (1997) called "third places" in *The Great Good Place*. Oldenburg explained that

> third places . . . serve as "sorting areas." The broad scale association which they provide ultimately leads to the stuff of "sociometrics." That is, people find that they very much like certain people and dislike others. They find people with similar interests. . . . Third places often serve to bring together for the first time, people who will create other forms of association later on. (p. xviii)

Although some heterotopic spaces satisfy Oldenberg's description, some are so specialized that they serve primarily as places of work rather than daily social interaction. This distinction is important because few of these kinds of spaces currently exist for academic purposes. They don't function like neighborhood bars, post offices, and community centers, which are the third places that Oldenburg described. These are places where an "individual can have many friends and engage them often *only* if there is a place he or she can visit daily and which plays host to their meetings." And the exchanges at these places are festive. He added, "The fun function of third places is better seen, perhaps, as the entertainment function," which is provided by the people themselves in extended conversations" (p. xix).

Unlike many of the publishing models that we have described previously in this chapter, most current heterotopic spaces online serve social functions that resemble third places. The metaphor of "homepage" is apt for such services as Yahoo, AOL, and ESPN's Sports Zone, all of which represent heterotopic homebases for certain sectors of users. Users turn on their machines and begin their online work and play from these sites. AOL, with its "buddy" software, its predictable links, its usergroups, and its chat rooms provides a "place" for users to "go." When they go "online" they go to this third place to follow their stocks, check their email, catch up on the latest news, meet with their cyberbuddies, discuss their work, and play games with others. Similarly, frequent visitors of the ESPN site visit for the latest sports scoop on their favorite teams and players and for updates on their fantasy baseball teams. Users log on during sporting events to chat with other aficionados. And they return to ask questions of guest sports stars or to read previous online interviews.

As corporate America relies more and more on the Web to do daily business and as users find more reasons to go online for services and goods, Web site owners scramble for ways to attract homebase customers. With a guaranteed daily userbase of hundreds of thousands, Web sites like AOL, Yahoo, Excite, and so on can successfully win advertising dollars and thereby grow their own businesses. Such heterotopic homebases are growing in number across our culture, as attested to by the recent proliferation of free e-mail providers online. They are giving rise to an emergent culture within our society that is coming to expect these kinds of services and interaction online.

These trends in the public and corporate sectors provide instructive models for academics and publishers. While academics affiliated with computers and composition have been working for the past 7 years to help publishers understand the potential of Web production, our ability to influence their publishing practices has been limited. We are a small, specialized segment of an already marginalized discipline of composition. Even though our small field could not serve as an emergent culture with the transformative potential of widespread heterotopic homebases, it has made significant contributions with online journals like *Rhetnet, Kairos, Computers and Composition*, and *academic.writing*. If we want to have a greater impact on what publishers do with our work and how it is disseminated, we must examine and learn from the growing homebase phenomenon. As Kuhn explained, "abnormal discourse" cannot become normal discourse until it is grounded in large segments of the dominant culture. Institutional change only occurs when multiple forces within a culture converge and collide with current practice.

Over the past few years, the computers and composition community has erected several sites that emulate heterotopic "homebases" online, like MOOs, OWLs, and, to a smaller degree, the NCTE, ACW, and CCC websites. The emergence of the Tuesday Cafe in Media MOO in the early 1990s provided highly specialized heterotopic spaces that sparked to life once a week. Similarly, some OWLs and professional Web sites have implemented synchronous components that turn primarily archival sites into temporary heterotopic spaces. Of all these spaces, only the Tuesday Cafes are characteristic of a "third place," and none of them serve as daily homebases for professionals in the field.

DISCIPLINARY HOMEBASE

We need to develop a comprehensive, heterotopic, disciplinary homebase, one that engages participants daily. Our listservs do not represent such a homebase because they do not reflect the space in which we live. In fact, they are distribution systems for communication, which increasing numbers of us are abandoning because they are too time intensive. Furthermore, our various Web sites, which are vital to our field, do not invite users to set their homepage preferences to them as their starting place for daily interaction.

We envision the Computers and Writing homebase as a central location that enjoins the personal and professional, serious and playful, challenging and accepting, trusting and skeptical. Upon entering this homebase, a combination Web site, virtual meeting place, smart search engine, and disciplinary archive, users will have at their disposal a communal living space that includes libraries, bookstores, daily news, meeting rooms (general and specialized), conference postings, game room, coffee house, pub, mailroom, and so on. In additionally, users would be able to program private spaces to include their own favorite links, resources, and personal touches. This space reflects and extends the various societies and cultures living within its borders.

This virtual living space could be available at a moment's notice. Upon logging on, priority announcements appear first, a buddy list opens in a designated corner of the screen, and a list of names and addresses appear in a pop-up dialogue box that represent researchers who have accessed the same materials you examined the night before. Your own search protocols have been downloaded and automatically linked in annotated hypertext. You see that you have three virtual conferences lined up for the morning and that the university link is down today, so you will have to go to school to teach. You see that four colleagues and a few others are chatting in the cybercafe and decide to fire up virtual reality to join the morning discussion.

You fly into the room with your usual panache and light on top of Sheldon's head for dramatic effect. He waves you off as you float lightly to the floor. Sheldon is saying, "But I don't see why writing in virtual reality must exist as hypertext or linear text. We have the ability here to write in three-dimensional space. . . ." Caroline rolls her eyes and looks at you, with a hopeful expression on her face. She whispers, "Have you heard anything about three dimensional writing? It seems like too much speculation to me." You say, "Hmm, I think I ran into a text last night in one of my searches. Ah, here's the reference, let me fly to the raw archive to see if I can find the text and its reviews. Be right back."

You fly over to the teaching library and see the shelf that contains all the sources that were linked in your last search protocol. The source you want is highlighted. As you grab it with your left hand, a translucent screen appears on your right. You use your index finger to select recent critiques and find that the book you are holding has not yet been filtered by any Web editors. But, it cites a majority of texts that have received Class 1 ratings from *Kairos* editorial group and Electronic Agents Inc.

You fly back into the cybercafe with the reference on three-dimensional writing and its reviews. Sheldon is still holding court, arguing that three-dimensional writing represents a new paradigm in cultural production. You remember that your graduate student, Eric, who regularly reviews and annotates raw archive articles for *Kairos*, is always complaining about the overuse of Kuhn's work and wonder what he would have to say to Sheldon. Checking, "Who's Online," you find he is reading the morning news, so you send him a note inviting him to join you in this discussion. He joins the group as you hand Caroline the references. Eric immediately jumps into the conversation, so you decide to take your leave. You say good-bye to Caroline and step out of virtual reality to enjoy a real cup of coffee and read your morning e-mail.

CONCLUDING THOUGHTS

This scenario of a Computers and Composition disciplinary homebase will likely emerge only if members of this community and academic publishers perceive the value of this new model and support its development. To imagine a disciplinary raw archive that includes all new knowledge in the context of a living space is to reconceive intellectual property, copyright, and fair use within research, promotion, publication, and teaching practices. On a broader scale, it will impact the dominant culture as it converges with the emergent online culture. We are currently witnessing a rapidly expanding financial base to support online infrastructure nationwide (mergers of AT&T with cable delivery systems and Microsoft, faster and tailored personal computers and WEB TV, etc.) and publisher-author relationships that are enabling new visions of online publication. These initiatives will help to fund the substantial financial investment necessary for developing such living archives. Additional grant sources, collaborative efforts among publishers, librarians, academics, systems analysts, and institutional support from individual campuses will also be necessary.

In the short run, we are likely to witness a proliferation of smaller scale interdisciplinary archives like Argos, the new WAC initiative, *academic.writing*, and publisher initiatives that collect copyrighted material, teaching and training resources, and interactive archival services. Publishers of such commercial archives would sell online access in place of traditional textbooks, which would make it possible for teachers to design and teach specialized courses easily and efficiently. Furthermore they allow online, for-profit publishers, electronic agents, and online services and electronic storage providers to link their own financial and cultural capital to the cultural capital of specialized and cross-disciplinary archives. Academics, professional organizations, and electronic journal editorial boards could build in value added resources that would encourage regular and repeated use of disciplinary homebases.

We realize that within 5 years new technologies and new communications systems will emerge that will substantially affect the outcome of our speculations. But, for the time being, the transition scenario we imagine here serves as a point of departure for discussion among academics, publishers, information managers, and systems analysts for a new vision of online heterotopic archives.

NOTES

1. This automated archive serves "over 35,000 users worldwide from over 70 countries, and processes more than 70,000 electronic transactions per day" (Ginsparg, 1996). Papers are "entered in the listings in order of receipt on an impartial basis (sic) and appearance of a paper is not intended in any way to convey tacit approval of its assumptions, methods, or conclusions . . ." ("General Information About the Archives"). The Advisory Board reserves "the right to reject any inappropriate submissions," and they state that any abstract submitted without a paper will be "rejected outright." <http://xxx.lanl.gov/help/general> (1-7-98)

2. Foucault's 1967 lecture served as the basis for the 1984 publication of "Des Espaces Autres." Although he never reviewed the piece for publication, it appeared in the French journal, *Architecture-Mouvement-Continuit* shortly before his death. The piece was then translated in 1986 by Jay Miskowiec and published in *Diacritics*.

3. MUSE also has search capabilities using SWISH (See FAQ sheet at http://www.press.jhu.edu/proj_descrip/faq/#subscription). Boolean searches can be applied to journal volumes, journal articles, authors, titles, and Library of Congress subject heading information in the table of contents.

4. In chapter 1 of *The Dialogic Classroom* (Galin & Latchaw, 1998), we discuss a multimedia program, *Litigation Strategies*, that was built to address criticisms of legal training by many newly practicing attorneys. We cite "[o]ne researcher [who] noted a serious gap in the education of lawyers, a majority of whom complain that the study of law has little to do with the practice of law. Notwithstanding Moot Court, learning how to deal with living, breathing clients happens as a kind of apprenticeship—on the job" (p. 5).

WORKS CITED

Argos. (1998, January 18). http://argos.evansville.edu/about.htm.

Barry, J. (1998, February 28). *Scrolls from the Dead Sea.* http://sunsite.unc.edu/expo/deadsea.scrolls.exhibit/intro.html.

Bolter, J. D. (1998). *Degrees of freedom.* http://www.lcc.gatech.edu/~bolter/degrees.html.

CIAO. (1998, January 22). http://www.ciaonet.org/.

Dobrin, S. (1997). *Constructing knowledges: The politics of theory-building and pedagogy in composition.* Albany: State University of New York Press.

e-print archives. (1998, January 22). xxx.lanl.gov.

Foucault, M. (1986). Of other spaces. *Diacritics,* 22-27.

Galin, J. R., & Latchaw, J. S. (1998). *The dialogic classroom: Teachers integrating computer technology, pedagogy, and research.* Urbana, IL: NCTE.

Getz, M. (1997, April). *Electronic publishing in academia: An economic perspective.* Proceedings of Scholarly Communication and Technology, Emory University. http://www.arl.org/scomm/scat/getz.html3.

Gibert, J. (1998, January 28). *CLAS/WMST 2100: Women in antiquity: Greece.* Perseus. http://www.Colorado.EDU/Classics/clas2100/.

Ginsparg, P. (1996, January 5). *Winners and losers in the global research village.* http://xxx.lanl.gov/blurb/pg96unesco.html.

Harnad, S. (1998, January 5). *Paper house of cards: (and why it's taking so long to collapse).* http://www.ariadne.ac.uk/issue8/harnad.

Healy, D. (1997). Cyberspace and place: The internet in middle landscape on the electronic frontier. In D. Porter (Ed.), *Internet culture.* New York: Routledge.

Hibbits, B. (1998, February 28). *Last writes: Reassessing the Law Review in the Age of Cyberspace.* http://www.law.pitt.edu/hibbits/lastrevp.htm.

JSTOR. (1998, January 15). http://www.jstor.org/aboutdemo/production.html.

Kairos: A Journal for Teachers in Webbed Environments. (1998, February 28). http://english.ttu.edu/kairos/.

Oldenburg, R. (1997). *The great good place: Cafes, coffee shops, community centers, beauty parlors, general stores, bars, hangouts and how they get you through the day.* New York: Marlowe.

Project MUSE. (1998, January 13). http://calliope.jhu.edu/muse.html.

RhetNet: a dialogic publishing (ad)venture. (1998, February 28). http://www.missouri.edu/~rhetnet/rhetnet.

Varian, H. R. (1997, April). *The future of electronic journals.* Proceedings of Scholarly Communication and Technology, Emory University. http://www.arl.org/scomm/scat/getz.html3.

Williams, R. (1981). Base and superstructure in Marxist cultural theory. In R. C. Davis & R. Schleifer (Eds.), *Contemporary literacy criticism and cultural studies.* New York: Longman.

chapter 2.5

WHAT ARE WE DOING TO OURSELVES?

(SOME MATERIAL PRACTICES OF DIGITAL PUBLISHING)

Dickie Selfe

collaborating with April Chapman, Allan Heaps, Heather Kreager, Brian Neuwerth, and Alanna Smith

This is a book of explorers, "early adopters"[1] of communication technologies, academics with a vision of what electronic writing might/should/will become. For reasons that become more obvious later, we have chosen a slightly different path; we have chosen to explore the underlying "materiality" of digital publishing. We chose this path because early in the process of developing this volume, the editors Dene Grigar and John Barber inspired us with the following question: What will writing have become and how will it have been used as we continue to test its materiality in electronic worlds?

We, however, recast that question this way: What will we become as we continue to test the materiality of "writing" in our new electronic worlds? Our discussions then resolved themselves into the two queries that dominated the writing of this chapter: What are we doing to students and students' prospects in the future? What are we doing to the English studies disciplines when, as a profession, we engage in and try to sustain the digital adventures represented in this volume?

Such questions are an important addition to this collection because academic explorers of the digital domain (myself included) are not particularly well suited to look after their own best interests (or those of their students) without some mediating influences. Two such influences are represented in this chapter. First, several undergraduate and graduate scientific and technical communication students provide academic explorers with a glimpse of the tensions that students feel as they head into a professional world imbricated with digital environments, environments that academics help create. Second, a group of 191 stakeholders—students, student workers, teachers, technicians, and administrators from 55 postsecondary institutions who responded to a questionnaire concerning technology-rich instruction—help illustrate what we are doing to the English studies disciplines in the last section of this chapter. Their mediation complicates issues such as "access to technology" and the "sustainability of our technology initiatives" in ways that are not always obvious to those of us focused primarily on the innovative potential of digital publishing systems. These stakeholders make it clear that academics exploring these digital domains have expanded and sometimes onerous responsibilities if we are to construct technical systems that are both humane and sustainable.

But to illustrate just why we need to take on expanded responsibilities, this chapter begins with some compelling testimony from technical communication students who stand on the brink of professional work tied closely to digital publishing. Their commentary helped move my attention away from the digital environments themselves and toward the inevitable struggle to live with the changes those environments produce in our personal and working lives. I hope it does the same for the readers of this volume.

WHAT ARE WE DOING TO STUDENTS AND STUDENTS' PROSPECTS IN THE FUTURE?

After reading a section of McLuhan's (1964) *Understanding Media*, Brian McIntosh, a student on the verge of graduating from Michigan Technological University's Scientific and Technical Communication program, offered our class this anecdote:

Chapter 33/Automation (pp. 300-311)

I've heard the term "global village" a great deal in the past two years (a result of being an STC [a student in the Scientific and Technical Communication program] and having a pair of ears), but I've never read a more interesting account of its roots than McLuhan's. Nor had I ever thought about our increasing technological innovation being a result of our own intrinsic needs...to free our hands, to interact, to learn.

Of all the things to chose from in this reading, I wanted to comment on these two lines:

Men could, for the most part, get through a normal life span on the basis of a single set of skills. That is not at all the case with electric speed-up. (p. 308)

Here, McLuhan is commenting on the fragmentization/division of labor that grew out of mechanical speed-ups (industrial revolution). He certainly seems to be right, as any GM [General Motors] worker could attest. I have a friend whose grandfather worked a lifetime at GM. He never graduated high school but managed to buy a large river front home, nice cars, a boat, and send his kids to college—all by repeating the same movements over and over for forty years. I will never experience this, and thankfully so. The trade-off is that I will have to deal with the constant demands of rapidly evolving technologies.

Brian McIntosh

McLuhan's "electric speedup" is the descriptive precursor to the primary focus of this volume: the new electronic worlds of publishing. In Brian's apparently simple observation that he (and we) will have to "deal with the constant demands of rapidly evolving technologies," I see a lifetime of change, potential, and struggle—a profound lifestyle change that seems to place Brian (and the rest of us) at odds with historical mentoring and learning relationships.

The first section of this chapter, then, begins our exploration of these questions in a term-long conversation held in the spring of 1997. These students and I have attempted to reconstruct the important moments of that conversation in a series of in-class, face-to-face and electronic discussions as we read, talked, and wrote about the working and public nature of digital publishing in a third-year, Scientific and Technical Communication course at Michigan Technological University. Our first recognition was that the digital world will influence not only the message (McLuhan, 1964) but the lifestyles and working styles of students, workers, parents, and citizens. That influence comes in the form of new sets of literacy practices.

Academic explorers who construct online publishing ventures are in fact helping to establish new sets of literacy practices that are likely to have repercussions for our students' lives. Those literacy practices are showing up in the commercial (academic and nonacademic) publishing industry as it goes through radical transformations: Digital technologies mandate changes in publication workflow, online promotional activities, interface designs, and just-in-time information management systems, and so on. Academics (as this volume suggests) are bent on taking successful advantage of these changes, and, as a result, they are changing the working conditions and expectations of graduating communicators.

Each year, scientific and technical communication students like these are poised to graduate into a world of online and electronic print publishing. This group of dedicated upper level undergraduates (and two graduate students) seemed the perfect consultants for an exploration of the implications of online publishing even though they would not likely be focusing their careers on academic publishing. You will hear in their words, I think, a reflection of our own ghostly concerns for the future. The syllabus described the object of the Print and Digital Publishing class in this way:

> We will all try to come to some understanding of work-related and social changes that are occurring as we move from traditional print publishing to digital, Internet publishing. Your one writing project will be to connect the issues covered in our discussions and readings to your personal expectations for work and life after graduation.

As they explored personal and professional concerns about and the exciting potential of these media, they revealed some issues that our student population in general (as well as academic professionals) will be facing. Some of these issues relate very directly to online publishing, whereas others illustrate how sophisticated these young people are at considering the implications that digital domains have for their personal, private lives. I chose to encourage this type of speculation because I saw no important reason to distinguish between the technological working world we and our students inhabit and our private adaptations to convenient and invasive digital technologies. Just as in the second section of this chapter I try to complicate our approach to the institutional uses of electronic/online publishing, these students pushed the boundaries of our technological infatuation into areas of immediate and intimate concern: family, attitudes toward work, access to technology, gendered approaches to technology, and many others.

What they have to say, I believe, is representative of many students' experiences: from first-year composition students who are being required to dabble with a seductive, even addictive, digital world to graduate rhetoric and composition students. Simply put, educators in the English studies (ES) disciplines (here referring to composition, literature, and technical and professional communication departments or programs) have tended to adopt technology-rich programs, teaching techniques, and publishing systems without considering the impact they might have on the students we teach. Students' comments on the influence of these new spaces served to ground, challenge, and complicate my own practical and theoretical understandings digital and print publishing. I hope those comments serve a similar function for others.

Our discussions in Print and Digital Publishing occurred in two venues:

1. The computer-aided publishing e-mail discussion list (CAP-L@mtu.edu) where we were joined by (about 50) other instructors, professional technical communicators, and students from other universities.
2. Weekly face-to-face (f2f) class meetings.

In both spaces, students were encouraged to use and discuss a series of readings assigned during the quarter. Those readings included in a 10-week quarter were as follows:

> Week 2: McLuhan, M. (1964). *Understanding media: The extensions of man.* New York: Penguin Books, pp. 23-45 & 300-311.
>
> Week 3: Bolter, J. D. (1991). *Writing space: The computer, hypertext, and the history of writing.* Hillsdale, NJ: Lawrence Erlbaum Associates, pp. 1-11 & 223-238.
>
> Week 4: Gomez, M L. (1991). The equitable teaching of composition with computers: A case for change. In G. Hawisher & C. Selfe (Eds.), *Evolving perspectives on computers and composition studies: Questions for the 1990s* (pp. 318-335). Urbana, IL: NCTE Press.
>
> Week 5: Birkerts, S. (1994). *The Gutenberg elegies: The fate of reading in an electronic age.* New York: Fawcett Columbine Books, pp. 210-229.
>
> Stoll, C. (1997). Lecture at Michigan Technological University about the influence computers and technology have had, might have on our future.
>
> Week 6: Roberts, P. (1996, June). Virtual Grub Street: Sorrows of a multimedia hack. *Harper's Magazine*, pp. 71-77.

Week 7: Landow, G. (1991). The rhetoric of hypermedia:
Some rules for authors. In P. Delany & G. Landow (Eds.),
Hypermedia and literary studies (pp. 81-104). Cambridge,
MA: The MIT Press.

Week 8: Howard, T. (1996). Who "owns" electronic texts?
In P. Sullivan & J. Dautermann (Eds.), *Electronic literacies
in the workplace: Technologies of writing* (pp. 177-198).
Urbana, IL: NCTE Press

After a week of online discussion, the class would meet for F2F
discussions during which I often attempted to take notes and
characterize their comments. In this section of the chapter, our
construction of these e-mail and face-to-face conversations is, of course,
partial and incomplete, but we do think it represents some of the
important implications that were discussed, implications that remain
important today. In retrospect student comments seemed motivated
largely by yet another iteration of previous questions: What are we
doing to the next generation of students and to ourselves as we help
develop and become more dependent on digital, online publishing
systems?

WHAT ARE WE DOING TO OUR WORKING "SELVES"?

The first reading (McLuhan, 1964) generated a strand of conversation
that was echoed throughout the term. It had to do with the working
world into which these students were about to step. Of course, it is
possible to find an academic discussions of many of the following issues
(see Gergen, 1991, *The Saturated Self* and Hecksher, 1994, *Post-
bureaucratic Organization* for observations on the personal and
institutional changes, respectively that seem to be occurring in a world
of technological innovation). Certainly, one of the central features of a
working world influenced by new communication technologies can be
found in the earlier comments of Brian McIntosh, probably one of the
most unabashedly enthusiastic technology advocate in the small class.

In a related observation, Alanna Smith is struck, as I am, by the
phrase, "learning a living."

I found McLuhan's article very interesting. Realizing that it was written
in 1964, it offers a lot of insight even in today's society.

Right off I found the subtitle "Learning a Living" to be a careful
thought. As I read on I came to this

Automation is information and it not only ends jobs in the world of work, it ends subjects in the world of learning. It does not end the world of learning. (p. 300)

After considering what McLuhan was trying to say, I came to this conclusion . . . in a factory, automation of an assembly line causes a loss of jobs for a number of workers. In conjunction with this, workers no longer need training to learn the skills they once needed to do the job. Therefore "it ends subjects in the world of learning," but learning doesn't come to an end, it just broadens into new subjects.

Alanna

By Brian's and Allana's accounts we will be, for the rest of our lives, "learning a living," constantly attending to new technologies and new content, and the prospect of this type of working lifestyle doesn't seem to bother these young adults a great deal. Had it occurred to me at their age, however, the prospect of life long learning in a constantly changing technological environment would have been frightening. I would certainly have felt exhausted at the outset and intimidated by the demands of assuming the role of a "beginner" so often, a role at the time that I was struggling to overcome. I would have been bewildered by the need to find help and support wherever I could inside and outside the traditional institutional hierarchy. Indeed, for many of our colleagues, the prospect of this type of continuous relearning, starting anew is not reassuring. This type of dread is what I suspect that many of my less techno-enthusiastic colleagues are facing as this new digital age is apparently foisted upon them. Their resistance is not surprising, it is, instead, surprisingly muted.

However, after a decade of working with student collaborators (like those helping me write this chapter) in technology-filled environments, I have apparently become somewhat accustomed to newness. And I have realized that students are coming, at least to this technological university with a slightly different attitude about their job prospects. They assume, as I did not when I left high school, that adjusting to new technologies is simply a part of their job or their content knowledge. It is not an additional requirement added on to some expertise; it is integral part of their literacy practices.

This last realization is an example why I continue to be fascinated by subtle changes in the modes of learning and awareness evident in the young people who roll through our program and our technical facility year after year. In general, they do not seem to be the apathetic, a-critical technological enthusiasts that many cultural critics sometimes assume (see, Birkerts, 1994). These young people are typically hyper-aware of the implications that new technological environments have for them professionally and personally, no matter how flashy the kaleidoscopic images of this brave, fun new world become. This exchange between Alanna and April is indicative.

> [Alanna wrote,]

> After consideration of what McLuhan was trying to say I
> came to this conclusion. In a factory, automation of an
> assembly line causes a loss of jobs for a number of
> workers. In conjunction with this, workers no longer
> need training to learn the they once needed to do the
> job. Therefore "it ends subjects in the world of
> learning," [McLuhan] but learning doesn't come to an end,
> it just broadens into new subjects.

[April responds,]

... [But] when we become more technologically advanced, a lot of the "middle steps" of production are lost. The people who once manned [sic] these steps either are eliminated or become jacks-of-all-trades, broadening their skills to adapt to a changing environment. This acquisition of additional skills is good for those people, but I'm not sure it's a very healthy trend over all. We end up with a work force that knows a little about a lot, instead of specializing in one aspect of the production process. Such specialization, especially in the world of printing and publishing, allows for true craftsmanship and products in which the crafter can take pride. It also gives one a feeling of stability— if you know that you're the only one in the shop who knows how to work a certain machine, you know you're not going anywhere, as opposed to a shop where there are only 5 or 6 people and *everyone* knows how to do *everything*—but not very well. More skills are great, but not at the expense of quality and workmanship.

April :)

So as attractive as the mobility of skills and intellectual effort may seem, April warns us to be concerned about the possibility that this mobility will replace the highly skilled craftspeople of our culture with a workforce of generalists who have little depth of skill or understanding. Online publishing is in itself an opening of the profession to a broader segment of society although, of course, the restrictive nature of technology access in our culture and across class barriers seems likely to reproduce the distinctions of haves and have-nots (Selfe & Selfe, in press). Still, it is a fact that many people who have not been able to publish, can now do so for the price of an account with an Internet provider or an account on some K-12 or university network. These new publicists are spared the costs of typical print publishing infrastructure at the same time they may also circumvent the advice, expertise, and valuable experience of writers, editors, graphic designers, typographers, and content consultants, as April indicated.

I have been convinced by student concerns and comments over the last decade that they often make this critical turn in their thinking. As educators and creators of digital environments, it is our responsibility to encourage this type of reflection by expecting it in our classes and by giving it a pedagogical space in which to flourish. I am also convinced that academics should be very attentive to students' abilities—that is, we should be trying always to learn what a life spent in the midst of new media has enabled. What, as a result of this life of media experiences can they do? What do they think? How do the learn? Taking advantage of their experiences is particularly problematic because our students are trained from an early age to think that they have nothing of value to teach us. But they do. And I often learned from these students during our F2F classroom discussions.

Each week, after reading and writing online, we would meet and dedicate an hour or more to a discussion of the lifeworld implications of these readings. As young and middle-aged adults—some with families and jobs—who were about to graduate into a world of print/digital work, it was not difficult to spark a conversation about the implications that communication technologies have for the culture and for individuals. The following are notes I took during one such meeting and posted via e-mail to class members so they might have a record of the gist of our conversation as they developed their final projects later in the term. Again, the topic of their future working world was central to the discussion, but they also revealed a bit more about their literacy habits and expectations as they talked.

[To the students in the class]

These are my notes on the class discussion between 12 people. All names are abbreviated. [Please remember that] none of this is a direct quote except the stuff in quotes.

B—On TBS he saw a cooking show at a time that seemed unusual (9:30 p.m.) and wonders if this is an indication that our working time/learning time/leisure times are getting all moved around.

A—We may never get away from work. [He describes a] cousin who begins work at 7:00 p.m. Sunday and never stops all week.

H—E-mail, voice mail, ... is creating a level of inconvenient access.

A—We are building expectations that people will always respond immediately [to electronic queries and publications]. The fact that the technology produces a disembodied memory—no face, no name—is changing our patterns of interaction.

A2—"Convenience to the point of inconvenience."

B—McLuhan doesn't seem to be very concerned about the changes media are making [to our culture].

A—McLuhan's trying to be descriptive and not be judgmental.

D—An ex-consultant in our computer lab now commutes to work with his laptop and a cellular modem and begins accounting for "billable hours" early in the day. Time literally becomes money.

A3—Lifestyles where you work all week and all weekend (like I did last summer) seem like lost time. No time for friends and important others.

A2—Working on something that you find enjoyable is OK, even if it takes up a lot of your time.

H—I think the PLACE of work is more important than the actual job. We have to set our own priorities, and I will only work in some parts of the country.

A2—I want to be a mother. I want to set up an at-home workplace to give myself more flexibility.

A [male] & L [female]—Kids find ways of making themselves the center. It's hard to work at home. [However,] digital technologies offer opportunities (home schooling programs) previously impossible for most folks to take on.

A—At home, work times for A are 10 p.m. to 4 a.m., sleep from 4-10 or so. Work until 5 to 7 and start over. Without a wife working at home even this would be a stretch.

D—What are the skills and perceptions that young people who have grown up with today's media have that older folks like me don't?

B—Principles of publishing stay the same: audience analysis, publishing guidelines, ... We [young people] seem to be [better] able to handle the interactivity of media.

A3—Parents are afraid of loosing stuff in the new digital age. The impermanence of digital media? We [younger people] are less concerned about that permanence.

D—What's going to happen when the kids of A come to school after working with digital media since the age of 2 ??

Everyone—All folks seemed to agree that it will be both a scary and exciting moment.

7 out of 12 folks talked.

If we extract from this conversation some potential literacy characteristics or attitudes of a new media-rich generation, they might include young people who

- learn, work, and play at any time of the day
- grow to expect immediate response to electronic queries
- resent levels of inconvenient access and protect the few distinctions between private and public (working) lives still available to them
- expect enjoyable and flexible work activities and work spaces (online and physical)
- have a facility with interactive media
- are less concerned (regrettably, from my perspective) about the permanence and an archival history of the generation's discourse.
- are both excited about and fearful of the coming generation of media-savvy youth.

In light of these potential characteristics, I came to this tentative conclusion:

Dickie's Final Comment:

We are going to have to reconfigure our teaching so that teachers are learning from young people about the new perceptual modalities young people bring to our classes. Older teachers will have to enter the classroom willing and anxious to learn from these young people but at the same time bring a larger, critical, thoughtful, historical perspective to the learning environment regardless of the topic of the class.

In that class discussion, we can hear echoes of several types of tension that these young professionals are experiencing:

- between buying into a 24/7 work life (working 24 hours per day/7 days per week) ("it seems like lost time") and the attractiveness of an exciting job worthy of commitment
- between the intriguing possibilities of telecommuting and the intrusive levels of electronic access to our personal lives ("levels of inconvenient access")
- between home-work environments that allow them to choose geographically where they live and the difficulty of working in a household full of lively children.

These kinds of tensions are not that far removed from those faced by the academics interested in the power of new digital communication systems. They are lifestyle considerations worth attending to even as we delve into the disciplinary and theoretical potential of these venues. We have, it seems, figured out how to publish electronically, broadly construed but not how to live within electronic environments.

This was not the end to our discussions centering around the question, "What are we doing to our working 'selves'"? Later in the term, after reading Roberts' (1996) "Virtual Grub Street: Sorrows of a Multimedia Hack," the strand about working lifestyles of those immersed in the digital age came roaring back to life. The conversation morphed slightly into concerns about the job itself, the job of an online media specialist.

[Jill quoting Roberts]

I never expected to be working like this. I once earned a respectable living writing long, earnest articles about spotted owls, riparian buffer zones, even, on one occasion, a 10,000-word treatise on the douglass fir, hero tree of the Pacific Northwest. (p. 72)

But now he claims to do nothing but produce "info-nuggets," informational segments to accompany the picture that replaced a thousand words. Roberts considers the expertise of writers to be decreasing, where they really need only be "filters to absorb and compress great gobs of information into small, easily digestible, on screen chunks." (p. 72)

A related point that [Clifford] Stoll mentioned in his lecture last week is that, it is almost impossible to read more than one page of text off a computer screen and retain most of it's [sic] information. So if as Jay Bolter states, "Print will no longer define the organization and presentation of knowledge, as it has for the past five centuries" is true and CD-ROMs [and other media] begin to replace books, magazines, articles, and school-teachers; will our new selectors of information be these multimedia informational hackers, with their "info-nuggets"?

Paints a scary picture doesn't it?

I agree with the concerns Roberts brings up about these "absorbers and compressors" replacing writers, yet I have another concern. Because of Robert's occupational decisions, I can only see him as a 34-year-old man with a 32-year-old wife, a 2-year-old daughter, and a 4-year communications degree, who, for the past year and a half, has been working as a blurb writer for a CD-ROM company and who is presently frustrated because he feels he sold out. Maybe he should just quit.

Then April let loose with this response,

> I was seriously angst-ridden after I read this article. This guy could
> make *anyone* depressed I think. I really don't know why he does
> what he does, if he gets so little joy and pleasure from his work (it's
> gotta be the money, that's all I have to say). I think he's really giving
> the medium, and the people who work in it (and *love* it), a bad
> name—calling himself a "hack" writing "the kind of pap . . . only the
> feckless and unprincipled had the nerve or need to take." I think his
> reflections on earning a "respectable" living doing environmental
> writing are belittling and extremely insulting. What right does he have
> to, on the one hand, moan and complain [about] how awful everything
> about the profession is, and then, on the other hand, not only take
> home his paycheck every week, but refer to himself and the rest of the
> MM writers as a collective we—as if he felt any camaraderie with
> them? If I were someone who made my living this way, and really
> *enjoyed* what I was doing, I'd be angry—I'd be angry that this man is
> whining and complaining about the thing I love, and yet keeps
> cynically writing (and complaining about it). I'd be angry that, with all
> the writers in the world who are struggling to survive and get
> published, this guy has the temerity to say "Look, I have a job, but I
> *hate* it—I used to be respectable and *now* look what I do . . ." And,
> I'd be angry that this man remains in the business, for whatever the
> reason, and continues to bad mouth the process and the products.
> Personally, I don't think he has any cause to complain—he got his first
> job through nepotism. :)
>
> Frankly, this article just made me furious. If I was supposed to feel
> sorry for Roberts, it didn't work—I just felt disgust. It reminds me of a
> Far Side cartoon: two people, husband and wife, sitting in a sumptuous
> mansion. The man is sitting at a grand piano, and the wife looks over at
> him and says: "Why don't you play some blues?" Mr. Roberts, as far as
> *I* can see, you have absolutely nothing to complain about, and to
> appeal to others to see your awful life is just self serving and pathetic.
>
> Just my $0.02,
>
> April :)

That in turn, made me a bit defensive about why I included Roberts in
the class readings in the first place:

> I guess I owe you people an explanation of why I included this piece in
> the readings for this quarter. First, it was someone actually working in
> the field. Many students seem to think that MM is the dream job. It
> might not be. Indeed if a lot of money is going into this type of
> production, the pap he writes might be an industry standard. Sad
> thought. Our objective would be to change that standard or set a higher
> one. But there was another reason. I found this article via another class,

a graduate class. In that class they were "using" this article to illustrate the potential for some of what Sven Birkerts was claiming, that we are becoming an illiterate society. I find Roberts' argument unconvincing for all the reasons April mentions. I can only hope that the other class (which I did not attend) was equally and eloquently critical.

Dickie

In a subsequent post, I added this:

> It seems like Roberts is complaining about a situation that is all too familiar to technical communicators: he's stuck in a production process that has him located at the end of the pipe. That is, others decide what the media is going to be like, what content is included, how much is included, and whose needs are primary (graphic designer's, videographer's, audio technician's, animator's, CD technician's, and then finally the writers' . . .).
>
> Technical communicators have had to deal with this syndrome from the beginning. Traditionally they have been asked to write documentation for projects in which they were not involved. In response STC students and faculty at most universities [I hope] have developed a sensitivity to the situation and methods for resisting it: avoid jobs where end-of-pipeline documentation is inevitable, lobby for production processes that include communicators from the beginning.
>
> Maybe that's why Roberts' position sounds so lame to the technical communicators on this list. Apparently he hasn't even begun to think about strategies that would have helped him avoid his current position. If he has, he certainly doesn't share those strategies in the article; he just complains.
>
> Perhaps an STC curriculum may have something to suggest to straight English majors [like Roberts] who are going to find work in the media industry?
>
> The very idea!
>
> Dickie

What struck me as important in this exchange is twofold. I was impressed by how ill at ease these students were with professionals who claim no agency, no ability to change their work-related station in life. And I was amazed by how much intellectual and occupational energy they were willing to put into making the digital publication one in which they could feel pride and excitement.

As technical communicators, they are in the awkward but powerful position of providing a new multimedia, digital interface between the general public and technical specialists. Those of us in academic environments who are willing, even enthusiastic, about plunging our disciplines and students into online publishing should be at least as concerned about providing students with strategies for avoiding the pitfalls of a media production process, whether that media ends up on a CD or the Internet: processes that Roberts suggested and April rejected so completely. Unfortunately, a concern about the media production process is not normally one of the pedagogical goals of an English studies course.

WHAT IS OUR RELATIONSHIP TO THE MEDIA ITSELF IN THE "LATE, GREAT AGE OF PRINT"?

Spurred on by some of the comments they read in Bolter's (1991) *Writing Space: The Computer, Hypertext, and the History of Writing*, the class also concerned itself with the media itself. April summarized and responded to the reading in this post:

> This article basically discussed many aspects that computers play and will play in the future of writing, print, reading, and perceptions about the world.
>
> I was most affected by the introductory chapter . . . , which discussed the emergence of "the electronic book" and its effect on traditional books. I have a great love for books and "traditional" reading, so the prospect of "this destroying that" (from the quote from Victor Hugo) is truly frightening.
>
> At first, I was confused by Bolter's use of the term "electronic book." He speaks of it in the context of "textual networks," which brings to my mind some sort of electronic "Choose Your Own Adventure," where every person takes their own path through a gargantuan bank of information, aided by search utilities to pick out the concepts which interest us. But as I thought about it, I realized that Bolter was talking about the Web. People don't take the same path through the massive network of "pages" (back to the electronic writing thing!), and are aided by utilizing search engines based on their interests.
>
> But is this an "electronic book"? How does this possibly compare with "traditional" books? Web surfing is chaotic, unconnected—books are coherent, linear. I really don't see how the "electronic book" could destroy the traditional book. I *do* agree that print will become a less influential medium than the computer. However, I think that there will always be people like myself who will take the romanticism of curling up with their favorite copy of White Fang by firelight over sitting down to a cold, impersonal laptop anytime, and that this type of consumption will not simply be a luxury, etc.

If we lose contact with the physical entity of print, the books which are the link back to our literary beginnings, then we lose the intimacy of the act of writing, the link with the author who pulled the work from their mind and soul. We forget that writing is truly an art. The idea of an electronic book as compared with a comfortably solid novel is vaguely obscene, like seeing the Mona Lisa on the Web, as opposed to viewing it in the Louvre. Writing, and reading, for that matter, is as dependent on the environment, the whole *experience*, as the work itself.

April :)

Brian responded:

This post is in response to April Chapman

>Bolter, Jay D. (1991). _Writing Space._

April says,

>>I myself have a great love for books and "traditional"
>>reading, so the prospect of "this destroying that"
>>(from the quote from Victor Hugo) is truly frightening.

Naturally we want to cling to what we know, thus I see your point. But the prospect of "experiencing" Beowulf as opposed to reading it is truly, truly exciting. And, how much more we could take away from it!

>>He speaks of it (electronic book) in the context of
>>"textual networks," which brings to my
>>mind some sort of electronic "Choose Your Own Adventure,"
>>where every person takes their own path through a
>>gargantuan bank of information,

Exactly. Pause the story to bring up a map of where your character is headed; pause the story to find out what a gauntlet (glove) is; pause the story to follow THIS historian's account of what happened or THAT historian's account of what happened.

>>However, I think that there will always be people like
>>myself who will take the romanticism of
>>curling up with their favorite copy of _White Fang_
>>by firelight...

Yep, one of my favorites.

>>Writing, and reading, for that matter, is as dependent on
>>the environment, the whole *experience*, as the work
>>itself.

Precisely! We will come to value different environments of experience.

Brian McIntosh

Brian also posted this comment after a class discussion:

On page 10, Bolter says, "Writing is the creative play of signs, and the computer offers us a new field for that play." He goes on further to say, ". . . we can only see and understand written signs as extended in a space of at least two dimensions."

But this is entirely not the case. As technology continues to make leaps and bounds, as virtual reality comes closer, as more VRML sites pop up on the Web . . . our ability to see and understand signs of more than two dimensions grows stronger; our "new field" to play on will be three-dimensional.

We all know "meaning" does not exist in the text but rather in the minds of the writer and the reader. Well, I see authors of the future unrestricted from conveying THEIR meaning. I see the writer and the reader achieving a greater sense of shared meaning in a 3-D world. Future readers will know how gray something is, how tall something is, etc. . . . without having to imagine it for themselves.

<——and this opens up a whole new can of worms, which I'll let someone else address.

Brian McIntosh

April, of course couldn't let this rest.

This is a response to Brian on Bolter . . .

On Wed, 19 Mar 1997, Brian L. McIntosh wrote:

> April says,
>
> Naturally we want to cling to what we know, thus I see
> your point. But the prospect of "experiencing" Beowulf
> as opposed to reading it is truly, truly
> exciting. And, how much more we could take away from it!
>

I don't know about you, but I will take the Beowulf I envisioned in my mind over *anything* some guy with a pocket protector could program into a computer :) I don't have anything against experiencing something a different way, but I must be getting ornery in my old age [under 22!]—I don't like people telling me how I should experience something. My Grendel doesn't (and *won't*, *can't*) look anything like that computer geek's Grendel, and I resent him imposing his vision on me. I know, I know—if I don't like it, don't use it. I guess I'm waiting for the day when VRML and other such technologies can be truly tailored to the user. When I can specify exactly what Grendel looks like, and how he acts, then I'll be happy. But only up to a point.

Will VRML kill the imagination, or make it stronger? I can see both sides of the argument . . . but as of now, with this technology still in its infancy, I fall on the "imagination killer" side. I want to be able to immerse myself in my own brain, and dislodge myself from the world for awhile, when I read a book. Die hards will tell you that you do the same thing when you use VRML or something similar, but the whole *flavor* of the experience is all different. I want the stimulation, the challenge of dredging up that character from my mind, much as the author might, rather than having it passively presented to me. I don't want to just *watch* the play in front of me, I want to recreate it, with my own actors and sets. Like I said, maybe when the technology evolves, this will be possible, but until that point, Mr. Pocket Protector can keep his VRML. :)

[Brian said]
>
> Exactly. Pause the story to bring up a map of where
> your character is headed; pause the story to find out
> what a gauntlet (glove) is; pause the story to follow
> THIS historian's account of what happened or THAT
> historian's account of what happened.

This just has this air of . . . fakeness is the word that springs to mind. There is the challenge of the hunt, of *physicality* that is lost here. It's like doing an "honest day's work" building a skyscraper, or playing SimCity. Same result (sort of), but sometimes you just want to . . . *get your hands dirty*. I just don't want to see the world turn into one big video game. It seems that way sometimes (and I'm not overly entranced with video games ;)

> >>Writing, and reading, for that matter, is as dependent
> >>on the environment, the whole *experience*, as the
> >>work itself.
>
> Precisely! We will come to value different environments
> of experience.

Precisely! Don't make things homogenously digital . . . leave me things to touch, to feel, with which to *commune*. Digital is getting very tired for me . . .

[from Brian's signature, April quotes the following]

> "Imagination is more important than knowledge."
>   -Einstein

Mr. Einstein says it best . . . imagination can take you to all those places and let you experience everything you can't program into a computer.

How 'bout you will me your copy of _White Fang_, Brian, and we'll call it even? ;)

April :)

April and Brian make the case well enough. We need to attend to literacy practices of both types: print and digital. Let us develop together standards of excellence and comfort zones of use in both domains.

I recognized in their conversation a literacy practice to which academics should pay heed if they are committed to developing in the digital domain: the power relationship between the author/designer and user. This is more than just the well worn concern for audience. It's a concern or respect for the materiality of the reader/user's experience. With what sort of control and feedback mechanisms are reader/users provided? How sincere is an author's attempt to take advantage of the "interactivity" inherent in these media? How free, really, is the reader/user to use this product? What comfort levels are online publishers providing or undermining? Students like Brian and April— who by the way are two of the most dedicated, self-taught online publicists that I have come across in our program—have what Giddens (1983) would call a deep and penetrating understanding of the social (and of course digital) systems around them. Given the chance, they can express their profound understanding of the implications of online publishing. However, our discipline and educational institutions rarely give them the opportunity to enter into our deliberations.

WHAT ELSE ARE WE DOING TO OUR CULTURE?

I was hoping during the quarter to hear from students about other cultural patterns of change as well, and I wasn't disappointed. They considered briefly what it means to own electronic "texts" and then moved onto issues of economic class, gender, gaming, and early exposure to technology.

Even as we struggle to establish standards for acceptable online development (Is the "info-nugget" writing that Roberts complained about or the CD version of Beowulf acceptable digital publishing?), standards for excellence and fairness in this medium are far from well established. This became quite clear when we began read Howard's (1996) take on intellectual property, "Who 'Owns' Electronic Texts?" April began the discussion with this comment:

I found this article especially interesting, because it involved exactly the topic which we were speaking about in Anne Wysocki's [a teacher in the Technical Communication program at MTU] Digital Photography class a few weeks ago. There, the issue was like that of a couple of the scenarios offered by Howard: if you take a part of a picture, spin it, color it, and blur it, is it copyright violation? These same issues are involved text—if you chop it, change the words around, etc., is it still the author's work, or is it yours? These are sticky issues, and, unfortunately, we do not have the infrastructure in place to deal with them. Hopefully, as electronic texts (and images) become more prevalent, we will be able to deal more successfully with these issues.

April :)

More was said online and in class about digital ownership. At one point, Howard, joined the discussion to clarify student concerns. What seems important here is that if we make online publishing part of the classroom practice, we should also make the electronic publishing process an object of investigation. If we do so, that investigation provides English studies professionals and students with an opportunity to combine more theoretical discussions of electronic policy with the practices of electronic production. (For extensive discussions of intellectual property and copyright see the August issue of *Computers and Composition* and the Spring 1998 Coverweb of *Kairos*).

But these young people were also concerned about more than the legalistic concerns that digital environments create. Alanna's comments started us into a thread that wound its way around concerns with class, economics, gender, and the computer game-making industry: I found Bolter perceptive, but parts of the article already seem outdated in a way. One specific example is in Chapter 13, page 223, where he begins:

> Some sociologists and economists feel that our society may be splitting into a technologically sophisticated upper class and a lower class lacking the skills required by the so-called information economy. . . . The computer illiterate will at best be passive/users readers of the machine. They may be able to enter data-as cashiers now do for cash registers that are already microcomputers-but they will not be able to write with the machine across the spectrum of semiotic communication. (pp. 223-224)

For a visual representation of this fact see Cathy Camper's "Note from the Future" cited in Hawisher and Selfe's (1997) *Literacy, Society, and Technology*. Wresch's (1996) book, *Disconnected: Haves and Have-nots in the Information Age*, explores these issues as well.

Alanna continued,

> I feel what Bolter is talking about has already taken place in society. But is it because the upper class is more technologically sophisticated, or is it because those in the lower class are put at a technology disadvantage therefore widening the gap? How many lower income people can afford to purchase a computer for their home? Not having the opportunity to access computers except while at school keeps them at a disadvantage, while the upper class becomes more sophisticated everyday with their car phones, beepers, and laptops with modems.
>
> Alanna Smith

And with that statement, Alanna took the discussion into new territory. Her response and our reading by Gomez (1991), "The Equitable Teaching of Composition with Computers" launched a discussion of some social, economic implications of our turn toward the digital domain.

Allan Heaps (a graduate students sitting in on the class discussions) responded"

> A couple of things I want to add to Alanna's post:

> Well, Alanna, I think you have only begun to get at one of the problems with technology use in our society. It is true that a segment of our society goes without computer and other communication technologies in their homes, but even more go without them in their schools. Struggling school districts can rarely afford the price tag on technology, even though most software companies offer a greatly reduced educational price. Some technology companies like Apple/Macintosh, Hewlett-Packard, and even IBM used to offer educational discounts on hardware as well (though in some cases it was mostly a way to get rid of outdated equipment while scoring a tax break) but those give-aways are a thing of the past.

> Paul LeBlanc [1994] tells a troubling story in his article "The Politics of Literacy and Technology in Secondary School Classrooms" about a woman in a workshop he ran who worked in a district that could not buy simple things like paper and pencils for the students, yet came up with enough money to put a computer in her classroom. She did not ask for the computer. She would have preferred up-to-date textbooks to replace the 15 year old versions they were using at the time, but there it was, and she had to deal with it. Paul asks the obvious question about why something like this happens. He also points to studies that show student improvement is based more on lower class sizes than on anything else. Yet when computers are placed in a classroom, most of the time the rationale is for them to be used to teach more students at a time instead of fewer. Troubling, troubling, troubling. What are we to do?
>
> Allan.

Feenberg (1991) would describe this phenomena (in *A Critical Theory of Technology*) as our cultural tendency to act "on" as opposed to acting "out of" the social technological context. That is, administrators act on the classroom setting without involving themselves in the daily practices of those classrooms. One has to wonder if many of the technological solutions recommended in academic articles and books like this volume might not fall into the same trap. All the more reason to attend carefully to the lived experience of those using digital environments and making local decisions based on those experiences and needs.

One other social issue that grew out of the "haves-have-nots" discussion had to do with the gendered nature of digital environments in general, and in gaming environments in particular. Alanna commented,

> This article [Gomez, 1991] caused me to evaluate a few things about the way I look at computers. It brought up an issue that we discussed briefly about the accessibility of computers to some groups of people. What I found interesting about this article is that it incorporated the stereotype that we come across, that women are less interested in learning about computers than men.
>
> [Gomez stated]
>
> Similar diminished expectations for females' potential to learn with, and about, computers have resulted in fewer opportunities for girls and women to use computer technology. A gender gap in computer use exists for three reasons. First, there are, as mentioned earlier, cultural biases regarding females' use of technology. . . . Second there is limited existing instructional software with female-oriented topics and formats. . . . Third, the content and structure of programming as a focus of entry-level computer literacy courses provides an additional barrier to some females as programming sustains an image similar to mathematics as male turf. (pp. 323-324)
>
> Although I have never been particularly interested in computer games or programming, I always figured there must be a number of women who are. But here at MTU [a technological university] I cannot name a single girl who is majoring in Computer Science. I also don't know any girls who play computer games.
>
> So I would like to know about others' views or discoveries on this topic.
>
> Alanna Smith

Although one particular strand embedded in April's comment (women computer science majors) did not continue on our class list, Amy Pearl and her colleagues provided an accessible and interesting take on the plight of women in computer science departments again in Hawisher and Selfe's (1997) *Literacy, Technology, and Society: Confronting the Issues.*

Brian McIntosh responded to Gomez with this summary and comment:

Gomez says,

Students of color and those of low socioeconomic status received instruction of a classic compensatory nature—practice in discrete "basic" skills—while their middle- and upper-class white counterparts received instruction in programming and problem-solving.

The underlying root for these inequities, of course, lies within us. . . .

The main point of this article is found at the end of page 325:

it is imperative that new models of instruction with computers be devised if these additional curriculum barriers to learning for nonwhite [sic] students, students of low socioeconomic status, and students of limited English proficiency are to be broken.

I came to understand that providing students with access to computers is not an end-all solution. Access does not equal equity. Computer instruction needs to be tailored to meet the needs of a diverse group of students. Thus far, the computer is simply another classroom tool for transferring our white, male-dominant culture to students that are female, nonwhite, non-English proficient, or poor.

Although Gomez provides no theoretical solution, she describes efforts that are underway to correct this aspect of a failing educational system.

Brian McIntosh

April responded out of her personal experience.

I found this chapter interesting, but not particularly surprising. I think that, even looking at the demographics of this university's computer department, that we could have figured out that white males in particular seem to be drawn to computers.

I did find interesting her discussion of efforts to make computers more inviting to women because I have always been interested in using and learning about computers. Not that I ever wanted to find out particularly about the guts of the machine, or programming it (although I *have* found myself embroiled in that process here at MTU), but using the applications available to me to create, especially word processors and graphics applications. I credit this interest to the fact that I was lucky enough to be exposed to computers very early in life. In my first grade class room, we had a really weird computer that looked like something out of 2001. But it was still there for us to acclimate to using. My family has had a computer for practically *forever*—at least back around 1984 or so. It wasn't even an Apple IIe—it was some sort of generic (Laser, I think) from *Sears*, of all places ;) It was about the cheesiest thing I can think of—5 1/4 disks and all. But it was also the coolest—we had great computer games, and I used to type stories using Appleworks. I think I *learned* to type on that computer. As the years went by, we upgraded to bigger and better things, but the computer was always a part of my life. Here at Tech, my horizons have opened. But I think that I was never intimidated by them, because I've always been exposed to them.

So, while this is probably not a viable option, I think that for females to really *truly* be comfortable using computers, they have to be exposed to them early in life. Having "female-friendly" content is helpful, too, but I think that if you're comfortable with the foundations, you can not only be comfortable with *any* content, but you will have the confidence and ability to learn new technologies and skills easily.

Just my $0.02,

April :)

April's call for early exposure to "female-friendly" content, set us off on a discussion of gaming software: software that often provides young people with their first exposure to computers.

As I read April's comment about making computers more female-friendly, I was reminded of my experience this weekend of trying to find a computer game for my daughter. Unless she wanted to be a Barbie Fashion Designer there wasn't a whole lot of choice. Her scathing look warned me not to consider the whole Barbie thing. Her remaining choices were Magic School Bus, Carmen SanDiego, and other titles either too educational or too juvenile to fit the bill. Meanwhile, my son was staggering under a mountain of games ranging from Knights Quest to NFL Action. Come on software designers, there are some girls out there who would like to play on the computer too!

Alison Buno buno@online.emich.edu

From an unidentified participant (unfortunately) came this reply,

Regarding trying to find Alison's daughter a computer game: With all the feminists that are out there, what's wrong with teaching her daughter to play Knight's Quest or NFL Action? Why are [these] games being strictly defined as boy's games? A girl could learn to play them as easily as a boy could. I know these are pretty corny ways out, but there are some really fun video games made from television game shows.

(Although I know that these could be limiting depending on how comfortable your daughter is with trivia.)

The Jeopardy game is great fun, and, if it's still out, so is the Wheel of Fortune.

Several years back, my family bought a game called "Coaster" manufactured by Disney. It was a great game. You got to design a roller coaster with a select number of pieces and twists and turns. Then you could "ride" it and have it judged by a panel of judges who all wanted different things out of your roller coaster in order to make it exciting. It's a great game!

Have you looked in to the Sim games? SimCity and SimTower are particularly fun. (I still play them!)

Alison responded,

True there's nothing stopping my daughter from playing Knights Quest or any other of the many conquest type games out there except for interest. They are not very interesting to her. Fighting and conquering are not very exciting to her. My son will play them for hours.

A working mother in the class provided another type of "reality check" to those of us too willing to dismiss the value of digital access (e.g., Clifford Stoll) at an early age.

April mentioned that Clifford Stoll believes that it is a myth that children need computers in education. I do not feel that computers are *vital* or life-sustaining to the education of children, but I do feel that they are more than "edutainment" [Stoll's claim].

Personally, I did not have access to a computer throughout my grade school or high school education. As a result, I came to college feeling "left behind". I was afraid to ask questions, fearing that I would look foolish.

I am now helping to raise a three-year-old girl. We are fortunate enough to have a computer at home, and I am amazed at her computer literacy. I will not deny her the right to any knowledge, be it books or computers or flash cards. I do not simply plop her in front of the monitor, run "Barbie Fashion Show" (which, btw, she would not be interested in!), and walk away. The computer serves as an interactive educational tool that we can share.

As far as the flashing lights and crazy sounds are concerned—I am well aware that *real* life is not a series a such splendid things. These lights and sounds serve only to attract the attention of a child. You can not teach anyone anything if you do not have their attention. If you have every tried to get the attention of a young child, you would appreciate flashing lights and beeping sounds.

Enough for now—

Heather Kreager

Then Brian broke the good-bad news,

> A couple weeks ago, we discussed here and in class how interactive boy games dominate the gaming industry, and how girl games are just about non-existent. Well, here's some good news for your daughters. According to a recent Wired magazine article—which you can find at http://www.wired.com/5.04/girlgames—200 girl games are expected to go on shelves this year, which is 10 times the amount available in 1996.

> [Although the link above is no longer active, check out <http://www.girlgames.com> as a starting point for games meant for young women.]

> For those of you who hate the traditional stereotype and the vehicles that support it, stop here.

> So, why the big push for more girl games? Well, according to the article, Mattel had the best-selling CD-ROM title last year. It was Barbie's Fashion Designer.

> Okay, fess up. Whose skin just crawled?

> Brian McIntosh

As is usual with e-mail list discussions, there was no substantial conclusion to what I call the "haves-have-nots" and "gender-bias" strands. But it is quite clear that students are willing to explore these issues if teachers are willing to make them part of the conversation about digital, online environments, and after all, what we call online publishing today is really in the business of creating digital environments. Students, after all, know quite well that they will face professional and personal decisions about their uses of the digital domain, and they are generally anxious about making those decisions in the normal rush of their working, personal, and parental lives.

ONLINE WITH THE ROLLER-COASTER RIDE

Finally, we can learn a great deal about the influence of digital environments on "readers" if we attend to personal reactions to the media on students. Those reactions, of course, vary. In "Reading and Writing in Hypertext" Johnson-Eilola (1997) described the experiences of vertigo and euphoria that teachers experience while reading literary, nonlinear hypertexts. He claimed, I think correctly, that this new genre of cyborg literature,[2] where a human reader and technical system co-exist in a new electronic relationship, engenders both excitement and bewilderment in readers. By attending to our students' experiences, we can see just how this sense of vertigo and euphoria manifest themselves, as these last two posts from April and Alanna attest.

[April says]

This is in response to the Landow reading for this week, "The Rhetoric of Hypermedia: Some Rules for Authors"

Ho hum . . . I knew that this would be a fairly dry piece of reading when I started into it, but I don't think that Landow could have sucked any more joy out of this topic. Rules for laying out hypermedia is about as exciting as reading about . . . oh, diagramming sentences. It makes it clear for the reader, sure, but . . .

For me, the excitement about hypermedia is that slight sense of adventure . . . you can't *really* know where exactly that link is going to take you. You have to trust the author to lead you where you think that they're leading you. Given a map of the entire place, I might just say "Huh . . . I guess I don't want to go there after all." I can absolutely understand using a map if I'm looking for something quickly. I think this is one of the fundamental ways Landow and I differ in our experiences. He seems to be coming from a scholarly, information-seeking Hypercard kind of hypermedia, whereas my background in hypermedia is pretty much limited to the Web (and we all know what a wacky carnival *that* is :) I wish he would have expanded a little more on what kind of environment he was picturing this rules working in—I think that I would have been a little more responsive to his ideas. Now, the "rules" themselves—some of them are pretty straightforward, no-brainer-type things (like "Don't make a link without telling the reader where it's going to go" Duh.) I enjoyed his take on authoring for a hypermedia. I'm at the point in my Web design where I want to examine these issues more closely—I'm past the "ok, what is the code to make this do this" and into the "ok, when they choose this link, where are they going to go? do I want them to go there? where will they go once they get there? what do they do if they want to get back to this point?" Pretty theoretical stuff, which, I think, involves not only "rules" like this, but also a pretty good analysis of the audience, something that Landow really doesn't discuss. I don't think that he gives users enough credit for knowing how to navigate—he acts like people get confused by everything, even though, the way he discusses it, these would be scholarly-types browsing for information. I think

Landow has some good thoughts, but I think he's too wrapped up in the rhetorical, glass bubble aspect of hypermedia authoring.

April :)

Actually, I might disagree with April here and give Landow (1991) credit for understanding the browsing academic pretty well. The older browsing public may indeed "get confused by everything." But I'm as guilty as any other academic of binding up dynamic and exciting literacy practices in rules and guidelines: sucking the joy out of the topic. Now there is a clear and useful warning to academic users and teachers of digital media! Don't suck the playful, exploratory spirit out of the digital media. But I am also aware of the anxiety created by that "slight sense of adventure . . . you can't *really* know where exactly that link is going to take you" on other readers of digital environments. Even within this one small class I found testaments to what Johnson-Eilola might call the "vertigo" that users experience in hypermedia systems, in this case the World Wide Web.

In a freewrite early in the term, Alanna Smith wrote,

In my work as a student, I can already see the changes of print and digital worlds taking place. While working on putting my resume online, I have been carefully considering what type of format I should use. As a novice web-site builder, . . . one pertinent question has occurred to me over and over. Is it better to place my resume on screen the same way it is on paper or in a new way. . . . To me the comfort of seeing a resume in a format I am used to makes it easier to find what I am looking for, makes it easy to scan and keep the information in order. Will business types who view the page feel the same way? Do they enjoy the comfort of familiarity? What about links? Should I furnish many jump sites or is it just a distraction from the purpose of my web page: to display what *I* have done. They may never come back to my page after they whisk themselves away through cyber-space, my site only a distant linked memory. It is easy to get tied up, drawn away from what you have gone in search of on the web. So much information, so quickly, so readily available, and yet I am not comforted by this. It seems disorderly, no format to follow just a jumble of thoughts people have randomly put on a screen. To a person who loves organization it can be quite annoying to find things scattered here and there, sometimes never finding what you want. Here one day, gone the next. How reliable is it? Do I dare ask? Do I put favorite pictures on the web only to have them copied by someone else and used on their page? What is the etiquette of this madness?

TURNING OUR ATTENTION TOWARD ENABLING INFRASTRUCTURES

Rarely have I seen a clearer example of what Johnson-Eilola (1997) meant by vertigo. Attending to our students' experiences with and expectations of the new digital era will no doubt provide us with insight into the special tensions that we are helping to create: some productive, some debilitating. What sort of world are we encouraging as we become habituated to the new online and electronic publishing environments? They can tell us their stories; we can adjust our instruction to accommodate and historicize the increasing range of literacy practices being introduced into our English studies disciplines. But oddly enough, as compelling as their stories are, those stories can not be the first thing to which English studies professionals attend. Quite obviously, these students would never have been able to talk of their digital publishing experiences unless the digital infrastructure had been put in place and maintained for them both at an early age and at the university they attended.

If we are helping to complicate our students' lives, we are also doing the same for ourselves. As online publication becomes an assumed condition—not exceptional but simply a part of the rich mix of information distribution systems—it will have serious repercussions for our academic lives. Unfortunately, English studies professionals are typically underprepared to watch out for their own best interests when it comes to digital infrastructures: human, electronic, and economic. The last section of this chapter—with the help of a range of questionnaire respondents—outlines a process for keeping our own best interests front and center.

WHAT ARE WE DOING TO OUR DISCIPLINE(S) WHEN WE ENGAGE IN AND TRY TO SUSTAIN DIGITAL ADVENTURES?

I approached this question from the viewpoint of an educator who depends on electronic environments in almost every course I teach and as a technology administrator who works to provide those environments (not just electronic tools) for educators and students engaged in digital communication practices. With the help of 191 colleagues from 55 institutions who replied to a questionnaire about technology-rich instruction in their departments, this last section outlines a research proposal, research that should be useful in constructing a picture of where our digital adventures are taking English studies disciplines.

Proposal. I suggest we form a consortium of research sites that will help us, as a discipline, construct a more accurate picture of where we are as a profession. The ultimate goal of this research and work would be to encourage students and academics alike to be critical technological activists: that is, thoughtful and informed participants in the construction of electronic environments.

From the vantage point of a teacher and technology administrator, the field of action in online publishing is quite complex. It requires me to attend to atypical concerns that lay behind the act of electronic writing or digital publishing, concerns dealing with supportive infrastructures. Technologies are of course important, but if they are to be functional for teachers and students, fairly extensive human, material, and institutional infrastructures have to be running behind them, infrastructures that depend on a number of important stakeholders: teachers, technical support personnel, student workers, training professionals, network engineers, and administrators of various stripes. These stakeholders attempt to supply and maintain budgets, networks, workstations, input devices, print and other output devices that, of course, are essential to the authors and readers who are taking advantage of the many publishing venues described in this volume: hardcopy, print/digital combinations, standardized publishing protocols (HTML, XML, and SGML), text-only venues (newsgroups, listservs, MOOs and MUDs), and other collaborative and interactive publishing systems.

The more theoretical aspects of pedagogy, authorship, and readerly practices are, to most academics, the most interesting and pressing issues that they deal with. But none of these fascinating new digital practices are likely to manifest themselves at a postsecondary institution unless the human and material infrastructures mentioned above are in place. The nub of the dilemma that English studies professionals face is that *if* they are interested in exploring the world of digital publishing, they will, at the same time, have to consult with those who attend to these infrastructures that make digital environments possible. These consultations will be necessary whether the infrastructure is primarily in-real-space (technology-rich labs, classrooms, or centers), entirely virtual (online universities, online publications, and virtual systems of all types), or, more likely, a combination of the two.

A Self-defeating Dynamic of Blame

In a 1996 questionnaire, despite the fact that most participants labeled themselves enthusiastic users of new technologies (4.4 on a scale in which 5 was the most enthusiastic), a substantial list of challenges accumulated as questionnaire participants described their experiences in technology-rich environments. When I looked at the challenges facing teachers in particular, a rather alarming, self-defeating dynamic of blame developed. Please keep in mind that what follows in Table 2.5-1 does not represent any one institutional response but is instead a synthesis of comments that appeared in the questionnaire and could occur on any campus at moments of concern or stress. The comments should sound familiar.

The dynamic can be summarized in this way. Students often said that they felt as if they knew more about technology than their instructors whom they considered ill prepared to teach with technology. Or, on the other hand, they complained of being intimidated by the range and scope of the technologies teachers assumed they knew or could master in one term. Additionally, both administrators and technical staff often saw teachers as incompetent technology users, unwilling to learn new systems well (even when supplied with training sessions) and unconcerned with instruction in new technological environments (particularly if they were on the tenure-track or had previously been tenured). On the other hand, early adopters (represented by authors in this collection) were viewed warily, as people likely to stretch human, financial, and technological resources. Clearly, in context, none of the claims just made are particularly inappropriate.

Table 2.5-1. A Summary of Challenges.

Comments from	To the average teacher	To the early adopters
. . . students	I know more than they do!	It's too much! I can't learn all this technology and the content!
. . . technicians	They know very little, and won't take time to learn on their own.	Too demanding. They don't seem to realize that I can't spend all my time on their projects!
. . . administrators	They won't even take advantage of the work-shops and technology I provide for them.	Too demanding! They don't seem to realize that I have severe budget constraints.

Teachers, on the other hand, pointed at administrators who provided few professional incentives, oversaw static pay schedules and increasing workloads, and failed to provide access to convenient equipment and time for project work and training. Faculty recounted problems with technicians who provided minimal technical support or who designed workshops that were not systematic or relevant to teacher's needs or technological situation. That is, they were being provided introductory, out-of-context workshops (both technically and educationally out of context) that simply introduced systems or software to faculty without discussing when, how, and why that system or software might be used to improve learning in a teacher's course. None of these claims were inappropriate either.

Administrators (facility, departmental, and upper administrators) also had a part to play in this dynamic. All too often they were described as looking for silver-bullet solutions to educational and technical problems. Teachers complained about one-time grants that within a few years led to support-challenged facilities. They also pointed to administrators teaching evaluations that discouraged experimental uses of technologies and tenure and promotion guidelines that ignored or penalized young faculty for nontraditional, technology-related scholarship. Once again, these concerns are legitimate. A graphic representation of this dynamic of blame adds a certain urgency or poignancy to the situation (see Figure 2.5-1).

Caught in this dynamic, stakeholders felt betrayed for the hard work they put in or the money invested in technological efforts. In this worst case scenario, stakeholders often seemed to blame others without examining the contexts in which others worked. They tended to ignore the important influence of infrastructure and institutional context that lay behind the commitment or lack of commitment to teaching well with technology.

It is clear that solutions to problems associated with integrating technologies and technological environments into instruction, challenge teachers to take into account issues with which they are not typically concerned: the past technical experience of students in their classes; the technical demands that their planning places on local, campus-wide, and Internet-wide communication systems; an expanded set of technical support responsibilities, often increasing programmatic responsibilities; and an understanding of the talents and availability of technical support personnel.

The following is an example that illustrates how these unusual responsibilities and our inability or unwillingness to talk to important stakeholders might devolve into a dynamic of blame. According to these questionnaire respondents, no one issue more influences online

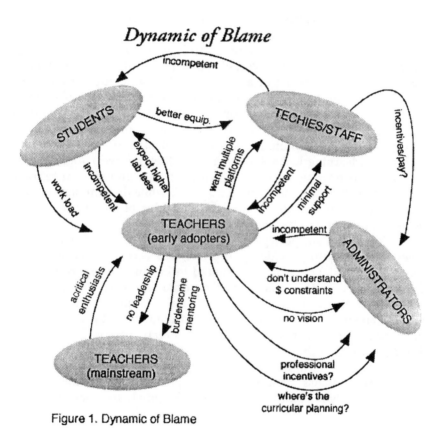

Figure 1. Dynamic of Blame

Figure 2.5-1. Dynamic of blame

publishing than the one I labeled *access to technology*. In light of that importance, these players combined to illustrate just how complicated issues related to access can become.

The Complexity of Access

The administrative committees at Michigan Technological University typically measure "access" in terms of a fairly reasonable statistical goal: provide one workstation for every 10 students. That goal, however, is also very simplistic, remarkably simplistic when compared to the synthesized definitions of "access" found in questionnaire responses. Students' measurements of access included safe, supported work environments on adequate workstations during schedulable times. Teachers suggested the need for timely access to several types of training and support in addition to safe, adequate working environments. They wanted workshops that offered them a situated approach to learning technologies—that is, they needed support while they learned new technologies, while they planned to integrate technology-rich instruction into their syllabi, while they implemented it in their classes, and while the assessed the value of the instruction for the next experimental class they would teach.

Technical support people have to consider another range of issues as they try to provide appropriate, safe access for teachers and students. For instance, they are required to institute secure, controlled, and authenticated access that also considers system loads and hardware/software bottlenecks. And finally, administrators added concerns about sustainable systems to the definition just given; to them access discussions must also take into consideration amortized budgets, hiring priorities, technology support for teachers and staff, and even changing tenure and promotion guidelines. If and when these players get together to discuss changes in access to publishing technologies, they all quite naturally imagine different sets of potentials and constraints.

Proposal for Local Action

What departments and those involved in publishing ventures want to avoid is the mutual blaming that can occur when stakeholders are not aware of the constraints and conditions with which others have to live. To avoid this dynamic of blame, representative role players must be willing to make clear their portion of the social context while valuing the responses of others. The strategy I suggest here as a result of the dynamic of blame is twofold:

1. We make time for earnest stakeholders to continually negotiate guidelines that make it possible to support technology while accommodating the constraints of others.
2. We find ways of reporting to the discipline what practices and conditions result from these negotiations.

This is not an extraordinary request. We make the same time for collaborating and scheduling in our online publishing efforts. We simply need to apply that strategy to planning for the infrastructure that lies beneath those online publishing adventures.

I am not recommending that we hold up our experimental use of online publishing while we get some all encompassing sense of the human, technical, and institutional infrastructure behind the effort. By all means forge ahead! Technologies are changing; our opportunities are fluid; the kairos of technological activism is compelling. But as the "access issue" illustrates, the value of involving multiple players in the design of digital environments is quite important if we are to avoid, as much as possible, versions of the dynamic of blame. And, of course, "access" was only one of many issues that should be considered. Other evolving and interrelated sets of issues that arose from the questionnaire included financing, establishing institutional relationships across campus, considering appropriate curricular developments, providing professional development opportunities, maintaining technical support, and making technical forecasts.

I would note that the final category here—making technical forecasts—is likely to be the least stable of all these categories. Even frequent updating of technical forecasts will only provide a snapshot of the technical possibilities with which we might experiment. I assume, instead, that attending to technological change will remain a constant, a never ending quest. It is, however and unfortunately, often the *only* issue that is consistently addressed on most campuses.

As we continue to invest in our digital adventures, if in addition to forecasting technological changes, we also attend to the issues just listed, individuals, programs, departments, and entire institutions will be in a much better position to sustain those creative publishing adventures. Consider the intellectual and human effort that is going into the projects discussed in other chapters of this volume, and consider the amount of potential students see in digital publishing adventures. In light of these considerations, sustaining the practice of electronic writing seems essential.

Call for Disciplinary Action: A Research Consortium

I mentioned earlier that I would like to try to answer this question: "What are we doing to ourselves by investing in these new digital communicative practices?" The answer for the discipline is that we just don't know. We pay so little attention to the human, financial, institutional, and technical infrastructures that support our work that it is hard to know what the infrastructure for higher education looks like now much less predict how it will look in 10 years.

I suggest, then, that the English studies disciplines form a research consortium: a group of collaborating individuals who are willing to invest intellectual energy into the development of shared planning strategies for technology and online publishing. The two most obvious attempts to encourage this type of collaboration have recently combined: The American Association of Higher Education's Teaching, Learning, Technology Roundtable (TLTR) program and the Epiphany Project. The first is an interdisciplinary attempt to encourage institutions of higher education to establish strategic planning processes that include stakeholders from around campus. The second was an organization that attempted to provide teachers with the means to learn about and engage in successful teaching with technology practices. These two organizations recently combined their efforts and offer a number of online and conference planning resources relevant to the consortium project I suggest here. However, neither really attempts, at this point, to deal directly with the focus of this volume: studying the new writing and new worlds of electronic environments.

As a first step in forming this consortium, I offer, in the appendix, a series of questions, each of which must first be asked in the context of an individual institution, and then shared and compared with other institutions. The objective of the consortium would be to better understand what "we are doing to ourselves" on the disciplinary level vis-à-vis online publications and other digital adventures. The following issue areas are contained in the appendix:

- Accessing technology and technological environments
- Financing
- Establishing institutional connections
- Considering appropriate curricular functions of online publishing
- Providing professional development opportunities
- Making technical forecasts
- Managing online publications

What are we doing to ourselves in light of the online publishing that the authors in this volume encourage us to imagine? At the very least, we are embarking on projects that will require us to broaden our horizons of responsibility, to consider the demands of infrastructure—human, financial, institutional, and technical—that English studies disciplines normally take for granted or ignore all together. The longevity of our efforts depends on splitting our collective attentions between the changed writing that goes on in these venues, the support structures that make them possible, and the lifestyle (and work style) changes that they encourage in ourselves and our students.

CONCLUDING REMARK

The tensions we deal with as we introduce our disciplines and our students to these new environments, are palpable. In each class, for every assignment, with each publication, we need to balance the excitement and potential of the media—the carnival spirit of adventure, transience, and whimsy—with the functional rhetoric of order, purpose, and sustainability. Our actions are ecological in nature: one decision influencing a number of others at many levels. I know that I wasn't as aware of those influences until I began listening to the students whose lives and careers depend, to some extent, on our media choices. Those student voices surprised me, or rather they upset my contained sense of just what is at stake in the process.

Let me illustrate just how challenging those voices can be by leaving you with a question posed by the graduate technical teaching assistant for the class, Deb Schueller. She is a quiet person who listened to our banter and concerns online and in class for most of the quarter and then asked this question:

> So, what do you think about the quote given below (definitely NOT web related)?

> A [person] of culture is [s/he] who understands the meaning of history, who appreciates the sacrifice involved in each new stage of knowledge: who accepts his [or her] share of responsibility in the particular social sphere in which [s/he] lives, be it family, professor, or country. What this world needs more than informed [persons] and technicians is better human quality, less selfishness, less useless pain, less exploitation of fellow [wo/men], more compassion.

> (Amanda Labarca qtd. in Manny Paul, 1968)

How does the mad rush to get stuff "online" defeat or enhance her conception? Do you think people have ethical considerations or concerns regarding the web and digital technologies other than whether or not "books" survive or perhaps whether or not we should hijack gifs, pirate software, or plagiarize ideas, or misrepresent commercial products? Or do we live in an age and place (late 20th century capitalist middle America) where ethics and culture, at least in their traditional definitions, no longer exist?

I hope the answer is "no." But that quite likely will depend on how well we attend to each other in the near future.

APPENDIX

Accessing Technology and Technological Environments

- What exactly do students, teachers, and professionals have access to? And is it adequate for supporting online publishing ventures?
- When and under what conditions can they work with, experiment with, and learn about communication technologies?
- What sort of support (human and otherwise) do students, teachers, and professionals receive as they first learn new technologies, as they incorporate them into their teaching or professional lives, as they actually begin constructing publications, and as they assess the success of those publishing adventures?
- Who makes access decisions and what is the process they go through? In other words, how can one become involved in that decision-making process?

Financing

- What exactly are the financial components of a digital publishing adventure: salaries, hardware, software, network connections, expendables, travel, ...
- How much should a department or program collect each year in order to support supplies, services, and equipment? That is, what is an amortized budget for each publishing venture?
- Where does that amortized budget come from? Does it come out of the institution's general fund, from a departmental

budget, from grants, out of student lab fees, from corporate support or ads associated with the publishing venture?

- How reliable is financial support? Does it depend on the benevolence of a single administrator, the success of the publication, or is it built into the curricular or institutional goals of the institution(s)?
- Which institutional stakeholders make key decisions when it comes to ongoing financial support? In other words, how can one get at the decision-making stakeholders and the decision-making process?

Establishing Institutional Connections

- Who are the important technical stakeholders across campus who make network access possible?
- What committees on campus are likely to set policy that influences digital publishing ventures? Which departmental, college-wide or institutional policies influence online publishing ventures?
- Who makes access decisions about publishing technologies and what is the process they go through? In other words, how can one become involved in those decisions?

Considering Appropriate Curricular Functions of Online Publishing

- Where in a curriculum are online publishing ventures appropriate?
- How much classtime should be spent teaching technology as opposed to teaching content? How do we minimize the first in order to maximize the second?
- How does online publishing change the literacy practices that are needed by 21st-century citizens? How do we teach those practices?
- What opportunities does online publishing bring to the classroom that were previously unavailable? How do we document these opportunities so that this expensive enterprise can be justified?
- What assessment challenges and opportunities do online publications present to educational institutions?
- To what are we exposing our students, if we publish their work (often in-process work by most standards) in a public venue? What are our objectives, and what are the risks for students and teachers?

Providing Professional Development Opportunities

- How are teachers and staff supported as they learn about new publishing technologies?
- Who are the advisors/mentors to those electronic publicists preparing for tenure and promotion?
- What monetary accommodations are made for technical staff who research, install, and maintain the technical infrastructure necessary for online publishing? Can they afford to go to the very expensive conferences, workshops, and EXPOS that allow them to stay current? How are they recruited, trained, and retained when industry salaries are so enticing?
- Are students (graduate and undergraduate) given professional development opportunities, since they are often leading the efforts to publish online?

Making Technical Forecasts

- What technical conditions are necessary at an institution for online publishing to occur?
- What technologies are most likely to influence online publishing ventures in the near future (1-3 years)?
- What technologies are most likely to influence online publishing ventures in the technologically distant future (4-5 years) ?
- Who determines what upgrade path is taken?

Managing Online Publications

- Who owns the hardware, software, and network infrastructure on which the publication resides?
- What are the intellectual property agreements between stakeholders in the publication: the (often multiple) owners of network systems, the publisher, and the authors?
- How are editorial policies determined and by whom?
- What do typical production schedules look like?
- How are editors, authors, and production staff recruited and compensated?

NOTES

1. A term referring to educators willing to put up with the trials and tribulations of new technologies in hopes of generating new instructional environments and improved learning (Green & Gilbert, 1995).

2. Here *cyborg literature* refers more to the process of reading than to the literature itself. This genre requires a reading process that joins the actions of the reader and an electronic infrastructure, which in turn enables this human machine to engage in the productive practice of reading. If we think of print products, the perfect bound book, as a machine, all reading can be assumed to have cyborg characteristics. But as Johnson-Eilola (1997) described the current practices, they are different enough to produce the experiences of vertigo and euphoria in the reader/authors of the 1990s.

WORKS CITED

Birkerts, S. (1994). *The Gutenberg elegies: The fate of reading in an electronic age.* New York: Fawcett Columbine Books.

Bolter, J. D. (1991). *Writing space: The computer, hypertext, and the history of writing,* Hillsdale, NJ: Lawrence Erlbaum Associates.

Feenberg, A. (1991). *Critical theory of technology.* New York: Oxford University Press.

Gergen, K. J. (1991). *The saturated self.* New York: Basic Books.

Giddens, A. (1983). *Central problems in social theory: Action, structure, and contradiction in social analysis.* Berkeley: University of California Press.

Gomez, M. L. (1991). The equitable teaching of composition with computers: A case for change. In G. Hawisher & C. Selfe (Eds.), *Evolving perspectives on computers and composition studies: Questions for the 1990s* (pp. 318-335). Urbana, IL: NCTE Press.

Green, K. C., & Gilbert, S. W. (1995, March/April). Content, communications, productivity, and the role of information technology in higher education. *Change*, 8-19.

Hawisher, G., & Selfe, C. (Eds.). (1997). *Literacy, technology, and society: Confronting the issues.* Upper Saddle River, NJ: Prentice-Hall.

Heckscher, C. (1994). Defining the post-bureaucratic type. In C. Heckscher & A. Donnellon (Eds.), *The post-bureaucratic organization: New perspectives on organizational change* (pp. 14-62). Thousand Oaks, CA: Sage.

Howard, T. (1996). Who "owns" electronic texts? In P. Sullivan & J. Dautermann (Eds.), *Electronic literacies in the workplace: Technologies of writing* (pp. 177-198). Urbana, IL: NCTE Press.

Johnson-Eilola , J. (1997). *Nostalgic angels: Rearticulating hypertext writing.* Norwood, NJ: Ablex.

Landow, G. (1991). The rhetoric of hypermedia: Some rules for authors. In P. Delany & G. Landow (Eds.), *Hypermedia and literary studies* (pp. 81-104). Cambridge, MA: MIT Press.

LeBlanc, P. (1994). The politics of literacy and technology in secondary school classrooms. In C. L. Selfe & S. Hilligoss (Eds.), *Literacy and computers: The complications of teaching and learning with technology* (pp. 23-36). New York: Modern Language Association.

McLuhan, M. (1964). *Understanding media: The extensions of man.* New York: Penguin Books.

Paul, C. M. (1968). Amanda Labarca H.: Educator to the women in Chile In *The work and writings of Amanda Labarca H. in the field of education in Chile.* Cuernavaca, Mexico: Centro Intercultural de Documentacion.

Roberts, P. (1996, June). Virtual grub street: Sorrows of a multimedia hack. *Harper's Magazine,* pp. 71-77.

Selfe, R., & Selfe, C. L. (in press). The relevance of technology use in English studies: Using technology-rich communication facilities as sites of teaching, learning, action, and response. In R. P. Yagelski & S. A. Leonard (Eds.),*The relevance of English studies.* Urbana, IL: NCTE.

Wresch, W. (1996). *Disconnected: Haves and have-nots in the information age.* New Brunswick, NJ: Rutgers University Press.

chapter 2.6
___

WRITING ELECTRONIC SPACES

Judith Kirkpatrick

___

FINDING THE DYNAMIC TECHNO-RHETORICIAN WITHIN US

Teachers do not usually change their methods much from the way they were taught, for their methods have come out of some practice from somewhere, often from the teacher's memory of what was a good learning experience. Many of us can remember teachers who even taught from their own college notes, and, I would argue, there are still many teachers swirling in the methodologies of their mentors of the mid-20th century. As students of the 21st century enter these classrooms created from industrial-age parameters and managed through schedules better suited to Grand Central Station, they have interests and proclivities unsuited to methodologies of the mid-20th century and will grow in their restlessness and dissatisfaction with outdated classroom practice. Just as a student of the mid-20th century would not have learned well through a method used in 19th-century schools, primarily the recitation, as a mode of learning, 21st-century students will thrive under new methods and in reinvented learning spaces developed from the possibilities of a new medium for communicating, computer networks. Some of today's educators may be unwilling to let go of the technologies with which they have practiced, the telephone, the typewriters, paper, the copy machine, blackboards, chalk, and transparencies, all products of the mid-20th century. These well-seasoned teachers who have been teaching with the technology they learned with, may be reluctant to change their habits for they are too comfortable with themselves, have control over their courses, and teach courses that will not be questioned, at least not until students experience learning using tools of technology previously unimaginable until the 1990s.

A creative, successful educator in the new millennium will not want to continue the industrial-age paradigm, however. Students need to gain information-age skills from teachers who are willing to experiment and reorganize classroom methodologies, who leave the comfort zone of time-honored practices, and who have embraced the new practices themselves, replacing the traditions that have been secure for the last 40 years or so. Educators can develop intersections for students at which students and teachers connect; these connections allow true learning to occur, that which remains after time, that takes hold and changes students. How does an educator craft the course so that these intersections are woven seamlessly into the fabric of the course? With care, with practice, and with solid reflection and assessment. This dispatch leads the practicing teacher through the changes that will allow an understanding of how student writing is moving away from traditional technologies and methodologies as writing in electronic spaces created by networked computers is transforming composing.

FINDING THE INTERSECTIONS AMONG US

What kind of a teacher would radically transform his or her methodologies after years of successful teaching? What kind of teacher would push and prod his or her own professional development in directions not considered previously? What kind of teacher would, with only distant incentives, open up his or her teaching to public spheres and inspection? In early 1993 Eric Crump invited those on the Megabyte University Internet mailing list to meet at the Techrhet Bar and Grill at MediaMOO (http://www.cc.gatech.edu/fac/asb/MediaMOO/), a synchronous multi-user space for professional media discussion on the Internet invented by Amy Bruckman, at that time a PhD student at MIT (http://www.cc.gatech.edu/~asb/papers/index.html). Bruckman was preparing for her dissertation at MIT's media lab on how to design computer-networked collaborative environments for children where especially girls would develop more affinity toward using computers. Bruckman's MOOse Crossing MOO, complete with its own client (a computer program made for connecting and programming at a MOO), was at the center of Bruckman's research from 1993 through 1996; meanwhile, MediaMOO evolved for adult media researchers almost as an aside to her work. Bruckman created MediaMOO as one of the first MOOs not constructed for role-playing games (RPGs) such as Dungeons and Dragons. Bruckman's voice at MediaMOO was always fair, supportive, creative, and, at times, inspirational as she designed MOOse Crossing for kids. At Media, anonymity was not condoned; instead, researchers were given the freedom to play with the toys that the MIT media lab offered, and play they did (Bruckman & Resnick, 1999).

In essence, one of the most active media groups, the techno-rhetoricians, were given the freedom to develop and practice among themselves. Most of the techno-rhetoricians were already good in the brick and mortar classrooms, were already competent at writing on a computer, and were seeing flaws in the current process-based composition theory as their own habits of writing changed.

Bruckman constructed an environment that allowed media researchers to practice what we began to define as new theory about using computers in teaching. What had been available in the Local Area Networked (LAN) classroom in the late 1980s to early 1990s, especially through such software programs as the Daedalus System (http://www.daedalus.com/) could begin to be understood through the social interaction, the collaboration, and the discussion that evolved at MediaMOO. Projects found at Media such as the Netoric (http://bsuvc.bsu.edu/~00gjsiering/netoric/intro.html) Tuesday Cafes found teachers each Tuesday at 8 p.m. EDT, from June 1993, discussing issues of teaching computers and writing, laying the groundwork for developing an online social constructivist pedagogy (Fanderclai & Siering, 1999). Bruckman's January 1996 *Technology Review* article, "Finding One's Own in Cyberspace," (http://www.techreview.com/articles/jan96/Bruckman.html) describes the sort of action that newcomers to electronic discourse often are challenged by.

> With the explosion of interest in networking, people are moving from being recipients of information to creators, from passive subscribers to active participants and leaders. Newcomers to the Net who are put off by harassment, pornography, and just plain bad manners should stop whining about the place they find unsuitable and turn their energies in a more constructive direction: help make people aware of the variety of alternatives that exist, and work to build communities that suit their interests and values.

Essentially, this Bruckman description is what the group of MediaMOO techno-rhetoricians were doing from 1993 forward as they reinvented their delivery of instruction. One could find them on the internet, but also find them at conferences, working in the NCTE Assembly for Computers in English (http://www.dsu.edu/ACE) booth, at the CCCCs Computers and Writing SIGS, at the Fifth C=Computers meeting at the CCCCs. This group of technorhetoricians, meeting regularly at this and other MOO-space on the Internet, have developed a community of like-minded scholars out of the rank and file of English teachers who emerge on many campuses as the innovators, the ones who dare to experiment, collaborate, and reinvent strategies and methodologies. The dynamic technorhetorician, coming out of educational theorist and social science research of such scholars as Papert (1996) who wrote for teachers and parents interested in bridging the generational gap that the digital age has brought into this late twentieth century society, and Turkle (1995) who examined the relationship between the mind and the intellectual life and commitments to online thinking and learning, has been a leader in circumventing time, discipline, and spatial boundaries so often associated with the industrial age paradigm, subsequently finding support for this experimenting and innovative teaching with colleagues in other disciplines not only locally, but also from a distance.

Let me explain how I found these conversations. As an adjunct, teaching 15 credits back in 1986, I began casually asking questions centered around who in our department was working on how our new fiber optic networked campus facilities at Kapi'olani Community College (KapCC) could be used for teaching. I was genuinely interested in finding the answers and had almost no notion myself as to how this could come about. I was not satisfied with: "Foreign Language is going to need that lab for its listening labs"; "No, the data processing department has priority on those classrooms"; "Let's look at Plato for individualized drill and practice at the remedial and developmental levels"; "We're going to be able to access the library catalogue from our offices someday."

FINDING OUT WHAT THE QUESTIONS ARE

Midway through the 1980s, my own writing process began to change because of my own computer literacy, but I hadn't yet imagined how to blend my Coles' collaborative writing community model with what I was hearing in answer to my questions. Our Provost, John Morton, was instrumental in planning to provide KapCC's new Diamond Head campus with fiber optics to every classroom and office. Those who have had to retrofit old campus structures with fiber optics will envy the timing of this newly designated campus being built through the 1980s. While I had had nothing better to suggest, I did go so far as to decide to make myself computer literate at that time, investing $4,000 in a Macintosh SE, taking mini-workshops on Wang word processing from our secretarial science department, and training my pinkie finger on my right hand to stop hitting return at the end of each line. I found myself on my computer daily, as early as 1987, amazed at the change in my own writing process and finding much of the challenges of revision disappearing from my past. I no longer planned my work in pencil on yellow pad. All drafts were written in a word processor. The notion of revision changed too as I watched my words appear on the screen, revising more as I wrote rather than after I wrote a first draft. In fact, the first drafts I produced were far more polished in content and sophistication than those previously written using a computer as a fancy typewriter. In 1986, I even electronically scanned 40 pages of Wang word-processed English 100 course work, which was not translatable into any other word processor, into Microsoft Word. My glee at having my course work available already in a word processor that I could modify encouraged me to revise, reinvent, and refine my assignments more readily due to the ease with which I could remake assignments. I found the ease and the convenience of having my course work on my computer a novel idea at that time. My computer began its transformation, also, into my filing space, supplanting the paper I was once tied to. The convenience, adaptability and speed of using a computer for writing, for me, was a first hook into a mode of work that was more productive and satisfying than previously possible with only a typewriter as my mode for word processing.

My first transformation began in the 1980s when I would be handed a textbook to teach from and do my best to pull from the text what I wouldn't mind my students doing. Then I discovered William Coles' works such as *The Plural I* (1988) and *Composing II: Writing as a Self-Creating Process* (1984). Coles led a 1-week colloquium in Honolulu that I attended and it was then that I discovered that there was no one right way to teach composition. The notion of academic freedom to craft a course, not as Sqwire and Chitwood had for me, but as Coles would— compelled me to write and rewrite a sequenced series of assignments, building on students' previous knowledge, requiring students to interrogate their assumptions in their previous knowledge and defend their work with and amongst other students. Student-written text was at the center of my pedagogy, collaborative writing groups, peer critique, writing for a broader audience than one (me), and writing in the presence of others (community) were the Coles driven practices that invigorated my teaching in the 1980s. Each year, however, from 1986 to 1991, I found little information about the possibilities of using computers for teaching other than drill-and-practice sorts of inventions. As a tenure-track professor (1989-1991), I concentrated on putting the pieces together to achieve excellence in the composition classroom, to develop curriculum, and to assess programs. After these 2 years in my 4-year tenure track in the University of Hawai'i system, teaching in a Coles' based collaborative, student text-centered brick and mortar classroom, I found what I had been looking for at a CCCCs conference in Boston in 1991. I was fascinated with the offering of a one day pre-conference workshop on New Directions in computer and composition studies, chaired by Gail Hawisher from the University of Illinois. I signed up, went, reconsidered what I wanted to spend my professional time and energies on, and experienced what I suppose I could call my radical transformation.

FINDING OUT THAT YOU ARE THE TECHNO-RHETORICIAN AND THERE ARE OTHERS JUST LIKE YOU

I joined an emerging community of scholars meeting regularly in the Internet in synchronous and asynchronous modes from across the United States, at various phases of movement into the possibilities that writing in a computer-networked environment offered. I read Handa's (1990) book *Computers and Community*, one of the few books whose articles were coming out of composition specialists who wrote to this audience of computers and writing specialists. Barker and Kemp's (1990) article, "Network Theory: A Postmodern Pedagogy for the Writing Classroom," described a way of using computer-networked classrooms to facilitate much of what I thought should be going on in a composition class anyway. The essence of the chapter dealt with how difficult implementing group work can be in the proscenium classroom, and how computer-networked software can enhance and make possible much of what I wanted to accomplish in designing the student text-centered composition classroom. I listened to representatives from the Daedalus Group out of Texas talk about using a powerful networked computer program as a tool with which to teach in the networked composition classroom. I joined the e-mail discussion list—Megabyte University—monitored by Fred Kemp, a Texas Tech University English professor. I started to consider the possibilities, on my own in Hawai'i with the support of others across the United States. The MediaMOO

Netoric sessions that had grown out of the collection of computers and writing teachers using computer networks for their professional collaboration and development allowed meetings online. First we would meet at Eric Crump's Techno-rhetoricians Bar and Grill where Locke Carter's Derrida robot and Becky Rickly's pony, along with the ever present surly bartender, would greet us. We could join Michael Day in his Panopticon for a game of Scrabble, share text from a gopher site, and visit the Beach and converse with Kimo the beachboy robot there. In June 1993, Tari Fanderclai and Greg Siering, both graduate students at the time, began organizing, formalizing, and archiving weekly discussions at the Tuesday Cafe, a space provided by MediaMOO (Fanderclai & Siering, 1999). The Netoric sessions in 2000 currently take place at Tari's MOO, Connections, housed at a server provided by the University of Florida, Gainesville. My amazement grew at the potentials for teaching that I was finding in networked writing. The engaging discourse that came out of the e-mail discussion, the distinct voices, the array of ideas, frustrations, challenges, and stories bolstered my own notion of reinventing the way I was delivering my courses, for if teachers could hold such challenging, focused, discussion on topics they were interested in, why couldn't this same model be a part of a discussion in a first-year composition course? I had known what I was not looking for, drill-and-practice, one-way communication, but I had not known until finding this community of scholars, what it was about using computers other than word processing that could enhance my teaching. If teachers could meet in synchronous group discussion, why couldn't students also benefit from the production of text in networked discussion? At this time in my teaching career, after 15 years in myriad classrooms, I stopped looking for that certain someone to lead our department into setting its agenda for the use of computers in writing. I knew that I had to be one of the ones to face the challenges of developing writing space and computer literacy that will lead students into a finesse with electronic communication in the 21st century. A primary challenge at this time was and remains developing computer competency levels and good access for students less privileged than myself. The community college system affords this possibility for students who are not able to have computer access at home. Students still arrive in most community colleges with little exposure or access to the Internet. From 1995 through 2000, the numbers did not change much; 6 students out of 20, on the average, were comfortable with word processing, saving to a disk, moving from platform to platform; 8 students out of 20 had been on the Web more than 10 times. I remember one of our computing center techies who was working on installing the Daedalus system for our classes saying to me in 1991, "We were waiting

for someone like you to come along." Why didn't they say so? But that's
another issue, for another dispatch, altogether.

FINDING THE CONFIDENCE TO PRACTICE NEW METHODOLOGIES

Teaching with technology requires the rethinking of fundamental
assumptions about the way learning occurs. I have often heard teachers
complain that although they had just finished lecturing on a topic for 40
minutes, the students did not seem to understand the topic well enough
to apply it to their work. Teachers then quickly dismiss this lack of
learning, blaming the students lack of focus, inattention, or poor
preparation for the challenges of the course. Teachers treat writing
assignments as isolated tasks, with multiple drafts, responded to for the
most part by the teacher. They usually leave students with a real reading
audience of only one, the teacher. Instead, teachers need to see how and
where writing is taking place in the world of work and even in the
world of research in academia. A teacher has to be willing to adapt his
or her teaching style—syllabus, assignments, classroom activities, and
relationship to the class—to the networked writing environment and all
of its possibilities, in order to reinvent the paradigm through which
learning takes place. In the workplace in the real world of the early 21st
century, writing on computers is the dominant way that writing is done.
I have heard Kemp admonish English teachers, on more than one
occasion, to simply get out and "Look around you!"

Doubts? Of course I had doubts, lost sleep, and fears in 1991, for
I was leaving behind some effective classroom strategies for peer
critique, collaborative group work, and oral presentation of arguments
that I had worked hard at developing. Student conferencing and group
workshopping techniques were well developed for all writing
assignments, and my students were satisfied with the course I delivered.
They accepted my system of marking and worked hard to develop their
own system of revision and correction. In fact, the closer time came to
begin my radical methodological shift, the more doubts I had, especially
in the middle of the night, as I thought about how to actually teach in a
computer-networked, student text-centered, collaborative classroom.
There was really nothing wrong with the way things had been going in
my classrooms. I was a successful instructor in the writing program. My
peer and student evaluations were high; the results were excellent. I was
half way through the tenure track. Two more years to go. . . .

After the first 6 weeks in a networked classroom, having spent
hundreds of hours on preparation (I estimate at least 6 hours preparation

time for each daily assignment that I posted during that first semester), I remember claiming that I never wanted to go back to the traditional classroom. In a number of ways, the course was working far better than I had expected. First of all, my students were excited about coming to class, often arriving early and staying late. They remained on-task and focused during the entire class hour and were not packing up at the end of class. In fact, many stayed on to work during subsequent sessions as long as there was room. The students were writing more vigorously and enthusiastically than I had ever observed before. The lure of the screen displaying their words that they could so easily change encouraged this engagement. As a result of their audience becoming broader, students took more care in clarifying their thoughts before publishing them through class discussion lists and during synchronous computer-networked discussion activities. Students who were shy in oral conversations found a new voice in written communication and enjoyed having their words be heard. Students spent more hours writing in a semester, most claimed, than they had previously, in their lifetimes. What was so novel about this for them was that they actually wanted to read each other's work and looked forward to the sharing and ease with which this sharing took place. Knowledge about each other's lives and attitudes became apparent much more rapidly as the community of students formed, and they became interested in each other, all through reading each other's writing in a computer-mediated environment. My evaluations remained high, and my commitment to computers and writing solidified as I assessed my students' progress as they worked their way through the curriculum in a LAN writing environment. Introducing this computer-intensive writing course into the information technology emphasis at a community college, where students often entered the class having no previous experience with computers, convinced students that their opinion that they could never learn how to work a computer on their own was wrong.

Over time these students become the monitors in the computer labs on campus, the desirable workers in the work-study programs, and the assistants to many faculty who learn new skills from their students. The students' writing has become more purposeful and task-oriented, they seek interaction and collaboration, and frequently enhanced their work with multimedia in finished forms. I keep that in mind when I teach writing now, knowing that, although traditional written work prepared in a traditional manner and submitted in traditional forms is still valued in some contexts, so is being able to use technology to create text that mirrors much of the evolving technology.

FINDING WHAT REPLACES WHAT WE LEFT BEHIND

Faigley (1996), in his chair's address (http://www.missouri.edu/ ~cccc96/faigley.html) at the general session at the CCCCs, echoed Kemp, who challenged teachers to look around as he charged them to go beyond the confines of the English department for a look at the revolution of digital communication technologies. He gave what many would call a wakeup call to the general assembly of the CCCCs by declaring, "With the coming of the Internet and the World Wide Web, another major renegotiation of pedagogy and authority is now in progress." He boldly predicted: "If we come back to our annual convention a decade from now and find that the essay is no longer on center stage, it will not mean the end of our discipline. I expect that we will be teaching an increasingly fluid, multimedia literacy and that we will be quite happy that attempts in the past failed to drop our fourth C—Communication." One of the primary benefits of writing in a networked environment is the ease with which communication can take place. In fact, most faculty using technology effectively describe their classes as using computer-mediated communication (CMC) as the primary organizational strategy for the course. The concept of organizing a composition course using the computer network as the mediator allows students to communicate to one or many, to write for clarification, for feedback, for discussion or analysis, and to engage in the text of others in ways previously not possible in the non-networked traditional space of the time- and space-bound limited classroom. In the end, Faigley challenged his audience to lessen the gap between the rich and the poor by inventing strategies to use the technologies that have the potential, instead, to further divide the enriched from the impoverished. The importance of this challenge should not be diminished, for the educational system could be further stratified without the intervention of teachers who develop a technology-rich learning environments for their students. Selfe's (1998) keynote CCCCs address, "Technology and Literacy: A Story about the Perils of Not Paying Attention" (http://www.ncte.org/forums/selfe/index.html), urges the members to pay attention to computer literacy. Her speech has evolved into a monograph published by the Studies in Writing and Rhetoric (SWR) series in 1999 and is a classic read for all teachers coming into the field of composition studies. She urged teachers to not ignore technology, for it should not be a question of whether or not we use technology, for "we have to pay attention to technology. When we fail to do so, we share in the responsibility for sustaining and reproducing an unfair system that, scholars such as Elspeth Stuckey (1991) and Mike Rose (1989) have noted in other contexts, enacts social violence and ensures continuing illiteracy under the aegis of education.

In the traditional teacher-centered classroom, I have always considered myself good at fostering discussion, and through this, encouraging the students in the class to construct their own knowledge. But there were always some students who did not speak unless they were called on. I engaged in a lot more "call-and-response" type interactions than I wanted to, where I would ask the question and the students who found seats closest to me would answer and monopolize the discussion if they could. I prefer lateral, student-to-student discussion in class, but the most dominant oral communicators often prevail with the rest of the class sitting silent, intimidated, bored, or distracted. When I began to use synchronous computer-networked discussion, in the Daedalus Integrated Writing Environment (1999) program called Interchange or at an educational MOO, I noticed that everyone (yes an absolute) was participating, that students were calling on each other to explain or clarify, that they were coming up with their own, socially constructed ideas, and that I was not as important to the pace and depth of the discussion as I had been. Students finally stopped waiting for me to answer their questions and as a result started thinking more. Their engagement in synchronous discussion was dependent on my letting go of the teacher-centered classroom and making the class, instead, student activity-centered. One activity that works especially well in this mode is clarification of a thesis for a researched project. Students quickly engage in this, for not only are they sending their own ideas out to the class, but they are reading and evaluating the ideas of others. A one-line instruction from the instructor who then steps back from the discussion provokes students to engage in discussion of ideas that they own, that they believe in, and that they know will be read and analyzed by their classmates. This choice of centering the classroom on student-produced knowledge requires conscientious commitment to new methodologies untried by many teachers who have come out of a papered environment. The computer network opens up a new world of possibilities for teachers that will improve students engagement in the content of the course and in their production of text, making them comfortable in the places where work will occur in the 21st century.

Essentially, I have taken myself off the podium and removed my voice as the only authority in the class. The pedagogy I espouse challenges students to dissent and encourages multiple positions to be expressed in the classrooms through e-mail, the sharing of texts and critique and through synchronous discussion. The technologically sophisticated learning space found in well-organized computer-networked course work provides a forum for what I feel is imperative as an outcome for a composition class. No longer is the classroom dialogic, teacher to student and student to teacher while others listen. Instead, the course becomes one long series of student conversations that develop the text of the course. Students are not reading dense prose, digging for obscured meaning that they feel only the teacher knows for sure. They are instead organizing their thoughts in an ever increasing level of complexity through their original discourse. Teachers willing to leave behind order and be left instead with open, unstable texts, move into the computer-networked classroom, out of the traditional process paradigm, and into a more interesting teaching and learning place that focuses on the art of questioning and discussion as the basis for what makes writing good.

My course now takes place somewhere in the wires that lie in between the screens in the exchanges of text and discussions that cyberspace affords. My methodologies with CMC were enhanced and enlarged through teaching in the wires. There are several fundamental beliefs about what many of us apply to these methodologies that I see at the core of the composition classroom and that are integral to the nature of the computer-networked environment.

1. We demonstrate rather than tell. For example: In looking at the transformation of Malcolm X after going to Mecca, students usually don't know what Mecca is, so in a class discussion, ask them to find out and share what they find with the class.
2. We create, sculpt rather than proscribe. For example: Students start with their own web page, made early in the semester from a template. This they turn into a webbed portfolio of themselves, their writing, their resume, their special interests, their aspirations.
3. We model behavior rather than dictate. For example: We create a mailing list from which students get information about the class and post questions and their own essays.
4. We simulate and ask writers to join a community rather than isolate. For example: Students are asked to share their writing with the class through e-mail and the Web. As a result, they often get positive feedback and encouragement from their classmates they never would have received otherwise.
5. We place students in a social context rather than individualizing. For example: Student group collaborative research projects result in presentations, analyses, and databases that will be useful for individuals in the class.
6. We treat writing as recursive and intertwined rather than as individual acts that can be completed, finished. For example: Each writing challenge builds on previous work

accomplished. Students grow through reflecting and revisiting their writing in written self-assessments.

7. We play with assignments, letting voices emerge in myriad ways rather than expecting the same voice from our students on the same kind of assignment. For example: Students' writing, on topics that allow their own voices to emerge, make interesting reading. Never have everyone write a paper with only one expectation.

8. We grow toward an understanding of the complexity of what makes writing good rather than accepting an explanation of the best ways of doing writing. For example: As students engage in their writing, frequently and vigorously, in public view of their classmates, their writing will expand and improve as a result of their interest in others' work and in improving their voice for their classmates.

9. We provide writing space that encourages expansion of the sense of what makes writing good rather than isolation of the act of exposition, written to limited audience. For example: After a first round of peer critique, students return to their own work with new, more objective vision about the challenges of the assignment and realize they are not alone in their struggles.

10. We try to interest students in committing to their work as writers by structuring the class and sequence of assignments through the posing of questions rather than the assigning of tasks. For example: Students, in answering questions in depth, will find the writing process becoming easier as a result of constant inquiry and explanation. Students might even be given a reading task with the challenge of asking the students to write an assignment series that can be chosen by classmates to read.

11. We bring students into discussion about issues of interest to them and ask them questions rather than ask them to report or analyze. As students grow in their ability to answer and ask questions on topics they are considering, their sophistication with their topic will grow into a more critical, analytical stance.

In other words, most teachers who challenge their students with problem-based learning, as many of our science and health courses have done since the early 1990s, will put students in a networked course that will train them to inquire and solve problems that they have posed. Many students are curious about some aspect of their rights, for instance, they feel has been violated, based on one of the amendments. After dealing with the issue over time, through Internet searching, through interviews with experts via e-mail, through resources previously unobtainable in the short time students spend on their work, students often emerge changed in their position on the key issues they researched. After this kind of writing experience, no matter what students decide to major in, they will have the tools necessary to solve the problems of the writing tasks that are created for them. The focus of the course lies in the students' process of answering questions, posing questions, and sharing those questions and answers with others.

Students are asked to engage in a long-term, term-long conversation about a subject in which they become vested and learn something. As students open up, one of the most engaging conversations they have is one with themselves. The course and the papers are not formulaic. The dialogue of the course is centered around student writings. I know this because students stay in touch with me via e-mail long after they leave the course, and they comment and respond to new ideas they are finding in their subsequent courses. A valuable course becomes one that is carried around in a student's head long after the course concludes.

Some of what I do could be done in a traditional classroom, granted, but it is done so much better in a computer-networked classroom, that I can see no possibility of my going back to teaching in any other kind of learning space. Computer networks allow immediacy in the sharing of texts through posting essays to the class mailing list; they encourage and facilitate synchronous and asynchronous electronic exchange of ideas in response to this immediate exchange of text. Meanwhile, the challenge of blending the construction of argument and persuasion with the advent of hypertext trickles into the students' repertoire of modes of discourse. The activities that previously were so cumbersome, they were not worth doing, become enjoyable and a matter of pride, for cyberspace has created a place for the ongoing conversations in a writing class that give a learning place the immediacy of the Burkean parlor where students improve as writers while increasing their awareness of their own thinking and its articulation and effect on others. I piece together and craft my courses as a work of art, weaving the threads from one assignment to the next that will invite students into a world of thinking and writing and talking and rewriting that helps them to be able to imagine ways to solve problems and challenges in writing in whatever venue they find themselves in. By pulling into the writing tasks the close reading, reflection, and predicting that students are capable of doing after analysis, and linking one writing task to the next, in what I call *low stakes writing*, students take risks with their thoughts that show them as thinking adults, struggling for the words to make their thoughts coherent.

The venue for this perpetual struggle for students to find the right words in their future jobs will take place in cyberspace where they compose themselves and find others. I leave my students with their own and others' text as the center of the course while their focus is directed toward reading and conversing and writing in electronic places. This is the place in their futures where they will be managing many aspects of their lives, doing their banking and shopping, pursuing hobbies, playing games, reading the news, writing to friends, while they will also be using computer networks for most fields of work. I encourage teachers to consider what happens in their classrooms, what holds, what is reconsidered, what makes a difference. At that point, teachers begin to know what to throw away and what to keep.

Radical transformation into the social constructivist, collaborative classroom requires teachers to write a sequence of tasks that asks students to use what they know to produce new knowledge out of a series of experiences that teachers need to constantly engage in dialogue about with their students. This dialogue, coupled with a movement in CMC toward a virtual classroom, allows an interconnectedness that for students makes the course one remembered as seminal in establishing their habits of thinking and learning in their university careers. The composition instructor who created the social-collaborative classroom that was validated in the early 1980s will move naturally into the use of CMC for writing classes. Most learning time is spent in the network, extending the borders of the class. I find the tensions stimulating, the rewards and results satisfying. Students are grateful for the computer and writing literacy they leave class with and often report back their successes. All students leaving a university-level writing class should be ensured that their media literacy needs will have been developed in order for them to research and write electronically. I can think of no one more qualified to assist students in achieving technoliteracy than the composition instructor.

FINDING THE ESSENCE OF WORK IN COMPUTERS AND WRITING

Although practice in the discipline of teaching composition may be evident, viewable, measurable to some extent, and pervasive, the principles and practices of computers and writing teachers, for teachers new to computer-networked communication pedagogy, may not be so evident. These new teachers might not master the shift into computers and writing all at once, but gradually, starting with learning the rules of computer networks and adapting these rules into their own professional and personal development. The first level of transformation comes from the teacher's adaptation and development of computer-networked practices that use an expertise in e-mail management, World Wide Web research and production, and participation in synchronous and asynchronous communication as part of the teacher's self-enrichment. The length of time new teachers take to develop this competence will be directly related to their access to a well-connected computer, but more importantly, to their willingness to learn through self-directed inquiry and to their ability to not be discouraged through failures. If teachers do not show this willingness to work on their own computer literacy, in the near future, they will not thrive in their profession.

After achieving this beginning computer literacy themselves, these new teachers begin articulating and speculating on the assumptions that are inherent in the new technologies they are learning, and with this speculating, the potentials of the enhanced practices in the teachers' professional and personal development become clearly related to how present teaching practices could be enhanced. Thus, the second transformation finds teachers beginning to articulate and experiment with practices of their own, carefully weighing, considering, and reinventing the way they conduct their classes. As teaching practices begin to change, the principles that guide teachers expand. Good teachers will find other ways to enhance their teaching and will experiment with the media accessible to their students.

But it is only with full and genuine articulation and experimentation over time that these teachers will move into cyberteaching, headed toward mastery of this new way of teaching. In this third stage, teachers can now think with a new vocabulary about networked pedagogy, can see clearly the best uses for various modes of electronic discourse, and will subsequently change the assumptions and values through which they create their teaching practices.

As teachers begin this movement toward professional expertise and development in turning themselves into techno-rhetoricians, there are a few prerequisites that need to be in place for this acquisition of knowledge and practice to be effective. To move toward incorporating CMC into teaching practice, teachers must first complete the following accomplishments:

THE TOP TEN LIST OF THINGS TO DO TO MORPH YOURSELF INTO A TECHNO-RHETORICIAN.

10. Get a working computer—Get a computer that works, all the time, at your office, and get one at home, with reliable connectivity. Have these computers be your own, not a shared computer with children and spouses. You might even have to pay for this at home connectivity, but it is important. Make sure your computer has plenty of hard-drive space, a couple of gigabytes, RAM, at least 128 megs, a fast modem for home use, 56K, and a fast processor, at least 300 megahertz. Don't ask me to explain gigabytes, megs, and megahertz. They are on all computers and you need them, the higher number the better.

9. Master this working computer—This does not mean to merely get the computer to print, but practice enough that you learn exactly what it takes to connect a computer via a modem to the Internet, using universal, free programs such as NCSA Telnet, Eudora, unix commands if you're so lucky as to have a unix account, file transfer programs (ftp) such as FETCH (for MACs) or CUTEFTP (for PCs), the latest version of NETSCAPE or EXPLORER. After these are mastered, that is, learned well enough that you could clearly teach others (your students), then work yourself beyond the beginner level in graphics manipulation, including scanning, and a powerful graphics program like Adobe Photoshop. You could probably learn many of these programs with the help of your students. Developing a support group as you work your way through learning these programs is important.

8. Become friends with the technical support staff—You and many others will be involved in working with technology at your school. Find anyone, everyone, and use your collaborative and rhetorical skills to draw them together; find out their names, their jobs, and understand that they are extremely busy people at most campuses. Let everyone know what each other is doing.

7. Read—All the back issues of the online journals, *Kairos* and *Computer Mediated Communication*, and subscribe to the paper journal, *Computers and Composition* edited by Gail Hawisher and Cindy Selfe. Then find the authors in

these journals at their sessions at NCTE and CCCCs. Sign up for pre- or postconference workshops at CCCCs on computers and technology issues. Join the Alliance for Computers and Writing (ACW) online for $10 and get a discount on the subscriptions to Hawisher and Selfe's journal. Attend the yearly Computers and Writing Conference.

6. Join—There are free international mailing lists on the Internet that have active discussions of issues in the discipline (i.e., ACW-L [the Alliance for Computers and Writing http://english.ttu.edu/acw/]; OCC-L [the online college classroom]; NCTE-TALK; RHETNET). There are many, many more. When you subscribe, remain a lurker for at least a couple of weeks to learn what is appropriate discourse for the discussion list before you begin to post.

5. Announce your new research and professional interest somehow—Let your departmental colleagues and others such as your chair, dean, provost, presidents, and so on, know of your interests. However, do not yet call yourself a techno-rhetorician.

4. Consider yourself a revolutionary—Have the confidence that what you are doing will be better for your students than what you were doing before, so if it is not perfect, then you can make it better the next time. Assess, assess, assess. As you assess, however, be sure to use measuring sticks that are also used in the traditional course. Your students' enthusiasm and your own revitalization will carry you out of your previous paradigms. Being a revolutionary is going to take time though. Fair warning; enough said.

3. Find and attend the Computers and Writing conference—This group of scholars meets at a campus each year in late May or early June. Each session throughout the conference will offer you a smorgasbord of presentations. If you have gotten through Steps 10 through 4, you will want to go to all of the sessions, so perhaps you should try to attend this conference with a colleague or two. This is the conference where computers and writing teachers find each other, often meeting for the first time face to face after working together virtually. Announcements for the conference and other regional conferences are always found on the ACW mailing list.

2. Become a participant at MOO (multi-user object-oriented) sessions held at an educational MOOs on the Internet, such as LinguaMOO, Diversity University MOO, ConnectionsMOO or DaMOO— After you learn how to discuss at a MOO, learn how to build yourself and your spaces. After you build, invite others to join you. When others join you, have a design for the session that will be productive, engaging, and focused.

1. Practice and model for your colleagues and your students what you believe to be a liberatory pedagogy through the exploitation of networked communication programs you have available for you—Your modeling will encourage those you affect to join as long as you are willing to share, tell your stories, listen to others, and provide multiple paths of connections for yourself.

NOW THAT YOU ARE A TECHNO-RHETORICIAN, WHAT CAN YOU DO?

One of the strengths of computers is that students can learn at their own pace as soon as they arrive at the course, whether it is through a campus or home computer, within whatever space it is the teacher designs. Making daily or weekly class assignments available through the Internet and giving students the opportunity to write to the class, to the teacher and to each other through e-mail and the Web allows for multiple forms of communication to occur. Students no longer can claim that they did not know about a due date or about some other sort of activity that was required and stated explicitly in class assignments. The daily individual student contact in the CMC environment prevents the lost student, the one who is about to give up, the disengaged student. Instead, the student can find the support and intervention that might be needed for the struggling student to do well. Before computer-networked conferencing, in my classes, small groups met frequently, using collaborative strategies I asked them to use. I found it difficult to have the one-to-one contact with students as they would be working in groups on a regular basis. As the class progressed, if groups did not seem to be working, I would change strategies for certain students, pulling them from large groups and assigning them to paired groups. This strategy was the best I had found for engaging students in working on their own writing with enthusiasm and with real audiences.

The power of group work without the face-to-face component sounded strange to me at first, for I valued group work, but was not sure of how effective it would be in the computer classroom. What was a pleasant surprise to me was that group learning in a computer environment is a valuable teaching strategy with even the shy or less vocal student, nontraditional students and non-native speakers; they can more easily accomplish peer critiquing through computer-networked discussions than in face-to-face work. The medium is quite engaging and egalitarian. Students who have traditionally removed themselves from voicing their opinions often find themselves involved. A psychology professor colleague, Langley Frissell, commented to me on this when he first experienced a student talking to him in an electronic Web chat mode who always sat on the fringes and said nothing in class. Frissell thought the students would talk to him through computer networks more readily than through face-to-face contact because they had never been taught to not communicate that way. But that comment and inquiry is for another dispatch, another time. The course materials I have developed lead students through a movement of discovering that they are responsible for whatever it is they want to make of themselves in their educational progress. I keep Frissell's observation in mind and hope parents keep not teaching their children to not communicate this way.

There are basic givens that most professionals in the field of composition instruction would agree to. Writing is an activity and beginning writers learn best through practice and feedback. A center to any beginning writing class should be student writing. When considered in a construct with computer-mediated classroom work, there should be student orientation to the use of computers, but always for a purpose. Yet I spend very little time teaching computer skills for the students teach themselves as a necessary adjunct to success in the course as long as modeling and directions are provided in a coherent manner. For instance, students soon learn to print as they download their syllabus from e-mail onto a disk and read it on the screen. They walk out of the class in wonder that they have their syllabus on their disk, captured in electronic pixels and databits. Not only are my sequencing of writing assignments refined, but also the sequencing of computer skills students learn is integrated with the writing strategies. For instance, students need to understand how to save text to their disks before they should begin to move blocked text. Students need to learn to backup their files before they begin to experiment with formatting techniques. I encourage students to experiment with both technology and the text that they create. All of the above can be done collaboratively, through computer-networked activities and assignments. What seems overwhelming to students at the beginning of the semester seems achievable at the end of 16 weeks. Students are grateful for the trouble a teacher goes through for them in helping them to develop their computer literacy skills. As they learn to talk the talk, bit by bit, their options widen and their marketability improves.

I want students to take an interest in their own metacognition, paying heed to knowing about knowing and its effect on the writing process. My students come to know themselves and others as thinkers, knowers, writers, and collaborators much more intensely in a computer networked environment. Saying this quite nicely in an end-of-the-year memorable quote, Spring 1993, by a first year English 100 student, Rommel Anacan, commented:

> I wrote about things that I never really thought about before! I wrote about stuff that I thought made me look so stupid and then lo and behold, the person who critiqued my paper went through something similar! Especially at this age, it's incredible to know that someone is going through what you are. It's really hard sometimes for any of us to communicate one on one.

A valuable course becomes one that is carried around in a student's head long after the course concludes.

The brick and mortar classroom of the last couple of hundred years cannot compete on even ground with a computer-networked classroom, once the potentials of this new learning space are practiced and understood. When teachers examine their belief systems through the processes of networked thinking and writing, they will have sharpened their awareness of the world outside their traditional classrooms. If they choose to reject the networked opportunities that computers offer, it will be an educated rejection, based on knowing the possibilities rather than a rejection due to their inability to imagine their mastery. They will have glimpsed the interrelatedness of academic disciplines, cultural awareness, and technologies that will make them have strong visions on global issues by socializing themselves in the community of academic discourse. By integrating my writing course with the use of computer technology, my students not only will develop a value for their own work and write with an authentic voice, but also they will find that in the end, this feels good. Please stop by at: http://leahi.kcc.hawaii.edu/~kirkpatr.

The future of virtual learning is in the hands of educators willing to take risks and lead this teaching revolution. If educators do not take this charge seriously, we will be at the mercy of others who preempt us, and that is not an option I am willing to consider.

WORKS CITED

Barker, T., & Kemp, F. (1990). Network theory: A postmodern pedagogy for the writing classroom. In C. Handa (Ed.), *Computers and community* (pp. 1-27). Portsmouth, NH: Boynton/Cook.

Bruckman, A. (1996, January). Finding one's own in cyberspace. *Technology Review*, <http://www.techreview.com/ articles/ jan96/Bruckman.html>.

Bruckman, A., & Resnick, M. (1995). The mediaMOO project: Constructionism and professional community. *Convergence, 1*(1) <http://www.cc.gatech.edu/~asb/papers/convergence.html>.

Coles, W. (1988). *The plural I: The teaching of writing.* Portsmouth, NH: Boynton/Cook.

Coles, W. E. (1984). *Composing II: Writing as a self-creating process.* Portsmouth, NH: Boynton/Cook.

The Daedalus Group. (1999). The Daedalus Integrated Writing Environment. <http://www.daedalus.com/>.

Faigley, L. (1996, March). Literacy after the revolution. General Session of CCCC's 1996 Chair's Address. National Council of Teachers of English—Conference on College Composition and Communication. <http://www.missouri.edu/~cccc96/faigley.html>.

Fanderclai, T., & Siering, G. (1999). The Netoric Homepage. 1999. <http://bsuvc.bsu.edu/~00gjsiering/netoric/intro.html>.

Handa, C. (Ed.). *Computers and community.* Portsmouth, NH: Boynton/Cook.

Papert, S. (1996). *The connected family.* Atlanta: Longstreet Press. http://www.connectedfamily.com/.

Rose, M. (1989). *Lives on the boundary: The struggles and achievements of America's underprepared.* New York: Free Press.

Selfe, C. (1999). Technology and literacy: A story about the perils of not paying attention. General Session of CCCC's 1998 Chair's Address. <http://www.ncte.org/forums/selfe/>.

Stuckey, J.E. (1991). *The violence of literacy.* Portsmouth, NH: Boynton/Cook

Turkle, S. (1995). *Life on the screen.* New York: Simon and Schuster.

CHAPTERS FROM NEW WOR(L)DS

Re-Vision+Expansion. *Techne* and art. A series of MOO sessions and subsequent e-mail, re-edited by Mick Doherty and Sandye Thompson, in which contributors discuss the theme of this book and the various ideas they address in their chapters. Unification.

chapter 3.1

MOO=PUBLIC+A(C)TION:

A MOO SESSION FOR NEW WORLDS, NEW WORDS

Mick Doherty and Sandye Thompson

A Mostly Un-Edited MOO Log
(by definition a contradiction in terms)

telnet purple-crayon.media.mit.edu 8888

connect guest

@join sandyet

1. Sandye's Tea Room

   You see Sandye's sanctuary, the place where she can unwind from the stresses of the day (or night) amidst the joys of gracious living. Please sit down (there's a chair, a sofa, and lots of floor space), relax, and partake in the pleasures of tea.

   obvious exits: north to Shamrock's Donut Shoppe

   sandyet, Mick, Dene, John_B, cyn, Jan, nickc, mday, beckster, traci, James_I, judi, Michael_S, jrg, Petes

   You see Sandye's Message Board, listener, blender, Tray of Sandwiches; Dessert Platter, toaster, Surprise Card, ST Plotmaker, proj1, proj2, and proj3 here.

2. Mick says, "We start in a few minutes if anyone needs to get food, use the facilities, or brush up on Foucault."

3. sandyet shows slide #1.

4.

   * * * * * * * * * * * * * * * * * * *

   WELCOME TO ::: Can Be an Editor!
   "You, Too, Can Be an Editor!
   Or, How MOOspace Puts the 'Public' back in publication."

   We will be logging this session for publication purposes, so we ask that you identify yourself for the record.
   * * * * * * * * * * * * * * * * * *

5. @who

Member name	Connected as	Location
Sandye Thompson	sandyet	Texas Woman's University
Mick Doherty	Mick	RPI (via telnet from Dallas)
Dene Grigar	Dene	Texas Woman's University
John Barber	John_B	Northwestern State University
Cynthia Haynes	cyn	University of Texas @ Dallas
Jan Holmevik	Jan	University of Bergen, Norway
Nick Carbone	nickc	Marlboro College
Michael Day	mday	South Dakota Tech
Becky Ricky	beckster	Daedalus Group (Austin, TX)
Traci Gardner	traci	Daedalus Group (Austin, TX)
James Inman	James_I	University of Michigan
Judi Kirkpatrick	judi	Kapi'olani Community College
Michael Spooner	Michael_S	Utah State University
Jeff Galin	jrg	Cal State Bernardino
Peter Sands	Petes	UW-Milwaukee

From: Cynthia Haynes <cynthiah@utdallas.edu>
Subject: RE: Collaborative MOO Session

1. Mick and Sandye,
2. Thanks for putting up the MOO logs. In what follows, I pasted in some of the comments from the first session that Jan and I did not get to attend. I took two of our comments from the second session (those are marked by @@ symbols) and used them as responses to people in the first session. And the ** comments are my comments now back to those in the first session...the $$ comments are from our chapter draft itself..and finally some additional comments at the end and that have to do with the checkpoint that occurred in the second session. Confusing?? I hope so! Do what you want with any of this :)

3. Cynthia and Jan

4. Mick says, *"Let's be honest ... no one in the broad global village culture needs MOOs to remain part of "the culture.' 'No one in academia as a whole does either. Aren't we, in the very act of trying to legitimate MOOs as publication, trying to re-invent what is "necessary" for cultural advancement and survival?"* [See also MOO 71]

5. **Cynthia says, "The effort to legitimize MOOs as publication, for us, is more about legitimizing 'activity' and 'community' as criteria for what counts toward promotion in academia—and about reconceiving publication in terms of getting out of binaries like the 'archive' vs 'real-time' and what that might mean. But this is giving away more than we should 'here' about our own chapter for the volume :)"

6. <snip>>

7. Dene says, *"Is MOOing valuable ... more valuable than say oral discussions?"* [See also MOO 110]

8. @@Jan says, *"as co-editor of a 13megabyte MOO :) I am not worried about selecting what is good and what is bad...what is good gets visited and read a lot, what is bad goes unnoticed until it's eventually recycled by either the author or by us...."* @@ [See also MOO 497]

9. <snip>>

10. Dene says, *"Herein lies a real value for MOOs ... digital communications and exchange of ideas outside of publication norms"* [See also MOO 130]

11. **Cynthia says, "But Dene, to say there is a value for MOOs more real than another value (say in the value of relationships formed in MOOs) is like saying that we must become as value-driven as the

6. John_B materializes out of thin air.

7. sandyet smiles at John_B

8. Mick says, "John ... didn't think you would make it?"

9. John_B says, "Got lucky. Been sitting on my internet connection for hours just to be able to be here."

10. sandyet [to John_B]: that must have hurt like the dickens....

11. Mick [to mday]: new words ... new worlds ... john what's the URL?

12. John_B says, "www.eaze.net/~jfbarber/worlds_book/worlds_book.html"

13. Mick says, "We plan to start around 7:35 ... give people time to straggle in ... and run exactly an hour to 8:35. That okay with everyone? Of course, stay as long as you can, leave whenever you like, join, talk, comment, mock, storm out in disgust ... whatever!"

14. Mday says, "Uhh, Mick invited me here, but I know nothing of this project. Just let me know if I should leave"

15. Mick [to mday]: no, no. One of the wonderful things about MOO publishing is that it involves the element of chance ... you happened to be logged on to the MOO at the right time, right place... very kairic of you! I would personally find it quite kewl if some random junior high student wandered in and commented on Negroponte."

16. John_B says, "Something like, wow ,that's digital dude?"

17. Mick wonders suddenly if we should establish a policy about correcting text in MOOs for book reprint ... will have to ask book publishers ...

18. Dene says, "I had this same discussion with Cyn and Jan about the MOObook. . ."

19. Mick says, "this is going to informally formal. San, you want to throw up the first slide and we can skate off into immortality?".

20. sandyet nods... no problem

21. sandyet shows slide #4.

22. * * * * * * * * * * * * * * * * * *
Michael Joyce:

The city of text is formed on a belief that we are the outcome of stories we tell ourselves as we come to know new things ... The problem we face is how to write in the interstices.
* * * * * * * * * * * * * * * * * *

23. Mick says, "And the partner slide to that one ... "

24. Mick shows slide #10.

* * * * * * * * * * * * * * * * * *

25. Porush's Law:
"Participating in the newest communications technologies becomes compulsory if you

administrators who form policies that affect whether we are granted tenure or promotion. Is it possible to steer away from codifying any values and move toward cross-codifying values? (This is a blatant allusion to the title of our chapter, "From Crossroads to Crosscodes: Hacking a New Intersection in Publication.")

12. <snip>>

13. jrg says, "No Mick, MOOing is not publication. It is public talking that is recorded. I really believe that" [See also MOO 138]

14. "Cynthia says, "WHOA, Jeff! Would you say that MOOing is not writing? Would you say that writing is not sometimes published? Would you say that MOOing is not sometimes publication? Am I lost in this syllogism? :)' [See also B-3 through B-6]

15. <snip>>

16. Mick [to mday]: I will be traditional for a moment here ... I can name 25 faculty I know VERY well who would say you're justifying electronic publication by dressing it up in a postmodern discourse that uses words to mean anything in ways that make them mean nothing. [See also MOO 140]

17. "Cynthia says, "I always bristle when someone says that 'postmodern discourse uses words to mean anything in ways that make them mean nothing'... (Mick, I take that to be your hypothetical 25 faculty, in this case)...so let me disrupt this whole reply with a metalepsis from the draft of our chapter that might lend "meaning" in a meaningful way to the charge of 'dressing up' electronic publication in some kind of postmodern discursive cloak:

18. $$Derrida notes that when people question your politics or ethics [or your language] it is often because "the first defensive and reactionary reflex is to accuse of ethico-political irresponsibility, even of nihilism," the very one who comes like this to question and disturb the "doxa" in its slumber"$$

19. <snip>>

20. nickc [to Mick]: but the MOO is here only so long as we're logged in, then it will be different when the recorder is turned off and we go offline—then it's just a transcript [See also MOO 248]

21. @@Cyn says, "not necessarily, Mick...the MOO is a database running a process in real-time...and of course it's also an archive"@ @ [See also MOO 301]

22. *** WARNING: Saving to disk in one minute. ***
23. *** Saving to disk. All activity will stop for a few minutes. ***
24. *** Last checkpoint took 17 seconds. ***

want to remain part of the culture.
* * * * * * * * * * * * * * * *
[See also P-2]

26. judi grins

27. judi says, "So what *is* the newest technology we're all participating in?"

28. Mick says, " ....Joyce seems to believe we are fortunate to be learning new things that enable a culture to evolve. Porush might be suggesting it is compulsory we are learning new things in order to keep up with an evolving culture ...In the late age of print, as Bolter named it, where and how are we creating the new culture of publication, and/or how is it creating us?"

29. Mick . o o O (thought we'd start you with an easy one ...)

30. Dene says, "but does technology alone guarantee that we are evolving? Is it the only sign?"

31. mday says, "Is there only one culture, or are there subcultures of publication? and will print culture necessarily die? Are we forcing its death?" [See also T-3]

32. Mick posits that we, right now, are in Joyce's City of Text, and at the same time, following Porush's Law ... I mean, at this moment. In this MOO. January 14, 1998, PM Central Time."

33. sandyet thinks Birkerts would impale himself on a fountain pen if he thought print would die out

34. Dene he thinks it will, hence the elegy

35. mday agrees with Sandye, and I would lament the death too.

36. John_B says, "we are (obviously) participating in the culture that is at the moment defining us. But, what will we have become at some time, any time, in the future when we choose to look back?"

37. sandyet thinks we have a tendency to think either/or... those binaries kill us...

38. mday likes having a choice between print and electronic

39. judi says, "so is MOO an interstice of the dominant technological culture we're all going to either survive in or become victims of?"

40. jrg [to mday]: "print culture won't be gone, not for a long hundred years or so, but lots of things will change in the meantime"

41. mday says, "maybe it's just that we'll have more choices and more venues for communication and publication. I think that's a good change."

42. John_B says, "good point jeff, but *how* will things change? And what will they change into? or away from?"

43. sandyet wonders what print culture will be... what is print culture now... many people don't 'read', not in the way we think of it... they get news from radio, tv, internet....

44. Dene says, "and is this really evolving? A progress?"

45. mday says, "electronic communication via networks certainly changes the speed and tone of text communication."

---

25. *** Finished saving to disk. ***

26. Mick says, "we're back live ..." [See also MOO 498-506]

27. "Cynthia says, "I rest my case :)"

B

From: Dene Grigar <dene@eaze.net>
Subject: RE: Collaborative MOO Session

1. It is very strange to read these comments out of context. Some of the ones I made here in this excerpt did indeed have more explanation to them than what is posted. Does anyone else have this same take on reading this? I know, for example, when I made the comment about MOOs and publications, I said right after that something like "traditional view of publication." Which changes the gist of the comment entirely.

2. Gets me to thinking about the notion of detextualizing...I have to think about this. Although it happens in any context, how much easier is it when we chunk text for online writing? And what does that do to our ideas? And more importantly, to us?

3. Hmm. Interesting.

4. Dene

C

From: Dene Grigar <dene@eaze.net>
Subject: RE: Collaborative MOO Session

1. Dene says, "How much of what is getting said here now is actually being read by us. The information overload is astounding?" [See also MOO 96]

2. Before finding this line in the MOOlog I had just been thinking this thought--again, since it was I who said it the first time. Trying to take in all of what is being said and who said it is not easy. And when this event was taking place and the screen was scrolling down like crazy and I was typing and reading at the same time...

3. How much of what anyone said during the MOO session really got read and commented on? I wonder. [See also J-2]

4. One comment a student of mine made during a particularly vigorous MOO discussion was that no one was listening to her, that everyone seemed to be talking 'out there' to no particular one person or about one particular idea. She said she felt isolated by this experience. [See also F-2 through F-5; H-2ff.; and J-7 through J-8]

5. Do any of you more experienced MOOers feel this same way as my student did when you are online in a MOO?

46. Dene says, "but text doesn't disappear. . ."
47. Dene says, "we are turing this into text, aren't; we:)"
48. Mick [kairic] . o o ("turing" this into text?)
49. mday does the Turing Test on this text. Yep, signs of intelligence!
50. Dene smiles at her pun
51. jrg [to John_B]: "Joan and I are theorize the ways in which digital archives are currently emerging as a new paradigm of production, distribution, and management of intellectual property. Once the institutional systems start to use new languages, change is internal to the culture as well
52. judi says, "I think we're going to be looking at our physical libraries/with paper books/as cultural markers of the 'late 20th century.'"
53. Dene says, "what new languages are these? "
54. mday says, "text becomes faster and more easily reproduced, but ephemeral, sometimes fleeting.
55. Mick says, "what is this "the culture" we are talking about. nail it down for me, the American postmodern academic publishing culture responding to the tenure process?"
56. Mick . o o (whatever THAT means)
57. mday can't think in monolithic cultures. Sorry. mday thinks of cultures. Pluralism.
58. Dene says, "what about joe schmoe in a chat room? isn't that culture?"
59. judi says, "What becomes troublesome is that there aren't many new depositories of digital work that will have a permanence for new technologies often don't *talk* to old technologies."
60. John_B says, "Porush used the term first, at the beginning of this thread. what does he mean by 'culture'?"
61. mday finds Porush's use of culture problematic
62. jrg agrees with dene, about questions of "progress" because progress is more myth than anything.
63. sandyet thinks it comes back to community... what one person values as culture, another person considers trash.
64. Mick says, "I think *Porush* finds Porush's use of "culture" problematic -- and ironic. But if we can't define what it *is* how can we reinvent it?
65. John_B says, "Community. . . a collection of diverse values, somehow working in collaboration?"
66. jrg [to Mick]: "cultures, more like it.
67. Dene nods to John_B
68. sandyet says, "isn't culture an agreed upon set of objects that we as a community agree to value? Culture has to be a collaboration."

6. Dene

D

From: Jeffrey Galin <jgalin@wiley.csusb.edu>
Subject: RE: Collaborative MOO Session

1. Cynthia,
2. I stand by the statement I made in that first session. I'll post it again below and your followup comment:
3. jrg says, "No Mick, MOOing is not publication. It is public talking that is recorded. I really believe that"
4. "Cynthia says, "WHOA, Jeff! Would you say that MOOing is not writing? Would you say that writing is not sometimes published? Would you say that MOOing is not sometimes publication? Am I lost in this syllogism? :)" [See also MOO 138, and A-13-14]
5. Cynthia, yes, I think the syllogism gets in the way here. Most MOO discussions are public talking that is recorded. On occasion, a log or snippets of a log are contextualized within more formal forms of presentation (Kairos, Rhetnet, quotes within published articles, etc.). When presented as such, these pieces are published. Publication is a highly institutionalized process that is culturally determined. Publication assumes some form of validation. Nearly 95% of even the enormous body of pre-print physics and math papers that are archived on the xxx.lanl.gov e-print archive site are later "published" in print journals. Public writing or speaking does not equate to publication. Audience, cultural capital, financial capital, and institutional recognition all play significant roles in what most people understand as a definition of publishing.
7. All that said, things are changing and new paradigms of presenting knowledge are emerging. But general MOOing, as far as I can tell, does not constitute publication.
8. cheers,
9. jrg

E

From: Dene Grigar <dene@eaze.net>
Subject: RE: Collaborative MOO Session

1. Jeff,
2. How about MOOing that is intended for publication, like the one we all participated in here? Or a piece of writing written in a MOOlog style, like the one John and I did for High Wired?
3. Dene

F

From: Mick Doherty <mdoherty@dallascvb.com>
Subject: RE: Collaborative MOO Session

1. Dene writes:

69. judi says, "Is Porush talking about the "bleeding edge" of digital communication? If so, he's right."

70. jrg says, "perhaps dissensus will play more of a role in community building and shifting. More voices, more communities, more clashing of ideologies?"

71. Mick says, "Let's be honest ... no one in the broad global village culture needs MOOS to remain part of "the culture." No one in academia as a whole does either. Aren't we, in the very act of trying to legitimate MOOS as publication, trying to reinvent what is "necessary" for cultural advancement and survival?" [See also A-4; T-6]

72. sandyet says, "maybe the idea of "community-at-large will collapse...spaces like this one will emerge, more tiny communities ... each with a particular need that this satisfies..." [See also T-8]

73. Dene says, "I wonder how much influence Bell had in making the phone important to culture?"

74. Dene smiles

75. mday says, "more people engaged an faster forms of agonistic communication yields more good ideas?"

76. John_B says, "Not reinvent, but extend the umbrella definition and acceptance of what communication technologies work (or are sanctioned to work) in the creation and evolution of "the culture.""

77. judi [mday]: that's the trouble with not knowing what came before or after in this quote.

78. Dene says, "we all know how much Ford promoted the use of autos"

79. Mick [to Dene]: Ford also said "History is bunk."

80. mday [judi]: yeah, context is everything.

81. Dene says, "yeah, easy to say when you make it"

82. jrg says, "I just read last week in an article by sherry turkle how micro-communities form online and maintain highly separate identity structures and rigid communal boundaries. Take Jayshouse for example".

83. Mick looks around the Tea Room and sees ... a micro-community!

84. jrg says, "maybe micro-communities fit our current notions of socially constructed identies that are manifesting themselves in virtual worlds in ways that were never so easily untangled in face to face interaction"

85. sandyet thinks of microbreweries... things attached to "micro" seem to have the image of exclusionary ... upscale....

86. Mick says, "so we have a community here that wants to publish a book -- more on that later, maybe. Consider this then:"

87. Mick shows slide #1.

88.
* * * * * * * * * * * * * * * * * * *
Marshall McLuhan used to remark, "Gutenberg made everybody a reader. Xerox made everybody a publisher. Personal computers are making everybody an author:

2. One comment of mine made during a particularly vigorous MOO discussion was that no one was listening to her, that everyone seemed to be talking 'out there' to no particular one person or about one particular idea. She said she felt isolated by this experience. Do any of you more experienced MOOers feel this same way as my student did when you are online in a MOO? [See also C-4]

3. My immediate reply to this ...

4. Several MOO participants have commented on the very point that Dene makes above -- both in the MOO session and in more recent followup e-mails, not all of which have been posted to everyone. (Is this like "paging" or "whispering"?) ...There has been another "thread" in the replies regarding whether or not printing (re-publishing?) the MOO Log, edited or not, is the same thing as the MOO itself ... and whether or not this is worthy of publication. I believe I see a connection.

5. In re-publicing (intentional mis-spelling) the MOO Log, we have overcome the lost text, re-explored the missing bits and bytes of Joyce's City ... allowed for the integration of web & paper, of synchronous and asynchronous, of traditional and postmodern... heh, I would say, even, of "kairic" and "chronos." MOOing "is" kairic .... which I guess suggests that paper publication is "chronic." Ain't heuretic reinvention of the media and its labels grand?

6. /mick/

G
From: Dene Grigar <dene@eaze.net>
Subject: RE: Collaborative MOO Session

1. Mick,

2. I disagree about print being Chronos and MOOing being Kairic. [See Also F-5] I still stand by my previous assessment based upon Platonic and Aristotelian views of reality that writing, any form of it, possesses both characteristics.

3. It's that Being in Time thing.

4. Dene

H
From: Jeffrey Galin <jgalin@wiley.csusb.edu>
Subject: RE: Collaborative MOO Session

1. One comment of mine made during a particularly vigorous MOO discussion was that no one was listening to her, that everyone seemed to be talking 'out there' to no particular one person or about one particular idea. She said she felt isolated by this experience. Do

E-mail, word-processing programs that make revising as easy as thinking, and laser printers collapse the whole writing-publishing-distributing process into one event controlled entirely by the individual". --Stewart Brand
* *

89. Mick says, "Let's see ... if we stretch that to "controlled entirely by the individual' community' ... what does that say about what we're doing here in public-a(c)tion?"

90. mday says, "er, you certainly can't judge quality in the same ways on computer nets. Everybody gets in, but does everybody get read?"

91. Dene thinks not

92. John_B says, "New communication technologies allow us new ways of looking at the larger surrounding world, and promote new ways of talking about that world as a way of understanding, and yes, controlling, it."

93. Dene says, "but not necessarily reading it :)"

94. mday says, "I think that after the first rush of being impressed with all the computer and net publications, people are starting to be more discerning, filtering out the garbage, and learning what counts to them and why."

95. sandyet [to John_B]: but who is looking, and talking and understanding and controlling the new technologies...

96. Dene says, "How much of what is getting said here now is actually being read by us. The information overload is astounding" [See also C-1; T-10]

97. mday is reading it all

98. jrg [to John_B]: "yes, in fact this also concerns Joan and my conception of the WWW as a heterotopia, in Foucault's language: a self-contained element of culture that mirrors or reflects or implies all other facets of culture ... at least that is part of a definition" [See also V3-5]

99. Mick says, "But on the PAGE ... when Sandye and I *edit* this (and how arrogant is that?) for the book ... is it still our micro-community's city of text?"

100. Dene says, "I would hope it expands into and across other communities"

101. sandyet [to mday]: I wonder if people are learning to be more discerning...what does that say if new technologies 'progress' ... the global village will be full of illiterates

102. John_B says, "[to sandyet] we are, here tonight. The people using the technologies, playing with them, experimenting with them, trying to find new words (or ways of expressing them) to describe new worlds (and our experiences in them)."

103. sandyet [to John_B]: I just find myself becoming more and more concerned about those not here... we are seeking out and describing new worlds... but they will never try to reach them. [See also P-10]

104. mday [sandyet]: I think people are becoming more discerning. It may be arrogant of me, but I feel that part of my role as a teacher of ethics and communication is to encourage students to develop skills of discernment, evaluation, etc.

105. Mick [to mday]: ethics? the Q-question?

106. Dene says, "Sandye, Plato and the cave syndrome ... you are trying to drag them up

---

any of you more experienced MOOers feel this same way as my student did when you are online in a MOO? [See also C-4]

2. Dene,

3. I and my students feel that way regularly, perhaps for different reasons. We are trained to expect responses from what we say. Students are used to performing for a grade. Student says x another student responds or the teacher responds. If students say things in class to the whole class and no one responds, students get upset. MOOs, do not work this way of course, but we are habitual creatures. Expectations often transcend contexts even if inappropriately.

4. One more thought Dene. You ever felt isolated in a crowd? I certainly do at times. In fact, generally avoid big crowds. I don't enjoy them for exactly the reasons that your student seems to have been frustrated. Like most folks, I like to be heard. In a MOO, much of what gets said does not get 'heard,' which gets me back to my point about MOOs and publication. One publishes to be heard. More importantly, however, being heard is tied to being enfranchised within a culture.

5. Charles Schuster writes in "The Ideology of Literacy: A Bakhtinian Perspective":

6. Literacy is the power to be able to make oneself heard and felt, to signify. Literacy is the way in which we make ourselves meaningful not only to others but through the other to ourselves._The Right To Literacy._

7. This is not to say that enfranchisement equates to publication. It is to say that publication generally does not occur without enfranchisement. I'll stop here. I need to think through these things further.

8. cheers,

9. jrg

From: Jeffrey Galin <jgalin@wiley.csusb.edu>
Subject: RE: Collaborative MOO Session

1. Dene Grigar wrote:

2. Jeff, How about MOOing that is intended for publication, like the one we all participated in here? Or a piece of writing written in a MOOlog style, like the one John and I did for High Wired? [See also E-2]

3. Dene

4. Dene, I think I addressed this one below [See also D-5], I said.

the rough ascent when they would rather stay in the cave?"

107.Mick <-- A Hugh Blair-ian Good Man Skilled In MOOing

108.sandyet says, "but who do we get to teach? we are teaching valuable skills... but who is exposed to them? students at university are the 'elite'... what about the majority of the population who don't have access to us?"

109.john_B says, "[to sandyet] yes, I'm with you on that concern. But explorers cannot always take everyone to the new worlds. We can send back dispatches, we can try and convince people to follow, to join us, but we can't make them.

110.Dene says, "Is MOOing valuable ... more valuable than say oral discussions?" [See also A-7]

111.jrg [to Dene]: "in what ways do you mean?"

112.Mick [to Dene]: in the larger concept of advancing academic knowledge *as it is currently conceived* I would have to answer "no."

113.sandyet nods mick....

114.Dene says, "well, we say MOO discourse is important but how and why? More than anything else we can teach? I am wondering ..."

115.mday says, "Not only the Q question, but the question of good and evil, of crime and harm, of stealing and privacy, copyright, ownership, pirating, Gilligan, and the rest."

116.jrg says, "seems like moos serve very specific functions for a very small elite group of folks, at the moment anyway"

117.Mick [to jrg]: micro-communities! Exactly what I was saying before!

118.Dene nods at Jeff's comments

119.john_B says, "[to Mick] but how about in the future, in the context of what the "larger concept of advancing academic knowledge "will have become?"

120.sandyet says, "I have to question the "value" of electronic publication.... who is our audience?"

121.john_B says, "who is our audience of *any* publication we produce?"

122.Mick [to sandyet]: who's our audience ... ?

123.Mick shows slide #2.

124.
```
* * * * * * * * * * * * * * * * *
Negroponte (Being Digital)
In the post-information age, we often have an audience the size of one.
* * * * * * * * * * * * * * * * *
```

125.Dene says, "but it is still an audience and it is outside of ourselves"

126.mday says, "we have met the audience, and she is ourselves."

127.jrg [to sandyet]: "digital publication has become a major concern of libraries for archival purposes and for writers who write not for money but to exchange new

5. On occasion, a log or snippets of a log are contextualized within more formal forms of presentation (Kairos, Rhetnet, quotes within published articles, etc.). When presented as such, these pieces are published.

6. But such MOOs are a different species than the ones that are not logged to be published. Granted, because of their archival nature, logs may be submitted for publication after the fact (though generally not because of permission problems). The very fact that publishing logs usually requires consent proves my point, I think anyway.

7. cheers,
8. jrg

J

From: Jan Rune Holmevik <jan.holmevik@hedb.uib.no>
Subject: RE: Collaborative MOO Session

1. Dene Grigar wrote [See also C-3]:

2. Dene says, "How much of what is getting said here now is actually being read by us. The information overload is astounding!"

3. I think the problem here is not really 'astounding' information overload, but rather the way information is delivered. With most clients, and in particular raw telnet, the output from the MOO become very hard to read and interpret. One reason may be that 99% of texts we are used to reading are 'static', that is, they don't scroll away from us as we read...we can go back and read it over again if there was something we didn't understand. Not so for the MOO newbie. When the text rapidly scrolls off the screen as people are talking it creates a frantic mode of reading where one is trying to read and understand everything while it is constantly keeps slipping away.

4. In our society we are well versed in dealing with information overload, just think of all the information we process every day just from news media. We are dealing with this 'overload' by selecting the information we want and need...we are dealing with a system that we've become used to...we know the rules...we know what channels to tune in to and what channels to over look.

knowledge."

128.Mick says, "Academia -- with departments, as we know them -- is less than 125 years old."

129.jrg chuckles at mday

130.Dene says, "Herein lies a real value for MOOs. . ."

131.Dene says, "digital communications and exchange of ideas outside of publication norms" [See also A-10]

132.Mick didn't like any existing electronic journals so started one. Talk about your audience of one.

133.sandyet nods Jeff, I agree, but many question digital publication because it *seems* transitory... I may get something from talking to you... but I have to "prove" it.

134.Mick screeches to a halt. Dene, MOOing, you imply, is NOT a publication?

135.Dene says, "it is outside of the norm, which many describe as print"

136.jrg says, "transitory in that forms will not remain. But translation schemes will not likely be lost, not if digital publishing becomes our primary means of archiving texts"

137.mday likes to think of what we do in terms of Deleuze and Guattari. Schizoanalytical, multicentered, rhizomatic, coloring outside the lines.

138.jrg says, "No Mick, MOOing is not publication. It is public talking that is recorded. I really believe that" [See also A-13]

139.Dene says, "Ronell says this too in the Telephone Book, Michael"

140.Mick [to mday]: I will be traditional for a moment here ... I can name 25 faculty I know VERY well who would say you're justifying electronic publication by dressing it up in a postmodern discourse that uses words to mean anything in ways that make them mean nothing. [See also A-16]

141.sandyet says, "how long has print been the norm? I have to start wondering how long it will be before something might be considered the norm..."

142.Dene says, "well, Sandye, I guess we can look at the last 100 years at least, right? More even?"

143.jrg says, "or it is public talking that gets excerpted and then printed on Rhetnet as a consumable object" [See also T-14]

144.mday says, "Like rhizomes it can grow around and through other institutions and supplant them, grow into them, morph in and around them."

145.nickc [to jrg]: that's more like narrowcasting, since so few people really can hear a moo talk at any one time

146.Mick [to jrg]: I disagree but can understand your definition -- if you define for me what "publication" *is* ..."

147.jrg [to Mick]: "can't do that of course, but as a new faculty member who must publish" I look to archives like xxx.lanl.gov for a close model to what I'd like to see happening in our community of computers and writing

5. I think most people are dealing with 'perceived' information overload in a MOO in exactly the same way, we read some things (maybe listen to some people more than other) and let other information scroll by.

6. One comment a student of mine made during a particularly vigorous MOO discussion was 'that no one was listening to her, that everyone seemed to be talking 'out there' to no particular one person or about one particular idea. She said she felt isolated by this experience. [See also C-4]

7. Do any of you more experienced MOOers feel this same way as my student did when you are online in a MOO?

8. This is a well known phenomenon, especially among new MOO users, but it can easily be avoided if we all start to pay more attention to- "listen" to-- what others say, instead of, as is often the case, being too busy talking ourselves :). Even just an acknowledging nod or a friendly smile will go a long way toward making people feel heard.

9. Cheers,
10. Jan

K

From: Dene Grigar <dene@eaze.net>
Subject: RE: Collaborative MOO Session

1. Jeff,

2. [See also H-4] If I were at a function at the 4C's for instance and had all of the people who participated online standing around me talking as we were doing online I do not think I would feel isolated among them. Big crowds of people I "don't" know, yes, I would certainly agree. A big crowd of close colleagues whom I feel especially close to, "that" is rare.

3. And my feeling of isolation did not occur because I was sitting alone in my garret-like office because right now I am sitting in the very same place and feel very warmed by our discussions about these MOO sessions. No feelings of isolation there.

4. But with all of cacaphonic commentary (and I mean that

148.Dene says, "I'm not agreeing, but ask any older faculty member what is valuable discourse and they will say print."

149.sandyet says, "if I publish a book with a publication number of 1 with my observations and such (a conversation I hope with my reader) and it is destroyed, it was still published...."

150.mday [Mick]: do you believe those 25 faculty, Mick?

151.Mick [to mday]: doesn't matter if I believe them ... they sit on the T/P committees. I speak, of course, from a seat outside academia.

152.jrg [to sandyet]: "actually, the rate at which change is occurring in our society is changing in interesting ways . . ."

153.jrg says, "I heard once that TV took 30 years or so to make into 40% of all homes, VCRs made it in less than 20 years ... Microwaves in 12 or so. Who knows for the internet?"

154.Dene says, "and computers since 1984."

155.Mick [to Dene]: nah. Macintosh since 1984.

156.Dene says, "Maybe Orwell's 1984 did not mark the death of the culture but the beginning :)"

157.nickc [to jrg]: with Microsoft bucks behind WebTv, and tv, rather than computer as interface, web will be in most homes in five years or so.

158.Mick says, "I'm not an Author. But I play one on WebTv."

159.sandyet nods... communication technologies move so fast... we can know almost anything as soon as it happens... the terrorist holding a hostage, the death of a politician, a new scientific discovery... news comes out so fast it doesn't "belong" to anyone anymore

160.nickc [to sandyet]: postman's right about news that's useless—one of the fallouts of t.v. and corporate consolidations of newspapers

161.sandyet says, "if the web is in most homes...and we link on top of each other... we all share the knowledge... who is the author?"

162.Mick says, "I'm not an author ... at least not according to Andrea Lunsford ..."

163.Mick shows slide #3.

164.

* * * * * * * * * * * * * * * * * * * *
Lisa Ede and I were stunned once we began to realize the degree to which all writing is social and, therefore (in our view, at least), collaborative. As a result of this recognition, we have attempted over the years to write "officially" with each other or with others, and to find ways to allow still other voices into our texts—as one way available to us to keep making the point that even when we seemingly write "alone" we are writing with others, with all those others whose words and voices we carry with us. Why all the credit should go to this supposed autonomous and stable and creative "self" has interested and puzzled us for fifteen years now.

                                            -- Andrea Lunsford
* * * * * * * * * * * * * * * * * * * *

metaphorically rather than literally), I felt like alone voice crying out in the night (and I mean that metaphorically too).

5.   Dene

L
From: Nick Carbone <nickc@english.umass.edu>
Subject: RE: Collaborative MOO Session

1.   Seems we've come down to two concerns: What is publishing, and Why publish.

2.   We also seem to be assuming an academic context, defined, at least in our training and prior and current practices, as peer-reviewed (and approved) writing that acknowledges sources (via citations) for various reasons (to borrow authority, to establish authority, to let the reader know where we're coming from, to set up a counter argument, to share our theoretical lineage [however unlinear it may be], to show that we know the stuff we're supposed to know in order to qualify for speaking to a particular community, to give thanks and praise to those whose shoulders we're standing upon, to situate our thinking, to define a still point in our reading history, and also to say we depend on what we're sourcing—its part of our intellectual complexion, part of the face we prepare to meet the faces that we'll meet).

3.   Here we are tooling along in the rhythms and cycles of print, it's comparatively leisurely recursiveness, establishing our own touchstones—the pieces we love or hate that come to us almost unbidden when we encounter other other works, especially our own, and we are, in this tooling, accustomed to editors, the limits of print, the demands of concision and the relatively straight and narrow, sequential order of the page, a process that takes a year, sometimes two, before a piece goes from writer to reader, and zap! we fall into this wired world where everything's accelerated "and", if we choose, saved.

4.   Because we can save random thoughts, freeze a dynamic discussion in a log, capture in the web thoughts on the fly, because the new technology can hold so much more, and because we can share it, broadcast it, recast it, hell, even print it.

165.Dene says, "Mick, Macs begin the onslaught of personal computing and the proliferation of this technology, yes?"

166.Mick would agree with that, Dene.

167.jrg [to sandyet]: "author as a concept will no longer mean what it currently does in the romantic senses

168.mday says, "Well, the Lunsford quote would certainly indicate a change in the nature of the subject, the author."

169.Mick says, "But if we're gonna name the starting point of the television in the 1940's then the starting point of the computer was the 1960's. Consistency in analogy and all that."

170.Dene says, "so who is writing this chapter??? who is the author here??"

171.mday is valiantly trying to worm his way into this chapter.

172.nickc [to sandyet]: there's the author of the whole--everyone who writes something combined, and the author of the part--the writer of the individual message, but ...

173.sandyet says, "isn't one of the reasons we cling to print publication is that we need to assign an owner?"

174.Mick says, " Sandye and me ... we're hosting, logging, and editing this chapter. we ain't *writing* it."

175.Dene laughs at the trouble she started ... that is the point guys. multiple authors."

176.Mick [to Dene]: don't think you drop this trouble. Blame Steve Jobs. Or Douglas Englebart. Or Vannevar Bush.

177.nickc [to sandyet]: no one will want to write parts much if they don't have a sense they're heard and appreciated and recognized by the whole--it won't work to be cogs in a writing machine

178.mday says, "Interesting concept, ownership. We're pretty retentive about ownership and copyright, but in other cultures, and in previous ages, it wasn't always that way."

179.jrg says, "Foucault's author functions need to be expanded, reconceived, so that we can begin again to see how the role of author functions in a digitalizing society"

180.Mick says, "What matters who writes? What matters who responds?" Hey ... that'd be a great title for a webtext ..."

181.jrg smiles at Mick

182.Dene says, "so does this text constitute a readerly or writerly text?"

183.Mick says, "OK, fine, *we're* reconceiving "author." Maybe even, much more slowly, *academia* is doing so as well. But my Uncle Don, the firefighter, isn't. Does that matter? Or are we completely elitist? Er, e-litist?"

184.sandyet says, "what, really, in the electronic space is the difference between an author, writer, reader, editor?"

185.jrg [to Dene]: "depends who is reading it I think

186.nickc says, "it matters a lot who writes and who responds because if it doesn't

5. If we define publishing as simply putting things where they can be read, then sure, everything we do online that can be seen is, in essence publishing. The question is, what's worth reading? What's worth someone's time and thinking, especially as the amount to be read grows exponentially?

6. If any of any of this ends up in a book, it will be by editorial graces; a decision will be made that says, 'this much can go between these covers.' And for all of a book's intertextuality, it has the comfort of a beginning, a middle, and end. Electronic forms are more permeable, less definite feeling for many for now. Books give the illusion, because they come to us more slowly, are more fragile (see Bernstein's piece in Chorus on this point), more self-contained in appearance, more expensive, and include 500 years of cultural capital and smashing success, of being--still--the preeminent form of publishing.

7. I don't believe they necessarily are, or need to be. But I also don't think any publishing, any pasting or posting or storing of words is the same thing as PUBLISHING. I like editors and peer-reviewers--they're really attentive readers in my experience.

8. I like being in a MOO a hell of lot more than I do reading MOO archives or logs. I don't think a MOO log has automatic value of the same kind I expect to find when I read a piece that's been recommended by a journal's editors and reviewers. If I come across a published MOO transcript, it's usually resituated with some preface, given a reason for being where it is. It's been revised most often, reshaped, no longer what it was, of different value. For me, the most value is always being present in a conversation. I like that more than reading a log of the same.

9. So if a MOO log makes it PUBLICATION--it really needs to be worked and recast for it make it worth my time. Otherwise it comes across as self-indulgence (in the end, a subjective determination, but then, that's what reviews are for).

10. Nick Carbone

M

From: Michael Spooner <mspooner@press.usu.edu>

matter, and you can distinguish voices, you can't have a community"

187. Mick [to sandyet]: that was the point of the McLuhan slide.

188. mday says, "doesn't technology always start in the hands of inventors, go to the elite, and then trickle down to others?"

189. nickc: not elitist so much as narrowly defined and expensive to start-but as product grows, gets easier to use, gets less expensive, it becomes more available

190. Mick says, "Trickle-down e-conomics?"

191. Dene says, "yes, but the first users are the ones who can afford to master it"

192. jrg [to Dene]: "who is writing depends on what the text is for, who is reading it, and where and how it was produced I think

193. Mick shows slide #2.

194.

```
* * * * * * * * * * * * * * * * * * * * *
Intellectual work flourishes in webs; writing is always a conversation, hidden or
not; and ideas should not be owned.
-- Donna J. Haraway
* * * * * * * * * * * * * * * * * * * * *
```

195. nickc [to Mick]: yeah, but each iteration of ease removes a layer of control and deeper understanding. Was a time only programmers could use computers

196. Mick [to nickc]: in a real way that's *still* true.

197. John_B says, "jeff, couldn't it just as easily be that the *text* depends on who is writing, for what purpose, and to whom?"

198. jrg [to John_B]: "sure, that is why we are arguing a new paradigm of publishing and authorship is at hand. Print terms are no longer working to describe what we do

199. mday says, "Amen to Haraway ... this notion of ownership of ideas has always puzzled me.

200. nickc [to Dene]: so you're right, each generation of expansion requires less active knowing from users, as a way to increase user base

201. Dene nods to Nick

202. sandyet wonders if each layer that moves away from those who have "mastered" it... means at each new generation has more reasons to misunderstand it

203. nickc [to sandyet]: or understand it differently ... but around here there's a lot of classes in school that teach t.v. literacy on the side-how to unpack a commercial, for example, to see it's cultural messages ... but computers are still gee whiz mystery items to a lot of people

204. sandyet [to nickc]: and I think that's valuable... but how many don't have that sort of exposure.....

205. nickc [to sandyet]: too many lack the exposure

206. mday says, "I think teaching classes like that, and including the web, is important, Nick"

Subject: RE: Collaborative MOO Session

1. I'll leave the theory to the theorists, but in any case, it seems to me that if you think it *is* a publication, a MOO's publication has been accomplished once the MOO closes. Then the chapter we're talking about becomes a sort of re/print-in any case, a different "moment," audience, rhetorical situation, etc, a different publishing. So different conventions apply, and we get into judgments about how successful it is in terms that Jeff alludes to with his reference to an institutionalized, culturally determined process.

2. And we knew this from the beginning, or we wouldn't have assumed the need to deal editorially with the MOO text when/as it is forwarded into print. The footnotes we're writing, I mean, the mechanical cleaning up, and inserting new texts as Cynthia was doing earlier today. I think we were aware from the beginning that these treatments were going to be needed as we changed venues from MOO to paper.

3. One thing I was trying to say in the session last week was that we "weren't" asking ourselves questions about the success of this MOOtext as a print pub in terms of that durned culturally determined process. We didn't ask "is this thing worth reading on paper?" We asked ourselves only "but what does 'worthwhile' mean?" We assumed that, with some editorial touching up, it would come out well enough to work. ... So here's where I am, and I don't expect this will be a popular view. Having read it now, I have to question going forward with it to print. We're not publishing for an audience of one anymore-or, ok: we're publishing for a "different" audience now-and we have to account for what our audience considers "substantial". I don't see it in this MOO.

4. Which is *not* to say it wasn't a valuable discussion. And not to say no MOO could ever turn into a good print pub. I just don't think this particular one will cut it. I'm imagining the review in College English, and it isn't a pretty vision.

5. Michael S.

N

From: Cynthia Haynes <cynthiah@utdallas.edu>
Subject: RE: Collaborative MOO Session

207. Mick says, "Steve Doheny Farina in his book -- what was it, the Wired Neighborhood -- claims strongly that our ability to understand computers and *use* them affects our persona -- if we type fast, are clever, and know commands, we are seen as Smart."

208. judi says, "if folks on the *bleeding edge* of technoculture who are teachers don't start to exploit these technologies in our work we'll become the victims of the entertainment and pleasure industries. Im not sure how to get this message out to teachers who choose to ignore cmc as a new way of writing." [See also P-13]

209. Mick [to judi]: why say "victim" in that context?

210. nickc [to Mick]: sdf also noted that identity and ability to be who one wants is limited by the code others supply and how well one chooses or can master it.

211. mday [Mick]: but you can't just be a good typist. There have to be good ideas and wit behind all that reading and typing.

212. Dene says, "as for the typing issue, it will be interesting to see the edited logs of this session"

213. sandyet says, "isn't part of the problem that many see cmc as a "new" way of writing... I'm writing the same way I always did... letters, words, sentences,...."

214. judi says, "victim because our audiences will be engulfed by other seekers of attention that are less academic!" [See also W1-5]

215. mday says, "Yes, Dene, I believe firmly that what we are creating could be a (not the) Belle Lettres of the late 20th century."

216. nickc says, "code is really interesting. I can't wait to see how Larry Lessig reports to the judge on the Microsoft case--he sees code as the unacknowledged legislator"

217. Mick says, "I feel weird quoting myself here, but ... there's another side to this. The responsibility of the writer to the reader."

218. Mick shows slide #3.

219.

* * * * * * * * * *
I tell my Tech/Pro students at the beginning of each semester, that if they have not captured their audience's attention within the subject line and the first glimpse of primary text, they have lost the battle to the delete button. We must pack meaning into a tight textual representation precisely because everything else about the electronic communication act is fluid. We may have to make the reader work harder to decode the text, but if we have kept her there to do so, we have engaged collaboration, and reinvented rhetoric as e-pistemic. -- Mick Doherty
* * * * * * * * * *

220. mday says, "Good point, Mick. You have to be skillful to get attention in such a fast, crowded, ephemeral medium."

221. PeteS says, "but sandye you're also writing both more publicly and with more *response* than any other way . . and with more opportunity for constant revision"

222. mday [sandyet]: well, the speed and connection and synergy of words that happens here is sort of new, sort of attractive about CMC.

223. Mick says, "the collaborative act is the rhetorical act, using Lanham's definition, of Getting Someone to Share Your Attention Structure.."

1. Oh wow...we're glad that we prompted such a rich vibrant discussion! After reading the day's postings, we have been thinking about this process and the fact that the specific topic of MOOs and/as publication has such an overlap with our chapter that we find ourselves in a conundrum, namely, making 'public' what will have been 'published' in our chapter for a real-time meeting that will have been published in Mick and Sandye's chapter. Whew! Now that's an interesting twist on everything! In our post today, (See A) playfully weaving together some decontextualized comments with our comments 'post facto', we mention that our chapter is in part an attempt to reconceive the notion of 'publication' itself. And yet, the responses we've seen today 'seem' to be putting what we said over against traditional modes of publication, and so of course our decontextualization of others' comments mixed with our own will fall short when measured against a conventional model. What to do about that? Well, we could discuss in this email exchange some of what is going in our chapter, but that has the feel of making 'our' chapter the subject of discussion... which we don't want to do. This is Mick and Sandye's chapter... this wondrous admixture of real-time, asynchronous, post-real-time REALized exchange we're having now. At least we think that is Mick and Sandye's aim, though we wouldn't presume to say.

2. We should probably say (about our chapter), however, that we were/are interested in valorizing 'real-time' and working at a kind of critical 'jarring' of the publication grip on academic mechanisms for promotion and tenure...AT THE SAME TIME (and for the most part) we are trying to explore, retrofit, temporarily don the garment of real-time publifying of our ideas in AND out of academia. Without saying what we will have been saying in our chapter (can we do this? :), we have NOT been saying that MOO logs should be/are publications. That is too narrow of a concern for the theoretical exploration we have in mind. We are trying to begin at the beginning, to ask the questions about what it means to have archived something, what it means to privilege the 'present' when we are in real-time, what is at stake when traditional modes of publication defend the system by asking what is 'worth' reading, what is worthwhile. We are interested in what and who gets to carve out the space of publication and the 'value' we place on it, but in relation to a real-time venue. We're NOT trying to knock down all of publication, or to reinvent MOOs under the old rubric of definitions of publication. Whether Mick and Sandye should publish

the MOO session and subsequent discussion should not, in our view, be determined by an imagined not-so-pretty review in College English. [See M-4] We wonder what we all would have missed if James Joyce or Virginia Woolf had decided not to publish based on whether the 'received' tradition reviewed their work.

3. In terms of the comments about isolation when MOOing. The MOO has that affect, among others. As Jan has said, much depends on how we control the overload of information, and much depends on one's personality, dispositions, learning styles, etc. But, the MOO ALSO has the 'potential' for being in the swirl of the social. The choice is there always beating like a pulse. We may even be alone in a MOO room, but we page one another (if we choose), we also page and emote across MOOs (through the InterMOO communication channels), we read texts of others while in the MOO (whether alone or in a MOOroom with others), we talk on inMOO channels as well, and we read and receive asynchronous MOOmails while doing all of the above. That is the POTENTIALITY always already available to MOOers. The feeling of isolation is (in our view) a function of the degree to which one takes advantage of these potentialities.

4. Cheers,

5. Cynthia and Jan

6. session and subsequent discussion should not, in our view, be determined by an imagined not-so-pretty review in College English. [See M-4] We wonder what we all would have missed if James Joyce or Virginia Woolf had decided not to publish based on whether the 'received' tradition reviewed their work.

7. In terms of the comments about isolation when MOOing. The MOO has that affect, among others. As Jan has said, much depends on how we control the overload of information, and much depends on one's personality, dispositions, learning styles, etc. But, the MOO ALSO has the 'potential' for being in the swirl of the social. The choice is there always beating like a pulse. We may even be alone in a MOO room, but we page one another (if we choose), we also page and emote across MOOs (through the InterMOO communication channels), we read texts of others while in the MOO (whether alone or in a MOOroom with others), we talk on inMOO channels as well, and we read and receive asynchronous MOOmails while doing all of the

---

224. nickc [to Mick]: that depends on the audience and the writer--there are some people who'll I read no matter what they post, like Marcy Bauman

225. sandyet [to Petes]: earlier we were talking about audience... what's more public... me here with you guys or my words in a book with a print of 20,000?

226. Mick [to Petes]: if you acknowledge that interactivity is a key part of "public"-ation, then THIS is more public.

227. sandyet says, "is what we do here or on the web as valuable as what we do in a book?"

228. Mick [to sandyet]: we ARE doing this for a book.

229. Petes says, "depends on whether anyone reads it, sandye, and who actually responds TO you. . . ."

230. traci [to sandyet]: it depends upon the setting of that book, no? 'me here w/you guys' has an implied audience. where is that in a book?"

231. nickc [to Mick]: 'public'-ation or 'public-action'? How is this any more public with just the ten or so of us?

232. Mick says, "I didn't say -action, you did."

233. sandyet says, "can I really know who reads it... and what impact anything has.... my words here could influence you and you could go influence others.. and so on and so on and so on."

234. jrg says, "but it becomes valuable because we are doing it for the book, primarily anyway."

235. Dene says, "and ultimately for each other and others outside of this room"

236. Mick [to jrg]: so the BOOK instantiates the validity of the MOO?

237. Mick whuffles at that.

238. nickc [to Mick]: in this one case, yes--we wouldn't have convened otherwise

239. sandyet says, "so if the point of the here and the book is enlightenment, to join the community.. then why can't *this* be publication?"

240. nickc [to sandyet]: because in action it's ephemeral, happening now--in stasis, as a log, half the value of the it is gone

241. Mick [to nickc]: we had a Kairos MOO last night -- we wouldn't have convened without the journal. That MOO will affect (and effect) the contents of "the journal without actually every being published in any form. Which MOO is more "public"?

242. nickc [to Mick]: the published moos are public--MOOs for meetings and planning may have public results, but the event itself is not public

243. traci says, "it looks to me like the rhetorical situations are being muddied. it's difficult to compare a conversation with a known audience validly to a book currently existent only in theory now you can perhaps compare a logged moo available to the world with a book available to the world, where the audience in neither case is 'set'

244. Mick says, "the MOO is here -- exists kairically, in the present re-invention of the text -- but the book is still a theoretical construct, existing (not yet) chronologically ..."

245. sandyet sees where mick is going...

246. jrg [to sandyet]: "no doubt, there has to be circulation and recognition. that is what tenure review boards look for, Being cited."

247. mday says, "and being published in venues that have "prestige""

248. nickc [to Mick]: but the MOO is here only so long as we're logged in, then it will be different when the recorder is turned off and we go offline--then it's just a transcript [See also A-20]

249. once some cobbled combinations of transcripts are published, you've got a reduced version of the MOO, an abridged sense, like a the tail end of breeze that sneaks in through the door before it closes."

250. mday says, "or an artifact of something that was once living..."

251. Mick says, "is editing a moo reducing it, Nick ... or "enhancing" it?"

252. nickc [to Mick]: reducing it--MOOing's more than just the words--it's the action of being presently engaged that matters as much to the meaning it holds

253. Mick says, "jeff, that MOO help page you did has probably had more readers than everything else you have or will ever write combined. Does that bother you?"

254. jrg smiles

255. jrg says, "I'm thrilled about the fact that MOOcentral will have been read by more folks than anything I ever write. But then again it is now being published by Jan and Cyn [in High Wired] and the website will move too"

256. Mick says, "Don't you mean it is now being *re*-published by Jan and Cyn?"

257. jrg says, "uhh, yeah, I suppose. But still not sure what we mean by publication, that damn new paradigm ain't in place yet"

258. Mick says, "so -- in praxis .... does the book chapter re-publication appear on your vita in place of the MOO website, or alongside it?"

259. traci says, "i'll be big-headed for a min, i'm in a situation sort of like Jeff's. The most read document on the daedalus web pages is that stupid MOO Teaching Tips page i created at the last minute before 4c's in DC. sometimes i feel guilty that of all the good things (and the many things we NEED customers to look at) the one the most people access is that thing i wrote which has nothing to do with daedalus"

260. jrg [to traci]: "no doubt, but look how much good it has done!

261. jrg says, "Clearly you produced something on the web that made it through the clutter. Maybe that is publishing?"

262. traci [to jrg]: i suppose... but you know i really don't think it's a good text

263. Mick says, "so traci .... if you apply for a faculty job someday, is that website a publication? academic service?"

264. traci says, "it's definitely a publication....it's been reprinted in several places, with and without my permission"

265. Mick [to jrg]: ooh. "making it through the clutter" as a definition of published. that's dicey, but I like where it heads.

above. That is the POTENTIALITY always already available to MOOers. The feeling of isolation is (in our view) a function of the degree to which one takes advantage of these potentialities.

8. Cheers,

9. Cynthia and Jan

O

From: Jeffrey Galin <jgalin@wiley.csusb.edu>
Subject: RE: Collaborative MOO Session

1. Indeed, there are a host of reasons why academics publish. Since so few of us make money at it, most are not looking for fortune. Certainly tenure and promotion stoke the fire. But, as you pointed out in the MOO session that we had, MOOcentral is probably one of the most read documents that I will ever publish. You asked me how I felt about that. [See MOO 253] I responded that I was thrilled that MOOcentral has proven useful to many people. After all, my goal in putting up the site was to share disciplinary knowledge and to provide resources for teachers using MOOs. You implied at that time that publication was about the desire of being heard but that it did not always work out in practice. In either case, I put up that website because I wanted to. But isn't desire culturally and institutionally determined as well?

2. Cheers,
3. jrg

P

From: Dickie Selfe <rselfe@mtu.edu>
Subject: RE: Collaborative MOO Session

1. Sorry if some of the points made here have already been discussed. A couple of points of contact for me.

2. At one point Porush's law appeared [See MOO 25]:

3. Porush's Law: "Participating in the newest communications technologies becomes compulsory if you want to remain part of the culture."

4. Then Mick said,

5. Mick says, "Let's be honest ... no one in the broad global village culture needs MOOs to reaming part of "the culture." No one in academia as a whole does either. Aren't we, in the very act of trying to legitimate MOOs as publication, trying to re-invent what is "necessary" for cultural advancement and survival?" [See also MOO 71 and A-4ff.]

6. While others were suggesting that "culture" was a collaborative construct that could not stand on its own, Mick posted this "reality check" for the group of MOO enthusiasts (or tolerants--those who tolerate).

7. Still Porush's law seems to apply to MOO folks in this way. We are part of the ongoing construction of a portion of what we collectively call culture. That being the case, when we engage in a new communication technology (those MOOs are one of the oldest interactive digital technologies) we form the justification for that portion of culture. More importantly, our choice of interactive publishing suggests that more static, broadcast technologies are wanting. The rhetorical moves we make in these interactive environments, makes it clear what this community (a small subgroup within a small subdiscipline) values. When we choose to take leadership roles in the larger community (publish books, lead workshops, ...) our valuing of the rhetorics of interactive discourses is compounded.

8. I dislike Porush's use of the word "compulsory" since we as a subdiscipline are already complicit in the computer industry's effort to produce a generation of cyber addicts with little tolerance for attitudes critical of a techno-mediated culture.

9. sandyet had one such critical concern.

10. sandyet [to John_B]: I just find myself becoming more and more concerned about those not here... we are seeking out and describing new worlds... but they will never try to reach them. [See also MOO 103]

11. What about the mass of other players in the world who are not in this particular game? I guess I would suggest that the choices we make about what we publish, in relatively privileged positions, where we

---

266.jrg says, "honestly traci, for me the goal of MOOcentral was to disseminate knowledge. Again I return tot he model of xxx.lanl.gov archive"

267.Mick says, "and when you say "reprinted" do you mean in *paper* ...?"

268.Dene says, "I cite every website and moo logs on my vita. I think they count"

269.traci says, "hmm. Although it's original 'form' was as a handout at 4C's. i guess it may have to be part of a presentation first."

270.jrg [to Mick]: "in part, unfortunately, that is the only way that the academic engine acknowledges contributions. Then again, I didn't build MOOcentral for recognition ... I built it because it needed to be built"

271.traci [to jrg]: i never meant for this handout to be anything but 'tips i wish folks on daedalusmoo would abide by' -- it was guidelines from the other side, from being an admin and trying to manage teachers who, brilliant tho they were/are, weren't thinking

272.Mick [to nick]: So this relates back to your idea bout a MOO being changed when it's committed to print ... I totally agree. But what if this MOO produces One Great Idea (collaboratively) and a bunch of clever aphorisms, wouldn't it be *enhancing* the text to edit it for presentation of that one idea?

273.traci says, "need it be enhancing or reducing? can it not be something different? is a play enhanced or reduced when it is in print on a piece of paper versus performed?"

274.nick [to traci]: sure it's different, but that's so vague, and for the sake of argument, I'd say it is reduced

275.Mick [to nick]: committing a MOO to paper does change it.

276.nick [to Mick]: sure, same as taxidermy changes an animal

277.sandyet throws her hands in the air...

278.SESSION II

279.sandyet says "for those of you who weren't here earlier ... we have some responses and ideas to share."

280.Mick posts slide #1

281.

```
***************************
John Barber writes in e-mail:
Everyone [in the previous session] seemed to be still focused on current problems
and concerns associated with writing about and in electronic environments
and ... implications for publishing, authorship, ownership, tenure,
promotion, voice, etc). But what will we be concerned with in the future, or more
to the focus of the book, and to draw on Victor Vitanza's notion of the future
perfect, what will we have been concerned with?
***************************
```

282.Cyn says, "Mick suggests we mention that we are involved with two electronic journals, Pre/Tex:Electra(Lite) (next thing in the works), and Elekcriture, a new journal with its first issue out sometime this spring."

283. Jan is co-editor [with Cyn] of Lingua MOO, a 13 megabyte hypertext with over 500 active readers and writers

284. Mick shows slide #5.

285.

```
*  *  *  *  *  *  *  *  *  *  *  *  *  *  *  *
```
In essence, Lingua MOO's purpose is much greater than it may seem upon first glance. If you can imagine walking into a virtual library and finding a rare book waiting to be read, a story waiting to be finished, then you are on the right track. We call it a text-based synchronous learning environment.
              -- Cynthia Haynes & Jan Rune Holmevik
```
*  *  *  *  *  *  *  *  *  *  *  *  *  *  *  *
```

286. Cyn says, "our chapter focuses on MOO as publication...synchronous, real-time, dynamic publication"

287. Mick says, "In the last session, Nick and several others -- including Dene -- suggested that MOOing was NOT a publication."

288. Jan says, "I need to correct myself...the MOO is a Cybertext or Cypher/TEXT...not a hypertext :)"

289. Cyn says, "and yes, since we will be MOOing parts of the next PTEL [Pre/Text Electralite] issue, that is, some of the articles in that issue will flip the viewer into the MOO by virtue of our web interface"

290. Mick says, "I know you get the question "define MOO" and "define cyphertext" all the time ... So don't answer that."

291. Jan grins

292. Mick says, "Instead, this: define "publication."

293. sandyet says, "that was the problem earlier... definitions"

294. Jan says, "the act of making something publicly available"

295. Mick says, "So publication requires chronological access -- archiving?"

296. Jan says, "not in my view, no"

297. Cyn says, "I want to take the notion of publication back a bit.... to ask the question "where does publication begin?""

298. sandyet [to Mick]: if the MOO isn't archived, it can't be published?

299. Mick says, "Well, Jan said "publicly available." A MOO isn't available *to the public* (define THAT) unless its archived."

300. sandyet [to Jan]: some would question that... a conversation makes something publicly available... is it publication?

301. Cyn says, "not necessarily, Mick...the MOO is a database running a process in real-time...and of course it's also an archive." [See also A-21]

302. Jan [to sandyet]: I would contend that this conversation here, for example, is publication...for the ones who are present...and will be later for those who read the logs

publish, who we involve in these interactive publishing ventures are crucial and in the long run determine whether we ever "do" reach beyond our narrow population of academic friends. For instance, I think the efforts of those involved in textual, virtual reality production are a welcome voice in a culture that is "going visual." I'm thinking, now, of those who think solely in terms of the WWW or multimedia publications.

12. I liked what Judi had to say.

13. judi says, "if folks on the 'bleeding edge' of technoculture who are teachers don't start to exploit these technologies in our work, we'll become the victims of the entertainment and pleasure industries. I'm not sure how to get this message out to teachers who choose to ignore cmc as a new way of writing."[See also MOO 208]

14. Agreed. Let the textually inclined among us stand up and be counted online and in print.

15. Dickie Selfe

Q

From: Mick Doherty <mdoherty@dallascvb.com>;
Sandye Thompson <sandyet@eaze.net>
To: Various Members of "The Computers and Writing Community"
Subject: Feedback Request: Book Chapter for MIT Press

1. Howdy from Texas -- hope the new semester is treating you well. Sandye and I are currently collaborating on a book chapter for a forthcoming volume from MIT Press edited by John Barber and Dene Grigar:

2. http://www.eaze.net/~jfbarber/worlds_book/worlds_book.html

3. The basis for this chapter is a MOO session which involved most of the contributing authors to the book, discussing the theme "Putting the Public back in Publication" and interactive MOO-based environments as/and scholarly work

4. The MOO discussion is archived here --

5. http://www.eaze.net/~sandyet/moo_logs.htm [Ed. Note: This site is no longer in place.]

6. What we are planning to do is edit and "annotate" the MOO log with "footnotes" and other "interstitial" commentary from the authors in the book and other "notables in the field" of C&W -- we certainly put you in that category, and invite you to come and play with us!

303.sandyet [to Jan]: I've been suggesting that any interaction (in text, written or oral) where we build community through sharing ideas is publication ...

304.James_I says, "for me, it's how we define public--does the public have access to a MOO? so maybe, in looking at John's comments, we're seeking a future perfect where access is more even?"

305.Mick says, "So, Elékcriture Editors, what will we have been concerned with about publishing in cyphertextual environments?"

306.Jan [to Mick]: first and foremost, I think, a re/thinking of the meaning of the publication

307.sandyet is interested in what the "author" will be if and when we focus communication in web-based spaces. [See also W7-12]

308.Cyn [to Mick]: we will have been concerned with integrating the reader/writer inside the text, and also with other readers/writers in real-time ... among other things"

309.Mick says, "So the text changes ... with the reader. Not just internally, but publicly. Is there a 'layered archive of all individual interactions with the text?"

310.Jan says, "and how new technologies open up new ways of expressing oneself and to share information and knowledge construction"

311.Cyn says, "we will have been concerned with research about how text AFFECTS in synchronous publication...the affective fallacy lives :)"

312.Mick reminds Jan of Porush's Law ... this was a point of real debate earlier.

313.sandyet says, "reader/writer/editor ... all become one ... everything is published... information is free!"

314.Dene says, "can people be part of the "culture" if they don't use the telephone?" [See also S-12]

315.Cyn [to Mick]: you mean some arguing against whether it is "compulsory"?

316.Mick says, "Are we changing the definition of culture? or participation? or both?"

317.Mick [to Cyn]: "it don't think it's compulsory."

318.Cyn says, "me either"

319.Jan is thinking about this

320.Cyn says, "it becomes part of the deep structure of culture"

321.Mick says, "there's a real arrogance -- one Porush happily admits to -- that claims it is compulsory."

322.Dene says, "to be able to search for a job one absolutely needs certain technologies: car, telephone, maybe computer ... it is somewhat compulsory"

323.Mick [to Dene]: only a certain kind of job.

324.Dene says, "yeah one that requires more than manual labor:)"

325.sandyet doesn't want to get off track here... we'll start debating what "culture" is again...

---

7. We're hoping you might feel inspired to dash off an e-mail response to some of the discussion this weekend, which we could then include also in footnote form.

8. We're not looking for anything formal; in fact, a "gut" response might be more in keeping with the original MOO discussion format. So you don't have to skim the entire log though you are welcome to ... Write as much or as little as you like; we will endeavor to include your commentary unedited, though of course we will also show the final draft to you for your approval lest we inappropriately decontextualize your work!

9. We are working on short deadlines, and would appreciate any response you might offer, even if simply "Sorry ... not interested" and/or "Don't have time this week ..."

10. Best,

11. Mick & Sandye

R
From: MJOYCE@vassar.edu
Subject: Re: Feedback Request: Book Chapter for MIT Press

1. Mick Doherty wrote:

2. *hoping you might feel inspired to dash off an e-mail response to some of the discussion inspired by your own words, which we could then include also in footnote form.*

3. *Write as much or as little as you like; we will endeavor to include your commentary unedited, though of course we will also show the final draft to you for your approval lest we inappropriately decontextualize your work! [See also Q7 and Q8]*

4. My god it's so hard to think what could decontextualize my work, or fail to, since it seems a process of decontextualization to me. Although the truth is that my first instinct here, as it often is with queries over the net for responses/interviews/etc, was to search through my recent writing and cannibalize (recontextualize?) what I've been thinking about lately, lifting up sections of writing like eggs from a short order grill and setting them over light(ly) into the new context.

5. Often or sometimes I feel abashed by this, as if I am somehow cheating, who I am not certain? my so-called self? whatever that linguistic complex might be, who no longer has an instrumental intelligence or memory short of the hard drive (that much of the cyborg seems true to me: in place of visual memory: photographs; in place of verbal memory: magnetic media) or you who expect (why? or why do I think this?) "fresh" language, a reciprocity, yes, for the session/chapter you seek comment upon.

6. What strikes me is that the medium here creates a false anxiety (to

326. Cyn says, "in my view, that isn't exactly an indicator of choice, or compulsion, so much as that these technologies operate beneath the surface, they become so ubiquitous as to be invisible"

327. Mick [to Cyn]: is ubiquitous not in some ways synonymous with "insidious"?

328. Cyn says, "not necessarily..."

329. Mick is either serious or playing devil's advocate. You Make The Call.

330. Cyn says, "Sandy Stone suggests that we are already in the age of ubi-comp ... ubiquitous computing"

331. Mick says, "Porush suggested that himself in CMC Magazine back in 1994."

332. Cyn says, "well, there you have it :)"

333. Cyn chuckles politely.

334. Mick says, "So .... again ... what will have been our greatest triumph in redefining publication? What will have been our highest hurdles? Greatest failures?"

335. Jan [to Mick]: those are big questions that I for one cannot answer until we've arrived....somewhere :)....

336. Cyn says, "ubiquitous would only be insidious if we define ubi as an ideology, which some may want to do ... and an oppressive ideology at that"

337. sandyet shows slide #7.

338.

```
* * * * * * * * * * * * * * * * * * * *
Lanham:
Keeping the process electronic from beginning to end would save much time and
effort. And it would make the apparatus of "published" scholarship available to
anyone anywhere in the world who had a computer terminal. Our sense of scholarly
research would change. Academic urbanity would no longer be an affair of big
research campuses. Such a system would be an extraordinary democratizing one.
* * * * * * * * * * * * * * * * * * * *
```

339. Mick always thought Lanham favored an elitist democracy anyway.

340. Jan says, "but I hope that we will have explored...and exemplified diversity in how knowledge can be shared...."

341. James_I nods to Jan--yes, and diversity necessitates access, maybe one of the high hurdles to change [See also U 4-5]

342. Mick says, "Well, I for one, have always expected kairos to fail ... in a big way. Porush, when I talked to him about "starting" the journal said "yeah, that won't work, eventually. Go down in big flames, though, and at least you'll be noticed. That can make a difference. I love that phrase -- that won't work, eventually."

343. Jan nods to Mick. I agree that our experiments may fail...but that is really beside the point, what is important is what comes after.

344. sandyet wonders if the whole concept of "scholarship" could change... everyone could plug in and pick out what information they needed... they would edit their own "texts" from all the data available to them

---

match, reciprocally, the false assurance) that a similar behavior (how, for instance, I handle a telephone interview while being much different except the medium of memory and the lossage due to my inability to generate verbally what I can rehearse from the disk-- though the truth is I somehow mix them, read from the screen in an interview while mimicking a conversational tone-- I've taken to doing as much in public talks where the language is clearly crafted--sometimes even projected behind me as I speak--and yet I offer the conversational tone as a likely to engender given our longer experience of it (my definition, circa 1974 of culture: "the experience of living in a place over time," where that 'culture' is neither unary nor ironic, rather inherently multiple).

7. Did I mention yet that I invented David Porush, or he me, sometime in Buffalo in the late 70s? It was my first city of text. Chicken wings preceded us. Frank and Teresa's Anchor Bar 19--.

S
From: David Porush <dporush@widomaker.com>
Subject: Re: Feedback Request: Book Chapter for MIT Press

1. Hey Mick et al,

2. I reviewed the whole dam archive off the web, I like the mixture of desultory/drunkard's walk cocktail chat and high-jynx, and liked Stewart Brand's [See also MOO 88] quote the best!

3. Of course I am being ironic and my first impulse on seeing one of my provocations put up as a slide for a MOO is to sort through all of Michael Joyce's old work and see how I can re-cannibalize it in order to deconstruct my text...especially since Michael invented me over a plate of buffalo wings sometime in the early 1970s at Frank and Teresa's Anchor Bar. Extra hot! [See also R-4 and R-7]

4. But seriously, Mick, the proposition that you must participate in the latest comm tech - or even the bleeding edge - in order to be a part of the culture is such an absurdity, I can barely take it seriously....On the other hand, I DO get to play the heavy in your MOO session, so let me not break character.

5. No, no, can't take Porush's Law seriously at all,

6. IF....

7. ...you are looking at it as an imperative from Microsoft or the State Regent, mandating computer literacy by the year 2002!

8. BUT....

9. ...it does capture the flavor of the imperative for resistance or inoculation against the Master Virus for any well-meaning guerilla, Burroughs-wise or Guevara-wise: there is no more privileged position than being in the belly of the beast. Where else can you get the

345. Mick says, "What are your expectations for Elekcriture? What do you want people to say about it in 1998? In 2002?"

346. Cyn says, "our greatest triumph, in my view, would be to dismantle the priesthood of publication, the grip that publishing industry has on academia (i.e. through credentialling mechanisms), and vice versa...this is NOT saying that we dismantle publishers or that we stop publishing...it means that we examine and intervene in the models of publishing that we know to be inappropriate mechanisms for conveying knowledge, for allowing people to connect with one another, and with determining institutional structures for conferring job security"

347. Cyn says, "sorry for the long post"

348. Mick shows slide #2.

349.

* * * * * * * * * * * * * * * *
Negroponte (Being Digital):
In the post-information age, we often have an audience the size of one.
* * * * * * * * * * * * * * * *

350. Mick says, "How's that work with cyphertext?"

351. Jan [to Mick]: like hand and glove :)

352. Mick says, "So with an audience of 1 ..."

353. Cyn says, "Victor [Vitanza] would say that we should say goodbye to audience, at least as an aspect that we consider when we write...sort of the message in the bottle notion"

354. Jan [to Mick]: an audience of 1 at a time.

355. Mick says, " ...: we throw out the norms. The expectations and editorial policies. These are vestiges of a long-dead process of meaning-making. Right?"

356. Jan [to Mick]: wrong

357. Mick <-- cranky old-guy

358. James_I grins at Mick

359. Cyn says, "this is NOT to say we don't NEED audiences, so much as the fact that audience can no longer be fictionalized...audience becomes something that has to include software agents, search engines, etc"

360. Mick says, "the writer's audience is always a fiction. Ong, right?"

361. Cyn [to Mick]: Ong, Barthes, Foucault

362. Jan says, "issues of quality will always be important BUT you will have to listen to what is being said...be MORE critical than ever before..."

363. sandyet says, "many complain that hypertext is too writer-based... and it is... but the reader is the writer...and they should determine the quality... but many say that we have a generation that isn't prepared to be critical... they don't have the skills"

364. Michael_S says, "damn, I feel like an atheist in church around here. there's a whole

leverage to re-program the machine with a positive feedback-looping message. its counter-viral message:

10. "Dismantle Thyself"?

11. Moses has to enter the court of the Pharoah in order to present the alphabet and demo its superiority -- only 22 characters! highly portable! laptop size! expresses abstractions like nobody's business! works in desert conditions!-- over the hieroglyphic system, with its thousands of characters and symbols and pictographic literalness. or, one might say, idolatry. Pharoah rejects it, Moses goes off and founds another culture, a nomadic one, doomed to exile and to the multiplication of voices. Hot damn, whoo-hoo, that's the kind of participation I'm talkin 'bout.

12. As to telephones (in answer to Dene) ... [See also MOO 314]

13. Yeah, you gotta get on the horn if you want to be part of the culture. The assumption that the default state of moral purity is some Waldenesque solitude of self-satisfied contemplation or hermetic retreat leads not to Thoreau (even he didn't give up his e-mail) but to the Unabomber. To derive some ethical design for utopia on that presumption, the presumption of privacy (which assumes ownership and property) or solitude (which breaks the circuit of responsibility) leads, IMHO, to a culture of Hobbesian ad execs and Bubba survivalists.

14. Whoa. Nuff ranting. Thanks for the opportunity and flattering billboard.

＝＝＝＝＝＝＝＝＝＝＝＝＝＝＝＝＝＝＝＝＝

15.
David Porush, Professor
Rensselaer Polytechnic Institute
Troy, New York 12180
e-mail: porusd@rpi.edu

＝＝＝＝＝＝＝＝＝＝＝＝＝＝＝＝＝＝＝＝＝

16. Nature was "finished" when it invented the human brain.
-- Porush's Law #17

17. "The purpose of art is to prolong the moment of perception."
-- Viktor Shklovskii

T
From: Eric Crump <eric@serv1.ncte.org>
Subject: Re: Feedback Request: Book Chapter for MIT Press

1. Here's some stuff, Mick. Hope it's not too late. Use what you can use & let the rest find its way to the bitbucket. What a great session. Wish I'd been there. Too much to comment on, so I just blabbed about what hit me first.

2. --Eric

3. mday says, "and will print culture necessarily die? Are we forcing its

lot of consensus that I just can't relate to."

365. Mick [to Michael_S]: worry not. My apparent consensus is largely ironic.

366. nickc says, "sandye, the reader is only the writer if they have the hypertext on their own computer?"

367. sandyet nods to nickc

368. Mick says, "Let the reader determine quality? When? At what level? Don't we NEED clearinghouse services like journals?"

369. Cyn [to Michael_S]: Michael, please note that I've NOT been saying NO publishing, I am always of the mind that we need to work within the belly of the beast (cf Haraway), and believe you me that to get tenure I'll need some hefty pulp publications, but we're here talking about the future, right?

370. Michael_S says, "I'm not worried about the future of publishing. publishing is utterly promiscuous. it will happen within in what ever technology is available ... for an audience of one or one million. why not? just like always.

371. James_I [to Michael_S]: how widely available?

372. Cyn [to Michael_S]: I agree, and what forms it takes will be novel, as in new and unimaginable

373. Mick says, "Gaonkar argues that "rhetoric is a whore" -- it relies on all other disciplines to even exist. Publishing is like that, too."

374. Michael_S says, "by "forms" you mean what? etext, for example? i'd say sure."

375. Cyn [to Mick]: I don't know this person, but rhetoric has been characterized as a whore for centuries, not for being that which all disciplines need to exist, but that which "embellishes" "paints" up language and thought

376. Michael_S says, "electronics is promiscuous, too. it will bed an advertisement as quickly as a dissertation. quicker, i bet."

377. sandyet has noticed that the distinction between advertisements and other form of communication is getting smaller

378. Mick says, "I thought it would be interesting if we posted two snippets of conversation from the earlier MOO session and asked those of you not then present to "join the conversation" (a/synch?)"

379. Mick says, "Here they are ..."

380. sandyet smiles at mick

381. Mick shows slide #6.

382.
* * * * * * * * * * * * * * * *
judi says, "if folks on the *bleeding edge* of technoculture who are teachers don't start to exploit these technologies in our work, we'll become the victims of the entertainment and pleasure industries. i'm not sure how to get this message out to teachers who choose to ignore cmc as a new way of writing."

sandyet says, "isn't part of the problem that many see cmc as a "new" way of writing... i'm writing the same way I always did... letters, words.

---

death?" [See also MOO 31]

4. eric says, "yes, yes. it will (eventually). we must. change is good. cave-drawing culture died. who mourns? netculture will die, too, someday. I hope! print culture will influence netculture for a good while yet, and its vestiges will be with us forever (forever, of course, being only as long as we keep hanging around). But any attempt to "protect" print culture from the onslaught of netish stuff is just nostalgia. Understandable, but sheesh, don't bet your house on its success. Porush has a point, ironic 'r not. There "is" an imperative to "get online" at all costs. In a way, it "is" a manufactured imperative. But it may also be that the real imperative in most everything we do--survival--is lost to our vision, but still operating. We may "have" to go digital for reasons we can't yet fathom.

5. Of course, as soon as I make some dumb statement about cave-drawing culture dying I come across this quote from Sun CEO Scott McNealy: 'The concept that every computer should speak one language was stolen from cavemen who wrote on walls.' (_Internet World_, Jan 98). But that, I guess, is what the vestigial influence of print will be like, too. We may always be finding new ways to do old stuff."

6. Mick says, "Let's be honest ... no one in the broad global village culture needs MOOs to remaining part of "the culture." No one in academia as a whole does either. Aren't we, in the very act of trying to legitimate MOOs as publication, trying to re-invent what is "necessary" for cultural advancement and survival?" [See also MOO 71; A-4]

7. eric grins & agrees with Mick. What else we got to do? If we weren't re-inventing necessities and hyping our own gigs, we'd have to do some real work or something. Just kidding, of course. Creating and promoting our own cultural imperatives is good clean decent work. The dirt under our nails is virtual, but it's there. We're sons & daughters of the digital soil, just trying to make ends meet.

8. sandyet says, "maybe the idea of 'community-at-large will collapse... spaces like this one will emerge, also more tiny communities... each with a particular need that this satisfies..." [See also MOO 72]

9. eric says, "yeah. isn't it weird? at the same time economies are globalizing at a furious pace. culture is maybe "more" fine-grained and particular than ever? and in spite of American media-culture spreading like a virus across the planet. This is just an impression from a US midwest-bound guy, but it looks from here like American culture spreads over the surface of the global web of cultures like a wave that has no real depth. It may be what we all end up having in common, but it will not displace original cultures, only give them a pair of bluejeans to wear over their eternal bodies. or something."

10. Dene says, "How much of what is getting said here now is actually being read by us? The information overload is astounding!" [See also MOO 96; C-1 ff.]

```
sentences.....:
* * * * * * * * * * * * * * *
```

383.Mick whistles, allowing everyone time to read before posting the second snippet

384.Mick says, "here we go ..."

385.Mick shows slide #7.

386.

```
* * * * * * * * * * * * * * *
```
Mick says, "Jeff, that MOO help page you did has probably had more readers than everything else you have or will ever write combined. Does that bother you?"

jrg says, "I said I'm thrilled about the fact that MOOcentral will have been read by more folks than anything I ever write. But then again it is now being published by Jan and Cyn and the website will move too"

Mick [to jrg]: this is an important micro-question ... Don't you mean it is now being "re"-published by Jan and Cyn?"

jrg says, "uhh, yeah, I suppose. But still not sure what we mean by publication, that damn new paradigm ain't in place yet"
```
* * * * * * * * * * * * * * *
```

387.Jan grins re re/publication :)

388.Mick says, "The common word in these two snippets is "new" ... when does it all stop being new?"

389.Michael_S says, "nothing personal, but i think judi's position is hype ... it's alarmist and utopian at the same time." [See also T-17]

390.james_I says, "i think judi wants us to be the driving force maybe, not to let the pleasure/entertainment folks drive everything—relates to what sandyet said about advertising a little earlier"

391.Cyn [to sandyet]: cmc as a new way of writing...I agree, we're pretty much writing the same ways in cmc, but I think the AFFECTIVE side of reader response...but almost back bit in cmc...it's not just the age-old question of HOW text affects us ... and I think we do to an Aristotelian pathos in which we write more descriptively, use more narrative, and probably a host of other modes.

392.Michael_S says, "the digitized word is already y a mass comm phenomenon. academics are just not going to dominate it. sorry."

393.sandyet has to wonder who "us" is... how much cmc stuff (muds, moos, web, email, etc) is "academic"

394.james_I [to Michael]: ahhh, not dominate, but certainly be stakeholders, not to be absorbed into mass comm completely [See also U 7-8]

395.Michael_S says, "no, it won't absorb academics. it will sleep with even us."

396.Mick says, "narrative ... right! Hold on ... This is a long one ... but it fits precisely with what Cyn is driving at ...."

397.Mick shows slide #8.

11. eric says, "you know, the current anxiety over information overload is kind of funny in a way. At some point, waaaaaaaay back when, the amount of information anyone had access to exceeded their ability to gobble and digest the stuff. I've never lived at a time when I could read all the books I could get my hands on, yet walking past a book store or library doesn't cause me to swoon from the weight of those unread words. Yet when the words arrive in our email inboxes, or come at us over 50 cable channels, we fret. why? There's always too much, if what you might like to consume is seen as a consumable possibility. Maybe we ought to just let go an unrealistic expectation and get to what we can, learn to navigate our infosphere nimbly and quickly as we find useful & let it go at that?"

12. jrg says, "No Mick, MOOing is not publication. It is public talking that is recorded. I really believe that"

13. jrg says, "or it is public talking that gets excerpted and then printed on Rhetnet as a consumable object" [See also MOO 138ff.; A-13 etc.]

14. eric says, "..and in the latter case, it's publication, yes? Publication, seems to me, has more to do with how words are used than with where they are created. Chitchat on a streetcorner, if put in a form that's accessible to a number of people over a period of time (the specific number or amount of time don't matter so much) is published. We have a habit of distinguishing between Published (stuff put in legitimized venues) and published (stuff put into a public forum; any stuff, any forum). But that's one of the cool things about the net (though it's fashionable these days to dismiss its radical democratizing features): anybody with access can P/publish (both senses of the word, simultaneously). RhetNet isn't particularly special in that regard except in labeling it a 'cyberjournal for rhetoric and writing' we're insisting that both senses can co-exist. Just a matter of keeping that point on the surface."

15. judi says, "if folks on the "bleeding edge" of technoculture who are teachers don't start to exploit these technologies in our work, we'll become the victims of the entertainment and pleasure industries. I'm not sure how to get this message out to teachers who choose to ignore cmc as a new way of writing. [See also MOO 208; P-13]

16. Michael_S says, "nothing personal, but i think judi's position is hype" [See MOO 389ff.]

17. eric says, "You make it sound so unsavory, Michael! Nothing wrong with hype. It plays an important role in the process of change. It's the competing self-fulfilling prophecies that lead us where we might not otherwise go. Carolyn Marvin wrote a great book about how societies grapple with technology-induced change: _When Old Technologies Were New_. She describes the hype surrounding the introduction of the electric light and the telegraph. Even she, of course, seems to disdain the outlandish claims made at the time, just as many people today want to disdain the outlandish claims being made now. But hype

shouldn't really be held to the standard of truth or prudence. Hype is a catalyst, an instigator of 'movement' and it serves well when it moves us in interesting and productive directions."

18. *Michael_S says, "the first question is whether anything the MOO here offers is worth reading. i mean serious reading. it's fun as we go, of course."*

19. *Michael_S says, "i'm not being heavy; i just mean can anyone who "would" read it learn from it anything significant?"*

20. *Michael_S says, "i'm guessing there are "some" things online that even eric crump won't read. why not? is a judgment."*

[See also MOO 437]

21. eric says, "Oh yeah! I skim & dive, delete buckets of email, blow right past most websites, etc. and without a twinge of conscience. As Mick noted in his slide [See also MOO 219], in a fast medium you have little time to capture attention, generally, I mean, I'll give a book 20-30 page to prove worth my time. I give email about 10 words. So it goes.

22. Of course, since I'm being held up as an example of the limits of infopromiscuity, I'll just note that it seems very unremarkable to me that there would be things even I wouldn't read. Michael makes it sound like a score for discrimination when I don't think I've ever argued against discrimination (that I remember, anyway; I might have). I do like to "reposition" discrimination, distributing the filters as well as the words. Let standards be applied ex post facto, in other words, and we can still make good use of standards. When filtering comes into play too soon in the process, it squelches the conversation, allows greater control by whoever happens to have the most power, and generally limits possibilities. Boo hiss.

23. And whether a MOO transcript is worth reading may imply that anyone would or should sit down and read the thing through. Read it like a book or article? That's not the only model of reading (never has been, perhaps). Skim & diver & "mine" may apply better. What significance there is in a MOOtext may be distributed since good stuff emerges unpredictably as a function of rhetorical reaction (sort of like chemical reaction: when certain minds/perspectives/words come together in certain combinations, boom, cool stuff happens). MOOtext is not crafted; it's evolved. So we might meander through it, skimming the surface, looking for gems, or we might use a program's search functions to look for comments by key people or the presence of key phrases that help us find the ideas we might find interesting.

24. The significance is there, it's just not arranged nicely like it is in a print document. It's worth publishing things like this, though, because when they are made available, people will learn good strategies for reading them and getting at their significance. If we dismiss MOOtext and other odd & exotic new forms, we're precluding the possibility that

398.
* * * * * * * * * * * * * * * * * *
Johndan Johnson-Eilola:
Communication used to be about telling stories, about listening to narratives of discovery, learning, redemption, and war. Not just little stories, but big stories: heaven, hell, utopia. Relatively recently, though, the map has started to replace the story as our fundamental way of knowing....I see the potential for increased responsibility, prestige, and influence for business and technical communicators, but only if we are able to reconceive what we think of as the value of our work; that is, we must reposition ourselves as mapmakers rather than authors.
* * * * * * * * * * * * * * * * * *

399.Mick thinks that because we are writing the *shape* at the same time as the *text* of a publication, that mapmaking *is* story-telling.

400.Cyn says, "the map is a metaphor I'm uncomfortable with, it is still a closed network, attempting to account for everything in text, when language and writing resist that kind of closure...writing is slippery, it defies even maps"

401.sandyet [to Cyn]: I agree... I'm concerned though that one refrain I seem to hear a lot from members of the c&w community is... you must embrace this *new* form of writing... we are using different methods, forms, etc... but at the core we are just communicating

402.Cyn [to sandyet]: I'm also uncomfortable with the MUST as the imperative...so I agree with you. I'm not one to say we MUST do anything. That we CAN do something now, writing differently, use different analytical modes of intelligibility...that is not the same thing as compulsory, which is where we began this discussion

403.Mick [to Cyn]: only if you define map in the traditional 2-dimensional way.

404.Cyn [to Mick]: then we should use another term :)

405.Mick says, "Why? we're using "writing" aren't we?"

406.Cyn [to Mick]: ... like rhizome or Klein jar' or Mobius strip (ala Vitanza)

407.Jan agrees with Cyn and Sandye...the best way to alienate someone is to tell them what they *must* do .

408.James_I [to sandyet]: and i like your use of 'communicating'--'writing' gives some folks problems since there's some links between e-comm and oral comm, as much as written.

409.Michael_S says, "i don't think anyone means compulsory so much as inevitable. eh?"

410.Mick says, "to tell someone something is inevitable is to give it a compulsory feel."

411.Cyn [to Michael_S]: I think some may mean compulsory, if they're in the context of what might get them a job over someone else without technological expertise, depends on the context really

412.mday says, "Better to suggest possibility, possible vectors."

413.Cyn nods vigorously in agreement with mday's ideas.

414.mday says, "Compulsory sounds like that's what Bill Gates wants. Big Bro!"

415.Michael_S says, "figures ;-)"

what value they have will ever be valued."

U

From: "James A. Inman" <jinman@umich.edu>
To: Mick Doherty <mdoherty@dallascvb.com>
Subject: Collab. Book Chapter Notes

1. Hi, Mick--

2. Thank you for inviting me to make some comments/notes about various parts of the MOO logs for your book chapter. What I've done, more or less, is to go in and generate more (well, sort of more) extended discussions of a couple of comments I made at Media. Please feel free to edit these freely into whatever form best suits your needs.

3. NOTE 1

4. *James, I nods to Jan--yes, and diversity necessitates access, maybe one of the high hurdles to change.* [See also MOO 341]

5. Additional note: Especially when we're talking about putting "public" back into "publication," the idea of access has to be central, at least in my mind. We need to start interrogating this term as more complex than just putting more people in front of more computers. Layers of access I see as relevant to this discussion include browser capability (if we're looking at web-based resources/publication) and the development of computer literacies. We need a population of users who have the opportunity to go online and who pair this opportunity with the skills and savvy to take advantage of what's there.

6. NOTE 2

7. *James, I [to Michael]: ahhh, not dominate, but certainly be stakeholders, not to be absorbed into mass comm completely.* [See also MOO 394]

8. Additional note: Here, I don't neglect the fact that our students, customers if you will, are going to be consumers of the entertainment industry and that, in that fashion, mass communication will exact some measure of control over academia. What I am getting at though is that we should have some stake in these matters as well, some influence over the tools our students development, the analytical skills they implement to evaluate, even to perceive what they see in the world. If the entertainment and other industries control what's seen, why can we not have some say in the construction of the lens through which our students view?

Thanks again! I hope these are maybe useful. (: James

V

From: Patricia Ericsson <ericssop@columbia.dsu.edu>

416.Cyn [to mday]: we talked about ubiquitous computing a bit ago, yes :)

417.Mick says, "No, seriously. I'm writing about -- what else -- how we name what we do and why it affects it."

418.mday is considering perhaps mentioning that connection to/from/with Bush and Nelson in a chapter he may do on research.

419.Mick says, "So let me ask this ... we log this MOO. We edit it. We make it into a book chapter. Who is the author? And is it still a "MOO"?"

420.Cyn says, "it's a Moobius strip :)"

421.Michael_S says, "i don't know what it would contribute to the book."

422.Cyn says, "couldn't resist"

423.nickc says, "the voices is the author, Mick, but it's not a MOO anymore--it's transcript. Or is that a magritte question C'est non le pipe?"

424.Jan [to Mick]: my answer to that is, we are co-authors, and no, it's not a MOO.... because that's where the electrons come in...."

425.Mick [to Michael_S]: you don't think the issues discussed here -- from both sides -- would contribute anything to the book?

426.mday [nickc]: we're back to where we were earlier. It is a MOObius strip.

427.Michael_S says, "the first question is whether anything the MOO here offers is worth reading. i mean serious reading. it's fun as we go, of course.... the form of it doesn't matter to me. is the content worth publishing? one would have to see the transcript, i guess."

428.nickc [to Michael_S]: you're right, what matters the transcript if the content doesn't speak to an audience beyond those of us here--will this matter to readers, will it help them to know something?

429.Mick says, "What is "serious reading" Michael?"

430.mday says, "do you mean worthwhile? reading of use, of worth, of value?"

431.nickc [to mday]: there's serious and there's serendipitous

432.Michael_S says, "i'm not being heavy. i just mean can anyone who *would* read it learn from it anything significant?"

433.mday says, "maybe the transcript should be annotated? Grin."

434.Mick [to mday]: well, the transcript *will* be annotated. And all book authors will be invited to annotate it.

435.Cyn says, "I was going to say that Geoffrey Sirc has a great article in Computers and Composition about the issue of placing value on productive and non-productive discourse online, it was a while back I think"

436.mday likes serendipitous. Likes synergy too. what gets in the book might illustrate that.

437.Michael_S says, "i'm guessing there are *some* things online that even eric crump won't read. why not? is a judgment." [See also T-21 through T-24]

438. Mick says, "Sandye and I literally see our "author" role -- if you use that word -- as host, editor, organizer ... of course, how information is organized and presented is a very real facet of authorship."

439. Mick [kairir] . o o (even Eric Crump?)

440. mday says, "er, a matter of time. If you can't get Eric's attention, then you are dead in the water."

441. Michael_S says, "Oh please."

442. nickc [to Cyn]: yes, margaret daisley also wrote about that in C&C--"The Game of Literacy"

443. Jan chuckles

444. judi thinks that a lot of synchronous as well as classroom dialogue recorded for posterity is of value to the teachers who evoke the discussion; however, without a connection to the speakers/writer, the value to the "reader would be limited unless the authority of the people discussing or the topic is compelling."

445. Cyn says, "sjrc's article is in vol 12 no 3, 1995 "The Twin Worlds of Electronic Conferencing""

446. Mick [to Cyn]: you are a bibliographic database.

447. Cyn laughs.

448. Cyn says, "I'm really an agent :)"

449. sandyet says, "can we ever know if what we produce will be of value to the audience? no matter what the form..."

450. nickc says, "logs are useful as reminders, but unless the discussion is a tad more formal, sometimes, and more directed, like an interview or forum discussion, the log might be a bore to someone who didn't participate in the first place"

451. Mick says, "*Everything* on line *does* get read -- *by* agents. (Neat how those two tied together.) It's [all] about information management. Which is precisely what Sandye and I are doing in this chapter ... authors as information managers."

452. sandyet nods mick.... and how will that impact publication in the future...

453. nickc [to Mick]: I still think there's a big difference between info management and knowledge making

454. Michael_S says, "you mean you're going to evaluate and choose! you gatekeeper!"

455. Mick [to Michael_S]: oh, absolutely. For a *hoo* no less ... boo ... BOOK. I can't even bring myself the TYPE the word!"

456. Cyn laugh.

457. mday hoos

458. Cyn says, "LOL"

459. Jan laughs

460. Mick says, "And the unedited version of these MOOs will sit in electronic space for

---

Subject: Re: Feedback Request: Book Chapter for MIT Press

1. You caught me at a good time and I'm now reading the transcript. I'll send you some of my reactions and commentary as I go, OK?

2. As I'm reading (and by the position of the slide, I guess I'm about 1/5 the way into it) I realize that even though I know most of the people in the conversation, I'm having a hard time keeping track of who is saying what, even though in MOO sessions I've participated in, that's not been a problem. In addition to reading the ideas, I'm trying to track who is developing what ideas. In a F2F conversation, this tracking wouldn't be nearly so difficult. So my first reaction is that reading something that is such a hybrid of communication is challenging me.

3. These two comments made me think of a quick count I did yesterday on a new book I received.

4. mday says, "I think that after the first rush of being impressed with all the computer and net publications, people are starting to be more discerning, filtering out the garbage, and learning what counts to them and why."

5. sandyet [to John_B]: but who is looking, and talking and understanding and controlling the new technologies... [See also MOO 95]

6. The book is _Composing Cyberspace_ by Richard Holeton (McGraw Hill). I read a couple of the essays, and then noticed that the DOB of each (almost--four exceptions) author was listed, do I decided to look at that. Which (kinda?) answers part of the question Michael and Sandye ask above. Here's my quick tabulation:

7. DOB not listed: 4
Pre-1940: 1
1940-45: 7
1946-50: 13
1951-55: 4
1956-60: 9
1961-70: 2
1971: 1
Dead: 1

8. The people who are composing cyberspace, "discerning, filtering out the garbage, and learning what counts" and "looking, and talking and understanding and controlling" [are] the ones who are getting into print? Do the ages of those who are getting into print make a difference? Is the culture (I know that's a problematic term, but. . .) being defined by (now I'm quoting Tim McGee's reaction [in an e-mail to me] to my tabulations):

9. "not just be a certain group of people, but by a group with certain life experiences, such as McCarthyism, Cold War, Kennedy Era, Vietnam.

the reader of the book to access if she so wishes. Not many standard authors leave drafts in public folios."

461.Michael_S says, "there are great unread archives in every university library."

462.Michael_S says, "can we agree that some things aren't worth reading? no probably not."

463.mday says, "depends on who you are and what you are looking for."

464.nickc [to Michael_S]: we can agree--a lot of the web is not worth reading

465.Jan says, "I agree to that....however it will be a subjective judgment"

466.Cyn says, "that's a question of value, which is a valuable question, but probably not one we could agree on"

467.nickc [to Jan]: yes, and subjective is good, because it frees one from being totally socially constructed

468.Mick says, "But for what it's worth -- Negroponte says 90% of the WWW is crap. And I think he's lowballing it."

469.Jan nods

470.Michael_S says, "fine. why should we add to it?"

471.nickc [to Michael_S]: because our crap don't stink

472.mday says, "But that means that up to 10% isn't, and that's pretty good, IF you can find it."

473.Michael_S says, "lol"

474.Mick says, "I think -- and I will be totally honest here .. That about a third of what we've published in Kairos is pretty bad. Not where I'd like to see us draw the line."

475.Mick says, "But at least that -- and probably more -- that I see in print journals is, to use the earlier term, "crap.""

476.Mick would conclude that it is *academia* not *media* that is producing the crap.

477.Jan agrees with Mick on this

478.Michael_S says, "Kairos is the best of its kind. but there's always going to be crap in any publication."

479.nickc says, "it's not a matter of technology that determines quality, but a matter of the ratio of good to bad in any scene--judgments are subjective, but also communal as well--"

480.Mick says, "well, Kairos is really the only of its kind ... until Elekcriture comes out! Electronic-only media-dependent publications are hard to come by in academic humanities."

481.beckster nods to mick. and hard to convince folks that they're worth their weight as publications.

482.Mick [to beckster]: of course e-pubs don't "weigh" anything.

---

etc. in our backgrounds. Therefore, we compose cyberspace in a particular way--to look the way we want it to."

10. This is enough for one message. I'll read more and see if I have any other earth-shattering insights. :)

W
From: Patricia Ericsson <ericssop@columbia.dsu.edu>
Subject: Re: Collaborative Book Chapter for MIT Press

1. A bit more.

2. Dene says, "as for the typing issue, it will be interesting to see the edited logs of this session."

3. sandyet says, "isn't part of the problem that many see cmc as a "new" way of writing... I'm writing the same way I always did... letters, words, sentences....."

4. judi says, "victim because our audiences will be engulfed by other seekers of attention that are less academic" [See also MOO 212-214]

5. Popped this chunk into the message so you can find it easily. I'm responding the Sandye's comment that's she's writing the "same way." I couldn't disagree more (well, maybe I could). She writing in a whole new environment that privileges certain ways of thinking, responding, and reacting. A MOO privileges fast readers, quick typists, those who are skillful on-the-fly wordsmiths. Additionally, the conversational nature of the MOO, without the need to "get a word in" like a F2F conversation, is a radically new form of communication.

6. Another snip:

7. sandyet [to Jan]: I've been suggesting that any interaction (in text, written or oral) where we build community through sharing ideas is publication...

8. Mick says, "So, Elekcriture Editors, what will we have been concerned with about publishing in cyphertextual environments?"

9. Dene says, "John and I are interested in what writing will look like when and if we are focusing our communications in webbed based and interactive spaces"

10. Jan [to Mick]: first and foremost, I think, a rethinking of the meaning of publication

11. sandyet is interested in what the "author" will be if and when we focus communication in web-based spaces. [See also MOO 304-307]

12. Just struck here by the use of the words "publication" and "communication." If an event isn't publicized, then no one will attend. Hmmm. Don't know where this might go or why. Maybe I'll know when

483.Mick snickers

484.Michael_S says, "if they're hard to come by, why add elikcriture to the picture. it divides a small supply of good stuff, no?"

485.Mick says, "geez, Michael, are you kidding? should we eliminate all print journals except Rhetoric Review?"

486.Cyn says, "Elekcriture will not overlap with Kairos, at least in mission...we're still developing it's mission"

487.beckster giggles and feels the weightlessness of it all crashing down upon her

488.Michael_S says, "it seems that way to me too."

489.nickc [to beckster]: all new publications struggle with that, don't they? they need time to build an archive, find an audience, have their pieces and authors cited

490.beckster [to nickc]: sure, sure, I just think that print pubs can do it more quickly

491.mday says, "they will eliminate themselves. cost, and practicality will do a Darwin on them ... but not all of them. Not yet."

492.Michael_S says, "i'm just pointing back to what you said about how hard e-articles are to come by."

493.Mick [to Michael_S]: No, I said e-journals are hard to come by. I did admit that we published more than we should. But that's a different statement."

494.Michael_S says, "oh, i thought you meant publications within [the journals] ... so if there are plenty of articles (are they articles?) to go around, then sure : why not another ejounal in this field."

495.Cyn says, "I think there are also elements of another Lanham articulation of the problems between print and digital words...publishers will be entangled (already are) in what Lanham calls the 'economics of human attention'"

496.Cyn says, "some WIRED contributor discusses this in a recent issue without ever citing Lanham, interesting"

497.Jan says, "as co-editor of a 13megabyte MOO :) I am not worried about selecting what is good and what is bad...what is good get visited and read a lot, what is bad goes unnoticed until it's eventually recycled by either the author or by us.... so I can't really understand what the big problem is here..." [See also A-8]

498.*** WARNING: Saving to disk in one minute. ***

499.mday [Cyn]: excellent mention of Lanham. I think that's what rhetoric may boil down to in this medium. Who gets attention, and why?

500.Mick says, "I quoted Lanham's definition of "rhetoric" in the earlier discussion. Getting someone to share your attention structure." Beautiful." [See also W13-14]

501.sandyet nods jan... isn't that the way it always is? lots of people read certain texts, listen to certain speakers...the individual determines what is elite

502.Jan [to beckster]: you let the works/texts speak their own value...

503.Jan [to sandyet]: exactly

504.beckster says, "I agree, but I also think that folks appreciate not having to weed

I read more.

13. Mick says, "[Rhetoric is] Getting someone to share your attention structure." [See also MOO 500]

14. Maybe this is the best definition of publication.

15. Mick says, "We post information daily. Who reads it? That's our challenge."

16. We make our students read it. :) [See also MOO 514]

17. Final comment:

18. My head's swimming. Maybe because it's Friday after 5:00. But lots of the movement is caused by what I call the "popcorn effect." All your ideas are like little warming kernels in my brain. I think more, they get warmer and they all start exploding. Great stuff. Eventually the metaphor breaks down, because I don't process the mental popcorn by eating your ideas. I have to revert to gelatin metaphors for the next process—Jell-O in my brain.

19. (I just re-read the above. Swimming in Jell-O with popcorn. It is time to give it a rest.) This was a good way to end the week. Thanks for giving me the opportunity to take and look and think.

Patty Ericsson

out as much"

505.

*** Saving to disk. All activity will stop for a few minutes. ***

*** Last checkpoint took 17 seconds. ***

*** Finished saving to disk. ***

506.Mick says, "we're back live ..." [See also A-22 through A-26]

507.Michael_S says, "i don't know. seems like it's just combining an archive function with a publishing one."

508.Mick says, "publishing is the archiving of ideas anyway."

509.beckster quotes mick

510.Michael_S says, "of *some* ideas"

511.sandyet shrugs... there are soooooo many academic journals related to my field(s)... I had to learn to determine what was valuable to me.... even with "filters" of publication, there was a lot of junk

512.Cyn says, "in my third year review last semester, the chair of the committee reviewing me wrote in his report that Lingua is a book..13MB worth of text, not all of which (of course not!) I wrote, but certainly some of it :)"

513.Mick says, "we get into the problem of determining what's good for A) us, and B) our microcommunities."

514.Mick reiterates Negroponte: "In the post-information age, we often have an audience the size of one." I think "post-information" is GREAT pun there,too. I wonder if Negroponte meant it? We post information daily. Who reads it? That's our challenge." [See also W15-16]

515.sandyet says, "but don't we read things lots of times because someone recommends it, reputation and individual "value" helps us weed..."

516.mday says, "ultimate-solipsism. And yet that's how much of academic specialization in publishing is heading. How many of you care very much about what's published in PMLA?"

517.Cyn chuckles politely.

518.Michael_S says, "have to go. gotta get back to editing the works cited list in the printbook on my desk."

519.Mick says, "post-Modern Language Association?"

520.Cyn says, "we should start an e-journal called SPAMLA"

521.Michael_S says, "LOL"

522.mday [Cyn]: YESS!

523.sandyet falls off her chair

524.beckster says, "we can only hope...."

525.Cyn laughs.

526.Jan says, "hey, electronic publishing is MORE fun than print publishing....can we agree on that? :)"

527.Cyn nods vigorously.

528.@quit

*** Connection Closed ***

ENDNOTES (IN MEDIA/S RES)

As editors of this chapter, our task has been—literally—mechanical. For the most part, the following notes reflect our decisions in the mechanics of presenting a MOO log and metatextual e-mail conversation in a codex book. We were surprised at how difficult it was to make decisions about spelling and grammar and at how much communication theory—speculative though it may currently be—was raised as we pieced this chapter together. What follows is our commentary on that process.

AA

An interesting phenomenon arose in the editorial process that can only be adequately expressed with some faux MOO dialogue; since the "we" in these notes refers to both of the editors of this chapter, we need to divide into our unique voices for a moment:

Mick says, "I keep getting the feeling that Dene, Jeff, or someone else is here in the room every time I decide to change a word. It's almost like they're on the screen with me, like in the MOO."

sandyet agrees. I know what you mean. I don't have the same problem making changes in text I edit at work—even though I know those people, the authors, too. Something is different here.

Mick says, "You know, it's kind of like when you get my voice mail at work and leave me one of those long, rambling three-minute messages . . . "

sandyet exclaims, "I do NOT ramble!"

Mick says, ". . . somewhere about midway through sometimes I actually find myself nodding and saying things like 'Uh huh' or even trying to interrupt. I forget that you're NOT there."

sandyet nods. It's the immediacy enabled by the technology. Same as in the MOO . . . we forget that we are not with the people who created the words we are editing because we were there when they were being uttered.

Mick says, "We were part of the dialogue then, so we feel they are part of the dialogue now."

sandyet says, "Exactly. That's what makes the editing process so difficult."

BB

We opted to change the names of some of the MOO participants, using our handy search-and-replace option in Microsoft Word. Unlike the old *Dragnet* reasoning, doing this to protect or obscure an identity, we did it to make the speaker's identity more obvious. Ericsson's comment [**see also V-2**] suggested to us that static reading of a MOO log could prove a chore unless speakers were adequately labeled.

That Dene Grigar was in the early session "Guest" and in the later session "Violet_Guest" served no purpose but to confuse. In fact, we opted to replace all "Guest" monikers with indicators of real names; John_B (John Barber) and Michael_S (Michael Spooner), for instance, do not have regular-named characters in MediaMOO and were assigned color+guest labels; these have been replaced for the reader's benefit. We concluded that this action did not affect the content of the MOO discussion, though various identity theorists (for instance, Turkle and Doheny-Farina) would probably argue otherwise.

CC

There were actually two separate MOO sessions, in order to allow the greatest number of possible contributors to this book to attend and participate. The second session begins at MOO #278. Both sessions were held and logged in "Sandye's Tea Room" [**see also MOO #1**] in MediaMOO, selected to facilitate the ease with which the "editors" of this chapter could capture and review the text in the session logs. We originally planned to hold the session in LinguaMOO, but decided instead on a more "neutral" site, as the co-founders of Lingua were participating in the discussion. Whether the "where" of the MOO truly affected the process (or product) of the discussion is, of course, another point for debate.

DD

One of the "cuts" made in editing involved the longstanding MOO tradition of personal introductions. There were several dozen lines of intros, hellos, discussion, and banter surrounding the act of each participant simply saying, for the record, "My name is, and I am from . . ." We collapsed these statements into the "@who" command [**see MOO #5**], as a result, leading with the impression that everyone was "there" at the same time rather than the actual situation: two different sessions, people wandering in and out based on their own class and work schedules, getting booted, signing back on, etc.

In retrospect, this particular editing decision probably *does* alter the content of the MOO discussion(s), but space constraints of the print medium demanded it. Additionally, we do believe that by removing the "enters" and "exits" statements from the MOO—a natural follow-up decision—we have made the text appear less "fluid," which may be positive or negative depending on your epistemological stance.

EE

Originally, only contributing authors to this book were "invited" to participate in this MOO session. After some short discussion with Barber and Grigar (as far as several rapid-fire, late-night e-mails can be called "discussion"), we decided that this was simply mis-using the medium to the point of absurdity; the potential for expanding discussion is one of the key intertextual (if not hypertextual) attributes of computer-mediated communication.

As such, several members of the *Kairos* editorial staff were invited to join the three of us already involved, and one—James Inman—agreed. Several times throughout the MOOs, colleagues and co-workers logged on for their own purposes and were "paged" with an invitation; Becky Rickly, Traci Gardner, Peter Sands, and Michael Day all joined us in that manner. Ironically, Day ended up with a chapter in this volume after learning about the book during the MOO session. Cross-media publication comes full circle, it seems.

FF

Frequently, experienced MOOers will eschew longer comments for several rapid-fire statements that end with an ellipse, indicating more is coming. This allows the others in the MOO to read at a more normal pace while the "speaker" continues to write. In many places, we simply collapsed these "ellipsoid" MOO comments into one longer statement. A good example is Mick's comment at MOO#342; is any meaning lost or changed by the fact that this was originally four separate utterances?

On the other hand, some of the longer statements in the MOO (**see traci's MOO#259**) were entered into the conversation all at once; because Gardner never dominates a MOO conversation and is well-respected in the C&W community, she is able to do this effectively. The fact that there were responses to Gardner's comment(s) is a reliable indicator that others took the effort necessary to read the long MOO entry.

We admit, too, to occasionally moving text around to make threads more consistent—several dropped connections, a couple of technological glitches, and some of our other editing decisions (discussed here) made this advisable, if not necessary. Honestly, this is the one decision that made us most uncomfortable—is our "for clarity's sake" reasoning enough of a reason to alter the order in which the text presented itself? We finally concluded "yes."

GG

Grammar is always an issue in editing MOO logs. Does "fixing" grammar somehow alter the "kairic" nature of the text as it developed? We believe that it does; yet, in a nod to the traditions of print culture that surround the development of a book like this one, we opted to make several categorical corrections.

We corrected errors of "Net grammar," such as mis-keyed URLS, in order to prevent perpetuation of a correctable error. Obvious spelling errors were fixed unless they were commented upon in such a way that added to the discussion (see MOO 47-50). We did not change capitalization. Actually, for the data-hungry, the original edited MOO log contained 10,698 words, according to our trusty spellchecker, of which only 339 were tagged as questionable. Of those, since many were proper names or technical jargon, we changed only 106—almost 1% of the text. Is this a significant amount? We would be curious to see other published MOO logs present similar data.

HH

While this is simple conjecture, there were periods during the MOO when we felt certain there was a fair amount of "paging" going on. Individual participants in a MOO are able to use simple commands to make comments, unseen by the group, to other individuals that were unlogged. One way to "check," though not confirm, this supposition is to use the "@who" command which not only identifies who is online, but when they were last active. There were numerous times unobvious in a log that several moments passed between comments, but all "players" appeared "recently active."

This kind of "meta-commentary" is one significant difference between MOOing and Galin's comparison to a discussion—in a polyvocal discussion, whispering or passing notes would be socially inappropriate. In a MOO, it is both unnoticed and expected; we often check with each other regarding reactions or comments we are considering making in a MOO, fostering a different kind of extratextual collaboration.

We, the hosts of the MOO, were engaged in what has been called "multi-MOOing." We each had another screen on our respective desktops open to the *Kairos* office in LinguaMOO, where we were able to discuss the progress of the meeting and decide which slides to show next, without fearing the dreaded mis-typed whisper that accidentally appears to everyone. There were at least two instances of that particular gaffe in our sessions and those have been removed in the editorial process, as they were never intended for the log in the first place.

II

Suggested for practice, how to read a MOO log: use the Find function on your computer. Interested in more about, for instance, the forthcoming journal *Elekcriture*? Don't scroll 800 lines skimming and diving; tap the word into the Find field, and hit return. MOO logs may not be hypertextual in the way Michael Joyce has defined the term, but the computer does allow for nearly all on-screen reading to be hypertextual, where the reader helps determine her own path. MOO logs are a perfect example of the kind of text which can be "enabled" by this kind of reading.

There are problems with this theory. If we don't know what a MOO was about, how are we to pursue find-n'-read methods? That's where the editors come in, the "gatekeepers" Michael_S accused us of being. Effective meta-commentary, a detailed bibliography, a clear title, and a set of accurate keywords provide starting points for the most jaded of paper-bound scholars.

JJ

<FWIW>Are personal politics important in MOOspace or in e-mail exchanges? Of course, no less so than in any other communication. We wondered if it would be appropriate, or even interesting, to point out that these MOO sessions and e-mail discussions featured two married couples and an engaged couple, several individuals who had been at each others' weddings, numerous co-authors (above and beyond this book), co-workers, half of a journal's entire editorial staff, and at least three faculty who sat on (or are currently sitting on) graduate students' dissertation committees. One contributor to this book claimed "A MOO like this one is easy and difficult for precisely the same reason—it's academically incestuous."</FWIW>

KK

We considered adopting the use of different fonts, or perhaps altered typefaces, to further enable a reader's possible navigation through the various texts in this "chapter." In fact, some MOO clients allow for this very feature. Most, however, including the commonly-used though widely-disparaged raw telnet, do not offer this function so we offer the proverbial lowest common denominator: text as text.

LL

We found it interesting, and at one point were counting in our multi-MOO window, how often MOOers tend to "name drop." Perhaps this was the tone set by the nature of the slides we used as discussion prompts—decontextualized quotations. Or, we speculated, perhaps it was a further attempt to somehow legitimize the action of creating text for publication in this medium. We even considered the Hawthorn effect—when you know someone is watching (or going to be reading), you act differently. Though citation is common in LinguaMOO's C-Fest series meetings, the rate of name-dropping in these MOOs was startlingly higher. Perhaps, we concluded, it is just the nature of academic discussion as a whole.

MM

We opted to leave emoticons in place when they were used, though their use was surprisingly infrequent compared to our experience and expectations. Perhaps the same awareness of potential *print* publication led participants, even subconsciously, away from use of emoticons. We are also presuming that the audience for this book will recognize :-) as a smile, and that readers of this endnote will not be annoyed by the fact that we have not offered a definition for the word "emoticon."

NN

Ericsson [see also V and W] and Crump [see also T] used their electronic mail to "insert themselves into the conversation" by selecting dialogue and responding to it in a similar voice. It would not be difficult to splice much of their text, unedited and unaltered, into the MOO log in such a way that no one would ever guess they were not actually in attendance during the generation of the conversation. (Crump, you will notice, even drops his name into lowercase letters in the manner of his own permanent character on MediaMOO.)

These two are doing what Joyce called in *Of Two Minds* "writing in the interstices." In this way, a MOO is the ultimate Burkean Parlor (let's say, "Cyberkean Parlor") in that we can not only enter into the conversation in mid-stream, we can insert ourselves into the conversation (inter)textually. Of course, metaphorically, this has always been true in academic publishing, but never at such an intense micro-level. Perhaps in this way, MOOing and other electronic writing forms will allow us to see things about the way we approach our epistemological processes in new and clearer ways.

Joyce [**see also R**] and Porush [**see also S**], two of the most interesting and accessible scholars in the field of electronic communication, did *not* do what Ericsson and Crump did in re-creating dialogue as they imagine it should have happened if they had been there. Though both did respond to statements made in the MOO, it was with a more traditional narrative commentary. It would be ludicrous to suggest that Ericsson and Crump are more comfortable writing in electronic dialogic style than Porush and Joyce—the latter two have dozens of electronic publications between them. But, we speculate that perhaps the fact that Joyce and Porush did their graduate work—learning their entry points into the academic parlor of conversation—in the 1970s, while Crump and Ericsson are completing PhDs in the post-Web 1990s determines their initial reaction in how to respond to the commentary.

OO

There was some argument from contributors to the book that an interesting, and perhaps integral, part of this chapter would be to make the MOO an "open hypertext." That is, put the log in a publicly available FTP folder, and allow all interested parties to read it and *write* to it. We could not overcome the practical problems of overwriting files to attempt this experiment.

PP

The two MOO participants who were "most responded to," not surprisingly, were the two editors of the chapter. We don't kid ourselves into thinking that this is because we had more important things to say (write); frankly, it's probably because we were the "hosts" and people expected us to lead the discussion. But, cynically, in our multi-MOO window, we wondered aloud to ourselves if it also wasn't in part due to a subconscious supposition on the part of the participants that such a reaction would better their chances of "making the editorial cut" into the book you are now reading.

QQ

The electronic mail from the book contributors is included in the order we received it [see also A through P] followed by the "invited" posts [see also Q through W] of people mentioned or quoted in the MOO session and few other notables in the field. The mail is unedited for content, though we used the same guidelines in the mail as we did in the MOO text, corrected for spelling but not capitalization. We also italicized all quoted material from the MOO or from earlier mail messages to facilitate reading. With one notable exception [Porush, see also S-16 and S-17], we also removed participants' signature files, as they were generally more like business cards than theoretical stances.

RR

There was much "off-list" mail—messages sent to us but not to the group as a whole—generated by those involved. We have not included any of it here, and did not seek permission to do so; we consider it to be in the same genre as "paging" and "whispering" in MOOspace. Inserting a page into a MOO or an offlist post into a collection such as this, even with the author's permission, would inappropriately alter the dialogic nature of the interchange.

SS

At one point we considered "saving a tree" by cutting from the MOO log the many utterances in the nature of "I agree" or "good point" to leave only the substance. That is, at best, an arguable point; we finally found comfort in our decision *not* to remove them. In fact, doing so would remove a natural calibration of the various ongoing threads. Response to an utterance, even in disagreement, is a validation of it. Many of our undergraduate students have said they would rather be flamed than ignored in MOOspace.

TT

Because MOOspace is fluid, it's not like an oral discussion in a classroom where you might write a phrase on the chalkboard (or its electronic equivalent) and leave it there for discussants to consider and pursue. In fact, we found ourselves having to continually re-post the slides we were using as discussion prompts because participants wanted to see them again, and then fielding complaints from others frustrated that the slides were preventing them from participating very well! We have removed dozens of lines of text by omitting the repeated slides.

UU

What use is a MOO log? You know, what practical Tuesday evening in the graduate rhetoric seminar use? We are loathe to suggest "exercises" for students in theory classes, but wonder if communication theory and "voice" might not get a real workout from using MOO logs in experimental ways.

Imagine distributing an edited MOO log with Michael Joyce and Mark Bernstein discussing hypertext (see *Kairos* 3.1) and asking students to actually *read* it—to try to find the voice of the speaker. Technophobic, or at least technoskeptic, they may be reading the words of Michael Joyce not in a brilliantly crafted essay, but aloud in what amounts to a script— *playing the role of Michael Joyce*—what an opportunity to experiment. Imagine holding a class MOO session on any topic and then distributing an unedited log and assigning them to read it aloud, as the script of a play. Only, assign them another participant's role . . . the opportunity to play the role of a colleague and to hear our own words in the phraseology of another speaker could open new avenues of thought regarding tone and interpretation in the written word. We would enjoy seeing some of our academic colleagues in this book venture experiment with just such an approach and report their findings.

VV

As Barber requested [see MOO 281], we kept trying to make the "theme" of this MOO discussion about the future of electronic writing. Yet the conversation kept coming back to the issue of whether or not what we were doing right then was a "publication." We were afraid this might be seen as inappropriate "navel-gazing"—and indeed, it still might! But we are left to wonder "what is the future of electronic writing?" and "is a MOO a publication?"—are these in fact the same question?

WW

This edited-for-print version of a MOO log and e-mail exchange may not really provide an accurate sense of the "new worlds" of these "new words" of our writing and communicative processes. We don't believe for an instant that a writing teacher totally disinterested, or even interested but unexperienced, in MOOing can read this chapter and have a sense for what the technology can and will do to the writing process. The text as it appears here is static; the loss of dynamic interaction reduces the kairotic feel of the electronic intercourse.

But, staying with the "new worlds" theme pervasive in this volume, we think that this artifact is very much like the moon rocks Aldrin and

Armstrong brought back from Luna in 1969. Those were tangible proof that there was something there, familiar yet different, ready to be explored. They were something we could touch, and we would wonder "what's it really like to be immersed in this material?" Similarly, this chapter, edited MOO log and all, might encourage someone to try to experience the "real thing." We are, of course, as Sandye has written elsewhere, simply "Speaking of the MOOn."

THIS IS NOT A BIBLIOGRAPHY

These Are the Slides We Used

We made 33 slides, but used only slightly more than a third of them. These "made the cut."

Barber, J. (1998, January 15). Today's MOO. E-mail to Mick Doherty and Sandye Thompson.

Brand, S. (1987). *The media lab: Inventing the future at M.I.T.* (p. 253). New York: Penguin.

Doherty, M. (1997, March). The RhetNet defense: A new academic forum toward "shooting hoops." *Rhetnet: A CyberJournal for Rhetoric and Writing.* http://www.missouri.edu/~rhetnet/hoops/.

Galin, J., & Doherty, M. (1998, January 14). Excerpt from MOO Session 1 at MediaMOO.

Haraway, D. J. (1991). *Simians, cyborgs, and women: The reinvention of nature* (pp. 175-177). New York: Routledge.

Haynes, C., & Holmevik, J. R. (1996, Summer). Lingua unlimited: Enhancing pedagogical reality with MOOs. *Kairos: A Journal For Teachers of Writing in Webbed Environments*, 1(2). http://english.ttu.edu/kairos/1.2/coverweb/bridge.html.

Johnson-Eilola, J. (1996, Spring). Stories and maps: Postmodernism and professional communication. *Kairos: A Journal For Teachers of Writing in Webbed Environments.* 1(1). http://english.ttu.edu/kairos/1.1/features/johndan.html.

Joyce, M. (1995). A memphite topography: Governance and the city of text. *Of two minds: Hypertext pedagogy and poetics* (pp. 105-116). Ann Arbor: University of Michigan Press.

Kirkpatrick, J., & Thompson, S. (1998, January 14). Excerpt from MOO Session 1 at MediaMOO.

Lanham, R. A. (1993). *The electronic word: Democracy, technology, and the arts* (pp. 21-22). Chicago: University of Chicago Press.

Lunsford, A., Rickly, R., Salvo, M., & West, S. (1996, Spring). What matters who writes? What matters who responds? Issues of ownership in the writing classroom. *Kairos: A Journal For Teachers of Writing in Webbed Environments,* 1(1). http://english.ttu.edu/kairos/1.1/features/lunsford.html.

Negroponte, N. (1995). *Being digital* (p. 164). New York: Knopf.

Porush, D. (1995, March). Ubiquitous computing vs. radical privacy: A reconsideration of the future. *Computer-Mediated Communication Magazine.* http://www.december.com/cmc/mag/1995/mar/last.html.

We Mentioned Some Journals

College English
Ed. Jeanne Gunner
National Council of Teachers of English, Urbana, Illinois
Editorial Offices: University of Massachusetts-Boston

Computers & Composition
Eds. Gail Hawisher & Cynthia Selfe
Ablex Publishing Corporation, Greenwich, Connecticut
Editorial Offices: Michigan Tech University

Computer-Mediated Communication Magazine
Ed. John December
http://www.december.com/cmc/mag/

Elekcriture
Eds. Cynthia Haynes and Jan Holmevik
Forthcoming

Kairos: A Journal For Teachers of Writing in Webbed Environments
Ed. Doug Eyman
http://english.ttu.edu/kairos/
Editorial Offices: LinguaMOO

PMLA
Ed. Domna C. Stanton
Publications of the Modern Language Association, New York
Editorial Offices: University of Michigan

PreText/ElectraLite
Eds. Victor J. Vitanza and Cynthia Haynes
http://www.utdallas.edu/pretext/index1a.html

RhetNet: A CyberJournal for Rhetoric and Writing
Ed. Eric Crump
http://www.missouri.edu/~rhetnet/

Rhetoric Review
Ed. Theresa Enos
Rhetoric Review Association of America
Editorial Offices: University of Arizona

Wired
Ed. Katrina Heron
Marketing Design Group, San Francisco

Lots of Times, We Name-Dropped

But we did so without citing a particular source, more or less aligning ourselves with (or against) a particular established scholar or scholarly tradition. These include:

Thomas Hobbes, Moses, Michel Foucault, Richard Lanham, Hugh Blair, Gilles Deleuze and Felix Guattari, Neil Postman, Sven Birkerts, Nicholas Negroponte, Steve Jobs, Jay Bolter, Douglas Englebart, Vannevar Bush, Marshall McLuhan, Donna Haraway, Walter Ong, Roland Barthes, Dilip Gaonkar, Jacques Derrida, Sherry Turkle. *Wouldn't you love to see a MOO session with those participants logged in?*

We Mentioned Some Websites

Does not include the electronic journals mentioned above.

C-Fest
http://lingua.utdallas.edu:7000/256

MOO Teacher's Tip Sheet
http://www.daedalus.com/net/MOOTIPS.html

LinguaMOO
http://lingua.utdallas.edu

New Worlds website
http://www.eaze.net/~jfbarber/worlds_book.html

There Were *Some* Particular Articles and Books and Stuff Mentioned

Does not include the ones used on our slides (see above).

Bernstein, M. Chasing our tails, chasing our tales. Reprinted from *Chorus* on the Eastgate Systems webpage. http://www.eastgate. com/tails/Welcome.html

Daisley, M. M. (1994). The game of literacy: The meaning of play in computer-mediated communication. *Computers and Composition,* 11(2), 107-120.

Doheny Farina, S. (1996). *The wired neighborhood*. New Haven, CT: Yale University Press.

Doherty, M., English, J., & Thompson, S. (1998, Spring). The impossible dream: An intermoo with Michael Joyce and Mark Bernstein. *Kairos: A Journal For Teachers of Writing in Webbed Environments*, 3(1). http://english.ttu.edu/kairos/3.1/features/intermoo/start.html.

Haynes, C., & Holmevik, J. R. (Eds.). (1998). *High wired: On the design, use, and theory of education MOOs*. Ann Arbor: University of Michigan Press.

Holeton, R. (1998). *Composing cyberspace*. New York: McGraw-Hill.

Marvin, C. (1988). *When old technologies were new*. Cambridge, MA: MIT Press.

McNealey, S. (1998, January). The best & worst of the net '97. *Internet World*, p. 56.

Ronell, A. (1989). *The telephone book*. Lincoln: University of Nebraska Press.

Schuster, C. (1990). The ideology of illiteracy: A Bakhtinian perspective. In A. Lunsford, H. Moglen, & J. Slevins (Eds.), *The right to literacy* (p. 227). New York: MLA.

Sirc, G. (1995). The twinworlds of electronic conferencing. *Computers and Composition*, 12(3), 265-277.

Stone, A. R. (1995). *The war of desire and technology at the close of the mechanical age* (p. 168). Cambridge, MA: MIT Press.

Thompson, S. (1997, Fall). Speaking of the MOOn: Textual realities in MOOspace. *Kairos: A Journal For Teachers of Writing in Webbed Environments*, 2(2). http://english.ttu.edu/kairos/2.2/coverweb/sandye/bridge.html

Turkle, S. (1996). Virtuality and its discontents: Searching for community in cyberspace. *The American Prospect*, 24, 50-57.

Cultural Quota

Since we were talking about community and shared language, we made sure (subconsciously, certainly) that we dropped all kinds of cultural references. In no particular, order, then, this MOO was hosted—this chapter was written by—a group of people that assumed each other would understand:

McCarthyism, the Cold War, Kennedyism, Vietnam, Jell-O, microwaves, VCRs, WebTV, trickle-down economics, klein jar, moebious strip, synergy, spam (and Spam), Dragnet, Aldrin and Armstrong, James Joyce, Virginia Woolf, Burroughs (William? John? Jeff?), Guevera, Walden (the book? the pond? the puddle?), Unabomber, Hobbes (the philosopher? the stuffed tiger?), Plato's cave, Gilligan's island, Belle

Lettres, Aristotle on pathos, Bill Gates, Lessig's report on Microsoft to the DOJ, Turing test, Heuretics, Burkean Parlor, Hawthorn effect.

What does this list do to define our micro-community?

@quit

*** Connection closed ***

Note: On page 391, line 326, what Cyn refers to as ubiquitous computing, Sandy Stone actually called ubiquitous technology. Ubiquitous technology which is definitive of the virtual age, is far more subtle. It doesn't tell us anything. It rearranges our thinking apparatus so that different thinking just *is* (168).

EPILOGUE

"THEY ARE ALREADY IN IT"

Lester Faigley

The debate over who has access to the Internet obscures the fact that almost every person of college age in the United States and Canada has been using extraordinarily powerful computers from the time of their earliest memories. Some of these computers in the year 2000 have more power than the most powerful computer that existed in the mid 1970s. They are called video games. Furthermore, a sizeable percentage of students entering college today acquired much of their abilities to read and write using computers. For many students, writing using computers seems as natural as a pen and pencil did for their parents. Indeed, it seems hard to believe for those of us who have been around long enough to remember that in the 1970s almost no one used computers for writing. The ordinariness of computer-mediated literacies today tends to make us forget just how new these literacies are. I have to make an effort to reconstruct my own writing history before I started writing on computers, but I do remember the transition.

In 1979, I moved from the University of North Dakota to join the faculty at the University of Texas at Austin. When I got to Texas, like other new faculty I soon discovered that the money from the

University's enormous endowment was not spread evenly across campus. Whereas museums, libraries, performing arts, and sports facilities appeared to have limitless funding, the English Department was a pocket of poverty in the midst of splendor. Colleagues from other universities who called would not believe that our offices lacked telephones and that the most basic support services were absent. I knew I could not retype my manuscripts every time I or an editor made a few changes without slowing my scholarship to a crawl, and I could not afford to have them retyped by someone else. Earlier that spring I had seen high-quality computer-generated laser printing from a program called Scribe, developed at Carnegie-Mellon University. Texas had a site license for Scribe and a laser printer, which was my only hope to continue publishing at the rate I had grown accustomed. But Scribe was still under development at that time and had many bugs, so I had to use what programming knowledge I had to produce citations in the correct format and other details. Furthermore, I had to work using a dumb terminal connected to a mainframe by a modem with the speed of smoke signals—300 bps—almost unimaginable today when 14,400 bps is considered very slow. But even with all these problems, composing online still was far better than retyping everything from scratch.

When the first Macs and PCs appeared in the early 1980s, they seemed like a gift from heaven (except for the cost). I was no longer dependent on access to the main-frame computers I had been using, which increasingly gave busy signals when I tried to connect from off campus. More important, the usefulness of PCs for teaching writing was immediately evident. The ease of revising on PCs fit hand in glove with the process pedagogy that was sweeping through writing instruction. Apple and IBM were eager to get students to use computers and equipped many new classrooms, including one at Texas in 1986. Not long afterward, our computers were connected on a local network, which also supported the popular student-centered approach to teaching writing. I and others have written about how these local networks led to significant changes in patterns of classroom interaction, but the emphasis of our writing courses were still on producing essays composed in multiple drafts with peer reviews.

In the 1990s new technologies did not so easily support the prevailing model for teaching writing. Under John Slatin's leadership of our Computer Writing and Research Labs, in 1991 our classrooms were connected to the Internet. At first it seemed like the benefits for our students would be limited to accessing from the classroom the growing online resources provided by our libraries. At that time, undergraduate students were not provided e-mail accounts, and they were not able to take advantage of the potential for global communications from the computers they used in class. A few graduate instructors, however, did find ways to get students online in the bigger world, even allowing students to log in using their own accounts and passwords. One of the most striking demonstrations was conducted by Noel Stahle, who in an elective course in Spring 1994 concerning South Africa, connected his students with people in that country, which allowed them firsthand information on the political process that brought Nelson Mandela to power.

Other graduate instructors were busy building MUD and MOO spaces at the same time, which also represented distinct challenges to the process model of essay writing that had reigned comfortably during the early years of computers and writing. These MUD and MOO projects were clearly a new genre that coexisted uncomfortably with traditional genres of classroom writing. But still bigger impacts were to come. In 1994, graduate students established one of the first Web servers on our campus. Like the other technical innovations, the Web did not seem at first that different from other forms of online communication, but it was not long until teachers and students began to use its graphic capabilities. The power of the early Web lay in the ease in which text and pictures could be combined. Very few writing teachers had experience teaching graphic design, and I was not among them. I dusted off old books on design that I hadn't looked at since I was an undergraduate studying architecture and bought more books, I went to Web publishing classes offered by my university, and I did the tutorials included in Photoshop and other graphics software packages.

But it wasn't just a matter of retraining myself. Even though the multimedia capabilities of the Web are both dazzling and daunting, they do not present the biggest challenge to writing instruction brought by the Internet. Until very recently, college writing teachers entered the classroom confident of two assumptions: first, that the essay is the foundation genre for writing in the academy, the professions, and public life; and second, that students do not write well because they do very little writing on their own. The first assumption can perhaps be maintained a few years longer, but the second is dispelled quickly if you teach in a networked classroom. More and more students come to college with years of experience writing online and now with publishing on the Web. The metaphor of conversation is frequently used by writing teachers to discuss how texts respond to other texts, and it is certainly appropriate for our students' online writing, but we do not have to introduce them to the conversation. They are already in it.

Advocates of teaching writing as a process often talked about "empowering" their students, although it was never very clear how students from economically secure backgrounds were to be "empowered" by writing essays. What was clear was that power was supposed to flow from the teacher to the student. Students who spend hours reading and writing online each day can hardly be represented as disempowered. If they are truly disempowered, it is not a condition we can remedy simply by teaching them to be proficient in writing essays. We can teach them to communicate more effectively in a variety of genres and media and to have a sense of responsibility and stewardship about the use of technology. We still have a great deal to teach them, but we should keep in mind that when we are exploring new pathways, some of our students have walked these pathways before us. We have a great deal to learn from them too.

AUTHOR INDEX

SUBJECT INDEX